MW00581398

PEACE AND PENANCE IN LATE MEDIEVAL ITALY

Peace and Penance
in Late Medieval Italy

Katherine Ludwig Jansen

PRINCETON UNIVERSITY PRESS
PRINCETON & OXFORD

Copyright © 2018 by Princeton University Press

Published by Princeton University Press,
41 William Street, Princeton, New Jersey 08540

In the United Kingdom: Princeton University Press,
6 Oxford Street, Woodstock, Oxfordshire OX20 1TR

press.princeton.edu

Jacket illustration: Workshop of Tederigo Memmi. Museum of Fine Arts, Boston.
Sarah Wyman Whitman Fund. Photograph © 2018 Museum of Fine Arts, Boston.

Library of Congress Cataloging-in-Publication Data

Names: Jansen, Katherine Ludwig, 1957–author.
Title: Peace and penance in late medieval Italy / Katherine Ludwig Jansen.
Description: Princeton : Princeton University Press, 2017. | Includes
        bibliographical references and index.
Identifiers: LCCN 2017035263 | ISBN 9780691177748 (hardcover : alk. paper)
Subjects: LCSH: Penance—History. | Peace of mind—Religious
        aspects—Christianity—History. | Peace—Religious
        aspects—Christianity—History. | Reconciliation—Religious
        aspects—Christianity—History. | Church history—Middle Ages, 600-1500. |
        Italy—Church history.
Classification: LCC BV840 .J36 2017 | DDC 282/.450902—dc23 LC record available at
https://lccn.loc.gov/2017035263

British Library Cataloging-in-Publication Data is available

This book has been composed in Miller Text

Printed on acid-free paper. ∞

Printed in the United States of America

10 9 8 7 6 5 4 3 2 1

In memory of

Janine Lowell Ludwig (1934–2012)

and

Fernanda De Vita (1911–2014)

CONTENTS

ILLUSTRATIONS

ABBREVIATIONS

AFH   Archivum Franciscanum Historicum

ASF   Archivio di Stato di Firenze

BAV   Biblioteca Apostolica Vaticana

BS   Bibliotheca Sanctorum

CASANAT.   Biblioteca Casanatense

CCCM   Corpus Christianorum Continuatio Mediaevalis

CCSL   Corpus Christianorum, Series Latina

DBI   Dizionario biografico degli italiani

MGH   Monumenta Germaniae Historica

NOT. ANT.   Notariale Antecosimiano

RIS   Rerum Italicarum Scriptores (Milan edition)

RIS2   Rerum Italicarum Scriptores (Bologna and Città di Castello edition)

RLS   Repertorium der lateinischen Sermones des Mittelalters

STATUTI   Statuti della Repubblica Fiorentina

A NOTE ON NAMES AND CURRENCY

I HAVE RENDERED most names into the Italian vernacular rather than using their Latin form. Thus I use the form Remigio dei Girolami rather than Remigius de Girolamis Florentinus. I have retained the Latin name only when a figure is commonly known by that name; e.g., Jacobus de Voragine, or when his or her place of origin is obscure. The primary exception to that rule is when a name has been Anglicized by tradition; hence Thomas Aquinas. The New Year in Florence began on 25 March, the feast day of the Annunciation. I cite two years for those dates that fall between 1 January and 24 March. Florentine currency and its rate of exchange always present a challenge as rates of exchange varied over time and place. In 1252 when the first gold florin was struck, it was worth one libra or lira (the money of account), which equaled 20 soldi. One lira was worth about one silver pound. The fiorino piccolo (picciolo), or penny (hereafter f.p.), was the Florentine equivalent of the denarius (12 f.p. = 1 soldo/solidus, or shilling). Therefore, 1 lira = 20 soldi/solidi = 240 denari/denarii or fiorini piccoli. See Carlo Cipolla, *The Monetary Policy of Fourteenth Century Florence* (Berkeley: University of California Press, 1982), viii–x.

ACKNOWLEDGMENTS

THIS BOOK has been a long time in the making. During its research and writing I have been the fortunate recipient of generosity from great institutions and individuals alike. It is both a pleasure and a relief to give thanks at last to all of them. Begun in Florence, under the patronage of Villa I Tatti, the Harvard Center for Renaissance Studies, the project also enjoyed support from the American Council of Learned Societies, the Fulbright Foundation, the Grant-in-Aid Program at the Catholic University of America, the Institute for Advanced Study in Princeton and the American Academy in Rome where, high on the Janiculum, I finished the first draft of the manuscript. I am grateful to the selection committees, directors, and staff of these institutions for providing me with funding and periodic intellectual homes over this last decade or so. The resident scholarly communities at the VIT, IAS, and AAR were all memorable groups who, around the lunch or seminar table, allowed me to bounce and refine the ideas that are the foundations of this book.

I am also particularly indebted to the many archivists and librarians at the Archivio di Stato di Firenze, the Biblioteca Apostolica Vaticana, the Berenson Library at I Tatti, the American Academy in Rome, as well as the interlibrary loan personnel at the Firestone Library, Princeton University, the Institute for Advanced Study, and the Mullen Library at the Catholic University of America. In addition, Colum Hourihane and Adelaide Bennett Hagens opened up the resources of Princeton's Index of Christian Art to me. Erica Buentello, Beth Newman Oii, Andrew Cuff, Nicolas Novak, and Nicholas Brown—CUA research assistants over the years—along with Ramon Sola kept pace with my endless requests for books and articles.

I am also grateful to the following institutions for inviting me to speak to engaged audiences who asked the sharp questions that contributed to making this a better book: the American Academy in Rome, Columbia University, Harvard Divinity School, Harvard University, Indiana University, Notre Dame, Princeton University, and Yale University.

By asking the well-posed question, sharing information, or passing on a bibliographical citation, friends, colleagues, and graduate students have provided invaluable inspiration over the years. I am grateful to Frances Andrews, Peter Brown, Barbara Bruderer, Gian Mario Cao, Giles Constable, Natalie Davis, Peter Dougherty, Pat Geary, Jim Hankins, Mächtelt Israels, Rebecca Johnson, Bill Jordan, Carol Lansing, Giuliano Milani, Maureen Miller, John Padgett, Irving and Marilyn Lavin, Bill North, Enrico Parlato, Ken Pennington, John Petruccione, Austin Powell, Louise Rice, Valentino Romani, Dennis Romano, Dan Smail, Franek Sznura, John Van Engen, Michael van Walt van Praag and Chris Wickham. Some of this group also read the manuscript in full or in part and offered valuable comments and criticism. For their collegial generosity and thoughtful feedback, I am indebted to Sarah Rubin Blanshei, Marie d'Aguanno Ito, Bill Jordan, Dennis Romano, Miri Rubin, Tom Tentler, and the two not-so-anonymous readers at Princeton University Press. Dan Smail, in particular, gave the manuscript the rigorous reading it required. It goes without saying that the mistakes and missteps that remain in the book are of my own making.

In the more than ten years I have spent working on this book, as is the historian's prerogative, I have changed my mind and reconsidered my opinions on more than a few topics contained within its pages. Or, as the politicians like to say: my thinking has evolved. This means that I have revised a number of the arguments and corrected mistakes made in various articles I have previously published. I would like to I thank Brill and *Speculum* for allowing me to republish the contents of those articles in amended form here.

I am also appreciative of the care and attention that Brigitta van Rheinberg, Quinn Fusting, Amanda Peery, Eva Jaunzems, Leslie Grundfest, and the entire team at Princeton University Press have taken in shepherding this book through acquisitions, editing, and production.

Finally, I would like to thank my extended postmodern family and dear friends who have been wonderfully supportive over the years, even if it wasn't always clear to them just exactly what I was doing for all this time. The ottimo Massimo, on the other hand, understood it all too well. He shared in the triumphs and tragedies along the way. It's trite but true: I couldn't have done it without him.

IN THE SECOND QUARTER of the thirteenth century, a Franciscan preacher
called Luca da Bitonto (fl. 1230s) explicated a familiar episode in the Gospel
of Luke (7:37–50) in which a female sinner, unbidden, enters the house of the
Pharisee where Jesus is reclining. Identified by medieval theologians as Mary
Magdalen, she throws herself contritely at Jesus's feet, washes them with her
tears, anoints them with her aromatic oils, and plies them with her kisses. It
was a dramatic conversion scene, well known to late medieval Christians, as
preachers had made it a focal point of sermons delivered in honor of the saint
on her feast-day. The scene concludes when the Lord absolves her with his
blessing: "Your sins are forgiven. Go in peace." An ordinary interpretation of
this passage underlined the Magdalen's humility and love for the Lord, the
impetus for her great penance. But by associating peace and penitence—as
the gospel passage had done—Luca da Bitonto added a new dimension to the
standard understanding of the passage when he preached:

> Just as enemies are accustomed to kiss each other when they meet to
> make peace, likewise this sinner [Mary Magdalen] who had waged war
> on the Lord, now came to make peace and gave kisses to his feet.[1]

For an audience already familiar with the rituals of peacemaking as practiced in the urban centers of northern and central Italy, the friar's aim was to
frame Mary Magdalen's penance in such a way as to make it comprehensible
to the citizens of late medieval cities. A comparison with the contemporary
practice of civic peacemaking was the preacher's ingenious solution to the
problem at hand.

Having read my way through more than a few model sermons, texts that
purposely purged the color, flavor, and local detail from their content so as
to serve as Latin templates that preachers in far-flung places and language
groups could personalize as they pleased, I was struck by the particularity of
Luca da Bitonto's words, which in those few lines seemed to capture in microcosm an entire world then unfamiliar to me, at that time a graduate student
embarked on dissertation research.[2] I wondered what peacemaking in the

---

1. MS Casanat. 17, fol. 66v; not in *RLS*. On the theme of Mary Magdalen and penance,
see my *Making of the Magdalen: Preaching and Popular Religion in the Later Middle Ages*
(Princeton: Princeton University Press, 2000), 199–244. The Magdalen's feast-day was a
holy day of obligation in the West, which meant that work was suspended so that people
could go to Mass, where they would have heard a sermon preached.

2. On the model sermon, see D. L. d'Avray, *The Preaching of the Friars: Sermons Diffused from Paris before 1300* (Oxford: Oxford University Press, 1985).

Italian communes (known for violence, feud, and vendetta) looked like, and if indeed such a practice ever even existed. If so, what forms did it take? Was it practiced under the auspices of the Church or the commune? How did it function within the judicial systems of the emerging popular governments? Who participated in these events? What was at stake when people made peace? What types of written or visual evidence documented this practice? And crucially for this study, what intellectual underpinning held together the architecture of ideas that allowed Luca da Bitonto to fasten peacemaking and penance so firmly together in his preaching? That brief encounter with the Franciscan preacher's sermon, which raised more questions about late medieval dispute resolution practices than I could then answer, was the genesis of this present study on peacemaking and penance in the age of the Italian communes.

PEACE AND PENANCE IN LATE MEDIEVAL ITALY

Introduction

If there is to be peace in the world,
There must be peace between nations.
If there is to be peace between nations,
There must be peace in the cities.
If there is to be peace in the cities,
There must be peace between neighbors.
If there is to be peace between neighbors,
There must be peace in the home.
If there is to be peace in the home,
There must be peace in the heart.

—ATTRIBUTED TO LAO-TZU (570–490 BCE)

AS THIS QUOTATION attributed to the ancient Chinese philosopher indicates, imagining peace is both a timeless and universal human inclination. This does not mean, however, that conceptions of peace and peacemaking efforts do not have their own rich and variegated histories within their own cultural contexts. Indeed they do, and this book is a contribution to the history of one of the most significant of them in the Middle Ages. Firmly contextualized in the peacemaking practices of late medieval Italy, with an eye trained on Florence in particular, this study frames the subject in Christian ideas about penitence, which were disseminated in a great whirlwind of mendicant and lay preaching that swept over the Italian peninsula, gathering force in the early thirteenth century.

The *Oxford English Dictionary* offers multiple definitions of "peace," of which the first five are relevant for our discussion. "Peace" is first defined as "freedom from, or cessation of, war or hostilities;" second as "freedom from civil disorder and commotion;" third as "quiet, tranquility;" fourth as "a state of friendliness, concord, amity;" and fifth as "freedom from mental or spiritual disturbance or conflict."[1] The semantic field of the term peace as used in the

---

1. *The Compact Oxford English Dictionary* (Oxford: Clarendon Press, 1991), 2nd ed.

Middle Ages is equally broad and encompasses all those lexical variations and more. If we were to be schematic we could categorize them as aspects of political peace, civil peace, and domestic peace, all of which overlapped and to some degree participated in one another because they were suffused and embedded in the meanings of peace as formulated in Christian religious culture.

Medieval theologians envisioned peace in its most perfected form as the eternal peace of heavenly Jerusalem, where the hope of life-everlasting at the end of time would be fulfilled.[2] The mundane world experienced a promise of this peace during the lifetime of Jesus when he bid farewell to his disciples with the words: "Peace I leave you, my peace I give you" (John 14:27), often interpreted as a prophecy of the peace to come in the Kingdom of God. Certain millennial and eschatological thinkers, on the other hand, believed that a time of tranquility on earth was nigh, one prophesied in the Book of Revelation 20: 1–7 (Apocalypse). Inaugurated by an angel who would vanquish Satan, Christ in the company of his martyr-saints would then return to rule the earth for a thousand years. This period would signal the imminent demise of the world before the Last Judgment, after which the peace of Jerusalem would reign supreme.[3] But for now, before the end of time, the world being an imperfect place, the only achievable peace was a pale imitation of heavenly Jerusalem, a limited peace at best. Even if it could never be realized fully on earth, eternal peace continued to be an aspirational model conditioning all thinking about peace in the Middle Ages.

The way in which fallen human beings could approximate and perhaps even experience heavenly peace and tranquility in a partial way was to convert and make peace with God. This is the sort of peace that Saint Augustine (d. 430), the theologian whose conception of peace influenced all medieval Christian thinkers who followed him, had in mind when he wrote in *The City of God* that "the peace of all things is the tranquility of order." For human beings, inner peace, on which all other types of peace were based, could only be achieved when both body and soul were brought into alignment to create harmonious order.[4]

2. The author of a twelfth-century tract called *De bono pacis*, most likely Rufinus of Sorrento, distinguishes three types of peace associated with three specific locations: that of angels was associated with Jerusalem; of men with Babylon; and of demons with Egypt. For a recent edition of the tract, see Roman Deutinger, MGH Studien und Texte 17 (1997). For recent discussions of the text, see Otto Gerhard Oexle, "Pax und Pactum: Rufinus von Sorrent und sein Traktat über den Frieden," in *Italia et Germania: Liber Amicorum Arnold Esch*, ed. Hagen Keller, Werner Paravicini, and Wolfgang Schieder (Tübingen: Walter de Gruyter, 2001), 539–55; and Jehangir Yezdi Malegam, *The Sleep of the Behemoth: Disputing Peace and Violence in Medieval Europe, 1000–1200* (Ithaca, NY: Cornell University Press, 2013), 286–96.

3. Robert Lerner, "Medieval Millenarianism and Violence," in *Pace e guerra nel basso medioevo: Atti del XL Convegno storico internazionale, Todi, 12–14 ottobre 2003* (Spoleto: Accademia Tudertina, 2004), 37–52, among his most recent works in a vast bibliography dedicated to this subject.

4. Augustine of Hippo, *The City of God*, trans. Marcus Dods (New York: Random House, 1950), Bk 19: 13, 690.

According to late medieval theologians, the only way to realize that inner peace, "the tranquility of order," was by means of penance, which, they argued, acted like a purgative to cleanse the soul of all earthly concerns, temptations, and evils. They further argued that peace with God, attained through the restorative power of repentance, was nothing less than the cornerstone on which all other versions of peace were erected. Domestic peace, neighborhood peace, civic peace, the security of the state—all these versions of exterior peace were predicated on an inner peace or "serenity of the soul" effected by penance.[5] This is the primary reason why medieval moralists, preachers, and politicians placed such stock in what we might call "penitential peace," because they understood it as a disciplinary practice that would lead to civic peace. Though Robert Bartlett was discussing peace in its legal milieu, his insight that "peace was thus not presumed as a universal given . . . breaches of which could be punished; rather it had to be created by a positive act" holds true in the religious context as well.[6] The positive act in this case was purgation through penitential action. In social practice, the enactment of a peace agreement created an analogous state. The act restored concord, the civic bond, and was a precondition for peace and tranquility in the city. Thus it is necessary to remember that when medieval people were engaged in peacemaking, they regarded it as an external act of reconciliation, predicated on an inner peace established through penance, both of which foreshadowed—through a glass darkly—the eternal peace of Jerusalem.

Consequently, Christian conceptions of penitential peace were never very far from the surface of any discussion of conflict settlement, which is why—even if it creates some semantic ambiguity—I prefer the medieval term "peacemaking" to "dispute resolution," the latter terminology having been drawn from contemporary legal lexicons. I would argue that the semantic ambiguity is useful in that it preserves and respects the medieval meaning of the practice. That ambiguity also allows for the religious, political, legal, and social aspects of peacemaking to be invoked simultaneously; whereas to employ the term "dispute settlement," "conflict resolution," or even "dispute processing" fences the procedure into a legal or political context, thereby draining it of all its religious connotations. The chasm between the modern and medieval meanings is brought into sharper focus when we examine the discourse and vocabulary underlying the medieval institution, which places the emphasis on the peace rather than the conflict. As the terminology implies, peace instruments look forward to the harmonious future rather than back to the contentious

5. The phrase is Jawaharlal Nehru's, excerpted from the full quotation: "Peace is not a relationship of nations. It is a condition of mind brought about by a serenity of soul. Peace is not merely the absence of war. It is also a state of mind. Lasting peace can come only to peaceful people."

6. Robert Bartlett, "'Mortal Enmities:' The Legal Aspect of Hostility in the Middle Ages," in *Feud, Violence and Practice: Essays in Medieval Studies in Honor of Stephen D. White* (Burlington, VT: Ashgate, 2010), 197–212, at 198.

past.[7] The legal agreement that recorded the settlement of a dispute was called an *instrumentum pacis*, a peace instrument, and was commonly referred to as a *pax* (peace). These are the terms enshrined in Florentine statute law and used by notaries who recorded such settlements in their casebooks. But it is not merely a question of usage that is at stake. I am arguing in favor of this terminology because the word *pax* signified more than dispute resolution in the late medieval period, so much more that the term habitually conjured all of these meanings together at one time. The word pointed toward the past, present, and future simultaneously. It referred back to what some have argued was the origin of the city, when communes were founded upon a sworn oath— often called a pax—of peace and protection, while at the same time the word pulsed with the energy of the contemporary political project of peace, public order, and security promoted by popular communal governments.[8] It also summoned the prophesied future described in Psalm 85:10, when the four daughters of God would return and Justice and Peace would embrace in a kiss.

In a sense this entire study is an effort to understand the multiple meanings of the term peace in the late medieval period by juxtaposing source materials that are not usually examined together, so as to facilitate conversation between disparate disciplinary fields that are not ordinarily in the habit of conversing. That is, to use the terms that medieval people would have understood, I have tried to unite the history of "inner peace," as it has been examined by historians of religion to the history of "outer peace," as analyzed by scholars of political, legal and social history. Peacemaking was a widespread and commonplace practice that permeated late medieval Italian society, but it has yet to be studied in a multifaceted way. It was deeply rooted in the religious culture of penance, which structured how it was practiced, a fact that the scholarly literature—hemmed in by disciplinary boundaries and an emphasis on the study of violence—has for too long overlooked. By illuminating the social practice of peacemaking and its penitential context, this book nuances our picture of faction-riven late medieval Italy, arguing that religious ideas shaped some of the most important secular institutions that emerged in this period to keep the peace. My twin emphases on the religious crucible in which penitential ideas of peacemaking were forged, and the secular institutions

7. This is an insight from Antonio Padoa Schioppa, "Delitto e pace privata nel pensiero dei legisti bolognesi. Brevi note," *Studia Gratiana* 20 (1976): 271–87, at 274.

8. For the link between the communes, oaths, and peace, see Otto Gerhard Oexle, "Peace through Conspiracy," in *Ordering Medieval Society: Perspectives on Intellectual and Practical Modes of Shaping Social Relations*, ed. Bernhard Jussen (Philadelphia: University of Pennsylvania Press, 2001): 285–322. See now Malegam's reinterpretation of Oexle in *The Sleep of the Behemoth*, 230–63. For a revisionist view of this theory of the foundation of the communes, see now Chris Wickham, *Sleepwalking into a new World: The Emergence of Italian City Communes in the Twelfth Century* (Princeton: Princeton University Press, 2015), which argues the communes in fact were "making it up as they went along," 19.

that realized them, helps us to see how the spiritual and political leaders of medieval cities sought to temper the effects of feud, violence, and vendetta by foregrounding the place of peace agreements in the communal judicial system.

My emphasis on both religion and society serves to bridge fields of scholarship, enabling us to see the dynamic whole that constituted medieval peacemaking more clearly than we can see it by examining its discrete parts.[9] Therefore, this book is neither a legal history nor a political history of dispute settlement. Nor is it solely a religious or social history of peacemaking. Instead, by fitting together the many individual tesserae that represent the diverse sources, approaches, and insights of all these fields, I hope to have constructed a mosaic that tells a larger story about peacemaking in the communal period, one that shows how peace was conceived, achieved, and memorialized in late medieval Italy.

I have chosen to focus primarily on Florence for three basic reasons. The first is source-driven. The Fondo Antecosimiano in the Archivio di Stato of Florence is arguably unparalleled in its richness, and a preliminary investigation of its holdings assured me that I would find the peace instruments I was looking for in the notarial records. But I wanted to read those legal sources against other pieces of evidence for medieval peacemaking such as political treatises, sermons, hagiography, ritual descriptions, and iconography produced in the same context. Florence offered that possibility, though in some cases—perforce—I had to gather contemporary evidence outside of the city's reach and influence. The second reason is that since I was undertaking a multidisciplinary project, I wanted to have a well-developed body of scholarly literature in the various fields that this book encompasses. Well-studied as Florence is, the scholarship would serve as my Virgil, helping to guide and test my interpretations in this new terrain. My debt to the (mainly) Italian and Anglophone scholarship on Florence is incalculable and is to be measured in the footnotes of this study. Third and finally, Florence provides a fitting laboratory to study peacemaking precisely because of its notorious reputation for violence, feud, and vendetta, to say nothing of the political factionalism and instability that characterized most of the Duecento. In the pages that follow, I outline briefly some of the important political developments of that century for those readers unfamiliar with Florentine history but who have an interest in peacemaking practices.

A BRIEF OVERVIEW OF THIRTEENTH-CENTURY FLORENCE

The troubles that would cast a long shadow over the entire thirteenth century began, according to one Florentine chronicler, in 1215 in the town of

9. Though not the synthesis called for by Mariaclara Rossi, ("Polisemia di un concetto: la pace nel basso medioevo: Note di lettura," in *La pace fra realtà e utopia. Quaderni di Storia Religiosa* 12, Verona: Cierre, 2005, 9–45, at 10 and 34), my study weaves together more disparate modes of scholarship on peace than has yet been undertaken.

Campi, host to a fête celebrating the knighthood of one of the city's elite sons. At the banquet a row erupted. Great platters of food were overturned and violence ensued. In the event, Oddo Arrighi dei Fifanti sustained a knife wound to his arm inflicted by Buondelmonte dei Buondelmonti. The dispute, which injured Oddo's honor as much as it did his flesh, was resolved when the Fifanti allies decided that Buondelmonte should marry the niece of Oddo Arrighi in order to bring peace to the families. The star-crossed betrothal was hurriedly arranged and then unexpectedly broken off when Buondelmonte subsequently engaged himself to another woman. Oddo Arrighi did not take this second affront to the family honor lightly; he consulted his allies who decided that Buondelmonte had committed a capital offence. Thus on his wedding day, on Easter morning, Buondelmonte was assassinated in cold blood at the foot of the Ponte Vecchio in front of the Amidei palace, the home of his jilted bride.[10] All reports note that this shocking act of violence immediately thereafter divided the city into political factions: the Guelfs, who supported the Buondelmonti, and the Ghibellines, who were allies of the Fifanti. The story, then, is not only one of personal vendetta, but also the origin story of the Guelf and Ghibelline parties in Italy, from which it should be clear that private enmity, local factionalism, and political alliances were so inexorably knotted together that they cannot easily be untangled, much less understood apart from one another. And though the politics and rivalries were much more complex than this brief explanation allows, in the grand scheme of political affairs on the Italian peninsula, the Guelfs now stood as papal allies, while the Ghibellines aligned themselves with the imperial party led by Frederick II.

John Najemy has astutely observed that the creation story of the two parties functions "as a parable of the original sin that required the popolo's punishment of the elite."[11] The *popolo* consisted of those of an intermediate social status between the nobility and the laboring classes. In a political context the term "popolo" also refers to the "popular" governments established by wealthy merchants and skilled artisans whose interests were distinct from those of both the noble grandees and unskilled labor. The first government of the popolo was established in 1250, when a popular revolt toppled the pro–imperial nobility as a response to crushing taxation and magnate violence against Florentine citizens. The *Primo Popolo*, as it was called, reigned for a decade, until the Battle of Montaperti, when the Ghibellines defeated the Guelfs, then recaptured

10. *Cronica fiorentina compilata nel secolo XIII*, in *Testi fiorentini del Dugento e dei primi del Trecento*, ed. A. Schiaffini (Florence: G.C. Sansoni, 1926), 82–150, at 117–19, a text also known as the Pseudo-Brunetto account. It is an old tale, often told by Florentine chroniclers, and here I have quoted one the earliest. For a very good contextualized analysis of the multiple versions of the tale, see Enrico Faini, "Il convito del 1216: La vendetta all'origine del fazionalismo fiorentino," *Annali di storia di Firenze* 1 (2006): 9–36. Later versions, such as the one I recount in chapter 4, situate the scene of the murder beneath the statue of Mars at the Ponte Vecchio.

11. *A History of Florence, 1200–1575* (Malden, MA: Blackwell, 2006), 13.

Florence, ruling briefly between 1260 and 1266. But the Guelfs again took power—this time for good—in 1267, the year after the French House of Anjou had defeated the Hohenstaufen in the Regno, the southern Kingdom of Italy. Allied with the papacy and the Angevins, now rulers of the southern Kingdom, Florence was rewarded with lucrative banking business and trading contracts. The Guelf government dealt with its Ghibelline enemies by confiscating their property and exiling them from the city. Consequently, hostilities, rancor, and warfare continued between the parties, making everyday life in the city almost untenable and forcing the Guelf leaders to turn to the papacy to provide non-partisan mediation. In 1280 it came in the form of Cardinal Latino Malabranca, a legate sent to Florence by the pope, whose peacemaking mission we will hear more about in chapter 2. For now, it is important to know that he made peace between the Buondelmonti and the Uberti families (allies of the Fifanti) and established the office of "conservator of the peace," a civic office whose charge was to impose peace settlements where warranted.[12] Significantly, the cardinal-peacemaker also allowed many of the Ghibellines to return home, even granting them a limited degree of power in the new executive magistracy he created called "the Fourteen," a form of government not destined for longevity. Two years later, in 1282, the Guelf party replaced the Fourteen with a magistracy led by guild priors. Membership in one of the city's important guilds was the criterion for election into the Priorate of the new guild government. Elected as prior in 1289, Giano della Bella, son of one of the elite families of Florence, surprisingly (given his social status) became the principal protagonist of the government of the *Secondo Popolo* of 1293, whose mandate was to curtail the privileges of the magnates, many of them (but not all) from old Ghibelline lineages.[13] The new government succeeded in circumscribing the power of the grandees by decreeing a constitution called the Ordinances of Justice, in which anti-magnate laws were enacted. The Ordinances of Justice (1293–95) was arguably the most important piece of legislation that the commune ever enacted. In essence, many of the old established lineages were penalized and blacklisted under this new legislation. Among other things, it decreed harsh penalties against magnates who assaulted or harmed popolani, and it excluded the grandees from the governing body of the Priorate. Though older scholarship hailed the advent of the popular governments, more recent scholars have argued that the Ordinances of Justice demonized the magnate

---

12. Nicola Ottokar, *Il comune di Firenze alla fine del Dugento* (Turin: Einaudi, 1962), 4.

13. For the make-up of the Florentine factions, see Sergio Raveggi et al., *Ghibellini, Guelfi e popolo grasso: i detentori del potere politico a Firenze nella seconda metà del Dugento* (Florence: La Nuova Italia, 1978); and Carol Lansing, *The Florentine Magnates: Lineage and Faction in a Medieval Commune* (Princeton: Princeton University Press, 1991). See now Enrico Faini, *Firenze nell'età romanica (1000–1211): l'espansione urbana, lo sviluppo istituzionale, il rapporto con il territorio* (Florence: L.S. Olschki, 2010); and Silvia Diacciati, *Popolani e magnati: società e politica nella Firenze del Duecento* (Spoleto: Fondazione Centro italiano di studi sull'alto Medioevo, 2011).

class in order to legitimize the popolo's governing authority. That may well be true; nevertheless, the guild government engaged in an active discourse that promoted itself as an architect of peace. The opening paragraph of the Ordinances of Justice says as much when it extols the saints and the new guild government, which promises to govern the city faithfully in perpetual concord and stable union, and to work toward augmenting the peace and tranquility of those under its dominion.[14]

The Guelfs had decidedly won the day, but within a few years the victorious party itself was riven by internal strife, such that by the last years of the thirteenth century the party had split into White and Black factions. The former stood in opposition to the expansion of papal power in Tuscany; the latter, many of whom were rich merchants and bankers, supported Angevin and papal policies. Using tried and true methods, the Whites sent the Blacks into exile, where they remained until 1301 when, under the leadership of Corso Donati, they engineered a coup d'état and grabbed the reins of government from the Whites. Members of the defeated White party, including the prior Dante Alighieri, were now condemned as political enemies and sentenced to exile, their property confiscated by the commune.

All this political upheaval and turmoil, often the result of personal animosities disguised as political rivalry, was reported in great detail in the bloodsoaked pages of Florence's chroniclers: Dino Compagni, Giovanni Villani, and Marchionne Coppo di Stefano Bonaiuti, among others.[15] It must not be forgotten, however, that in that same period of widespread violence and vengeance, the commune experienced unprecedented demographic and economic growth, accompanied by an unparalleled cultural efflorescence. Undergirded by the activities of the textile and banking industries, Florence in this era was also home to the creative forces of Dante and Giotto, whose monumental talents inexorably reshaped the history of literature and the visual arts on the Italian peninsula and well beyond. The city was also a center of great religious learning and popular fervor inspired by the mendicant friars, who were targeting the urban centers of Italy—those perceived dens of iniquity—with their preaching campaigns intended to revitalize religious belief and practice. As early as 1221, the Dominicans had planted themselves outside the city walls in the northwestern section of Florence, where construction of the convent-church complex of Santa Maria Novella continued throughout the century. A few years earlier, the Franciscans had staked out a place on the opposite

14. For a new edition, see *La legislazione antimagnatizia a Firenze*, ed. Silvia Diacciati and Andrea Zorzi (Rome: Istituto Storico Italiano per il Medio Evo, 2013), 57.

15. Dino Compagni's chronicle is now translated as *Dino Compagni's chronicle of Florence*, trans. Daniel E. Bornstein (Philadelphia: University of Pennsylvania, 1986); Giovanni Villani, *Nuova Cronica*, ed. Giovanni Porta, 3 vols. (Parma: Ugo Guanda, 1991); *Cronaca fiorentina di Marchionne di Coppo Stefani*, ed. Niccolò Rodolico, in RIS 30, Part I (Città di Castello: Lapi, 1903).

side of the city near the river, building a small oratory there, which would eventually be transformed into the friary and church of Santa Croce. Both Orders regarded the call to penance and peacemaking as fundamental aspects of their mission, and they often wove the two themes together in the fabric of their sermons, the subject of the first chapter of this book.

In order to contextualize all that follows, chapter 1 traces the arc of the penitential peace movements led by laymen and friars, a story that begins at the turn of the thirteenth century, and follows it through to the mid-fifteenth century, the age of the Observant friars, heirs to what had by then become a well-established tradition of pacification through preaching. Though some of this material will no doubt be familiar to those who study the history of religious movements, it will be less so to those who concentrate on dispute resolution from a legal point of view, making its presence here at the outset all the more important. Synthesizing the work of scholars who have studied the various religious movements of the later Middle Ages as separate and unconnected phenomena, this chapter makes a new argument that binds all these movements together, suggesting that they shared one common trait: they were peace movements that took the form of penitential processions. It furthermore examines the development of religious ideas that linked peace to penance, and shows how inspired laypeople and mendicant preachers pressed these views into civic action. Here I show how the friars and their like-minded allies sowed the seeds that contributed to a confessional culture—itself tied to penitential reforms of the thirteenth century—that was to flourish throughout the Middle Ages. And it was that confessional culture in which urban peace-making practices matured. Though I cast my net widely throughout central and northern Italy in order to bring as wide an array of evidence as possible into view; nonetheless woven throughout the discussion is an account of how peace movements and preaching emerged in and impacted the city of Florence and its *contado*, its subject towns and territory.

Though perhaps expected, I do not trace this story back to the Peace of God movement of the tenth and eleventh centuries because, in my view, the character of that movement was fundamentally different from the penitential peace that I have identified as an animating force of the later medieval movements. That is, the Peace of God, which began in France in 975 at a church council in Le Puy, originated as a reaction against the private warfare that was widespread in southern and central France. Some have argued that the movement was also apocalyptic and millenarian in character, traits shared with some of the later peace movements, but that is where the similarities begin and end.

The earlier and later movements diverge first of all in respect to their leadership. Bishops guided the Peace of God by convening a series of councils to protect churches, clergy, peasants, and the poor from marauding warriors.[16] They imposed sanctions—usually in the form of excommunication—on anyone who broke the peace. The aim of the Peace of God was to protect the weaker (and unarmed) members of society against the bellicose knightly class. This was not a primary objective of the peace movements of the later Middle Ages. Nor were the clergy the prime movers behind them. The decisive difference, however, is that the Peace of God was not a penitential movement so far as I can see, which should not surprise us given that this was not yet the great age of penance ushered in 1215, in the wake of the Fourth Lateran Council, when the sacrament was reformulated. Canon 21 joined individual annual confession to the long-standing obligations of contrition, satisfaction, and absolution. Now in order to receive communion, a Christian was obliged to confess and repent at least once per year.[17] This new stress on sacramental penance manifested itself in society in a wave of feverish preaching in the piazzas, and provided the early friars with endless subject matter for their sermons. It is well known that Francis of Assisi and his early followers often preached on penance, high theological matters being off limits to these unschooled preachers; yet the Dominicans too, their well-trained counterparts, took up the mission to preach penance with great zeal. Domenico Cavalca, O.P. (d. 1342), one of the great vernacularizers of our period, wrote: "Those who are the successors of Christ and of the apostles, such as prelates, religious, and priests, are obliged to preach the gospel and to call people to penance: they cannot keep quiet without committing a grave sin."[18]

The friars preached that penance would lead to inner peace, the soil in which exterior peace could take root. Significantly, a penitential framework for understanding the civil act of reconciliation was crucial for its success, as it allowed both parties to avoid slights against honor, shame, or humiliation. As God's will, preachers and moralists noted that peacemaking was an act of humility, inspired by love of God and elicited by a gift of grace.[19]

Evidence for this argument comes in the form of sermons, theological tracts, chronicles, hagiography, and visual evidence, traces left behind by preachers, penitents, and religious movements ranging from the Great Devotion of 1233 to the preaching campaigns of the Observant friars in the first part of the fifteenth century. In analyzing this material, I am indebted to

16. *The Peace of God: Social Violence and Religious Response around 1000*, ed. Thomas Head and Richard Landes (Ithaca, NY: Cornell University Press, 1992); and Dominique Barthélemy, *L'an mil et la paix de Dieu: La France chrétienne et féodale, 980–1060* (Paris: Fayard, 1999).

17. For penance in the early and central Middle Ages, see Rob Meens, *Penance in Medieval Europe, 600–1200* (Cambridge: Cambridge University Press, 2014). For confession, see Thomas Tentler, *Sin and Confession on the Eve of the Reformation* (Princeton: Princeton University Press, 1977).

18. *Frutti della lingua* (Rome: Antonio de' Rossi, 1754), 214.

19. For more on this theme, see Ottavia Niccoli, "Rinuncia, pace, perdono. Rituali di pacificazione della prima età moderna," *Studi Storici* 40.1 (1999): 219–61.

the work of a number of scholars who emphasized the central place of peace-making in the individual religious movements they studied. André Vauchez noted that pacification was a primary concern of the Allelujah movement, while Arsenio Frugoni, noted that the Bianchi made peacemaking their apostolate.[20] More ambitiously, Clara Gennaro linked some of the fourteenth-century religious movements together under the rubric of peace.[21] None of them, however, put these peace movements into dialogue with the civic practice of peacemaking emerging in the communal judicial system, nor did they undertake to analyze how closely theologians linked these two concepts.

In Anglophone scholarship, meanwhile, John Bossy began examining the social nature of early modern Christianity and its focus on peace. In *Christianity in the West 1400–1700*, where the theme of peace is a leitmotif throughout, he showed how ecclesiastical institutions shared rites and practices that aimed to create a sense of community among Christians. "The characteristic of [a] Christian relationship was peace," he remarked, and although the medieval period was not his subject, he did note in passing that "brotherhood and peacekeeping were associated throughout the Middle Ages."[22] As we shall see, he returned to the theme of Christian peace in a series of lectures he gave a decade later, but for now we should note that his portrait of the church and its emphasis on peacemaking likely helped set the stage for two monographs on religious peacemaking published in quick succession in the early nineties.

The first, *Revival Preachers and Politics in Thirteenth-Century Italy: The Great Devotion of 1233* by Augustine Thompson, O.P., revised Vauchez's discussion of the mendicant pacification campaign in northern Italy and observed that notable among its characteristics was the use of preaching as a launch pad into civic peacemaking.[23] One of the book's most important contributions was

20. André Vauchez, "Une campagne de pacification en Lombardie autour de 1233: L'action politique des ordres mendiants d'après la réforme des statuts communaux et les accords de paix," *École Française de Rome. Mélanges d'archéologie et d'histoire* 78 (1966): 503–49; repr. in Vauchez, *Religion et société dans l'Occident médiéval* (Turin: Bottega d'Erasmo, 1980), 71–117. After a long absence Vauchez returned to the theme of peacemaking with "La paix dans les mouvements religieux populaires (XIe–XVe siècle)," in *Pace e guerra nel basso medioevo. Atti del XL Convegno storico internazionale Todi, 12–14 ottobre 2003* (Spoleto: Centro italiano di studi sull'alto medioevo, 2004), 313–33. See also Arsenio Frugoni, "La devozione dei Bianchi nel 1399," in *L'attesa dell'età nuova nella spiritualità della fine del medioevo. Atti del III convegno del Centro di studi sulla spiritualità medievale.* (Todi: Accademia Tudertina, 1960), 232–48, at 239.

21. "Movimenti religiosi e pace nel XIV secolo," in *La pace nel pensiero nella politica negli ideali del Trecento, 13–17 Ottobre, 1974. Centro degli Studi sulla spiritualità medievale* 15 (Todi: L'Accademia Tudertina, 1975), 93–112.

22. John Bossy, *Christianity in the West* (Oxford: Oxford University Press, 1985), 57–58. See also his "The Mass as a Social Institution, 1200–1700," *Past and Present* 100 (1983): 29–61; and *Disputes and Settlements: Law and Human Relations in the West*, ed. John Bossy (Cambridge: Cambridge University Press, 1983).

23. (Oxford: Clarendon Press, 1992), 12. It is an irony that no sermons survive from this movement propelled by preaching.

to show how charismatic preachers associated with the movement inserted themselves into municipal governments to reform statute law.

Though it produced no celebrated preachers, the Bianchi were similarly oriented toward linking peace to penance. Daniel Bornstein's *The Bianchi of 1399: Popular Devotion in Late Medieval Italy* tracked the path of this religious revival at the end of the Middle Ages. The Bianchi, known as such for their characteristic white robes, were dedicated to penitential practices and peacemaking. Indeed, as Bornstein remarks, peacemaking was "among the most prominent of the Bianchi's described activities."[24]

As noted earlier, Bossy returned to the topic in a series of lectures published as *Peace in the Post-Reformation*, in which he reflected on early modern Christianity through the lens of the Church's social agenda of peacemaking. Here he sketched a portrait of ecclesiastical institutions that contributed to peace, order, and stability in Italy, Germany, France, and England. Shortly after its publication, but from the standpoint of very different archival evidence, Ottavia Niccoli posed related questions about religious peacemaking in this period, specifically in Italy.[25] She argued strongly that the study of dispute resolution must never be detached from its all-important religious context, because peace constituted a human relationship as well as a divine one, and therefore could serve simultaneously as both a political and religious instrument."[26] Furthering this point of view, by examining the pacification campaigns of the early fifteenth-century, Cynthia Polecritti put Bernardino of Siena's sermons under the spotlight to illuminate how he mobilized the crowds who flocked to his preaching events to make peace.[27] Mario Sensi did similarly by mining the textual treasure trove left behind by lesser-known preachers of the Franciscan Observance. In two densely packed but erudite articles, the first published in 2000, the same year as Polecritti's monograph, he examined the Observant friars' techniques and sermon texts, as they took to the streets of central Italy to call for peace.[28]

Most recently Rosa Maria Dessì has heeded the beck and call of the mendicant preachers. In a suggestive essay featured in a collection that she edited

24. (Ithaca, NY: Cornell University Press, 1993), 45.

25. First delivered as a series of four lectures at Trinity College, Cambridge, they were subsequently published as *Peace in the Post-Reformation* (Cambridge: Cambridge University Press, 1998); and Niccoli, "Rinuncia, pace, perdono," 219–61.

26. Niccoli, "Rinuncia, pace, perdono," 252.

27. Cynthia L. Polecritti, *Preaching Peace in Renaissance Italy: Bernardino of Siena and His Audience* (Washington, D.C.: Catholic University Press, 2000).

28. Mario Sensi, "Per una inchiesta sulle 'paci private' alla fine del Medio Evo," in *Studi sull'Umbria medievale e umanistica in ricordo di Olga Marinelli, Pier Lorenzo Meloni, Ugolino Nicolini,* ed. Mauro Donnini and Enrico Menestò (Spoleto: Centro italiano di studi sull'alto medioevo, 2000), 527–59; and "Le paci private nella predicazione, nelle immagini di propaganda e nella prassi fra Tre e Quattrocento," in *La pace fra realtà e utopia,* 159–200.

entitled *Prêcher la paix et discipliner la société: Italie, France, Angleterre (XIIIe-XVe siècles)*, she looks at peace as a social practice in the Italian communes from the age of Saint Francis to the end of the fifteenth century.[29] Based on hagiographical and sermon sources, and informed by Pierre Bourdieu's concept of *habitus*, she suggests that the mendicant friars should be regarded as spiritual propagandists for the new popular republican governments, which themselves had made peace an integral part of their political agenda. It is an argument that coheres well with the thesis of Massimo Vallerani's ambitious essay in the same volume. Looking at Perugia as a test case, he convincingly links the flagellant movement led by Raniero Fasani to the Ordinances enacted by the popolo of Perugia, both dating from 1260.[30] Here the association of penance and peace manifests itself as a political project of the popolo, an approach I apply to Florence in chapter 2 of this present study.

Turning to a body of discursive material concerned with political and "outer peace," chapter 2 looks at how those texts began hammering out an ethic of civic peace. In an age of urban growth, when the populations of Italian cities expanded enormously, and the population of Florence alone tripled, or "even quadrupled, to an estimated 120,000" due to continuous waves of migration from the contado over the course of the thirteenth and fourteenth centuries, the city's political structures, infrastructure, and resources were put to the test.[31] Such is the milieu for the factionalism, private vendetta, and everyday violence that emerged from this new demographic reality. Medieval political theorists, responding to this new situation, imagined peace on earth (while always pointing forward to the peace of Jerusalem) as the highest good of society and the end toward which all government should aspire. They understood concord, or civic harmony, as the means by which society attained its end, conceived as the common good of peace. By cultivating the civic bonds of concord, the city could achieve peace. Crucially, it was the dispensation of justice that produced concord, the harmony of wills, on which the peace of civic society depended.

Starting with political manuals such as the anonymous *Oculus pastoralis* and Brunetto Latini's *Li Livres dou tresor*, both of which found an avid readership in the communal period, I flesh out a thirteenth-century tradition (grounded in Ciceronian and Aristotelian thought) which was beginning to

29. Rosa Maria Dessì, ed. (Turnhout: Brepols, 2005), 245–78. She had earlier published on this theme, examining the preaching of James of the March in "Predicare e governare nelle città dello Stato della Chiesa alla fine del medioevo: Giacomo della Marca a Fermo" in *Studi sul Medioevo per Girolamo Arnaldi*, ed. Giulia Barone, Lidia Capo, and Stefano Gasparri (Rome: Viella, 2001), 125–59. Her "Pratiche della parola di pace nella storia dell'Italia urbana," in *Pace e guerra nel basso medioevo. Atti del XL Convegno storico internazionale, Todi, 12–14 ottobre 2003* (Spoleto: Centro italiano di studi sull'alto medioevo, 2004), 270–312, is an Italian version of the French essay.

30. Massimo Vallerani, "Mouvements de paix dans une commune de *Popolo*: les Flagellants à Pérouse en 1260," in *Prêcher la paix et discipliner la société*, 313–55.

31. John Najemy, *A History of Florence*, 97–98.

theorize a vision of the common good premised on a community united in
the bonds of concord.[32] Like Brunetto, Remigio dei Girolami was a native
son of Florence, and his *De bono pacis* (1304) is arguably the highest expression written in the period of a theory that equates peace with the common
good, though such ideas can be found in his earlier sermons also examined
here. A Dominican friar and scion of one of the city's prominent lineages,
Remigio laid out his ideas in sermons and treatises, which crystallized the
views of the popular government that held political power in Florence at the
turn of the thirteenth century. The guild government wrapped itself up in a
mantle of peace (and Remigio's political theology) for three primary reasons.
The first consideration was protection from magnate violence. In this case the
new merchant elite who now ruled Florence could defend the Ordinances of
Justice, which circumscribed magnate political power, as a piece of legislation
promoting peace. Second, peace and tranquility were necessary preconditions
for trade and commerce—the city's passport to prosperity—to flow freely.
And third, a state of peace ensured security from domestic enemies who had
been banned from the city and were now living in exile. My reading of these
texts—especially Remigio's work—has been aided enormously by the scholarship of Charles T. Davis, Quentin Skinner, Matthew Kempshall, and above
all, Fr. Emilio Panella, on whose meticulous editions and commentary on the
sermons and treatises I have relied.[33] With the exception of Panella, scholars
have tended to approach these tracts from the standpoint of the development
of political philosophy. Their interest, for the most part, is in tracing a lineage
of ideas: where, for example, do the ideas of Remigio or Brunetto fit in relation to Dante's or those of other political philosophers of the period? Though
that is a profitable and time-honored way to read these texts, my approach is
more culturally specific. It tries to analyze these treatises, especially those of
Remigio, in the light of the specific factional violence and social tension that
exploded on the streets of thirteenth-century Florence in the wake of the political, social, and cultural changes brought about by the city's unprecedented
economic and urban growth. And unlike the work of my colleagues, my analysis of Remigo's political work shows how bound up it was in the penitential

32. Brunetto Latini, *Li Livres dou Trésor*, ed. Francis J. Carmody (Berkeley: University
of California Press, 1948); and *Speeches from the Oculus Pastoralis*, ed. Terence O. Tunberg
(Toronto: PIMS, 1990).

33. Charles T. Davis, "An Early Florentine Political Theorist: Fra Remigio de' Girolami,"
Proceedings of the American Philosophical Society 104.6 (1960): 662–76; Quentin Skinner,
"Ambrogio Lorenzetti: The Artist as Political Philosopher," *Proceedings of the British
Academy* 72 (1986): 1–56; M. S. Kempshall, *The Common Good in Late Medieval Political
Thought* (Oxford: Clarendon Press, 1999). The editions of Remigio's works are published
by Emilio Panella, O.P., *Dal bene comune al bene del comune: I trattati politici di Remigio
dei Girolami (†1319) nella Firenze dei bianchi-neri* in *Memorie domenicane* 16 (1985):
1–198; 2nd. ed. (Florence: Nerbini, 2014). The editions also appear on his website: http://
www.e-theca.net/emiliopanella/remigio2/8500.htm [consulted 6/20/17].

discourse that was emanating from the universities, particularly from Bologna and Paris, the city where the Dominican preacher had studied as a student of Thomas Aquinas.

In chapter 3, I turn to the documentary evidence on Florentine peacemaking, which takes the form of notarized peace agreements, of which I have analyzed a database of over five hundred contracts covering the period from 1257 to 1343. The agreements depict peace as an act of mutual consent between parties, in that they are drawn up as bilateral pacts, which entrust the power to make peace to the adversarial parties themselves. Despite the tendency still present in some of the scholarly literature to call these agreements *paci private*, or private peace contracts, they were anything but private settlements. Though they were agreements between private citizens, they were not separate, apart, or outside the public justice system, because as the jurist Alberto Gandino (d. 1299) was to argue: every crime offends not only the victim, but also the entire community.[34] And conversely, as Niccoli remarks, every individual peace agreement also had bearing on the peace of society at large.[35] But to point this out is also to draw attention to a terminological difficulty that results from an out-of-date view of medieval justice that distinguishes between private and public systems of dispute processing. In this formulation, private or personal justice, which frequently took the form of negotiated settlements or other informal practices, is ordinarily associated with the early and central medieval period, often construed as a "stateless society."[36] This positivist narrative of medieval legal history further argues that concomitant with the rise of the state, a strong public judicial system emerged which arrogated to itself the coercive power to punish, replacing more personal and private forms of justice. But as a generation of legal historians led by Massimo Vallerani, Mario Sbriccoli, and Thomas Kuehn has now shown, there is "no nice contrast between private and public systems;" nor can a rigidly evolutionary model be traced from "private grievances to public prosecution of crimes."[37] The very existence and continued use of peace agreements (and for that matter

---

34. . . . "quia omnis delinquens offendit rem publicam civitatis," Alberto Gandino, *Tractatus de maleficiis*. Quoted by Padoa Schioppa, "Delitto e pace privata nel pensiero dei legisti bolognesi," 286–87.

35. Niccoli, "Rinuncia, pace, perdono," 252.

36. For a good introduction to the problem, see Patrick J. Geary, "Living with Conflicts in Stateless France: A Typology of Conflict Management Mechanisms, 1050–1200," in *Living with Dead in the Middle Ages* (Ithaca, NY: Cornell University Press, 1994), 125–60; originally published as "Vivre en conflit dans un France sans état: Typologie des mechanisms de règlement des conflits, 1050–1200," *Annales ESC* 41 (1986): 1107–33.

37. Thomas Kuehn quoting Massimo Vallerani, "Social and Legal Capital in Vendetta: A Fifteenth-Century Florentine Feud in and out of Court," in *Sociability and its Discontents: Civil Society, Social Capital, and Their Alternatives in Late Medieval and Early Modern Europe*, ed. Nicholas A. Eckstein and Nicholas Terpstra (Turnhout: Brepols, 2009), 51–72, at 62; and then Kuehn himself at 69.

arbitrations) in the age of popular governments and their communal courts belies this tidy narrative. My work on peace instruments supports these revisionist interpretations.

But it is equally important, as Vallerani observes, to discard another piece of that older narrative which regards peace agreements as a "sign of backwardness and weakness in juridical systems."[38] Toward this end, scholars have now reached a new consensus that understands peace instruments as "infra-judicial" forms of dispute settlement instead of private resolutions. Not divorced from the courts, they frequently interacted with legal processes already underway and indeed had the imprimatur of statute law and the judiciary.[39] Sbriccoli takes the argument even further; he suggests that in the podestarial courts of the communes, the peace instrument evolved from a personal to a public remedy or what he calls a *pax publica, seu civitatis*.[40] Furthermore, he regards the pax as a form of procedure in itself, a third form alongside accusation and inquisition.[41]

All this is to say that recent legal scholarship gives the peace agreement an important place in the communal courts, or as Sarah Rubin Blanshei so well observes:

The case, dispute, or trial is not the only focus of the study of law. The emphasis is on reconciliation as much as, if not more so, than punishment, and therefore the use of a peace accord, or pax, to conclude a trial is not a sign of the weakness of the legal system, not a relic of an earlier, atavistic system, but a means of dispute resolution that meets the needs of that society. Dispute resolution is treated as a positive process, not as a barometer of a society's pathology.[42]

Such scholarship, built on the insights and methods of legal anthropologists, has been of the utmost importance in guiding my analysis and contextualization of the mountain of peace instruments I have collected from the archives.[43] The "approach" they advocate necessitates seeing each case

38. Massimo Vallerani, *Medieval Public Justice*, trans. Sarah Rubin Blanshei (Washington, D.C.: Catholic University Press, 2012), 6; originally published as *La giustizia pubblica medievale* (Bologna: Il Mulino, 2005).

39. Kuehn, "Social and Legal Capital," 62.

40. Mario Sbriccoli, "'Vidi communiter observari:' L'emersione di un ordine penale pubblico nelle città italiane del secolo XIII," *Quaderni fiorentini per la storia del pensiero giuridico moderno* 27 (1998): 231–68, at 236.

41. Sbriccoli, "'Vidi communiter observari,'" 235–36. As should be evident, these revisionists, led by Vallerani, also reject the older narrative that posited a linear progression from accusatorial to inquisitional procedure. For an admirably clear précis of that historiography, see Sarah Rubin Blanshei's foreword to Vallerani, *Medieval Public Justice*, ix-xii.

42. Blanshei, foreword, *Medieval Public Justice*, ix.

43. All are indebted to Max Gluckman, "Peace in the Feud," *Past and Present* 8.1 (1955):

holistically; that is, as a process that takes into account prior relationships, background history, the dispute, the court case (if there is one), and the settlement. The larger whole is made up of unfolding episodes, each shedding light on the other. Though our documents rarely allow us to ascertain the backstory; they do furnish us with information about the dispute and its resolution, the subjects of the central chapters of this book.

Chapters 3 and 4 use the methods of social history—quantitative analysis and sampling—to excavate the crimes and wrongs for which Florentines made peace. Chapter 3 can be considered a contribution to the history of crime in so far as I have formulated typologies of crimes and misdemeanors and offer some revealing statistics on disputes that were remedied with a peace contract.[44] They ranged from fists fights to homicides, but also included cases of theft, domestic violence, violations against the *gabelle*, and even rape. This is to say that there was a surprisingly wide array of issues that could be resolved with a notarial pax, but bare-fisted brawling was by far the crime that most peace agreements sought to address. The processual model of dispute settlement has taught us that any discussion of a conflict must include an analysis of its resolution. Consequently, the chapter articulates in detail how a peace settlement was envisioned as an act of mutual consent, given documentary form by public notaries, and embedded firmly in the judicial system. As distinct from the impression given by chroniclers, those making peace in medieval Florence were everyday folk—both women and men—not just the local grandees. Because of its low cost and speed, along with its apparent ability to restore social equilibrium by not assigning blame to either party, it was a procedure that clearly fulfilled a public need.

As distinct from the everyday street violence analyzed in the previous chapter, chapter 4 foregrounds those peace agreements meant to put an end

---

1–14. See also, among others, Sally Falk Moore, *Law as Process: An Anthropological Approach* (London: Routledge, 1978); Simon Roberts, *Order and Dispute: An Introduction to Legal Anthropology* (New York: Penguin, 1979); and *Disputes and Settlements*, ed. John Bossy.

44. For some representative works on medieval crime, see Trevor Dean, *Crime in Medieval Europe* (New York: Longman, 2001); Barbara Hanawalt, *Crime and Conflict in English Communities, 1300–1348* (Cambridge: Harvard University Press, 1979); Hanawalt and David Wallace, *Medieval Crime and Social Control* (Minneapolis: University of Minnesota Press, 1999); and the many works of Andrea Zorzi, including *Istituzioni giudiziarie e aspetti della criminalità nella Firenze tardomedievale*, ed. A. Zorzi, *Ricerche storiche* 18.3 (1988); "Giustizia criminale e criminalità nell'Italia del tardo Medioevo: studi e prospettive di ricerca," *Società e storia* 12 (1989): 923–65; and *Rassegna a base regionale delle fonti e degli studi su istituzioni giudiziarie, giustizia e criminalità nell'Italia del basso Medioevo*, ed. A. Zorzi, *Ricerche storiche* 19–22 (1989–1992). See also Garthine Walker, *Crime, Gender and Social Order in Early Modern England* (Cambridge: Cambridge University Press, 2003); and most recently, Hannah Skoda, *Medieval Violence: Physical Brutality in Northern France, 1270–1330* (Oxford: Oxford University Press, 2013).

to vendetta, an institutionalized form of enmity and itself a legal remedy in Florence for processing disputes. While almost anything could lead to the violence that manifested all too often as revenge killings, this chapter reveals how notaries modified their legal agreements to facilitate peace, while at the same time distinguishing with linguistic subtlety this form of violence in the contracts. I have learned much from the scholarship produced over the decades by early medievalists on the topic of vengeance and peacemaking, though a consideration of penance has not ordinarily informed studies of these interrelated topics.[45] As in the previous chapter, my analysis is also indebted to a new generation of anthropologically minded historians working in the later medieval period who have revised the ways in which we understand vengeance, violence, and dispute processing.[46] That is, their work has shown that violence should be analyzed as a cultural construct that expresses meaning. Or, as Anton Blok has observed, "rather than defining violence a priori as senseless and irrational, we should consider it as a changing form of interaction and communication, as a historically developed cultural form of *meaningful* action."[47] Thus it is important for historians interested in human behavior to examine the cultural context of violence to decipher

45. There is now an enormous body of research on violence, vengeance, and dispute resolution in the early and central Middle Ages. I limit myself to citing a few key recent studies. William Miller, *Bloodtaking and Peacemaking: Feud, Society, and Law in Saga Iceland* (Chicago: University of Chicago Press, 1990); the collected essays of Stephen D. White, *Feuding and Peacemaking in Eleventh-Century France* (Burlington, VT: Ashgate, 2005); Paul Hyams, *Rancor and Reconciliation in Medieval England* (Ithaca, NY: Cornell University Press, 2003); *Feud, Violence and Practice: Essays in Medieval Studies in Honor of Stephen D. White*, ed. Belle S. Tuten and Tracey L. Billado (Burlington, VT: Ashgate, 2010); Warren Brown, *Violence in Medieval Europe* (London: Routledge, 2010); and *Vengeance in the Middle Ages: Emotion, Religion and Feud*, ed. Susanna A. Throop and Paul R. Hyams (Burlington, VT : Ashgate, 2010).
46. See, for example, Thomas Kuehn, "Dispute Processing in the Renaissance: Some Florentine Examples," in *Law, Family, and Women: Towards a Legal Anthropology of Renaissance Italy* (Chicago: University of Chicago Press, 1991), 75–100; Kuehn, "Social and Legal Capital in Vendetta," ibid., 51–72; Andrea Zorzi, "'Ius erat in armis': Faide e conflitti tra pratiche sociali e pratiche di governo," in *Origini dello Stato: Processi di formazione statale in Italia fra medioevo ed età moderna. Atti del convegno internazionale, Chicago, 26–29 aprile 1993*, ed. G. Chittolini, A. Molho, and P. Schiera (Bologna: Il Mulino, 1994), 609–29; and "La cultura della vendetta nel conflitto politico in età comunale," in *Le storie e la memoria. In onore di Arnold Esch*, ed. R. Delle Donne and A. Zorzi (Florence: Reti Medievali— Firenze University Press, 2002) [E-book, reading 1], 135–70; Daniel Lord Smail, "Common Violence: Vengeance and Inquisition in Fourteenth-Century Marseille," *Past and Present* 151 (1996): 28–59; Smail, *The Consumption of Justice: Emotions, Publicity, and Legal Culture in Marseille, 1264–1423* (Ithaca, NY: Cornell University Press, 2003); Chris Wickham, *Community and Clientele in Twelfth-Century Tuscany: The Origins of the Rural Commune in the Plain of Lucca* (Oxford: Oxford University Press, 1998); and Trevor Dean, *Crime and Justice in Late Medieval Italy* (Cambridge: Cambridge University Press, 2007).
47. Anton Blok, *Honour and Violence* (Malden, MA: Blackwell, 2001), 104.

the meanings its enactors intended to communicate with their actions, and to distinguish, so far as it is possible, instrumental uses of violence from expressive uses.[48]

In a similar vein, this chapter argues that we must look at the willingness of those accused of perpetrating a crime to undergo banishment as a meaningful action. That is, rather than focusing on contumacy rates as a weakness of the court system, we should be looking at banishment—the judicial outcome of contumacy—as a strategic choice made by individuals. A peace instrument, when drawn up after banishment, could yield a more positive outcome than a court case. Instead of standing trial and risking a harsh penalty, one could choose to flee Florentine jurisdiction, endure banishment, and then use a peace agreement to return under more favorable conditions that might include reduced penalties or cancelled sentences. It was a strategic risk, but one many Florentines were prepared to take. My work shows that the use of the pax for this purpose was second only to its use for ending unarmed violence. Towering over this chapter is the work of Andrea Zorzi, the trail-blazing historian of medieval Florence, whose many innovative studies on vendetta, violence, and their place in the Florentine legal system have shaped my own interpretation of the material. I close the chapter with a reading of Albertanus of Brescia's *Liber consolationis et concilii* (ca. 1246), an anti-vendetta tract, which, I suggest, partially lifts the veil that ordinarily conceals the "behind the scenes" negotiations of most dispute settlements.[49]

Just as the previous chapter emphasized vendetta as a communicative form of violence, chapter 5 insists on regarding the rituals of peacemaking as an expressive and performative language, one often overshadowed by the more seductive topic of ritual violence. Unlike historians of the early medieval period, Italian scholars of communal Italy have been somewhat reluctant to study rituals, regarding them as "relics of pre-political practices."[50] In my view, rituals in the communal period were anything but relics of a stateless past. To disregard the ritual kiss associated with peace agreements is to miss the rich symbolic meaning that is incorporated into the choreography of peacemaking. In an attempt to decipher the meaning of the kiss of peace, I trace

48. Blok, *Honour and Violence*, 107. For similar observations on the medieval context, see Skoda, *Medieval Violence*, 1–8.

49. *Albertani Brixiensis Liber Consolationis et Consilii, ex quo hausta est fabula gallica de Melibeo et Prudentia, quam, anglice redditam et 'The Tale of Melibe' inscriptam, Galfridus Chaucer inter 'Canterbury Tales' recepit*, ed. Thor Sundby (London: N. Trübner & Co., 1873).

50. Marcello Fantoni, "Symbols and Rituals: Definition of a Field of Study," in *Late Medieval and Early Modern Ritual: Studies in Italian Urban Culture*, ed. Samuel Cohn, Jr., Marcello Fantoni, Franco Franceschi, and Fabrizio Ricciardelli (Brepols: Turnhout, 2012), 15–40. It should be noted that a generation ago American scholars such as Ed Muir and Richard Trexler were analyzing the early modern cities of Venice and Florence through the lens of ritual studies.

its evolution, showing how it migrated from the Mass to the civil ceremony of peacemaking and how it continued to function therein. [51] An element of the Christian Mass, itself a rite that, according to Durkheim, is a "symbolic act that implies the involvement of a supernatural entity,"[52] the ritual kiss of peace retained its association with the holy, even in its civic context. As witnessed by the visual evidence, I argue that the meaning of the kiss of peace on the mouth, now embedded in civic practice, continued to resonate with that sacred power. The work of ritual theorists and anthropologists such as Catherine Bell and Paul Connerton, among others, has informed my treatment of this topic, helping me to put the body at the forefront of my analysis, and to consider more fully how the ritual enactment of the kiss may have been experienced, understood, and remembered by both those who participated in it and those who witnessed it.[53]

The chapter then analyzes a few extended ritual performances, as outlined in some extraordinary peace agreements from Rome and San Gimignano, in order to disclose the penitential context that informed them. In the case of San Gimignano, a number of marriage contracts issued from the peace, which provide the basis for my discussion of marriage alliances made "for the good of peace." The final contribution of this chapter is to interpret the iconography of peacemaking offered by the visual evidence. By incorporating the visual imagery of the kiss of peace into the discussion, I show how the peacemaking act was inscribed into social memory in late medieval Italy. Having collected a corpus of images depicting the kiss of peace, comprised of wall paintings, ex-voto panels, tomb sculpture, and manuscript illuminations, I use these materials to make the case for the critical role ritual continued to play in dispute processing in an age that few would regard as "pre-political."[54] Close attention to the visual material ultimately also throws light on the iconographic function of the angel, who appears in a great many of the images, but whose role as a mediator of peace has never before been problematized or indeed analyzed in relation to the medieval theology of angels. Nor have the images ever before been put into dialogue with each other to underscore their shared theological and social matrix, and to demonstrate what they—as visual evidence—can contribute to the late medieval conversation about peacemaking. In tandem

51. For the kiss in the Mass, see John Bossy, "The Mass as Social Institution, 29–61.

52. Quoted by Fantoni, "Symbols and Rituals," 17.

53. Catherine Bell, *Ritual Theory, Ritual Practice* (Oxford: Oxford University Press, 1992); and Paul Connerton, *How Societies Remember* (Cambridge: Cambridge University Press, 1989).

54. My work also contributes to the debate about historians' use of ritual analysis. For the two poles of the debate, see Philippe Buc, *The Dangers of Ritual: Between Early Medieval Texts and Social Scientific Theory* (Princeton: Princeton University Press, 2001); and Geoffrey Koziol, "The Dangers of Polemic: Is Ritual Still an Interesting Topic of Historical Study?" *Early Medieval Europe* 11.4 (2002): 367–88.

with the kiss, the angel's presence imparts sacrality to the scene, elevating the
civic transaction of peacemaking above the mundane world and into the tran-
scendent state of holy peace that human beings can reach only through an act
of repentance. The visual evidence, then, returns us to the religious context
of peacemaking with which we began. It does so by depicting how intimately
entwined are the civic and sacred settings. The angel, the mediator between
God and humankind, and denizen of the heavenly city of Jerusalem, presides
over the ritual enactment of civic peace on earth, protecting its enactors in the
merciful embrace of his outstretched wings.

Peace of course is one of the most important subjects of any age, but it has
not had the attention that it demands, especially in the medieval period. This
may be for any number of reasons, among them the perception epitomized in
Thomas Hardy's oracular pronouncement in *The Dynasts*: "War makes rat-
tling good history; but peace is poor reading." In the event, I hope that this
present study, which looks at conceptions of peace, its social practice, and its
commemoration in late medieval Italy, will make a first step toward dispelling
that impression.

CHAPTER ONE

Preaching, Penance, and Peacemaking in the Age of the Commune

Blessed are the peacemakers
for they shall be called children of God.

—MATTHEW 5:9

IN 1425 THE RULING MAGISTRACY of Siena invited Bernardino of Siena (d. 1444), one of the great lights of the Franciscan Observance, to preach a cycle of sermons for the moral edification of its citizens. During his three-month residency in the city, he preached at different venues, including the Sala dei Nove, a chamber of government sometimes called the "Hall of Peace," in the Palazzo Pubblico, Siena's town hall. In a sermon given on Sunday, June 3rd, he invoked the hall's celebrated murals, painted by Ambrogio Lorenzetti, another celebrated son of Siena. Those frescoes, executed almost a century earlier, depicted an allegory that illustrated the positive effects of good government and the prophecy of a dire future if tyranny were allowed to reign in its stead.[1] Bernardino had been preaching on the theme of peace for some

---

1. The literature on these wall murals is vast; I list here only the works that have influenced my thinking about them. Quentin Skinner, "The Artist as Political Philosopher," *Proceedings of the British Academy* 72 (1986): 1–56; Randolph Starn, "The Republican Regime of the 'Room of Peace' in Siena, 1338–40," *Representations* 18 (1987): 1–33; Jack Greenstein, "The Vision of Peace: Meaning and Representation in Ambrogio Lorenzetti's Sala della Pace Cityscapes," *Art History* 11. 4 (1988): 492–510; Randolph Starn and Loren Partridge, *Arts of Power: Three Halls of State in Italy, 1300–1600* (Berkeley: University of California Press, 1992); Randolph Starn, *Ambrogio Lorenzetti: The Palazzo Pubblico, Siena* (New York: George Braziller, 1994); Nicolai Rubinstein, "Le allegorie di Ambrogio

years, and had established so sterling a reputation as a peacemaker that, by the time of his death, it was cited as proof of his sanctity during his canonization process.[2] Burnishing that reputation in 1425, Bernardino used the Hall of Peace murals as both stage set and heuristic device when, gesturing toward the frescoes on Good Government, he informed his audience that his theme for the day was "War and Peace":

> Turning toward Peace, I see goods circulating, I see dancing, I see the building of houses, I see fields and vines being worked and planted, I see people going out on horseback to the hot springs, I see young women on their way to be married, I see flocks of goats and sheep. And I see a man hanged to uphold holy Justice. And to facilitate these things, everyone lives in holy peace and concord.

But then, turning toward the opposite wall, which shows the misfortunes that bad government and discord have the potential to unleash, Bernardino conjured a hair-raising description that matched the pictorial narrative point-by-point:

> On the contrary, turning to the other side, I don't see any goods; I don't see any dancing. Instead I see someone being killed; I don't see any houses being built; instead I see devastation and arson; no one is working the fields or pruning the vines, no one is sowing, no one goes out to the hot springs or pursues pastimes anymore; I don't even see anyone venturing outside the city walls. O women! O men! The dead man, the woman assaulted, flocks only as prey, treacherous men killing each other. Justice, her scales broken, lies bound hand and foot on the ground.[3]

One can only imagine the shudders that ran down the collective spine of the audience as Bernardino prophesied a future without peace. Surely it must have stirred the city fathers' corporate will to prevent such a terrible fate. For over a century the republican governments of central and northern Italy had envisioned peace and security as the ends of good government, but the persistent

---

Lorenzetti nella Sala della Pace e il pensiero politico del suo tempo," *Rivista Storica Italiana* 109 (1997): 781–802; Robert Gibbs, "In Search of Ambrogio Lorenzetti's Allegory of Justice: Changes to the Frescoes in the Palazzo Pubblico," *Apollo* 149, no. 477 (1999): 11–16; and Quentin Skinner, "Ambrogio Lorenzetti's *Buon Governo* Frescoes: Two Old Questions, Two New Answers," *Journal of the Warburg and Courtauld Institutes* 62 (1999): 1–28.

2. The canonization process noted that "he brought peace and concord to enemies, he ended quarrels, fights, and discord; he disseminated peace, concord and love everywhere and he extinguished old hatreds." Celestino Piana O.F.M., "I processi di canonizzazione su la vita di S. Bernardino di Siena," *AFH* 44 (1951): 87–160, and 383–435, Article XIII, 387; other mentions at 120, 156, 158 n.1, 88, 419, 421, 424, and 431. Cited in Polecritti, *Preaching Peace*, 85.

3. *Le prediche volgari. Predicazione del 1425 Siena*, ed. Ciro Cannarozzi, 2 vols. (Florence: Rinaldi, 1958), vol. 2: Sermo XL, 254–75, at 266–67.

question had become: how to achieve those ends? How could war and discord be transformed into peace and concord? Naturally Bernardino had the solution to hand. Repentance. Through penance one made peace with God. It was the foundation stone upon which every other type of peace—peace with one's family, one's neighbor, one's enemy—was to be constructed. Two years later, in another sermon cycle also delivered in Siena, the preacher refined and reframed his discussion, noting, "There are two types of peace: the one within and the other without."[4] The one within—the peace of the heart—was attained only through moral reform, the result of true penance.

Bernardino stands near the end of a long line of medieval preachers who entwined the topics of penitence and peace in their sermons, the subject of this chapter. The deep connection between the two subjects may not be self-evident today, but it was an affiliation that medieval Christians regularly encountered if they were attentive to the messages transmitted in the sermons of their preachers.[5] The sermon of Luca da Bitonto, invoked in the preface of this study, is a case in point. This chapter shows that the various religious movements of the later Middle Ages, usually viewed as distinct and independent entities, should be understood collectively as peace movements that took the form of penitential processions. Led by laypeople or friars, all these movements shared a theology that linked peace to penance, the motor, they believed, that drove social and political change. I argue, moreover, that civic peacemaking practices of the late medieval period can only be fully understood as products formed in the religious matrix this chapter establishes, one that firmly yoked together peace and penance. Forged in the crucible of late antiquity, the marriage of peace and repentance developed out of the ritual kiss embedded in the Mass. Its original function was to bind and unify in peace and fraternity what was sometimes a fractious early Christian community. As we shall see in chapter 5, by the late antique period, theologians had added a new layer of meaning to the kiss, construing it as a ritual of reconciliation, our point of departure.[6]

4. *Prediche volgari sul Campo di Siena 1427*, ed. Carlo Delcorno, 2 vols. (Milan: Rusconi, 1989), vol. 1, 383–84. On which see Polecritti, *Preaching Peace*, 124. In this case, sent by Pope Martin V and Bishop Antonio Casini to reestablish the peace, he began his sermon cycle on the feast of the assumption. See Piana, "I processi di canonizzazione," 387 n.2.

5. An insightful article on the subject is Clara Gennaro, "Movimenti religiosi e pace nel XIV secolo," in *La pace nel pensiero nella politica negli ideali del Trecento, 13–17 Ottobre, 1974* Centro degli Studi sulla spiritualità medievale 15 (Todi: L'Accademia Tudertina, 1975), 93–112.

6. Michael Philip Penn, *Kissing Christians: Ritual and Community in the Late Ancient Church* (Philadelphia: University of Pennsylvania Press, 2005), 43–45. Significantly, Penn finds scant evidence in the Graeco-Roman tradition that the kiss was understood as an act of reconciliation, thereby lending more credence to the argument that this was a late antique Christian innovation. For an extended discussion on the kiss of peace, see chapter 5 of the present work.

Reconciliation was at the very heart of the sacrament of penance as it developed and was then subsequently codified by Pope Innocent III (d. 1216) at the Fourth Lateran Council in 1215. Canon 21, *omnis utriusque sexus*, decreed that every member of the Church was now required to make an annual confession of sin in order to partake in communion. The council furthermore compelled the Christian faithful to fulfill all penances imposed by priests. Excommunication and the prohibition of Christian burial awaited those who did not comply. Henry Charles Lea likely overstated its significance when he called canon twenty-one "perhaps the most important legislative act in the history of the Church," but his point is well made that this was a new and very different expression of the sacrament.[7] Though auricular confession had been part of local practice before the thirteenth century, it had never before been decreed as an obligation on a universal scale, supported by the full weight and power of ecclesiastical sanctions. This newly reformulated idea of penance was important for many reasons, not the least of which was that, as we shall see, it became the primary message broadcast by the friars through their preaching. Reconciliation was the connective tissue that linked the ideas of peace and penance together. Through the sacrament of penance—which now included a confession of one's sins— one reconciled with God, while one reconciled with one's enemy by means of a peace contract, a different but analogous sort of confession of guilt.

The interlocking story of peace and penance begins in the years just prior to the Fourth Lateran Council. It was a period in communal history when the cities of central and northern Italy had liberated themselves from imperial and episcopal yokes, and had begun experimenting with new popular forms of government. But it was a time not without tribulations. From local feuds and factions involving magnates and popolo, to Guelf and Ghibelline strife within and without the city walls, to wars against the empire or papacy—not to speak of the Crusades and other external conflicts—blood feud, violence, and warfare dominated the landscape up and down the Italian peninsula. Nor should we forget the strain put on ordinary citizens inside the urban walls, as demographic pressures caused cities to expand at previously unheard-of rates. In the case of Florence alone, the commune's population tripled (perhaps even quadrupled), as immigrants from the countryside migrated to the city over the course of the thirteenth century. It is no wonder that violence often exploded on the streets, as already teeming urban spaces became even more overcrowded, and city dwellers were forced to accommodate newcomers, particularly in the Oltrarno neighborhood.

7. *A History of Auricular Confession and Indulgences in the Latin Church*, 3 vols. (Philadelphia: Lea Bros. & Co., 1896), vol. 1, 230; but see also Thomas Tentler, *Sin and Confession on the Eve of the Reformation* (Princeton: Princeton University Press, 1977) and Alexander Murray, *Conscience and Authority in the Medieval Church* (Oxford: Oxford University Press, 2015), a collection of previously published essays, all of which treat the topic of confession.

One response to the pervasive violence that characterized the period was to form peace movements. Cries of "peace and mercy" were the sparks that flew from a sort of spontaneous combustion that galvanized everyday folk who, in the second quarter of the thirteenth century, began to search for a way to usher in the period of respite prophesied by Isaiah, who foretold: "My people will sit in the beauty of peace" (Isaiah 26:3). In surveying the terrain from the thirteenth to early fifteenth century, we will meet many people—both men and women—who were peacemakers or leaders of religious revivals that were dedicated to peace. All were shaped by convictions, imagery, and ritual rooted deeply in the soil of medieval Christianity. Many were priests, but many were laypeople, the latter often penitents, who lived their lives according to the precepts of penance, imagined as a life converted from sin and devoted to acts of repentance, expiation, self-mortification, and alms-giving, not infrequently held together by the bonds of voluntary poverty. This path was envisioned as a permanent process, a life's work, which called for constant vigilance and attentiveness to the pitfalls of the secular world. Those pitfalls included vanity, lust, gambling, magic, and usury, a catalogue made famous by Bernardino of Siena's fire-and-brimstone sermons denouncing them.[8]

The polemics of the preachers notwithstanding, many of the movements and practices that emerged in this period were led and inspired by laypeople. Indeed they were often first on the scene to agitate for peace. We shall see, however, that the mendicant orders, which arrived in the urban centers of Italy in the first quarter of the thirteenth century, often co-opted local nonviolence movements. The resulting pacification campaigns led the friars to work closely with city magistrates to promote peace and concord through the reform of local statute law. By leveraging their spiritual authority, the friars acted as mediators and facilitators to settle what were often deep-seated antagonisms and conflicts that, left unchecked, had the potential to explode and wreak havoc in the crowded urban spaces where people lived cheek by jowl. But it was their sermons, some still extant, that formulated a path to peace and rallied their followers toward action. They showed how peace could be achieved by putting it into a Christian framework of penance and reconciliation. This chapter, then, examines some notable examples of preachers of peace (be they clergy or penitents), their sermons, and the penitential peace movements that

8. It should be noted that popular preachers such as Bernardino, along with some of his predecessors and disciples—Franciscan and Dominican alike—also denounced Jews, sodomites, witches, heretics, and prostitutes, groups of people they believed were especially associated with these sins. The preachers had the rhetorical power to mobilize their listeners against these groups, often with predictably ugly results. For two studies that examine this subject with regard to the fomentation incited by the Observant Franciscans, see Jeremy Cohen, *The Friars and the Jews: the Evolution of Medieval Anti-Judaism* (Ithaca NY: Cornell University Press, 1982); and Franco Mormando, *The Preacher's Demons: Bernardino of Siena and the Social Underworld of Renaissance Italy* (Chicago: University of Chicago Press, 1999).

periodically burst onto the urban landscape throughout the thirteenth and fourteenth centuries. It also begins the work, continued in subsequent chapters, of examining the social practices their words and deeds inspired. I range widely through the territory of central and northern Italy in order to bring as many voices into the conversation as possible, but attentive readers will note that throughout this chapter I periodically return to Florence to analyze the impact that these religious peacemakers and practices had on the city.

"THE TRANQUILITY OF ORDER": SAINT AUGUSTINE AND THE PREACHERS

Like so many medieval ideas, the intertwining of peace and repentance was indebted to Augustine of Hippo, who formulated a definition of "peace" in *The City of God.* He argued that "the peace of all things is the tranquility of order."[9] As always, his meaning is far more complex than that deceptively simple sentence suggests at first glance. Above all, he meant that the body and soul maintain equilibrium—peace—when all parts are arranged in fitting and harmonious order. But that harmonious order had been disturbed notoriously through original sin, when the will itself became unhinged, at war with itself, and at odds with the Lord. The fall of man had brought about a *discordium malum* that was incompatible with the tranquility of order.[10]

By the later Middle Ages, the healing balm of the penitential sacrament—administered through equal parts contrition, confession, and absolution—was the medicament believed to restore the delicate balance that ordered body and soul and its relationship with God. When an individual came to the Lord with a contrite heart, peace was established, an inner spiritual tranquility. And interior peace was imagined as the bedrock on top of which exterior peace and concord could then rise. Indeed it was the prerequisite for familial peace, harmony between neighbors, and civic concord, all of which adumbrated dimly the glorious peace of the celestial city, "the perfectly ordered and harmonious enjoyment of God, and of one another in God."[11]

Caritas, or love, was the key. Its blazing heat melted even the hardest hearts. Aldobrandino Cavalcanti (d. 1279), a Dominican preacher who spent most of his career in Florence, citing Job 41:24, likened the heart, hardened through sin, to a cold stone; but that spiritual hardness—much like ice—could be liquefied, thawed through the fire of ardent *caritas.*[12] Love, or more

---

9. Augustine of Hippo, *The City of God*, trans. Marcus Dods (New York: Random House, 1950), Bk 19: 13, 690.

10. Peter Brown, *The Body and Society: Men, Women, and Sexual Renunciation in Early Christianity* (New York: Columbia University Press, 1988), 404–408.

11. Augustine of Hippo, *The City of God*, Bk 19: 13, 690.

12. MS BAV Borgh. 175, fol. 27v; *RLS* 1: 340; and for liquefaction through the application of caritas, see a sermon by the Franciscan Iohannes de Castello, MS Assisi 470, fol. 495r; *RLS* 3: 726.

specifically love for Christ, would ignite the flame of contrition, leading to the penitential act of confession. The culmination of the rite looked forward to a reconciliation in the form of forgiveness or absolution, whereupon inner tranquility or peace would be restored.

Thomas Aquinas (d. 1274), a contemporary and confrère of Aldobrandino, made a similar argument in the *Summa Theologiae* while clarifying the relationship between charity and peace. Love, according to Thomas, is to be understood as a constituent element of peace. Though not itself a virtue, peace was an attribute of charity, the highest of the three theological virtues infused at baptism. Peace "is the work of charity directly, since charity, according to its very nature, causes peace." Quoting the tract on divine names by the late antique Neoplatonic Christian philosopher now known as Pseudo-Dionysius the Areopagite, Thomas argues that "love is a 'unitive force' as Dionysius says (*Div. Nom.* iv): and peace is the union of the appetite's inclinations."[13] In addition to Pseudo-Dionysius, Thomas was clearly echoing Augustine, who had suggested that peace "of the irrational soul is the harmonious repose of the appetites."[14] And that union or inner peace, the two great theologians agreed, was the basis for establishing exterior peace with family, neighbors, and fellow citizens, otherwise designated as concord.

Giordano da Pisa (d. 1311), a Dominican friar steeped in Thomastic thought, whose career was spent preaching in the public squares of Florence, took the message of peace and charity to the streets. In a sermon given on January 31, 1304 (1305), during a particularly violent period in which both the Whites and Blacks, the Guelfs and Ghibellines, were causing such turmoil in the city that the pope was forced to send Cardinal Niccolò of Prato to Florence as special envoy to negotiate what turned out to be a failed peace, Giordano waded into the fray to preach a message of peace. Preaching in the vernacular at Santa Maria Novella, he informed his audience in no uncertain terms that peace depended on the indwelling of Christ in the heart:

> It's not peace, no, when you don't forgive from the heart but remain in bad faith. But when Christ is the mediator, it's the real thing because it's from the heart. And when is Christ the mediator? When a person is moved to pardon his enemy solely out love for Christ: "I don't want to lose Christ on account of your enmity: I want to pardon you to have Christ." Now these are good peace settlements, secure ones, because they are the ones where Christ is the mediator.[15]

13. *Summa Theologica,* trans. Fathers of the English Dominican Province, 3 vols. (New York: Benzinger Bros., 1947–48), II pars IIae, *Of Peace,* q. 29, a. 3. Online at: http://dhspriory.org/thomas/summa/SS/SS029.html#SSQ29OUTP1 [consulted 6/21/17]

14. Augustine of Hippo, ibid.

15. *Prediche del Beato Giordano da Rivalto dell'Ordine dei Predicatori*, ed. Domenico Maria Manni (Florence: Viviani, 1739), Sermo XXX, 134. Delivered in the vernacular,

Invoking as he did *le paci buone* and *le paci secure*, Giordano knew well the profile of good and secure peace settlements made in accordance with the norms prescribed by Florentine statutory law.

Even if the Dominican firebrand Savonarola (d. 1498) thought otherwise, the Order of Preachers did not stand alone as peacemakers in this period.[16] Peacemaking and penance were a natural fit for the early Franciscans too, as the pope had mandated expressly that they exhort penance in place of preaching on the mysteries of the Church, difficult matters which required a more advanced and rigorous theological education. And there was no doubt that the faction-riven communes were in need of models and brokers of peace. Thus the marriage of peacemaking and penance turned out to be a felicitous union, well suited to both the needs of the Friars Minor and society at large.

Some of the earliest Franciscan documents testify to Francis's preoccupation with peacemaking. His testament discloses that the Lord revealed to him his familiar salutation, "May the Lord give you peace." But Francis did more than greet people in the name of peace; he actively sought to craft it. Though none of his sermons survives, Thomas of Spalato paints a vivid portrait of the efficacy of the saint's preaching on peace in Bologna in the year 1222:

> In the same year on the Feast of the Assumption of the Mother of God, when I was a student at Bologna, I saw Saint Francis preaching in the piazza in front of the Palazzo Pubblico, where almost the whole city had convened. The beginning of his sermon dealt with angels, men, and demons, and continued to discuss the three rational spirits. The

---

Giordano's lively sermons were taken down in *reportatio* format by an eager listener. Consequently they have retained much of the flavor they had when delivered "live." For Giordano, see Carlo Delcorno, *Giordano da Pisa e l'antica predicazione volgare* (Florence: Leo S. Olschki, 1975); and most recently, Cecilia Iannella, *Giordano da Pisa: etica urbana e forme della società* (Pisa: ETS, 1999), along with her "Predicazione domenicana ed etica urbana tra due e tre trecento," in *Predicazione e società nel medioevo: riflessione etica, valori e modelli di comportamento / Preaching and Society in the Middle Ages: Ethics, Values and Social Behaviour. Atti/Proceedings of the XII Medieval Sermon Studies Symposium Padova, 14–18 luglio 2000*, ed. Laura Gaffuri and Riccardo Quinto (Padua: Centro Studi Antoniani, 2002), 171–85. On peace and this text specifically, see Ianella's "La paix dans la prédication de Giordano de Pisa (vers 1260–1310), in *Prêcher la paix et discipliner la société: Italie, France, Angleterre (XIIIe–XVe siècles)*, ed. Rosa Maria Dessì (Turnhout: Brepols, 2005), 367–82, at 378 n.44.

16. In a sermon given on 20 January 1495, Savonarola reminds his Dominican confrères that the Order of Preachers was celebrated for its peacemakers, including, Saint Dominic, Saint Peter Martyr, Cardinal Latino Malabranca, Saint Catherine of Siena, and Saint Antonino Pierozzi. "Tell me," he asks, "who should pacify and compose the city of Florence? Certainly there is no need of those who are already partisans. Therefore, the mediator should be someone dispassionate in-between." See *Prediche sopra i Salmi*, ed. Vincenzo Romano, 2 vols. (Rome: A. Belardetti, 1969–1974), I: 107–108, cited in Dessì, "Pratiques de la parole," 259 n.54.

sermon of this ignorant man seemed worthy of no little admiration, even though he did not keep to the method of a preacher but of a *concionatore*. Indeed, the whole manner of his speech was calculated to extinguish enmities and to encourage the making of peace agreements. His tunic was dirty, his person unprepossessing and his face far from handsome; yet God gave such power to his words that many factions of the nobility, among whom the fierce anger of ancient feuds had been raging with much bloodshed, were brought to reconciliation.[17]

There is much to be said about this description of Francis's preaching, including what appears to be an allusion to Rufinus of Sorrento's categories of peace; but let us concentrate on his efforts at restoring peace to the city of Bologna. His exhortation that day was aimed at reconciling the powerful factions in a city torn apart by blood feud. The saint's humble demeanor, coupled perhaps with persuasive rhetoric stressing love and penance, pacified the belligerents and brought about the hoped-for peace between long-standing enemies.[18] Thomas of Spalato's description conjoins preaching and peacemaking. Pointedly his prose transcends platitudes when describing the peace made between factions. He stipulates that the parties drew up peace agreements, documents that signaled that this was no informal peace, but a legal peace sanctioned by and presumably registered with the civic authorities.

Another account dating from the 1240s shows Francis making the link between peace and penance explicit. The *Compilatio Assisiensis* recalls an episode near the end of the saint's life when the bishop and *podestà* of his hometown found themselves caught up in a prolonged dispute. The situation had escalated to the point that the bishop had excommunicated the podestà, who in turn retaliated by putting an embargo on all the bishop's commercial transactions with Assisi's merchants. Discord reigned. Bedridden with illness and unable to mediate in person, Francis directed his companions to extend his invitation to the podestà and grandees of the city to gather at the episcopal palace. Once there he instructed them to chant in unison his "Canticle of

17. I have used, but slightly altered to better reflect the Latin original, the translation by John R. H. Moorman, "St. Francis Preaches at Bologna," in *St. Francis of Assisi: Writings and Early Biographies: English Omnibus of the Sources for the Life of St. Francis*, ed. Marion A. Habig (Chicago: Franciscan Herald Press, 1983), 1877. For the original source, see Thomas de Spalato, *Historia Salonitarum*, ed. P. A. Lemmens, "Testimonia minora saec. XIII de sancto Francisco," in *AFH* 1 (1908): 69–84, at 69. See chapter 1 n.2 for Rufinus of Sorrento.

18. For further comment on this passage, see Rosa Maria Dessì, "Pratiques de la parole de paix dans l'histoire de l'Italie urbaine," in *Prêcher la paix*, 245–278, at 245 n.2. On the concionatore, see Carlo Delcorno, "Professionisti della parola: predicatori, giullari, concionatori," in *Tra storia e simbolo: Studi dedicati a Ezio Raimondi, dai direttori, redattori e dall'editore di Lettere italiane*, ed. Ezio Raimondi and Carlo Delcorno (Florence: Leo S. Olschki, 1994), 1–21.

Brother Sun," with particular emphasis on a brand-new verse he had penned for the occasion. They performed as directed, their voices ringing out as one:

Laudato si, miu Segnore,
per quilli ke perdonano per lo tuo amore
e sustengu enfirmitate et tribulatione;
beati quilgli kel sosteranno en pace
ka da te, Altissimo, siranno coranati.[19]
[Be praised, my Lord,
through those who forgive for love of You,
through those who endure sickness and trial.
Happy are those who carry on in peace,
for by You, Most High, they will be crowned.]

Invoking at the same time the Lord and Francis, the absent mediator whose presence was conjured among "those who endure sickness and trial," the *lauda* sung by the townspeople melted two hardened hearts that day. In an act of penitence worthy of Mary Magdalen herself—the exemplar of perfect penance—the podestà flung himself at the feet of the bishop, seeking his forgiveness.[20] The bishop received him in the same spirit of reconciliation, apologizing for his own intemperate behavior. The parties then embraced and exchanged the kiss of peace as a public sign that their quarrel had been settled.[21]

On another more famous occasion around 1220, Francis played the tripartite role of procurator, mediator, and guarantor of the terms of a peace pact when he negotiated an agreement between the city of Gubbio and a ferocious enemy who lately had been terrorizing the local citizenry. The story of the "Wolf of Gubbio" is often told as an exemplum highlighting the saint's harmonious connection with the natural world, but as some scholars have pointed out, it is also doubtless a metaphorical description of civic peacemaking practices.[22] Recounted in the collection known as *The Little Flowers of Saint Francis*, a relative latecomer to the Franciscan hagiographical canon (circa 1330s), the narrative recalls how Saint Francis negotiated with the wolf:

19. *Compilatio Assisiensis dagli scritti di fr. Leone e compagni su S. Francesco d'Assisi dal MS 1043 di Perugia*, ed. Marino Bigarmi (Assisi: Tipografia Porziuncula, 1975), 238–43.

20. Katherine Ludwig Jansen, *The Making of the Magdalen: Preaching and Popular Religion in the later Middle Ages* (Princeton: Princeton University Press, 2000), 199–244.

21. On this scene, see Thompson, *Revival Preachers*, 149–50; Dessì, "Pratiques de la parole," 246. Similarly Margaret of Cortona (d. 1288) helped to reconcile the bishop of Arezzo to the citizens of Cortona. Iuncta Bevegnatis, *Legenda de vita et miraculis beatae Margaritae de Cortona*, ed. Fortunato Iozzelli, O.F.M. [Bibliotheca Franciscana Ascetica medii aevi 13] (Grottaferrata: Editiones Collegii S. Bonaventurae ad Claras Aquas, 1997), 219, 306.

22. Thompson, *Revival Preachers*, 137–38; Polecritti, *Preaching Peace*, 88–89.

"And you, Brother Wolf, do you promise to observe the peace pact, so that you will offend neither men nor animals or any other creature?" And the wolf, kneeling and bowing his head, with tame movements of his body, tail, and ears showed how he wanted to observe each clause of the pact. Saint Francis said, "Brother Wolf, I want you to vow here before everyone, just as you promised me outside the gate, that you will not deceive me about the guarantee I've made for you." Then the wolf raised his right paw and placed it in the hand of Saint Francis.[23]

The agreement stipulated that the wolf would cease to menace the town-folk, while the citizens of Gubbio promised to keep the wolf fed so long as he should live. The once-violent wolf, now docile as a lamb (or the podestà of Assisi), gestured his penitential submission and repentance by genuflecting and bowing his head.[24] The parties sealed the contract with yet another gesture, performed in the presence of the assembled townspeople: the wolf lifted his right paw and placed it in the hand of the saintly peacemaker, acting on behalf of the town of Gubbio.[25] Given that one of the parties to peace was a wolf, it is hardly surprising that in this account a handshake rather than the standard kiss of peace on the mouth ratified this particular contract. Nonetheless, it is a nod at the ritual gesture—the kiss of peace—that ordinarily sealed an agreement of this sort. The reciprocal gesture, made in the true spirit of penance, was one meant to restore equality between the two feuding parties.

The visual tradition of this story is likely linked to the translation in the 1380s of *The Little Flowers* into Italian from Latin, for that is when our first depiction of the scene appears. In a fresco cycle in the Church of San Francesco at Corsignano, now Pienza, Francis is shown as mediator, the physical link between the city fathers and the wolf: his hands reach out to both parties (Fig. 1). The wounds of the stigmata, the manifestation of God's love for Francis, are featured prominently, emphasizing the role that charity plays in peacemaking.

A later vision of this scene from Sassetta's Borgo San Sepolcro altarpiece, painted for the church of San Francesco between 1437 and 1444, adds a significant detail (Fig. 2). The panel shows one of the wolf's victims dismembered in the background; it is the crime scene, a representation of the violent act for which a peace was required. But more to our point, it shows Francis taking the paw of the wolf in one hand, while with the other, instead of clasping the hand of a town official, he turns and gestures toward a seated notary, who is drafting a peace agreement on parchment draped over his lap. Certainly by the fifteenth century most everyone, including Sassetta, would have known that notaries were officials endowed with the public authority to draw up

23. *I Fioretti di San Francesco,* ed. Cesare Segre and Luigina Morini (Milan: Rizzoli, 1979), 123–27, at 126.
24. *I Fioretti,* 124.
25. Ibid., 126.

FIGURE 1. *Saint Francis of Assisi and the Wolf of Gubbio Make Peace.* Fresco by Cristoforo di Bindoccio and Meo di Pero, ca. 1380. Church of San Francesco, Pienza. Photo: author.

peace agreements. It is even possible that the Sienese painter had witnessed Bernardino of Siena preaching peace in the Campo ten years prior to this commission in San Sepolcro. If he had, he would have seen notaries drawing up peace agreements, a sign of verisimilitude that made its way into his rendering of this scene.[26] By inserting the notary (and his legal document), the painter seamlessly creates a narrative that invokes the union between religious and civic peacemaking. The wolf, having committed a violent crime, is brought to heel through the auspices of Saint Francis. His peace is preserved in a *pax*, a notarized legal document that is at the core of civic peacemaking.

26. Roberto Cobianchi also puts the scene into an Observant peacemaking context in "Franciscan Legislation, Patronage Practice, and new Iconography in Sassetta's Commission at Borgo San Sepolcro," in *Sassetta: The Borgo San Sepolcro Altarpiece,* ed. Machtelt Israëls, 2 vols. (Florence: Villa I Tatti, 2009), vol. 1: 107–19, at 116. This scene, from the dismembered Borgo San Sepolcro altarpiece, is now in the National Gallery, London. Machelt Israëls and a team of scholars have recently reconstructed the entire polyptych in the volume listed above. For the Pienza scene by Cristoforo di Bindoccio and Meo di Pero, see vol. 1: 134; for the iconography and the technical information of the Sassetta panel itself, see vol. 2: 511–15. The "Wolf of Gubbio" is the only scene from the life of Saint Francis not from Bonaventure's *Legenda Maior,* the source for all the important fresco cycles of the saint's life, including the Upper Church of San Francesco at Assisi, the most important of them all. The back of the altarpiece, decorated with scenes from Francis's life, was visible to the friars in the choir during Mass and to the laity at other times, particularly during visits to the tomb of Fr. Ranieri, a local saint, who was buried in the high altar.

FIGURE 2. *A Notary Records the Peace of Saint Francis of Assisi and the Wolf of Gubbio.*
Sassetta, scene from the San Sepolcro Altarpiece, ca. 1437–1444. National Gallery
of Art, London. Bought with contributions from the National Art Collections Fund,
Benjamin Guinness and Lord Bearsted, 1934 (NG4762). Photo: © National Gallery,
London/Art Resource. Reproduced by permission of Art Resource, New York.

FIGURE 3. *Two Aragonese Knights Make Peace with the Intervention of
Suor Sara and Saint Francis.* Votive panel attributed to Antonio Orsini (da
Venezia), 15th c. Musée des Arts Décoratifs, Paris. Photo: Jean Tholance.
Reproduced by permission of the Musée des Arts Décoratifs.

Long after his death supplicants continued to call on Saint Francis to mediate disputes. In 1432, one Suor Sara prayed to the saint to stop two Aragonese
knights from engaging in judicial combat that would have led to at least one
certain death. He reconciled the parties and they made peace "without any
impediment to their persons," explains the ex-voto, a panel—*dicto lavoriero*—
commissioned to commemorate the event.[27] (Fig. 3) The ex-voto is meant to be
read from the middle, where Suor Sara prays to Saint Francis on the left, who
is receiving the stigmata. On the right is the outcome of her successful prayer.
Francis has intervened to stop the two antagonists, identified as Joan Tolsà and
Joan Marrades, two Valencian knights, who had been called to the court of
the marquis Niccolò d'Este in Ferrara to fight their duel to the death. Instead,
thanks to the intervention of the saint and Suor Sara's timely prayer, they cast off
their arms, transformed their enmity into friendship, and embraced each other
in the kiss of peace. In the ex-voto, the knights are framed by their lances; their
helmets and shields, replete with heraldic devices, lie discarded at their feet.[28]

The central caption reads: "In 1422 on the 14th of October, two knights
were called to fight to the death. And the venerable Lady Madonna Suor Sara

27. It has recently been attributed to Antonio Orsini (da Venezia). For the ex-voto see,
C. S. d'Hiver, "Ex voto de San Francisco de Asis," in *A la búsqueda del Toisón de oro.
La Europa de los príncipes; la Europa de las ciudades,* ed. Eduard Mira and An
Blockmans-Delva, (Valencia: Generalitat, 2007), catalogue entry 35 and color plate,
100–101; 459–60 (English translation). For the complicated story, see Martín de Riquer,
Cavalleria fra realtà e letteratura nel Quattrocento, trans. M. Rostaing and V. Minervini
(Bari: Adriatica, 1970), 236–51.

28. My thanks to Giovanni Pagliarulo at the Villa I Tatti Fototeca for bringing this image
to my attention and supplying me with a study photo from the Kaftal study collection.

prayed to God and Saint Francis that she would have this work painted if the same knights would make peace or that they not kill each other, as appears in this present picture. And so by the grace of God and the efficacy of prayer these knights made peace without any impediment to their persons." The banderoles identify each of the Valencian knights.

PENITENTS

Suor Sara commemorated her central role in fostering this peace, but not all women were so bold in celebrating their public roles as peacemakers. Indeed, Margaret of Cortona (d. 1297), a Franciscan penitent, tried to resist her commission as peacemaker, one that the Lord himself had bestowed on her in a vision. Calling her a *clamatrix pacis*, he invited her to call the citizens of Cortona to peace, a role for which she deemed herself unworthy.[29] On another occasion, when Margaret prayed to the Lord asking for peace among the factions of Cortona, he replied with another assignment: "Daughter, tell your confessor to urge the citizens of Cortona to first acquire interior peace, and then exterior peace will follow," a refrain in the preachers' repertoire we have already heard them articulate.[30] For the most part, rather than serving as a public *clamatrix pacis*, Margaret seems to have stayed behind the scenes, praying for peace and serving as a conduit, delivering messages concerning peace sent from the Lord to her confessor, Fra Giunta.

The behind-the-scenes peacemaking activities of the Dominican penitent Catherine of Siena (d. 1370) resembled Margaret's, though they often went far beyond the local level. In his testimony in support of her canonization, one of her disciples, Stefano Maconi, highlighted her role as peacemaker between the papacy and the cities of Florence, Pisa, and Siena during the War of the Eight Saints.[31] More than once, he testified, Gregory XI sent her shuttling between Avignon and Florence in an effort to make peace. What interests us here, however, is the role that she undertook as a local facilitator of peace. Catherine's outsider status as a holy person who lived a life of penance, along with her perceived impartiality, sealed her reputation as a peacemaker, as was the case with many other penitents. In her short lifetime she assisted in settling a number of disputes in her native Tuscany. Stefano eulogized her as a peacemaker— one who could transform enmity into friendship—and noted that he once

29. Iuncta Bevegnatis, *Legenda de vita et miraculis*, 360–62. For a translation, see *The Life and Miracles of Saint Margaret of Cortona, 1247–1297*, trans. Thomas Renna (St. Bonaventure, NY: Franciscan Institute Publications, 2012), 16.

30. *The Life and Miracles of Saint Margaret*, 215.

31. For Caffarini's testimony, see *Il Processo Castellano*, ed. M.-H. Laurent, in *Fontes vitae S. Catharinae Senensis* 9 (Milan: Fratelli Bocca, 1942), 260, 300. On this aspect of her life, see F. Thomas Luongo, *The Saintly Politics of Catherine of Siena* (Ithaca, NY: Cornell University Press, 2006), 148. Savonarola noted in a sermon that "Santa Caterina of Siena made peace in this state [Florence] at the time of Pope Gregory," in *Prediche sopra i Salmi*, 107–108.

asked her to intervene in a long-standing feud between local magnates on the advice of one of his neighbors, a nobleman, who, many years previously, had been entangled in a similar feud. After speaking with Catherine, the nobleman had been persuaded to make peace and thus was recommending her dispute resolution skills. When asked to mediate this new conflict, Catherine accepted, and "with her mediating," Stefano recounted, "we have peace."[32]

Raymond of Capua, first Catherine's confessor and later her hagiographer, highlights another episode illustrative of the impending saint's talents as a mediator of disputes. In that case, she convinced Nanni di Ser Vanni Savini, a wealthy banker, who was involved in at least four feuds, to make peace with his enemies. Initially, Nanni proved a tough nut to crack, as he was deaf to both the saint's and her confessor's entreaties for peace. It was not until he saw Catherine rapt in ecstasy, praying for divine aid, that he saw the error of his ways. Then and there he vowed to make peace to save his soul "from the devil's clutches." Once his heart was softened, Catherine admonished Nanni to do penance for his sins. Raymond recalls with satisfaction that "Nanni with great grief confessed all his sins to me, through the virgin he was reconciled with all his enemies, and following my advice, he was also reconciled with the Most high whom he had for so long offended."[33] It was an exemplary story: the holy woman, through prayer, brings Nanni to recognize himself as a sinner. She then admonishes him to do penance, paving the way for him to make peace with his enemies, while Raymond—the priest—hears his remorseful confession that will lead to reconciliation with God. The story touches upon all the elements necessary for a good peace, highlighting important markers along the way: the intervention of the saint, her appeal to do penance, the role of confession leading to reconciliation with the Lord, and finally, the making of civic peace among enemies.

It should be noted, however, that while female mediators (apart from female saints) are generally obscured in the historical record, their male counterparts, such as Fra Alberto of Mantua, a little-known contemporary of Saint Francis, appear with some frequency. A Bolognese chronicle records that in 1207 Fra Alberto, an itinerant preacher, served as a peacemaker in northern and central Italy. In Faenza alone, he reconciled forty-five parties involved in homicide. From there he went on to Bertanoro, Siena, Castel Nuovo, Forlì, and Imola, where in this last city he made another twenty-seven peace contracts for homicide.[34] Tellingly, there is no evidence that Fra Alberto was associated with any religious order; *fra*, a contraction of *frater* (brother), was a title liberally bestowed on holy men, but not indicative of sacerdotal status. We will meet a number of these peacemaking *frati* in the pages to come; notably, only a few of them had taken clerical vows.

32. For the "eulogy," see *Il Processo Castellano*, 316; for the feud, ibid., 259.

33. Raymond of Capua, *The Life of St Catherine of Siena*, trans. George Lamb (London: Harvill Press, 1960), 212–15, at 214. For more on Nanni, see Luongo, *The Saintly Politics*, 132–33.

34. "Cronaca B," *Corpus chronicorum Bononiensium*, ed. Albano Sorbelli, in RIS2: 18 Part 1 (vol. 2 of text): 69. I discuss peace agreements for homicide in chapter 4.

At about the same time, Raymond "the Palmer" of Piacenza, a lay penitent, was making a name for himself as a peacemaker in his native city. Called "the Palmer" on account of the palm fronds he collected while on pilgrimage, Raymond is known to us from a hagiographical text, a vita written by one Rufino in 1212, about a dozen years after his death. Commissioned by Raymond's son, the vita traces the arc of the shoemaker's journey to patron saint of the city of Piacenza. Raymond's vocation became clear when he experienced a vision of Christ while on pilgrimage in Rome. Under the portico of the basilica of St. Peter, Christ commanded him to return home to urge his fellow citizens to convert, give alms, and lead "rival parties to peace."[35] Rufino tells us, "Raymond held peace . . . in such high regard that when he sensed contention or hatred between people he would not rest until he had recalled them to concord." Sometimes that took the form of a scolding, such as this one: "Are you ignorant, my children, that the Son of God himself descended from heaven to earth and that he was placed on a most cruel cross, so that he might reconcile men to God? Why then do you want to be enemies to one another? Those who have enemies never have peace." In another instance, Raymond took up a heavy cross, made his way to a public piazza, and prophesied that unless the Piacentine people extricated themselves from civil discord, God would have his revenge. His harangue seems to have had the desired effect: Rufino recounts that "not a few, influenced by his pious warnings," came to the saint to mediate their disputes.[36] Though primarily concerned with civil strife in his own city, when Piacenza went to war with neighboring Cremona he tried valiantly (though unsuccessfully) to make peace between the opposing armies through preaching. Rushing out onto the battlefield, invoking the name of Christ, he cried out: "Remember that you are Christians; imitate your Savior! Forgive, forgive, and make peace! Commit the whole matter to me, whom you should consider to be the fairest arbiter." In this instance his words went unheeded. The Cremonese army took him captive and dragged him off to prison.[37]

PENITENTIAL PEACE MOVEMENTS

Wielding their influence as "living saints" to quell feuds and ancient rivalries, Raymond, Alberto, Francis, Margaret, and Catherine engaged society as "freelance" peacemakers. Others became leaders of penitential peace movements. Let us turn first to examine the "Great Devotion," also known as the "Great Alleluia," the first of these movements, which, for a period of ten months in

35. The text has been translated by Kenneth Baxter Wolf as "Life of Raymond 'the Palmer' of Piacenza (1212)," in *Medieval Italy: Texts in Translation*, ed. Katherine L. Jansen, Frances Andrews, and Joanna Drell (Philadelphia: University of Pennsylvania Press, 2009), 357–76, at 366.
36. "Life of Raymond," 369.
37. Ibid., 370.

1233, swept through northern Italy. Though André Vauchez and Augustine Thompson have sensitively analyzed different aspects of the movement, a sketch of its aims and accomplishments will add useful context in which to ground our subsequent civic story.[38]

THE GREAT DEVOTION

Salimbene de Adam (d. 1288), the Franciscan chronicler and an eyewitness to the Devotion from its very beginnings, recalled it as a time of peace and tranquility, a time of respite from the weapons of war, a time of happiness and joy, of praise and jubilation. It was also a time when soldiers and civilians, city dwellers and rustics, men and women, young and old, all harmonized their voices in song. It was a time, moreover, Salimbene recalled, when "everyone was drunk on divine love.... [When] there was no anger, no perturbation, no disputing, no rancor ... and I saw it with my own eyes."[39] In the spring of 1233, when the friar was just a boy in Parma, a layman called Frate Benedetto da Cornetta appeared out of nowhere preaching peace and repentance. Salimbene remembered him as a sort of John the Baptist figure with a long dark beard, who wore a tunic of black sackcloth emblazoned front and back with a ruby-red cross. He was "a simple man, uneducated, but of goodness and innocence who lived an honest life.... Though he belonged to no religious Order; he lived according to his own devising, endeavoring solely to please God." As it turns out, Fra Benedetto was probably the accidental founder of what became the Alleluia movement, named after the cry of "Alleluia" that he taught his followers to exclaim in praise of God. His sermons began memorably with a trumpet blast that he himself sounded from a small horn he carried with him, and they often concluded with a candlelight procession that snaked its way through the city streets, punctuated by preaching and prayerful pauses to praise God and the Virgin Mary.[40]

The leadership of the Devotion was ultimately commandeered by a number of charismatic mendicant preachers—both Franciscans and Dominicans—who helped the movement burgeon throughout northern Italy, in the Po River Valley of the regions today known as Emilia-Romagna and Lombardy, and also in the Veneto. "Its most noticeable characteristic,"

38. André Vauchez, "Une campagne de pacification en Lombardie autour de 1233: l'action politique des Ordres Mendiants, d'après la réforme des statuts communaux et les accords de paix," *MEFR* 78 (1966): 503–49; repr. in Vauchez, *Religion et société dans l'Occident médiéval* (Turin: Bottega d'Erasmo, 1980), 71–117; Thompson, *Revival Preachers*; Daniel A. Brown, "The Alleluia: A Thirteenth Century Peace Movement," *AFH* 81 (1988): 3–16; and Daniela Gatti, "Religiosità popolare e movimento di pace nel'Emilia del secolo XIII," *Itinerari storici: il medioevo in Emilia* (Modena: Mucchi, 1983), 79–107, at 90–91.

39. Salimbene de Adam, *Cronica*, in *CCCM*, 2 vols. (Turnhout: Brepols, 1998), vol. 125: 102–103.

40. Salimbene, *Cronica* I: 103.

notes Thompson, "was the use of preaching as a springboard into direct political involvement and peacemaking." While many of the friars associated with the Alleluia movement brought about reconciliations between feuding parties, especially political parties, some of them—such as the Dominican preacher John of Vicenza (d. ca. 1265) and the Franciscan Gerard of Modena (d. 1257)—also revised city statute books to promote and ensure lasting peace in urban centers such as Padua, Verona, Vicenza, Bologna, and Parma. In Verona, John of Vicenza was given podestarial powers to do so; at Parma, where Gerard of Modena was invited to participate in the reform of the city statutes, the lion's share of his legislative contributions centered on the area of peace and justice. Guided by the notion that reconciliation would lead to permanent peace, Gerard was particularly keen to ease the way for those whom the city had banished to make peace with their enemies. Toward this end, he rewrote a number of the municipal statutes. Before such reforms and reconciliations took place, however, the friars laid the groundwork by whipping up religious fervor in sermons that cried out for peace. In a great rally in Paquara, a few miles south of Verona, John of Vicenza had a sixty-foot wooden tower constructed so that the thousands who attended could hear him preaching on John 14:27: "My peace I give you, my peace I leave you," a favorite theme of sermons on peace. After he wrapped up his sermon, John announced the political peace treaties he had negotiated between the party leaders of Verona, Padua, and Mantua.[41]

It was not unusual for the friars' well-organized campaigns to combine spectacular miracle-working and penitential rituals meant to soften hearts as tearful participants recalled the sufferings of the Lord.[42] Such was the case when John of Vicenza addressed the council of Bologna and presided over the subsequent reconciliation of the bishop to his city in the late spring of 1233. At that time, the preacher marched the entire population, barefooted, in a penitential procession through the streets. The chronicler of these events made a point of noting that those participating in the Devotion were awash in a great effusion of tears.

The preaching of the friars and the penitential rituals they encouraged set the stage for civic peace. Indeed, their preaching on peace created the expectation that civic peace could not be achieved without personal penance. Moreover, a penitential understanding of the civic act of reconciliation was crucial for the success of medieval peacemaking as it allowed both the injured and offending parties to avoid appearances of weakness, dishonor, or humiliation. Buonaccorso Pitti, an important Florentine citizen and officeholder, seems to have absorbed this by now venerable message when he settled a long-standing feud on Good Friday 1374, the most fitting day of the year for repentance. He notes in his diary,

---

41. Thompson, *Revival Preachers*: quotation at 12; preachers and statute reforms at 180; Gerard's legislation at Parma at 183 and 202–203; Paquara, 72–76.

42. Thompson, *Revival Preachers*, 154.

"I pardoned him [Cione] freely and, many years later, after repeated entreaties, was even prevailed upon to forgive his mother. He wanted me to forgive his cousins, the Mannelli, too, but this I refused to do until, one Good Friday, fully thirty years afterwards, when so as to earn grace in the sight of God, I summoned them to the chapter house in Santo Spirito and, with God as our only mediator, made them an offer of peace which they accepted in a humble and contrite spirit."[43] If peacemaking was construed as submission to God's will, it could not be construed as weakness. No one had to lose face or honor if peace was inspired through Christian charity. And as we shall see when we turn to analyze the kiss of peace in chapter 5, the kiss of reconciliation was meant to bring about a new social reality in which equilibrium would be restored to relationships that had been disrupted by feud or violence.

FRA RANIERO FASANI AND THE *BATTUTI*

Only a few decades after the Great Alleluia petered out, another penitential peace movement emerged in central Italy when, in Perugia around Easter 1260, Fra Raniero Fasani (d. 1282) inspired a fresh wave of agitation for peace and repentance. Like the Alleluia, its catalyst was an ascetic layman who preached penance. What little we know of Raniero comes from the *Lezenda de fra Raniero Faxano*, written by an anonymous, probably Bolognese, author.[44] He tells us that Fra Raniero, who had spent eighteen years in eremitical seclusion, first appeared in Perugia in 1258 preaching penance. Like Fra Alberto and Fra Benedetto before him, Fra Raniero was a freelance penitent. He was affiliated with no religious order; in fact, he was a married man with children.

Like Saint Francis, Raniero probably preached extemporaneously, leaving no trace in the written record of the nature of his words. But perhaps we can reconstruct the essence of his message, if not the exact form, by turning to a sermon on peace by his contemporary, Federico Visconti (d.1277), archbishop of Pisa. In 1267, at the behest of the pope, Federico preached a sermon to the city council of Pisa, urging its members to swear a peace with Charles I of Anjou, appointed by Clement IV as peacemaker of Tuscany. Even though Federico, a prelate of the church, delivered his sermon to an exalted audience, which included the podestà, his message was simple and meant to be adopted by others, as the text bears all the hallmarks of a model sermon.[45] Taking his theme from

43. *Two Memoirs of Renaissance Florence: The Diaries of Buonaccorso Pitti and Gregorio Dati*, ed. Gene Brucker, trans. Julia Martines (New York: Waveland Press, 1967), 24. Many thanks to both Tom Tentler and John Padgett who, on separate occasions, each reminded me of the value of this diary.

44. "La Lezenda de Fra Raniero Faxano," ed. G. Mazzatinti in *Bollettino di Società Umbra di Storia Patria* 2 (1896): 561–63.

45. *Les sermons et la visite pastorale de Federico Visconti archevêque de Pise (1253–1277)*, ed. Nicole Bériou, Isabelle le Masne de Chermont et al. (Rome: École Française de

John 14:27, "Pacem relinquo vobis, pacem meam do vobis," Federico suggested
that three senses of "peace" informed that memorable phrase Jesus uttered to
his disciples at the Last Supper. The first was "peace of heart," meaning peace
with oneself and God; the second was temporal peace, peace with family, kin,
neighbors, and fellow citizens. Both of these senses, he argued, were present
in the first half of the phrase, "My peace I leave you." The second part of the
phrase, he suggested, citing no less an authority than the *Glossa Ordinaria*,
"pacem meam do vobis" (my peace I give you), signified the peace of eternity.

The body of the sermon expands on these themes and is pitched on two
levels. For the learned he wraps Augustinian thought in scholastic language:
"We ought to have peace of heart, that is, tranquility of mind, in which flesh
obeys spirit, sensuality reason; and having overcome those enemies, then *synderesis* will lie quiet in peace." For the less learned he counsels: "You, dearest
brothers, ponder this when you are lying awake in bed at night, particularly
during those long winter nights: reflect on the state of your soul and consider
your mortal sins." He advises his listeners to take stock through internal re-
flection. That exercise, in turn, will lead to the self-realization that "I am in
sorry shape." Then, one's sins should be reckoned and confessed "so that you
will have the peace of heart that is the tranquility of mind with God: and this
is the first peace he leaves us: 'pacem reliquo vobis.'"[46] Recognition of sin,
contrition, and confession are here envisioned as the first rungs on the ladder
leading to the peace of eternity.

Even here, on this political occasion, one in which the city fathers were
being asked to sign a peace with Charles of Anjou, Federico's message was
that contrition, repentance, and confession were essential preconditions for
peace. These were also the essential ingredients of Raniero's new movement,
as Salimbene, again an eyewitness, observed. He noted that when Raniero's
followers arrived in Modena, they made peace and brought men who had been
mired in evil to confess their sins. In a characteristic postscript, the friar added
that there were so many people seeking reconciliation that day that the priests
hearing confession scarcely had time to eat.[47] Be that as it may, Raniero had
fostered the expectation that penance would precede peace.

This movement distinguished itself from its predecessors by inscribing
penitential practice on the body as a first step toward peace. Indeed, Raniero
was told to do so by Bevignate, a local Perugian saint, who notified him that
the Virgin Mary had demanded such practice in order to save mankind from

---

Rome, 2001), Sermon 14, 450–58. The evidence that it was meant as a model sermon runs
as follows: "Item, si vis dilatare sermonem, potes dicere quomodo Christus dicitur pax
propter quadruplicem pace quam fecit, secundum quas habet quattuor nomina," at 457.

46. *Les sermons et la visite pastorale*, 450–58. *Synderesis* is the moral habit of inclining
toward the good, at 452.

47. Salimbene, *Cronica* II: 703.

the wrath of God: "She wants the discipline that up to now you've practiced privately to be performed publicly."[48] The saint had then handed over a letter of instruction from the Virgin Mary addressed to the bishop of Perugia. It directed the good pastor to promote the practice among his flock. With due haste, the bishop promulgated the contents of the letter from the steps of the town hall.

Up to that moment, the "discipline," known since the early medieval period, had been an ascetic practice normally associated with monasticism and practiced in the privacy of one's own chamber.[49] Now it became a shockingly public means of atonement. Shouldering the sins of the world, the *battuti*, as Raniero's followers became known, publicly lacerated their flesh in expiation for the sins of humankind. It was nothing less than a collective and public sacrifice for peace.

Not without a bit of hyperbole, the author of Raniero's vita tells us that the practice was such an immediate success that by the second day after the announcement there was not a person left in Perugia who hadn't stripped down and taken up the discipline.[50] At the beginning of May, a fifteen-day holiday was declared to celebrate the devotion, and five months later a majority of the population had been won over to the practice. "And all who hated one another made peace and concord. In that way, as everyone knows, this form of penitential discipline spread throughout the Christian world."[51] Soon afterward, the brothers in blood, crying out for "peace and mercy," processed as far south as Rome, then turned round and marched north in procession from Italy over the Alps and into Northern Europe, all the while attracting new adherents to their movement.[52]

What was the result of all this religious fervor? Just as the Great Devotion only a few decades earlier had brought about legal change in northern Italy—it will be remembered that statute law was revised to promote peace—so too was reform brought about in Perugia. Raniero's penitential peace movement achieved civic change. Confraternities of the discipline were founded to pursue peace, a mission codified in their statutes. Moreover, as Massimo Vallerani points out, the rise of the popolo in Perugia was coterminous with Raniero's penitential movement. And their ambitions for peace mirrored each other. In fact, the leaders of the popolo profited from the spiritual clout of Raniero and his *disciplinati* to codify peace in the Ordinances they wrote in 1260.

48. "La Lezenda," 562.

49. Previously the discipline had been used as punishment by episcopal courts; see John Henderson, "The Flagellant Movement and Flagellant Confraternities in central Italy, 1260–1400," in *Studies in Church History* 15 (1978), 147–60, at 147–48.

50. "La Lezenda," 563.

51. The chronology is according to Henderson, "The Flagellant Movement," 150; quotations are from "La Lezenda," ibid.

52. Henderson, "The Flagellant Movement," 151.

Indeed, the last two chapters of the Ordinances direct the *podestà* and the *capitano del popolo* to pursue communal peace. Ultimately, Vallerani argues, the popolo was proposing a new model of society under the sign of peace.[53] It is an important argument and one to which we will return in the next chapter. For now it shall suffice to underline again that the penitential peace movements of the later Middle Ages frequently had the clout—and used it—to influence and structure civic peacemaking institutions.

THE *BATTUTI* OF 1310

It is possible that Raniero's movement inspired another group of *battuti*, who made their appearance in 1310, emerging first in the Piedmont region. Giovanni Villani (d. 1348), the Florentine chronicler, describes them as a great number of *gente minuta*, men, women, and children who had left their work and homes to wander from place to place, flogging themselves as flagellants. As Raniero's penitents had done, they also carried a cross before them and cried, "Misericordia, misericordia!" And like their predecessors, they "made many peace agreements between men and turned even more people to penitence."[54]

Though they may not have had a charismatic leader as the face of their movement, the *Battuti* of 1310 had taken to heart the lesson that where there is penance there is peace. The illustrated manuscript of Villani's *Cronica*, now in the Vatican Library, includes a miniature of this *grande maraviglia* (Fig. 4). It faithfully renders a small group of *battuti* stripped to the waist, whipping themselves as they gaze up at their standard emblazoned with the scourging of Christ, the divine intercessor, who sacrificed himself to mediate the fate of humankind with God. The artist, perhaps Pacino di Bonaguida, amplifies Villani's text with a telling visual detail. Unlike Sassetta's, Pacino's image of peacemaking includes neither notary nor document; what he does depict, however, is two *battuti*, their arms crossed over their chests. It is a gesture of submission, reminiscent of that of the Virgin Mary at the Annunciation. Furthermore, they are pictured exchanging the kiss of peace.[55] As we have

---

53. Massimo Vallerani, "Mouvements de paix dans une commune de *Popolo*: les Flagellants à Pérouse en 1260," in *Prêcher la paix*, 313–55.

54. Giovanni Villani, *Nuova Cronica*, ed. Giovanni Porta, 3 vols. (Parma: Ugo Guanda Editore, 1991), vol. 2: Bk. 9, chap. 121: 209–10. Villani mentions yet another similar movement, which descended on Rome in 1338. Villani, *Nuova Cronica*, vol. 3: Bk 12, chap. 96: 205.

55. For an annotated facsimile of the MS, see Chiara Frugoni, Alessandro Barbero, et al., *Il Villani illustrato: Firenze e l'Italia medievale nelle 253 immagini del ms. Chigiano L VIII 296 della Biblioteca Vaticana* (Vatican City: Biblioteca Apostolica Vaticana, 2005). Many thanks to Giusi D'Alessandro at the Biblioteca LUMSA for helping me get my hands on this volume. The manuscript dates to ca. 1340–1348 and the miniatures are attributed to Pacino di Bonaguida. See Alda Labriola, "Pacino di Bonaguida," in *Dizionario biografico dei miniatori italiani, secoli IX-XVI*, ed. Milvia Bollati (Milan: Sylvestre Bonnard, 2004),

FIGURE 4. *The Battuti of 1310*. Manuscript miniature by Pacino di Bonaguida. On the far left, two *battuti* exchange the kiss of peace, their arms crossed over their chests in a gesture of submission. From Giovanni Villani, *Nuova Cronica*, ca. 1340–1348. MS BAV Chigi L VIII 296, fol. 197v, Biblioteca Apostolica Vaticana, Vatican City. Photo reproduced by permission of the Biblioteca Apostolica Vaticana. © 2018 Biblioteca Apostolica Vaticana.

841–43; and Giusi Zanichelli, "Pacino di Bonaguida: Un protagonista della miniatura fiorentina," *Alumina* 18 (2007): 24–33. It has been suggested that Amaretto Mannelli, scion of one of the old Ghibelline lineages who later turned Guelf, commissioned the illustrated manuscript. Marco Cursi, "Un nuovo codice appartenuto della famiglia Mannelli: la cronica figurata di Giovanni Villani (Vat. Chigi L.VIII. 296)," in *Segni: per Armando Petrucci* (Rome: Bagatto, 2002), 141–58.

already noted, and shall examine in more detail in chapter 5, the kiss of peace on the mouth is the concluding ritual of civic peacemaking, symbolizing fraternity and reconciliation.

VENTURINO OF BERGAMO AND THE COLOMBINI

Unlike the spontaneous *Battuti* movement of 1310, which lacked a named founder, the penitential peace movement that arose a quarter of a century later, in 1355, was a deliberate foundation. Its leader was a young charismatic Dominican preacher called Venturino of Bergamo (d. 1346).[56] Venturino's movement began in his hometown of Bergamo when he organized a pilgrimage to Rome to gain papal indulgences for his followers, among whom were repentant murderers and robbers. An act of expiation in itself, the pilgrimage emphasized the nexus of peace, penance, and mercy. Later in life Venturino recalled that he had facilitated more than one thousand peace agreements between mortal enemies.[57] It is an exaggerated figure no doubt, but one that nevertheless serves to underscore the partnership between peace and penance.

The author of the "Legend of Blessed Brother Venturino" describes how well over a thousand Lombard pilgrims traveled to Rome in brigades of twelve, all the while crying out "Mercy! Peace! Penance!"[58] One of the obligations of Venturino's pilgrimage was that inveterate enemies should walk side by side as an act of peace and reconciliation, sharing food, even using the same bowls, ladles, and knives.[59] His followers dressed themselves like Dominican friars, in white tunics and black mantles. Embroidered insignia that showed a white dove bearing three olive sprigs in its beak distinguished Venturino's

56. Clara Gennaro, "Venturino da Bergamo e la Peregrinatio Romana del 1335," in *Studi sul medioevo cristiano offerti a Raffaello Morghen: per il 90° anniversario dell'Istituto storico italiano, (1883–1973)*, 2 vols. (Rome: Istituto Storico per il Medio Evo, 1974), 374–406; and more recently Dinora Corsi, "La 'crociata' di Venturino da Bergamo nella crisi spirituale di metà Trecento," in *Archivio Storico Italiano* 4 (1989): 697–747; Frances Andrews, "Le voci della *Legenda beati fratris Venturini*: tra santità e condanna," *Cristianesimo nella storia* 34.2 (2013): 507–41, and Andrews, "Preacher and Audience: Friar Venturino da Bergamo and 'Popular Voices,'" in *The Voices of the People in Late Medieval Europe. Communication and Popular Politics*, ed. Jan Dumolyn, Jelle Haemers, Hipólito Rafael, Oliva Herrer and Vincent Challet (Turnhout: Brepols, 2014), 185–204. For this last I thank the author for sharing the article with me prior to publication. On the vita, see E. Hocedez, "La légende latine du B. Venturino de Bergamo," *Analecta Bollandiana* 25 (1906): 298–303; and for the edition, "Legenda Beati Fratris Venturini, O.P.," ed. P. A. Grion, O.P., *Bergomum*, n.s. 30.4 (1956): 11–110, vita: 38–110.

57. "Legenda," 87. Selections from the vita have been translated by Ronald G. Musto, *Catholic Peacemakers: A Documentary History*, 2 vols. (New York: Garland, 1993), 1: 556–66.

58. "Legenda," 68; and in his own words, Venturino himself also remembers the cry: "Legenda," 88. Villani's version in the *Nuova Cronica* claims that there were ten thousand Lombard pilgrims. See *Nuova Cronica*, vol. 3: Bk 12, Chap. 23: 66–8.

59. "Legenda," 69.

followers from the Order of Preachers and indicated also the group's mission of peace.[60] Though none of his sermons survive, it is possible that Venturino explicated the symbol of the dove and the olive in a manner similar to Robert of Anjou (d. 1343), who held forth on the historical significance of the symbols to the nuns of Santa Chiara when preaching at their convent in Naples.[61] Turning first to Roman history, he told them that Aeneas, when navigating the Tiber, sent his envoys to the king of Latium bearing olive branches. Then he recounted the story of the flood, noting that the Lord had sent a dove carrying an olive sprig to Noah as a sign of peace and reconciliation. In the event, Venturino's followers were so identified with the sign of the dove that they came to be called "Colombini," little doves.[62]

According to the chronicler known as the Anonimo Romano, Venturino's pilgrimage was launched in early February and reached Rome on the 21st of March, after winding down the peninsula through Cremona, Ferrara, Bologna, Florence, and Siena, and attracting followers who took up the discipline to beat themselves while chanting their mantra of "Penance, peace and mercy!" rhythmically to the strokes of the whip. Once in Rome, Venturino preached for ten days at San Sisto, Santa Maria Sopra Minerva, San Giovanni in Laterano, and even on the Campidoglio, where ultimately his movement began to unravel. According to the Roman chronicler, Venturino began to lose control of his audience during a sermon when he scolded the Romans for not removing their shoes while standing on holy ground, meaning that they should show some respect for the hallowed ground beneath their feet in which the bones of many martryrs lay buried. The Romans, never known for their courtesy, began to heckle him, laughing outright in his face. Fra Venturino unfortunately further misjudged his audience by proceeding to deliver an ill-timed plea for alms, wrapped up in another scolding. He reminded them that the games had not yet been played at Piazza Navona, and that instead of throwing their money away on the devil's sport, they should donate it to him. As a good custodian, he would dispense it to needy folk: those pilgrims, for example, who wanted to see the Veronica but were unable to do so. That proved to be his undoing:

> Then the Romans began to mock him and say that he was crazy. They said they wouldn't stick around any longer, so they got up, took off, and left him all by himself. Then he preached at San Giovanni. The Romans

60. The description of their garb differs from author to author. I have used Villani's description (ibid.), but see also the Anonimo Romano, *Cronica*, 24. The anonymous "Legenda" (68) describes their garments as "a white tunic with a tabard of sky blue trailing to black, with caps on their heads of the same weave as the tabard. On the right above the tabard they had two crosses of cloth: one red, the other white; on the left a white dove with a branch of green on gold and on the front of the caps a Tau." Translated by Musto, *Catholic Peacemakers*, 1, 560–61.

61. Angelica MS 151, fol. 73b.

62. Gennaro, "Movimenti religiosi," 102.

didn't want to hear another word of out him so they chased him away. At that he became furious and cursed them and said that he had never seen such a perverse people. He didn't show his face again; instead he high-tailed it out of Rome, leaving in secret for Avignon.[63]

A perverse people they may have been, but it is striking that the Romans received him so poorly when the Florentines, as we know from Villani, welcomed Venturino and his followers with open arms. For fifteen days they collected alms for the penitent pilgrims. They also fed them in turns at tables set up in the open air in the piazza of Santa Maria Novella, and they listened to the friar's sermons, which attracted "all the people of Florence, as if he were a prophet."[64]

As we have seen, no one took Venturino for a prophet in Rome. Ill-informed or maybe just naive, he seems not to have understood the workings of the Holy See in absentia. In trial documents from a subsequent case against him, Venturino admits that he left Rome in haste, but not before leading his followers in procession from Santa Maria sopra Minerva to Saint Peter's. In a candlelight vigil they all cried out for "penance, peace, and mercy." [65]

THE BIANCHI OF 1399

All these elements and more converged in a new peace movement that flowered on the Italian peninsula in 1399. Much like the supernatural impulse that marked the foundation of Raniero's *disciplinati* movement, the Bianchi too were born of a revelation, this one an apocalyptic vision of the Madonna weeping over the fate of humanity, with whom, she said, her son was losing all patience because sin perdured in the world. Death and destruction could be avoided, she warned, only with the institution of a new devotion that she instructed be performed in this way:

> Let every man, woman, and child, priests and friars, and people of all ages dress in white linen as I am dressed, or like the *battuti*, with head covered, and a red cross on the heads and shoulders of men and women alike. And they should beat themselves, and go for nine days in procession with a crucifix carried before them, flogging themselves and crying "mercy, mercy, mercy, peace, peace, peace" as loud as they can.

She continued by prescribing a novena of vigils, pilgrimages, the celebration of the Mass, and sermons, in addition to a regimen of dietary restrictions, fasting, and bare feet. She also required the singing of laude and the recitation of prayers. In conclusion Mary commanded: "repent and forgive each other and

63. Anonimo Romano, *Cronica*, ed. Giuseppe Porta (Milan: Adelphi Ed., 1979), 26.
64. Villani, *Cronica Nuova*, Bk 3: 23.
65. "Legenda," 93.

make peace and concord."[66] The Bianchi devotion seems to have taken up the gauntlet that Venturino abandoned so hastily when he suddenly decamped from Rome for Avignon.

Though the Bianchi first appeared in Liguria, the devotion spread quickly, making its way southward through Tuscany, and reaching Rome two months later. They had great success in Tuscany, where they attracted devotees from all stations of life, including Francesco di Marco Datini, the wealthy merchant of Prato. Living in Florence at the time, the sixty-five-year-old merchant and his "famiglia" participated in one of the nine-day devotions, which took the form of a penitential pilgrimage from Florence to Arezzo from August 28 to September 5, 1399. In his *ricordanza*, his daybook, Datini described his group of intimates, as "all dressed in white and barefoot, with scourge in hand, beating ourselves."[67]

Notwithstanding Datini's description, Daniel Bornstein, the movement's most prominent historian, argues that the Bianchi put peacemaking front and center, relegating to the margins the Virgin Mary's demand for flagellation.[68] Indeed, peacemaking became the Bianchi's defining characteristic. No less than Coluccio Salutati (d. 1406), the chancellor of Florence, identified the Bianchi with peace activism: "They seek peace, they pray for peace, they repeat peace, and all in one voice they call for peace, they clamor for peace."[69] Peace coupled with social reform, was their identity, their cri de coeur, and their objective. To this end, they sought the release of prisoners, the return of exiles, and the prohibition of usury, all of which were known to create acrimony and ill will that, if left to fester, could ulcerate into a disease marked by endless cycles of feuding and vendetta. The Bianchi were so successful in their mission that Luca Dominici, an eyewitness and chronicler, describes how in Pistoia on August 14, 1399, "innumerable peace agreements were made, so many that I couldn't say, let alone count."[70]

As peace activists, members of the Bianchi also mediated disputes. Dominici describes how two days later the city awoke to a procession, confession, and penance. Then just about every other activity came to a standstill

66. Luca Dominici, *Cronaca della venuta dei Bianchi e della morìa, 1399–1400*, 2 vols., ed. Giovan Carlo Gigliotti (Pistoia: Alberto Pacinotti, 1933), vol. 1, 50–54. This is one of a number of foundation legends.

67. On which see Joseph P. Byrne, "The Merchant as Penitent: Francesco di Marco and the Bianchi Movement of 1399," *Viator* 20 (1989): 219–31.

68. *The Bianchi of 1399: Popular Devotion in Late Medieval Italy*, (Ithaca, NY: Cornell University Press, 1993), 45. See also *Sulle orme dei Bianchi dalla Liguria all'Italia centrale. Atti del convegno internazionale Assisi-Vallo di Nera-Terni-Rieti-Leonessa (18-19-20 giugno 1999)*, ed. Francesco Santucci (Assisi: Accademia Properziana del Subasio, 2001).

69. *Epistolario*, ed. Francesco Novati, 4 vols. (Rome: Istituto Storico Italiano, 1891–1911), 3: 359, as cited and translated in Bornstein, *The Bianchi*, 50. I have slightly adjusted his translation.

70. Dominici, *Cronaca* 1: 67–68.

so that peace agreements could be drawn up to put an end to factions and divisions in the city. Indeed, Niccolò di Grimo, a public notary, was kept busily employed for the entire day doing nothing but drawing up peace contracts.[71] Another Tuscan witness noted that in the city of Prato, the Bianchi devised a weapons amnesty program: peace agreements were exchanged for arms. It was so wildly successful, he notes, that two mules were needed to cart away the surrendered arms.[72] To celebrate those peace agreements, Prato's most important relic, the *sacro cinto*, was displayed on that day.[73] A similar program, instituted in Florence, was even more successful as it took four pack animals to haul away the mountain of arms discarded at the hospital of San Gallo. Each time a peace was made and weapons turned in, a celebratory cry of *"Pace!"* would go up from the crowd.[74]

Documenting the great success of the Bianchi in central Italy, an anonymous Florentine chronicler with a good eye for detail noted: "first they confessed, took communion, and rendered peace out of love for the Crucified One and for all those they had offended; then they dressed in white and followed the Crucifix for nine days . . . and they fasted faithfully, always crying out to the lord for mercy and peace."[75] Like other Tuscan cities, Florence gave the Bianchi a royal welcome, especially those penitents from Lucca who mediated peace between mortal enmities in the city and the contado. Afterward Florence received them with great honor, giving them "wine and bread, alms, and everything else they needed to live."[76] By the end of August, as we have seen, the Florentines themselves (with the help of the priors and the bishop) had organized their own brigades of Bianchi. Donning white robes—some made of bedsheets—one large group processed within the city walls, while another, the group Francesco Datini joined, embarked on a nine-day pilgrimage to Arezzo. The devotion was so popular, our chronicler reports, that a good forty thousand people took part in it! In the unlikely event that his figures are correct, this would mean that almost 75 percent of the Florentine population assumed the aspect of Bianchi penitents for a short period.[77] Chronicle figures, however, are notoriously inaccurate; nonetheless, his point is well made that this was an extraordinarily popular devotion. It also seems to have had some tranquilizing effects on the quarrelsome population, for "wherever

71. Dominici, *Cronaca* 1: 71–72.

72. Correspondence between Francesco Datini and Domenico di Cambio (27 Sept. 1399) from the Archivio Datini di Prato, no. 864, lett. Firenze-Barcellona, Associazione "ai veli," quoted by Bornstein, *The Bianchi*, 50.

73. Dominici, *Cronaca* 1: 111.

74. Dominici, *Cronaca*, 1: 91.

75. *Cronica volgare di anonimo fiorentino dall'anno 1385 al 1409 già attribuita a Piero di Giovanni Minerbetti*, ed. Elina Bellondi, RIS2: 27.2, Part II, 240–42.

76. Ibid.

77. Najemy estimates the post-plague population in 1380 to be 55,000. See *A History of Florence*, 225.

they went, they made agreements of peace and concord with great devotion, and then, having spent nine days, each one returned home, and because of this the city remained in a state of concord."[78]

A remarkable visual souvenir of the Bianchi's presence in central Italy is painted on a wall of the little church of San Francesco (now rechristened Santa Maria Assunta) in Vallo di Nera, Umbria.[79] Occupying the wall of the nave to the right side of the entrance, the seven-meter mural unfolds a "newsreel" of sorts, which documents contemporary Bianchi peacemaking activities in the hilltop town at the end of the fourteenth century (figs. 5 and 6).[80] Men and women, clerics and laypeople, are shown in their characteristic white robes, emblazoned with red crosses on their shoulders and cowls, exactly as the Virgin Mary had specified. Like Francesco Datini, some of them are girded at the waist with scourges. They are gathered around the church of San Francesco carrying stalks of lilies and olive branches, a crucifix, and standards picturing the image of the Madonna and child. Mouths open, a number of them sing a song in praise of peace and the Madonna. The lyrics, inscribed on a parchment held by one of the tonsured men, exclaim: "Misericordia, o Vergine pia, pace o Vergine Maria."[81]

In another scene, the Bianchi—both men and women—continue to sing from a text, while others worship at the foot of a crucifix. A banderole announces that one Giovannone had the fresco made to bring peace to his town[82] (fig. 7).

The centerpiece of the fresco, however, is an act of peacemaking in which two men kneel face to face (fig. 8). It is a snapshot of the moment before they will exchange the kiss of peace. The artist Cola di Pietro da Camerino has conceptualized the reconciliation of the parties on two registers. On the temporal

78. Ibid.

79. The church was rededicated in 1652. See Sandro Ceccaroni, "Testimonianze del movimento dei Bianchi a Vallo di Nera agli inizi del XV secolo," *Spoletium: Rivista di Arte Storia Cultura* 27 (1982): 39–44, at 39 n.6.

80. On the frescoes, see the following essays in *Sulle orme dei Bianchi*: Elisabeth Bliersbach, "I Bianchi nell'arte Umbro-Laziale," 363–405; Maria Cecilia Giraldi, "Il passaggio dei Bianchi a Rieti nelle testimonianze iconografiche," 325–37; Paolo Renzi, "La devozione dei Bianchi a Terni negli affreschi di S. Maria al Monumento," 273–306; and Mario Sensi, "Le paci private nella predicazione, nelle immagini di propaganda e nella prassi fra Tre e Quattrocento," in *La pace fra realtà e utopia. Quaderni di Storia Religiosa* 12 (2005), 159–200, at 168–69.

81. Elisabeth Bliersbach notes that this phrase is a quotation from a lauda recorded in the Assisi laudario. See her "I Bianchi nell'arte umbro-laziale," 389. For the lauda, see Arnaldo Fortini, *La lauda in Assisi e le origini del teatro italiano* (Assisi: Edizioni Assisi, 1961), 42. For analysis of the many laude, see Bornstein, *The Bianchi*, who transcribes a number of them, 117–45; and Francesco Santucci, "Il passaggio dei Bianchi in Assisi," *Sulle orme dei Bianchi*, 155–71.

82. Mario Sensi fills in the missing words as: "hoc opus fe(cit fieri) Iuvannoni (a Vallo et Dio)/Li dia pace," in "Le paci private nella predicazione," 168.

FIGURE 5. *A Bianchi Peace Procession in Vallo di Nera.* Both women and men carry lilies and olive branches. Scene from a fresco by Cola di Pietro da Camerino, 1401. Church of S. Maria Assunta (formerly San Francesco), Vallo di Nera, Umbria. Photo: author.

FIGURE 6. *The Bianchi Chanting with their Standard.* Women and men carry a standard emblazoned with the Madonna and Child, who gives a blessing. A group of tonsured clerics at the left chant a lauda, lyrics of which, "Misericordia, o Vergine pia, pace o Vergine Maria," are written on the scroll held by one of the men. Scene from a fresco by Cola di Pietro da Camerino, 1401. Church of S. Maria Assunta (formerly San Francesco), Vallo di Nera, Umbria. Photo: author.

FIGURE 7. *The Bianchi Worship Christ on the Cross.* The bandarole proclaims
that Giovannone had the fresco made as a votive offering for peace:. *Hoc opus
fe*[cit fieri] *Iuvannoni a* [Vallo et Dio]. *Li dia pace.* (Giovannone of Vallo
[di Nera] and God commissioned the fresco to bring peace.) Scene from
a fresco by Cola di Pietro da Camerino, 1401. Church of S. Maria Assunta
(formerly San Francesco), Vallo di Nera, Umbria. Photo: author.

FIGURE 8. *The Kiss of Peace.* The central bandarole announces that in the
month of July 1401, "Cola of Master Pietro of Camerino painted me." Scene
from a fresco by Cola di Pietro da Camerino, 1401. Church of S. Maria Assunta
(formerly San Francesco), Vallo di Nera, Umbria. Photo: author.

plane, a Bianchi penitent on the right, possibly the mediator of the peace, gently nudges the shoulder of one of the pair forward toward his soon-to-be erstwhile adversary. On the spiritual level, a miniature angel hovers over their heads, encouraging the two of them to lean in toward the kiss that will seal their reconciliation.[83]

Though we do not know the identity of these particular peacemakers, nonetheless, we know of at least one important Florentine *personaggio*, whom we have met before, who credited the activities of the white-hooded activists with motivating him to put an end to a blood feud in which he was a protagonist. Buonaccorso Pitti noted in his memoir that while in Florence the Bianchi brought about many reconciliations, including that of "our family, the Pitti, [who] made peace with Antonio and Geri di Giovanni Corbizi, the nephews of Matteo del Ricco whom I had killed in Pisa, and with Matteo di Paolo Corbizi." A peace agreement to settle a homicide? Surprisingly, as we will see in chapter 4, peace instruments could be used even to dismiss charges of such gravity.[84]

The Bianchi movement, like the Great Devotion and the *disciplinati* movement of 1260, and to some degree Venturino's Colombini, took form as a penitential peace movement that aimed not only to pacify society by quelling strife, factions, and violence, but also to reform it by mitigating the underlying reason for those symptoms. Among their "action items" were liberating those in exile, under banishment, or in prison and canceling usurious debt. Most important was bringing about peace and reconciliation between those ensnared in a state of enmity. Each of these movements tried to usher in a new age of peace heralded by the angel of the nativity who, in the Gospel of Luke, announced "Peace on Earth to men of good will" (Luke 2:14).

CODA: PEACEMAKERS OF THE FRANCISCAN OBSERVANCE

The banner of penance and peace was picked up in the early fifteenth century in the peacemaking campaigns of the Observant friars, led most famously by two pillars of the Franciscan Observance, the super-preachers Bernardino of Siena (d. 1444) and James of the March (d. 1476).[85]

Bernardino of Siena was a young man when the white-cowled Bianchi swept through his native Tuscany. And though there is no direct evidence linking him

83. For further interpretation of this image, contextualized within a repertoire of peacemaking images, see chapter 5.

84. *Two Memoirs of Renaissance Florence: The Diaries of Buonaccorso Pitti and Gregorio Dati*, 62.

85. Yoko Kimura takes the story up to the end of the fifteenth century through an examination of Bernardino da Feltre's peacemaking campaigns (1483–1495) in central and northern Italy: "Preaching Peace in Fifteenth-Century Italian Cities: Bernardino da Feltre," in *From Words to Deeds: the Effectiveness of Preaching in the Late Middle Ages*, ed. Maria Giuseppina Muzzarelli (Brepols: Turnhout, 2014): 171–183.

to that movement, it is certainly possible that their memory provided fuel, if not inspiration, for his own fiery subsequent preaching campaigns. From 1417, during his visit to Lombardy and the Veneto, to 1425 when he settled conflicts in Assisi and Perugia, to Siena in 1427, and up to 1444, the year of his death when he preached in his hometown of Massa Marittima, the subject of peace and concord was never far from the friar's lips. An inveterate peacemaker, Bernardino preached a message of peace, which, as we have seen, was already long established: inner personal conversion facilitated outer reconciliation. Peace with the Lord was the prerequisite for harmonious relations in the world. And sermons about peace and concord were inevitably entwined with sermons on conversion; that is, conversion to penance, the subject matter of most medieval sermons. "Women: do you want peace?" Bernardino asked his female audience in Siena. "Yes? Then you have to get rid of vanity, pride, superfluous clothing, and luxurious fashions."[86] Moral reform, as will be remembered, was the first step toward repentance and reconciliation, from which civic peace could then follow.

On his first crusade for peace in 1417, Bernardino's words inspired reconciliations between political parties and individuals in Belluno, Crema, Verona, Como, Brescia, Bergamo, and Bologna. Though we do not have his sermons from this early period, we do have the preacher's own recollection of the role he played in pacifying Crema.[87] It comes in the form of a sermon he preached in Siena a decade later, recorded by Benedetto di maestro Bartolomeo, a cloth-worker who faithfully transcribed the entire sermon cycle Bernardino preached while in residence that year.

Bernardino tells his Sienese audience that when he arrived in Crema he found that partisan conflict had so sundered the city fabric that about ninety men and their families had been sent into exile. It was late summer, the period of the grape harvest, so Bernardino was forced to preach in the wee hours of the morning in order to attract an audience. No matter. He rose to the challenge and preached for a good four hours until dawn. The response from the townspeople was immediate: after the sermon, they flocked to him, informing him that if he genuinely wanted peace he would have to plead his case to Lord Giorgio dei Benzoni, who had banished the exiles. Not even the powerful lord could withstand Bernardino's powers of persuasion, for in no time the preacher was sent out to bid the exiles to return home. According to Bernardino's recollection, one of them, after arriving home, encountered an enemy in the piazza. Instead of drawing his weapon, he ran to embrace his adversary, and invited his newly found friend to dine with him that evening. By the next day the former exile's confiscated possessions, including his bed, his chests, linens, silver, along with his draft animals and sheep had been returned. Bernardino concluded his story with this rhetorical question: "And how pleasing do you think all this was to God?"[88]

---

86. *Prediche volgari sul Campo di Siena 1427*, ed. Carlo Delcorno, 2: 1261–62.

87. On this sermon, see Polecritti, *Preaching Peace*, 108–10.

88. *Prediche volgari sul Campo di Siena 1427*, 1: 366–69.

No doubt the story is a good exemplum; yet we should note that it also points to the very real issue of exile and the confiscation of goods, a double-barreled political problem that had been vexing city leaders for some time. The communes meted out the two punishments liberally, especially to political enemies, and both were resented bitterly by those who had to submit to them. We need only think of Dante who, in his own words, was "undeservedly in exile." The communes were not unaware of the difficulties these sentences created on both sides. As we shall see in chapter 4, city magistrates worried about the problem of exiles and *banniti*, whom they considered a political threat. Exile also had an economic impact on the city: when political exiles and banniti abandoned their hometowns, they took with them their labor and skills, and, for good measure, reduced the city's tax base as they left.[89]

Throughout his long career Bernardino continued to preach and act as a facilitator to peace. During Holy Week 1424, he gave a sermon on forgiveness in Florence in which he recounted yet another exemplum that modeled his message of peace and reconciliation.[90] Somewhere across the Alps, he told his audience, the husband of a very pious woman was killed by his sworn enemy. Instead of taking vengeance on him, the woman forgave her husband's murderer and reared her son in peace by withholding from him the circumstances of his father's death. In an extraordinary turn of events, after the son had grown up, he and his father's assailant became friends. Soon, however, gossip about the true identity of his new friend reached the ears of the young man. Thunderstruck, he swore to avenge his father's murder. He planned vendetta for Good Friday, and lay in wait to ambush his father's killer as he passed on his way to church. Brandishing a sword, the young man attacked, shouting out, "Stand still traitor, you are about to die!" But the day was not an auspicious one for revenge. The killer threw himself to the ground beseeching forgiveness, and in that instant, the young man, overcome by the love of God, pardoned his enemy. To celebrate their reconciliation they went off to Mass together, where a great miracle, a witness to their peace occurred. After the crucifix was uncovered, the Christ-figure on the cross miraculously came to life. Wearing his crown of thorns, his wounds still open, and his face covered in blood and spittle, Christ descended from the cross, parted the crowd, and made his way over to the young man who had freshly renounced vengeance. The Lord then embraced and kissed him three times before returning to the cross.[91] That day the young man reconciled with Christ, an act that made

89. On this problem, see Randolph Starn, *Contrary Commonwealth: The Theme of Exile in Medieval and Renaissance Italy* (Berkeley: University of California, 1982) and Fabrizio Ricciardelli, *The Politics of Exclusion in Early Renaissance Florence* (Turnhout: Brepols, 2007), along with the notes in chapter 4.

90. *Le prediche volgari*, ed. Ciro Cannarozzi, 5 vols. (Pistoia: Pacinotti, 1934), "Del Perdonare," 2: 230–47. On which see Polecritti, *Preaching Peace*, 176.

91. The story bears a resemblance to the one told about San Giovanni Gualberto whom Bernardino mentions at the end of the sermon. For further analysis of Giovanni Gualberto as peacemaker (and Bernardino's story about him), see chapter 4.

possible his reconciliation with his enemy. It is a skillfully wrought tale, one that encapsulates the preacher's pacific message so perfectly that his disciple James of the March borrowed it in a slightly less elaborated version in one of his own sermons on peace and the remission of injuries.[92]

James considered himself Bernardino's disciple; in this role, he adopted not only his rhetorical flourishes, gestures, and props, but also his master's themes. Indeed James became such a noted preacher of peace that he almost upstaged his teacher. But unlike Bernardino, who had learned to prefer preaching peace to direct intervention as a conflict mediator, James seemed to relish the challenge of entering the fray of political and civil discord in order to quell it. In this regard, he followed not in the footsteps of Bernardino but in those of his Franciscan forerunner Gerard of Modena, whom we have already glimpsed at work rewriting the statutes of Parma during the Great Devotion of 1233.

Only a few years after he entered the Order of Friars Minor and received permission to preach, James turned his attention to peacemaking. In 1425 we find him in Visso, in his home territory of the Marche, where he created a peace tribunal for civil cases. Within a year a member of the town council was implicitly comparing James's pacification of the city to the Bianchi when he noted: "A peace has been concluded in this territory of Visso and its countryside between all those who were living in hate and enmity on account of homicide and other excesses, from the time of the Bianchi up until today."[93]

In the final years of the decade, before he was sent to Eastern Europe to preach against the Hussites, James reduplicated his efforts throughout the Marche in the towns of Jesi, Macerata, Ancona, and Recanati. There, or at least in Macerata, according to one witness, James resurrected a venerable strategy for promoting peace that had been operative in city statutes since as early as the thirteenth century. Our source relates that "out of his love for God, James sought that the commune release some of those convicted and banished and readmit them to [the city]."[94]

Upon his return to Italy, after more than a decade abroad, the preacher took up where he had left off by preaching peace, reforming statute law, and creating new municipal offices dedicated to maintaining the peace. Beginning in 1444, for example, the year of Bernardino's death, James engaged in a flurry of peacemaking activities, particularly in Umbria, again in the Marche, and in northern Lazio.[95]

That year the town council of Rieti asked him to assist in reforming the city statutes and to establish a committee charged with keeping the peace. He

92. Sermo 91: "De pace et remissione iniuriarum," in Giacomo delle Marche (S. Iacobus de Marchia), *Sermones Dominicales*, 3 vols., ed. Renato Lioi, O.F.M. (Falconara Marittima: Biblioteca Francescana, 1978) 3: 280–93, at 292.

93. Sensi, "Le paci private," 167.

94. Sensi, "Le paci private," 179. On peace and its relationship to banishment, see chapter 4.

95. For a list of James's interventions in other city statutes, see Alberto Ghinato, "Apostolato religioso e sociale di Giacomo delle Marche in Terni," *AFH* 49 (1956): 106–42, at 121.

did so only after delivering a sermon to the assembly reminding them that "concord and peace of sweet name" should be served and augmented among the citizens, while noting that sedition, civil hatred, rancor, ill will and discord should be extirpated and eliminated. He may also have told them that the derivation of the word *pax* was from *placeo*, because it is pleasing to all.[96] Taking a page from Bernardino's sermon book, James further harangued his audience by putting them on notice that they also needed to address the underlying causes of these problems. This meant self-reform, with special attention given to moral defects such as taking part in quarrels and hatreds, cultivating bad habits and poor judgment, indulging in frivolous pleasures, or practicing craftiness, deception, lust, fraud, intrigue, vanity, lying, and all the other miserable failings of this world.[97] It should be noted that James's catalogue was the fifteenth-century iteration of Augustine's "appetites," those it was necessary to put in a state of order before peace and tranquility could be achieved.

James put his preaching into practice at Terni, the next stop on his busy agenda. There he met with members of the town council to advise them on how to improve their existing system of *pacieri*, officers of the peace. His reforms were enacted in a statute that created the office of *Conservatori e difensori della pace*, which provided for 360 pacieri entrusted to compose discord, extinguish hatred, and prevent vendetta.[98] Hand in hand with the statutory revision aimed at pacification of the city, the legislature also drafted a number of new statutes that penalized those engaged in "moral crimes" such as usury, blasphemy, gaming, and the breaking of sumptuary laws, many of the hot-button issues close to the hearts of the Observant preachers.[99] Conversion to penance continued to be the path to peace.

The preachers' message was familiar: conversion to penance was the necessary precondition to peace. This was possible only by addressing the underlying

96. Sermo 61 : "De honorificentia pacis & indulgentiae," in *Sermones Dominicales,* 2: 392–402, at 395: "Unde pax dicitur a *placeo, places* quia omnibus *placet* nisi dyabolo et suis membris."

97. Angelo Sacchetti Sassetti, "Giacomo delle Marche paciere a Rieti," *AFH* 50 (1957): 75–82, at 79. The gist of his sermon is recorded in the minutes of the assembly meeting by the chancellor Lucas Bartholomei Ballutii de Montefalcone, in Sassetti, "Giacomo delle Marche," 78–79.

98. Ghinato, "Apostolato religioso," Part II, *AFH* 49 (1956): 352–90, at 359 (numbers) and 352 (job description).

99. Polecritti, *Preaching Peace,* 105–106. See also Ghinato, "Apostolato religioso," Part I: 124–32. As it turned out, the decade of the 1440s proved particularly receptive to peace campaigns in Umbria and the Marche. James moved on to Convarianti and Todi in 1444, while in 1445 he pacified Foligno, and in 1446 both Ascoli Piceno and Fermo, while further pacifications punctuated his long career.

problems that began with the self. As we have seen, Federico Visconti had preached that the first step toward social reform was self-reform. What was needed was a long, hard look in the mirror that would result in a change of heart, just as Nanni di Ser Vanni had done, inspired by Catherine of Siena. Begin with the reform of the will, and the appetites would follow. Only then could "the tranquility of order," as Augustine defined peace, be established. After all, preachers suggested, civil discord and warfare were merely the symptoms of an underlying malady of the soul. Once the disease had been diagnosed, a salve to treat the symptoms could be applied.

In the Christian tradition, repentance was the medicine that brought about "serenity of the soul." Contrition and confession served as sacramental keys that opened the door of reconciliation with the Lord, the basis for all other forms of peace. Peace within the family, with neighbors, between city factions, and with other polities: all depended on inner peace that could be restored to the human person only through penance. Preachers and the laity understood this well. The penitential peace movements on the Italian peninsula, led alternatively by laymen and preachers, had this message at their core. Cries for peace were inevitably coupled with penitential practices such as flagellation, bare-footed processions, songs, and sermons exhorting repentance for mortal sins.

Such movements were no doubt a response to the combination of everyday violence ubiquitous in over-crowded cities, the partisan strife of factions, and the internecine warfare between the Guelf and Ghibelline parties both inside and outside the city walls. Indeed, it has been argued that the shockwaves generated by the Guelf defeat at Montaperti in 1260, a battle whose death toll was massive, was the watershed moment that transformed Raniero's flagellants from a local to an international movement.[100] Only through the violently bloody laceration of their own bodies in imitation of Christ could the *battuti* atone for the violence, destruction and warfare tearing apart city and countryside alike.

As we have seen, processions, rituals and sermons could activate revisions of local law, encouraging civic concord and tranquility. Indeed preachers transformed their words into action when, entrusted by magistrates to assist in rewriting the statute books, they instituted officers of the peace, enabled legislation allowing exiles to return to their native cities, imposed heavy fines for breaking the peace, and encouraged acrimonious parties to make peace agreements. In this they supported local officials in an effort to bend the arc of justice toward peace.

As will be clear by now, city magistrates were often eager to collaborate with the demands of the laity and preachers in their pacification efforts. They too had a vested interest in establishing peace in their cities. Indeed, the republican governments, which were taking root in the thirteenth century,

100. See, for example, Henderson, "The Flagellant Movement," 149–50.

emphasized peace initiatives as never before. Peace in all of its interlocking manifestations was integral to a new political ideology of the cities, one that was busy fashioning a social "imaginary" of peace and inventing civic institutions to foster it. Among those institutions was the peace instrument we shall examine in chapters 3 and 4, whose essential form, I suggest, was an echo of the penitential culture from which it emerged. At the core of all this civic enterprise and activity, however, was the question of how to implement changes to bring about a society where "Mercy and truth have met each other and justice and peace have kissed" (Psalm 84 (85):10–11). It is also the question at the heart of the next chapter.

CHAPTER TWO

Pax et Concordia

Peace I leave you, my peace I give you.
—JOHN: 14:27

AT THE SAME time as Luca da Bitonto was using the figure of Mary Magdalen to preach his message of conversion to inner peace through penance, an anonymous author was composing a handbook for municipal officers advising them on the importance of "outer" peace in the cities. Aimed at those assuming the office of podestà, the chief justice of the commune, the text took the form of a collection of model speeches. The office of podestà, borrowed from imperial administrative practice, required first that its occupant be a "foreign" magistrate, and second that the term be limited ordinarily to six months or at the maximum a year. These restrictions were meant to ensure the podestà's impartiality, segregating him from the fray of local factional politics. His primary function was to protect the peace of his city by dispensing justice.[1] The link between justice and peace is one of the themes running throughout this chapter. To establish it, we shall analyze a number of texts that suggest that a state of civil peace, what we have seen called "outer peace" in the previous chapter, could only be achieved through the proper administration of justice, assisted by civic concord. This conviction explains why the leaders of those penitential peace movements we examined in the previous chapter often trained their attention on revising statute law, or seized upon reforming those judicial punishments which, in their view, gave rise to discord. It also explains why they encouraged the practice of making peace agreements, because without justice they knew there could be no peace.

Written in the decades between 1220 and 1240, the *Oculus pastoralis*, is a handbook to guide the foreign podestà in his role as chief magistrate. More

---

1. On this office, see *I podestà dell'Italia comunale,* ed. Jean-Claude Maire Vigueur (Rome: École Française, 2000).

specifically, it is a collection from which the busy podestà could crib ideas for speeches. Significantly, several of them are exhortations to peace.[2] Indeed the collection opens with a ready-made speech that the podestà could use to urge his citizens to cultivate peace and perfect love among themselves by renouncing all violence and rancor.[3] The oration invokes images of the tranquil city where love, in concert with her companions, peace and concord, keeps warfare and discord at bay. "If there should be civil discord between citizens," the title of the second speech in the collection announces a more cautionary tale. [4] Here the podestà first outlines the social and economic benefits that accrue to the city when quiet, tranquility, and peace reign: the population grows, wealth increases, honors are bestowed, and friendships multiply. Indeed, the benefits of peace are immeasurable. Then, ominously, the speech turns dark and enumerates the dangers of discord, which are summed up in one portentous word: destruction. Discord, the podestà's speech suggests, can arise from even the most trivial cause and, at the instigation of the devil, has the power to unleash untold horrors: divisions between families and neighbors, physical damages from arson or the loss of property. Even worse, if discord is allowed to reign, violence against the human body will follow. Mortal wounds, mutilation, dismemberment, and bloody massacres become routine. The worst effect of discord, however, is that it threatens the very salvation of the immortal soul.[5]

In another speech the podestà warns of the dangers of warfare, noting that any spark of discord warrants an immediate reaction "lest that awful little scintilla grows and kindles hatreds." The antidote is to "let concord rule and flourish as the healthier medicine. For concord nourishes love. Peace gives birth to good will." As a reminder and possibly an incentive for his profit-minded audience, the author of the *Oculus* then makes a significant point: peace "also preserves and increases wealth."[6]

To underscore the importance of civil peace, he then turns to the gospel to observe, "With Christ's birth, God gave that gift to men when he said, 'Peace on earth to men of good will'" (Luke 2:14). And he bequeathed it when he ascended into heaven saying, 'Peace I leave you; my peace I give you'" (John: 14:27).[7] Like any good preacher or *concionatore*, the *Oculus* writer drew on key

2. *Speeches from the Oculus pastoralis*, ed. Terence O. Tunberg (Toronto: Centre for Medieval Studies, 1990).

3. Ibid., 24–25.

4. Ibid., 26–27.

5. It is a vision that predates Ambrogio Lorenzetti's great wall mural of the "Allegory of Good Government" in Siena's Palazzo Pubblico by more than a century. For the literature on it, see chapter 1, n1. Quentin Skinner argues forcefully that the fresco draws not on Aristotelian thinking as filtered through Aquinas, as has frequently been suggested, but on "pre-humanist" sources such as the *Oculus pastoralis*. See Skinner, "The Artist as Political Philosopher," *Proceedings of the British Academy* 72 (1986): 1–56, at 3 et *passim*.

6. *Oculus*, 65.

7. Ibid.

gospel passages to emphasize his points about civil peace, the first being that
the birth of Jesus ushered in an age of peace on earth to men of good will; and
second, that upon his Ascension, the Lord had both conferred that peace to
humankind and promised it in the world to come. It was the great challenge
of civil society to cultivate that peace, which the *Oculus* author framed unapol-
ogetically in Christian terms.

To a secular-minded western sensibility, one accustomed to the separa-
tion of Church and State, a civic goal framed in such starkly religious terms
may strike a discordant note, raising an eyebrow or two at the least. But we
must remember that such a worldview is not concordant with a medieval out-
look, one thoroughly suffused in Christian doctrine. It is worth highlighting
this point at this particular juncture, because this chapter offers an analysis
of visions of civic peace imagined by statesmen, their counselors, and urban
citizens, as distinct from the specifically religious viewpoint that structured
the material in the previous chapter. In that chapter we looked at how certain
visions of earthly peace were ineluctably connected to, and inevitably pointed
toward, the eternal peace of heaven, calling for a Christian understanding and
response to violence and warfare. This chapter, on the other hand, examines a
body of textual evidence concerned with civil peace. I argue that by the end of
the thirteenth century, the term *pax* came to be identified more with the ends
of civil society, the common good (which at the same time pointed toward the
eternal beatitude in the city of God), while *concordia*, or civic harmony, was
understood to be the means by which civil society attained this end, conceived
as the common good of peace. Thus one of the central aims of this chapter is to
show that the phrase *pax et concordia* was more than an empty catchphrase,
for it deliberately bound together two "goods" important for the health of civic
society. And though at least one legal commentator tried to draw a distinction
between the two for the sake of legal practice, in political thought the former
regularly represented the ends toward which the polity was meant to strive,
while the latter was a means to arrive at that destination.[8]

Though an association of ideas links the material in chapters 1 and 2, I nevertheless present the two bodies of material separately for the purpose of analysis, while bearing in mind that civic and religious voices were almost always

8. For example, William Durand (d. 1296), canonist and liturgist, argues in his *Iuris
Speculum*, 3 vols. (Venice: Società dell'Aquila che si rinnova, 1585), 3, Pars IIII, particula
I, *de tregua et pace*, 107 (nn.3–4): "item nota quod si non fiat pax, sed sola concordia, tunc
non fiet in instrumento de osculo mentio, nec de pace. Item si ex altera parte tantum
iniuria sit illata, tunc non fiet mutua pax, promissio seu concordia, sed solum fiet simplex
remissio inferenti a passo.... Hoc quoque nota quod si haec fiant per procuratores, debent
ad hoc speciale mandatum habere, de quo etiam in pacis instrumento fiat mentio special-
is." Cited in "Le paci private nella predicazione, nelle immagini di propaganda e nella prassi
fra Tre e Quattrocento," in *La pace fra realtà e utopia* (Verona: Cierre, 2005), 159–200, at
163, where Mario Sensi cites the Durand passage as if it were actually put into legal practice. I have seen no such distinction made in the Florentine documentation.

in dialogue, indeed often indistinguishable, and not infrequently were one and the same, as is the case with Remigio dei Girolami (d. 1319), a Dominican preacher, whose work features prominently in this chapter. Therefore, it is not only unwise, but also foolhardy, to attempt to disentangle the threads of religion from the whole cloth that made up medieval society, political philosophy included. The teachings of the Christian church informed everything from the rhythms of everyday life to the rhetoric of the highest secular magistrate of the city, as is evident in the *Oculus pastoralis* speeches we have just seen. Thus, even if this chapter examines notions of peace as conceived for civil society, it is necessary to remember that the ideas, framework, and vocabulary that comprise the politics of peace are deeply informed by scripture and the medieval Church's teachings on the subject.

Consequently, this chapter concerns itself with selected texts that were attempting to formulate a civic ethic of peace, one that emphasized the preeminent place of peace in civil society, the dangers of faction and vendetta, and the necessity of creating bonds of concord between citizens to unite them in common purpose, leading them to peace. But *caveat lector*: my intent here is not to offer a comprehensive survey of all possible materials pertaining to the topic, but rather to treat a few selected texts particularly relevant to thirteenth- and early fourteenth-century Florence, which may have been read, heard, or discussed within that particular urban context. I focus on these texts precisely because they are the ones whose echoes may have lingered in the minds of those charged with enacting the peace: officers such as the podestà, his retinue of judges, and the notaries who drafted peace instruments, agreements we will examine in depth in chapters 3 and 4. With that in mind, I have not selected texts that rank among the celebrated treatises of political philosophy; instead, I focus on a few representative texts from two genres of literature meant to guide statesmen and citizens of the Italian cities. On the one hand are two practical handbooks of governance, the *Oculus pastoralis* and Book Three of Brunetto Latini's *Tresor*, both of which offer insights into the importance of peace in civil society, though that is not necessarily their primary objective. On the other hand are the ethical tracts and sermons of Remigio dei Girolami, which receive the lion's share of the analysis in this chapter, because these works are concerned almost exclusively with an examination of peace in civil society, with an eye toward practical application, especially in Florence. All these texts are at the same time both descriptive and prescriptive; and all were written either as handbooks or direct responses to the local crises of Florentine politics rather than as comprehensive political treatises designed to argue for one form of government over another.[9] Reading these works within

9. For this reason the present discussion does not include texts such as Rufinus of Sorrento, *De bono pacis,* ed. Roman Deutinger, MGH Studien und Texte 17 (Hannover: Hahn, 1997); or Marsilius of Padua, *Defensor pacis,* ed. C. W. Previté-Orton (Cambridge: Cambridge University Press, 1928).

the political and religious context of thirteenth- and early fourteenth-century Florence (rather than as links in a great chain of political philosophy, as they often have been read), serves another goal of this chapter, which is to show that the descriptions of political violence and social discord found in all of these treatises were diagnoses of the situation "on the ground," as it were; thus they can be read as responses to the heartfelt cries for *pace e misericordia* we saw emerge from the penitential peace movements analyzed in the previous chapter. As this is prescriptive literature, we should read these texts first as tracts promoting the cultivation of virtue and moral reform; but no less important, we should also read them as discourses promoting the virtues of an efficacious judicial system, possessed of peace instruments able to play an important role in establishing civic peace. In the event, this chapter lays out the sociopolitical context for the emergence of civic peacemaking on a grand scale by arguing that the bonds of civic concord, the necessary preconditions for outer peace, could only be forged in the crucible of justice, or as the Psalmist envisioned it: only when justice and peace have kissed (Psalm 84 (85):10–11). Reframed in a Christian context, medieval preachers and moralists might have said that outer peace is possible only when justice and penitential peace have kissed, the context, I suggest, that gave rise to the *instrumentum pacis*, examined in chapters 3 and 4.

The *Tresor*, written in the 1260s by the Florentine Brunetto Latini (d. 1295), who began his career as a public notary and ended it as the chancellor of his native city, dedicates one quarter of Book Three to the "government of cities" in the Italian manner.[10] Composed during his exile in France, after the 1260 Ghibelline coup in Florence, Brunetto's text envisioned the lord or podestà of the commune as its primary peacemaker, even in an age when the new popular governments were coming to power. His discussions of peace appear both in his chapter on the virtues and vices, and in the section conceived as a handbook for future podestà.

Celebrated as a "pre-humanist" by a generation of contemporary scholars, Brunetto lives up to that name in his treatise, which is steeped in Ciceronian rhetorical theory and ancient political philosophy. (It is known that he had an early translation of Aristotle's *Nicomachean Ethics* by his side as he composed the *Tresor*.) In his discussion of "magnificence in the time of peace," citing Plato as his source, Brunetto notes that in order to maintain a peaceful society, the ruler must 1) defend the interests of the citizens by, for example, ensuring that there is an ample supply of food; 2) protect the entire community, not just certain interests; and 3) maintain justice by defending the interests of every person, not just a select few: "for those who help some against others

---

10. *Li Livres dou Tresor*, ed. Francis J. Carmody (Berkeley: University of California Press, 1948), 391–422, at 392; in English as *The Book of the Treasure (Li Livres dou Tresor)*, trans. Paul Barrette and Spurgeon Baldwin (New York: Garland, 1993). Henceforth I cite their translation. On Brunetto, see G. Inglese, "Latini, Brunetto," DBI 64 (2005), 4–12.

bring perilous discord to the city. The lord and governor of a city must see to it that there are no disputes among them."[11] In his section on concord, "a virtue which links in one law and one dwelling place those who are in the same city and country," we find Brunetto formulating a theory of the "common good" that is premised on concord among citizens. In this case, the condition of living under the same law fashions bonds of concord among its citizens. As for the nature of the common good, he calls on the wisdom of the pagan sages: "The philosophers called Stoics say: all things were created for the usage of men, and men were created for one another, that is, that they help one another, and for this reason we must follow nature and place the common profit above all else. . . . Sallust says: through concord small things grow and through discord great things are destroyed."[12]

Brunetto, like the author of the *Oculus pastoralis*, on which he drew, was elaborating a theory of the common good premised on yoking the community together in bonds of concord, while extinguishing the embers of discord. In the final section of the *Tresor*, he lays out his plan for so doing. He advises the potential chief magistrate that immediately after he has taken the oath of office—even before going to church to pray—he must discern whether there is any discord inside or outside the city. Should there be, he ought to take immediate steps to quell it and make peace, unless the citizens for their own reasons are against it. In the spirit of establishing peace and concord, which cannot exist without justice, the podestà should establish fines and punishments for crimes with the advice of his council and in accordance with statute law.[13] Pursuing the links between concord and justice, Brunetto argues that the good magistrate should "hear the extraordinary quarrels often and resolve them and diminish the complaints of all the people; for it is a good thing for the lord to hold his subjects within the bounds of the law, so that they do not reach the point of discord, for a flame which is not extinguished oftentimes becomes a roaring fire."[14] As the chief magistrate of the city, the podestà's chief duty was to dispense justice to keep the peace. Dispensing justice, it should be noted, meant above all else resolving disputes that were the cause of discord. It also meant supervising the punishment of convicted criminals. Justice, in Brunetto's eyes, was the key to concord, and it was among the podestà's primary duties as supreme magistrate to administer it. Statute law, upheld through fines and punishments, and the hearing of disputes in court, were the means by which the podestà could establish concord and ultimately peace. As we will see in chapter 3, it is not coincidental that our first peace agreements in Florence date from precisely this period, when statute law was being hammered out and the communal courts were coming into their own with the podestà as their highest magistrate. Significantly, the peace agreement

11. *The Book of the Treasure*, 233–34.
12. Ibid., 257.
13. Ibid., 365–66.
14. Ibid., 369.

was one among the resources that the communal judges had at their disposal to establish justice, which in turn fostered concord, the companion to outer peace. As a notary himself, who may well have enacted peace agreements in Florence before his exile, Brunetto understood better than most the relationship between justice, concord, and peace. He was among a number of political thinkers who imagined the judicial process as a means to promote concord, from whose bonds peace could then emerge and flourish.

REMIGIO DEI GIROLAMI

The writings of Brunetto's fellow Florentine, Dominican theologian and preacher Remigio dei Girolami (d. 1319), exhibit a similar concern that peace and harmony prevail over the social discord that so frequently engulfed his native city. The two authors also share the belief that justice is the key to outer peace. But Remigio's thinking on the matter, as we might expect given his education at the feet of Thomas Aquinas in Paris, expresses itself in a different register.[15] We will analyze Remigio's writings in a moment, but first it is important to sketch out some biographical context for the friar and his family.

The Girolami, though not among the magnate lineages, was by the mid-thirteenth century an important Florentine family aligned with the Guelf party and, after the split, mostly with the party's White faction.[16] Members of the Arte della Lana, the powerful Florentine wool guild, the Girolami had achieved such significant political clout by the end of the thirteenth century that they ranked as the top officeholders of the commune during the decade between 1282 to 1292.[17] Their service to the city dated back to 1250, when Remigio's father Chiaro was seated among the *Anziani* or Council of Elders of the government of the Primo

---

15. The discussion that follows owes much to the scholarship of Fr. Emilio Panella, O.P., who has edited Remigio's body of work on peace, which includes a corpus of peace sermons along with two tracts, *De bono comuni* and *De bono pacis*. The editions and commentary were published originally as "Dal bene comune al bene del comune: I trattati politici di Remigio dei Girolami (d. 1319) nella Firenze dei bianchi-neri," in *Memorie Dominicane* n.s. 16 (1985). It has recently been republished as a stand-alone volume, *Dal bene comune al bene del comune: I trattati politici di Remigio dei Girolami (d. 1319) nella Firenze dei bianchi-neri* (Florence: Nerbini, 2014). See also Panella's comprehensive website on Remigio: http://www.e-theca.net/emiliopanella/remigio/index.htm [consulted 6/21/17]. And Sonia Gentili, "Girolami, Remigio de'," DBI 56 (2001): 531–41. For a good English introduction to Remigio's political theology, see Charles Till Davis, "An Early Florentine Political Theorist: Fra Remigio de' Girolami," *Proceedings of the American Philosophical Society* 104. 6 (1960): 662–76; repr. Davis, *Dante's Italy and Other Essays* (Philadelphia: University of Pennsylvania Press, 1984), 198–223; and most recently M. S. Kempshall, *The Common Good in Late Medieval Political Thought* (Oxford: Clarendon, 1999), 293–338.

16. Another branch of the Girolami, sons of Remigio's first cousin, was associated with the Black Party and held office after 1303. On the Girolami family, see Panella, *Dal bene comune*, 58–100.

17. Panella, *Dal bene comune*, 78–81.

Popolo. Remigio's brother Salvi, a representative of the wool guild, was among the original priors of the newly established guild government of 1282. Salvi's sons, Chiaro, Girolamo, and Mompuccio, all continued the family tradition by serving as priors during significant turning points in the city's history. For example, Mompuccio served in the Priorate that decreed the Ordinances of Justice in January 1293, while Girolamo's term in office was cut short by deposition in 1301, just before the entrance of Charles of Valois into the city as a papal envoy, charged with making peace between the Guelfs and Ghibellines.

Florence's turbulent recent history, punctuated by numerous efforts to make peace between political factions, social ranks, families, and individuals, no doubt provoked Remigio to think long and hard about war and peace, discord and civic harmony, violence and tranquility; thus we find a number of his works dedicated to these subjects. They consider such questions, among others, as what are the reasons for warfare, factionalism, and violence? What prerequisites are needed for peace? How can peace be achieved? What institutions are necessary to promote peace? How are they justified? Among his works that take up these questions, are twelve sermons on peace written at various times for diverse occasions, another addressed to the Florentine priors and delivered around 1295, and his treatise *De bono pacis* (1304), a companion piece to his *De bono comuni*, written two years earlier in 1302.[18] Given the political importance and status of his family, combined with his own prominent position at the convent of Santa Maria Novella, it is not an exaggeration to call Remigio a political theorist in the service of the popular government of Florence. The remainder of this chapter therefore examines his sermons and treatises on peace, reading them not as political theory, as has been the scholarly accomplishment of others, but rather within the particular context of the sociopolitical and religious history of Florence. In this way we can grasp Florence's very particular problems, which resulted in social discord, along with Remigio's very particular prescriptive ideas on how to resolve them.

All this is to say that neither his sermons nor his treatises were written in a vacuum. Each was a response to the events of violence, factionalism, and all out warfare that were tearing his native city apart. Since at least four of the sermons likely predate *De bono pacis*, let us begin with Remigio's homilies on peace, which are every bit as much political interventions as they are sermons, made from the bully-pulpit he occupied as lector at Santa Maria Novella, an appointment he held for more than forty years. His written work was meant

18. Panella publishes sermons I-IX as an appendix to *Dal bene comune*, 248–78. All these sermons are from Remigio's *de tempore* collection found in MS Florence, Bib. Nat. Conv. Soppr. G4. 936. fols. 351r-64r. Editions of the other three sermons (occasional sermons) are interlaced in the introduction as follows: "Si Linguis," 37 (MS Conv. Soppr. G 4. 936, fols. 42r-42v); "Omne Regnum," 138–39 (MS Conv. Soppr. G 4. 936, fols. 76r-76v); "De domino Carolo. Accingere gladio tuo," 55–57 (MS Conv. Soppr .G 4.936, fols. 353r-353v).

to be used "in house" for teaching purposes, but his ideas nevertheless were publicly broadcast throughout the city, first in the form of sermons he himself delivered at political occasions, and second in a slightly different format, when his student, Giordano da Pisa, disseminated them in a simplified version in the vernacular sermons he preached in the streets of Florence during his many years in residence there.

"Si linguis," the first of Remigio's sermons devoted to peace, was likely written between 1279 and 1280, the period of Cardinal Latino Malabranca's (d. 1294) mission to Florence as legatine peacemaker.[19] The cardinal had been appointed as paciere in 1279 by his uncle, Pope Nicholas III Orsini, who sent him to Florence to impose a peace and complete the work left undone in 1273 by his predecessor Gregory X (d. 1276). Gregory's peace between the Guelfs and Ghibellines had lasted a mere four days, with the result that the pope laid an interdict on the city as punishment.[20] Requested by the Florentine magistrates, who wished to have the interdict lifted and the violence and warfare afflicting the city pacified, the two parties beseeched the pope in the summer of 1278 to send an impartial paciere to negotiate a peace. Accordingly, the Guelfs and Ghibellines then signed an agreement to abide by any decision the pope (or his representative) made as arbiter. With that guarantee, Nicholas III sent his nephew, the Cardinal-bishop of Ostia and Velletri, whom he referred to as *tamquam pacis angelus*, both a nice turn of phrase and a pun, since Cardinal Latino's full name was Latino d'Angelo Malabranca.[21] Even for an angel, the cardinal's mandate was a tough one: negotiate a peace between the parties whose conflicts had been wreaking havoc on the city for decades.[22]

19. Though this date (suggested by others) is not firm, I think there are two reasons to support it. The first is that it makes use of the terms Guelfs and Ghibellines (not Whites and Blacks, a later division), the factions into which the Florentines had recently split. The second is that Remigio was a great supporter and admirer of his Dominican confrère, Latino Malabranca, so much so that he gave a funeral oration memorializing him: "Oriundus de Roma que anthonomastice vocatur Urbs, et quantum ad modum, scilicet sue conversationis et suorum morum; item in nobilitate, qui ex parte patris filius fuit domini Angeli Malabranche qui fuit potestas istius civitatis et septies fuit Romae senator; ex parte autem matris fuit filius sororis pape Nicholai de Ursinis." Cited by Marco Vendittelli, "Malabranca, Latino," in DBI 67 (2006): 699–703. In *Dal bene comune*, Panella suggests two possible dates for the sermon: one coinciding with the legation of Cardinal Latino in 1279–1280, the other with Cardinal Pietro Duraguerra da Piperno in 1296 (139).

20. For this and what follows about the peace of Cardinal Latino, see Mario Sanfilippo, "Guelfi e Ghibellini a Firenze: la 'pace' del Cardinal Latino (1280)," *Nuova Rivista Storica* 64 (1980): 1–24; and Isa Lori Sanfilippo publishes all the relevant documentation: "La pace del cardinale Latino a Firenze nel 1290. La sentenza e gli atti complementari," *Bullettino dell'istituto storico italiano per il medio evo e Archivio Muratoriano* 89 (2001): 193–259. See also Vendittelli, "Malabranca, Latino," ibid.

21. M. Sanfilippo, "Guelfi e Ghibellini a Firenze," at 2, quoting the registers of Pope Nicolas III.

22. Villani recounts the Guelf-Ghibelline split in *Nuova Cronica*, vol. 1: Bk 6: chaps. 38–39: 267–71.

In November 1279, Cardinal Latino convened the citizens and representatives of the communal government in a great meeting in the piazza of Santa Maria Novella, where he had them confirm his authority as mediator and then lifted the interdict on the city. He requested and received the power to banish, imprison, fine, detain, and confiscate the property of those who refused to abide by his decisions, thus taking into his hands all the coercive power the government ordinarily held over its citizens. First he pacified the internal divisions within the Guelf party by making peace between the Adimari and their rivals. He then turned to the seemingly intractable problem of Guelf-Ghibelline strife as embodied in their relentless wars. Toward that end, he created The Fourteen, a new executive magistracy that included representatives of both parties: eight Guelfs and six Ghibellines. One of the many innovations of Cardinal Latino's "sentence" of peace, ratified in February 1280, was that eight guilds promised allegiance to the agreement, opening the door to what would eventually become the guild government of Florence. Also of great import was the "humanitarian aspect" of the peace: the provision that most of the Ghibelline exiles (pointedly excluding the Uberti) were allowed to return home and reclaim their confiscated goods and property, or at least partial reimbursement for their losses. [23] Giovanni Villani gives us this celebratory narrative account of the peace:

> The legate favorably concluded it the following February, when the entire people assembled in the old square in front of the aforementioned church [Santa Maria Novella]. The square was draped with cloths and great wooden platforms on which the cardinal, many bishops, prelates, clergy, monks, and the podestà, the captain of the people, all the councilors, and other officers of Florence were convened. The legate delivered a fine sermon with many lovely authorities thoroughly fitting the occasion, for he was a wise and skillful preacher. When he had finished, representatives of the Guelfs and Ghibellines *kissed one another on the mouth*, thus joyfully making peace among all the citizens. There were 150 on each side. Then and there the legate announced the terms each side was obliged to observe, confirming the peace with solemn, *duly authorized documents* and proper *guarantees*. From that moment the Ghibellines could and did return to Florence with their families and were *absolved from all banishment and condemnation*. All the books of *banishment and condemnation in the chamber were burned*. These Ghibellines also *received their possessions back*, but to ensure the security of the territory it was decreed that some of the principal Ghibellines leaders should remain within certain boundaries. When the cardinal had finished with the Guelfs and Ghibellines, *he made peace among individual families*, starting with the greatest of all, that

23. M. Sanfilippo, "Guelfi e Ghibellini a Firenze," 24.

of the Adimari with the Tosinghi, Donati, and Pazzi, *arranging several weddings* between the families. In similar fashion he *settled all the feuds* in Florence and throughout the countryside, some by the will of the parties involved and others by command of the commune, sentence having been pronounced by the cardinal *with solid sanctions and guarantees.* The cardinal derived a great deal of honor from these peace agreements, almost all of which were maintained, for they allowed the city of Florence to remain in a peaceful, good and tranquil state for some time.[24]

Excellent observer that he was, Villani here draws our attention to a number of important points, which I have italicized and to which we will return in subsequent chapters. Among them are the ritual kiss of peace on the mouth (chapter 5) exchanged to ratify the agreement; the duly authorized documents, sanctions, and guarantees (chapter 3); the feuds, condemnations, and judicial banishment (chapter 4); and the arrangement of several weddings (chapter 5). It is a "thick description," but for now let us focus on Villani's approving comments that the "legate delivered a fine sermon with many lovely authorities thoroughly fitting the occasion, for he was a wise and skillful preacher." Remigio's sermon does similarly, and given his personal relationship with Cardinal Latino, it seems to provide internal evidence that "Si linguis" was delivered on the very same day as the sermon of his Dominican confrère. The first line of "Si linguis" observes: "the Lord C. has given you today the delicate food of cardinals; I will give you something refreshing to imbibe with it, lest you have a meal without drink." Emilio Panella, the great authority on Remigio, suggests that the "Lord C." should be read as the "Lord Cardinal," another indication that the sermon dates from 1280, when Cardinal Latino was either hammering out or promulgating the terms of his peace. [25] It must be remembered that sermons delivered on important political occasions would by no means have been out of place. We have already witnessed Federico Visconti, Bishop of Pisa, delivering one to the city council on the occasion of a peace treaty sworn in 1267.

24. Villani, *Nuova Cronica*, vol. 1: Bk. 8, chap. 56: 498–501. The emphases are mine. The account continues: "The legate decreed that the city should be governed by fourteen good men drawn both from the Grandi and from the Popolani. There were to be eight Guelfs and six Ghibellines. Their term of office was to be two months, and a means of election was established. They were to assemble at the Badia of Florence, above the gate that goes to Santa Margarita, returning to their own homes to eat and sleep. . . . Having accomplished these things, Cardinal Latino returned with great honor to his duties in the Romagna."

25. He also notes that no cardinal associated with Florence in the second half of the thirteenth century had a name that began with the letter C; therefore, Panella proposes that the abbreviation is short for "Dominus Cardinalis" (the Lord Cardinal) in Panella, *Dal bene comune*, 139.

Remigio takes his theme for "Si linguis" from the first few words of the famous Pauline passage on love, "If I speak in tongues" (1 Cor. 13:1). Drawing a stark contrast between a state of discord and peace, Remigio first lays out the picture of discord, one epitomized by the political and social divisions paralyzing his city. He notes three major divisions, each of which he pointedly symbolizes with an animal figure. Because the proud Ghibellines on occasion had used the king of the beasts as their symbol, Remigio calls them lions; he symbolizes the Guelfs as calves, because, he explains, they are sacrificial animals.[26] He represents artisans and members of the popolo with the emblem of the lamb. Catering to his Florentine audience, a city built on the production of woolen cloth, Remigio explains that he is associating them with the lamb because they are woolworkers, merchants of the Calimala (the wool importers' guild), cloth-makers, shoemakers, cheese-makers, butchers, stationers, and peddlers, all of whom, like the lamb, are useful to society. Moreover, they share the lamb's quality of innocence, and all of their crafts depend on that self-same animal. Of course the spiritual symbolism would have been lost on no one: as Christians, they made up the flock tended by Jesus, the Good Shepherd.

The theme of Remigio's sermon is charity. It is a theme with which we are already familiar, but the friar presents it in his own particular admixture of Pauline and Augustinian precepts on love. Charity is like a flame, such that its heat fires clay into terracotta, he preaches; it also dissolves ice, it warms, it incinerates. Yet as Augustine says, it is like honey. Charity fosters concord between neighbors and peace in the city. And like a skilled craftsman, he shows how this works by interweaving a critique of contemporary society with the words of the celebrated Pauline passage on love. The preacher notes that in respect to evil deeds and malintent, charity protects against these things because *it does not act falsely*, and it acts likewise in regard to the evils of guilt and punishment because *it does not rejoice in inequity*. And because *charity is not envious*, it guards against thinking darkly about neighbors, for *it thinks not of evil*. "And likewise, in regard to the commune, *charity does not seek advantage for itself.*" As it is honey, *charity is not provoked to anger* against others. And because charity is fire, with regard to property and desires, it *is not swollen*, for *charity is not ambitious* and it reduces all to ash. Remigio sums up with a warning to his quarrelsome listeners: "He is not a good citizen, business partner, or ally who does otherwise [who violates the order of charity]." In the end, he circles back to the three beasts, his symbols of the social and political divisions in his city. Citing Isaiah 11:16, he preaches that "the lion, calf, and lamb will lie down together with a little boy to lead them," from which his audience was presumably meant to extrapolate the message

26. Panella notes that the Ghibelline coat of arms occasionally used the image of Hercules mounted on a lion. *Del bene comune*,137, n.3. There is no mention of the Whites and Blacks because the split had not yet occurred.

that it was possible for Ghibellines, Guelfs and the popolo of Florence to live together in the peace and harmony of God, if only they would live according to the teachings of Jesus. He concludes the sermon with the observation that "all these things secure the preservation of peace."[27]

As preachers had done before and indeed would continue to do well after him, Remigio preached conversion to charity as the balm that would heal society's wounds and divisions, which were the consequences of moral failings—among them falsehood, inequity, envy, malicious thoughts, greed, anger, and pride. As we have already seen, Remigio was not alone in maintaining that such moral defects could be assuaged by conversion to love through penance.

But in "Si linguis" Remigio also puts his finger on the problem of the city's social and political divisions. It is worth noting that although in this sermon he makes much of the political fissures in Florence, he takes little notice of the social stratifications that also characterized his city. Like the cardinal, he concentrates on the political factions dividing the city, and by deploying the symbol of the lion, he suggests indirectly that ferocious Ghibelline pride may be responsible for the city's troubles. Remigio at this point makes no attempt to confront social discord among the people of the lamb—the popolo. His analysis of Florentine social tensions would grow more sophisticated, however, only a few years later in his sermon, "Omne regnum."

Remigio probably wrote "Omne regnum" during the period between 1293 to 1295, when Giano della Bella was leading the popular uprising against the magnates, which resulted in the *Ordinances of Justice* and the establishment of the guild government. Among other things, that set of laws blacklisted magnate families from holding political office and decreed heavy penalties for violence committed against any member of the popolo. In this fractured political climate, Remigio was forced to reevaluate the causes of factionalism and violence and to take into account the new sociopolitical groupings he had not even countenanced in "Si linguis." In "Omne regnum," a Lenten sermon on the biblical theme "Every kingdom divided against itself shall be brought to desolation; and house upon house shall fall" (Luke 11:17), Remigio observes that his great city, like the one in the Book of Revelation (Rev. 16:19), has been fractured into three parts:

> One rift is because the Guelfs badmouth the Ghibellines saying that they don't ever cooperate, and the Ghibellines badmouth the Guelfs saying that they want them expelled. Another rift is because the artisans badmouth the magnates saying that they are being devoured

---

27. "Si linguis," in Panella, *Del bene comune*, 137. The italics indicate the quotations from 1 Cor. 13:4–6. This is a particularly thorny passage because it is an unfinished text. I am grateful to John Petruccione for his aid in helping me smooth out the English translation.

by them, that they commit treason, that they confiscate the property of their enemies, and so on. And for their part, the grandees badmouth the artisans saying that they aspire to govern, but they are so ignorant that they blame the land for their problems, and so on. The third rift is between the clergy and religious on one side, and the laity on the other, because they say that laypeople are traitors, perjurers, adulterers, and thieves, and this is true of many. The laity, on the other hand, say the clergy are fornicators, gluttons, and slothful, and that the religious are vainglorious thieves, and this is true of some. [28]

Apart from the dry wit exhibited at the end of this passage, we should note that Remigio's portrait of Florence in "Omne regnum" is of a city divided against itself in its politics, and by its social distinctions, economic interests, and religious affiliations. It is, therefore, a more trenchant sociological analysis of the city than that offered in "Si linguis." The preacher is not reticent about naming names or isolating root causes. Guelfs have turned against Ghibellines, magnates against the popolo, and clergy against the laity. Guelfs are at odds with the Ghibellines, who continue in their efforts to bring down the government; Ghibellines complain about the unfair punishment of judicial exile; the magnates complain that the ignorant popolo now rules the government, and the popolo in turn lament that the magnates despoil them of their goods and engage in treason against their rule. In this picture of social discord, even the laity and clergy are at each other's throats.

The preacher's remedy, however, is the same one that we have seen him offer in "Si linguis:" self-reform and conversion to the penitential path through God's grace, the first step toward civic harmony:

> Dearest brothers, only our Lord Jesus Christ can unite and mend these rifts through his grace, since "he is our peace who has made us one" (Ephesians 2:14). . . . And he wants to unite us, so long as we are willing to prepare ourselves. Therefore let us withdraw from sinning which divides us from God and in this way we unite with God and our neighbor, here on earth through his grace and in paradise through his glory.[29]

It is a refrain we have heard from other preachers; however, in a sermon on the common good of peace (Sermon VIII), probably delivered circa 1297, Remigio begins to modify his message, proposing civil remedies for civil disputes, another contributing factor to social discord.[30] Here Remigio is partic-

28. "Omne Regnum," in Panella, *Del bene comune*, 138–39.
29. Ibid, 139.
30. Sermo VIII: "Vade in pace," MS Florence, Bib. Nat. G.4.936, fols. 359v-60r; *Dal bene comune*, 264–65. I follow Panella who argues for the date based on manuscript evidence. The word "saint" was inserted in the margin of the manuscript in reference to Louis IX of France, canonized in 1297. For the dating, see Panella, *Dal bene comune*, 132–33.

ularly alive to the symptoms of violence and enmity and his sermon proposes solutions for treating those social ills. Preaching on a verse from Mark 5:34, the woman healed of her hemorrhage by Jesus, Remigio employs a traditional medieval metaphor to represent the city or society—the "body politic." Here the preacher informs his audience that a peaceful city is like a healthy body in nine ways, each of which he then explicates. It is not necessary to adduce them all here; three of his explanations will suffice to give us the flavor of his argument.

Inspired by a line from Proverbs (20:1)—*luxuriosa res vinum et tumultuosa ebrietas*—Remigio counsels that just as a strict diet preserves a healthy body, good citizens should do likewise by abstaining from gaming and drinking in taverns, because such things stir people up against each other and drunkenness invites only trouble. Extending the metaphor, Remigio observes that just as harmony is restored to the body when a tumor is lanced or an enema administered to flush out waste, so humility of spirit is the salve to treat the swelling of ambition, a not so subtle warning to those who were puffed up with the sin of pride. In his final analogy, Remigio compares civil peace to bodily health by noting the similarity between punishments and medical treatments. Noting that society's criminals are not unlike a disease afflicting the body politic, the preacher proceeds to show how judicial punishments have their analogues in medicine: financial penalties are comparable to bloodletting, exile to purgation, and execution to the amputation of a limb, all done to return the body to a state of equilibrium and the body politic to a state of harmony.

It is important to emphasize the implicit comparison Remigio draws between the practice of medicine and judicial practice. Medieval medicine, as is well known, drew on the ancient principal of establishing harmony between the humors that governed the body. The objective of medical practice, then, was to reestablish harmony in the body, when the humors became imbalanced. Bloodletting and purgation were the common treatments toward this end. We can see the same objective governing judicial practice. Remigio suggests that when judges use the instruments of the judicial system such as exile and financial penalties, or even corporal punishment, they do so to restore harmony to the body politic after a crime has been committed. While the aim of medical practice was to restore harmony (or health) to the body, judicial practice had a similar goal: to restore harmony (or concord) to the body politic.

On the individual level, Remigio was advocating abstinence from gaming, drinking, and frequenting taverns, all of which in his view led inevitably to violence. And like other preachers we have seen in the previous chapter, he was calling for a conversion to "inner peace" through moral reform, a curbing of the temptation to fall into the sin of pride by practicing humility. On the civic level, Remigio endorses the financial penalties or judicial punishments of banishment, exile, or execution, meted out routinely to criminals and political enemies in medieval Florence because, he argues, they lead to concord, the prerequisite for "outer peace," which is the proper end of good government. Indeed, as we shall see, Remigio believed that the function of the justice system was to foster concord, the preconditions under which outer peace could be established.

Sometime during the years between 1295 and 1300, when the political sands had shifted yet again, and the Guelf Party had split into White and Black factions, all of Cardinal Latino's legal remedies to maintain the peace were put to the test in Florence, whose problems were threatening to destabilize the political order of the entire Italian peninsula. The Whites now held the Priorate and war between the parties appeared likely to consume the city. According to the chronicler Dino Compagni (d. 1324), a prior at the time and loyal member of the White party, the Blacks sought the mediation of their ally Pope Boniface VIII to establish peace, and in the Jubilee year of 1300, the pope dispatched the Franciscan cardinal Matthew of Aquasparta to Florence as paciere. The cardinal's efforts came to naught, however, because the factions refused to grant him full powers to arbitrate their dispute. Moreover, his suspected partisanship for the Black cause was soon unmasked. After a bungled assassination attempt, in which an arrow shot through a window failed to strike the Cardinal's breast, he took flight, abandoning his mission in humiliating disgrace.[31]

In 1310, impatient to pacify Florence, the pontiff tried again, this time sending a secular paciere into the Florentine political quagmire. The brother of King Philip IV the Fair, Charles of Valois, had a mandate to impose a peace on the ruling White party, led by the Cerchi family, and the Blacks of Corso Donati, staunch papal allies. As he had come to Italy to help his Angevin cousin retake Sicily for the papal cause, the count's impartiality was (with good reason) suspect from the outset, so it is not surprising that he too failed utterly to bring the parties to peace. Indeed, no sooner had Charles negotiated his entry into the city in early November than the Blacks pulled off a coup d'etat. Dante, a White Guelf and a city prior, was declared a rebel in March 1302. He is the most famous casualty of this regime change, but we should also note that Remigio's nephews—Girolamo di Salvo, Chiaro, and Mompuccio—politically powerful members of the White party, were also sent into exile at this time.[32]

But all of this political chaos was yet to unfold when Remigio wrote his sermon "Accingere gladio tuo" for the advent of Charles of Valois's embassy into Florence.[33] Early November 1301 was still a moment of hope, and Remigio urged due deliberation and caution. Wearing his deep learning less than

---

31. Dino Compagni, *Cronica*, ed. Gino Luzzatto (Turin: Einaudi, 1968); I use the translation by Daniel Bornstein, *Chronicle of Florence* (Philadelphia: University of Pennsylvania Press, 1986), 24–25.

32. Panella, *Dal bene comune*, 84–91.

33. "De domino Carolo. Accingere gladio tuo," in Panella, ibid., 55–56 (MS Conv. Soppr. G 4.936, fols. 353r-v).

lightly, he peppered his sermon with an array of pagan and Hebrew sources to underpin the advice that one "should not act suddenly and hastily." Armed with Seneca, Proverbs, Ecclesiasticus, Cicero, and Suetonius, Remigio argued for proceeding in a measured way. Judging from the text of the sermon, he took his own advice and delivered an oration that was as cautious as it was circumspect.

Preached during a procession for peace, possibly one that Compagni noted in his chronicle, Remigio's second sermon, written to mark Charles's arrival in Florence, spoke more directly to the question of the factional strife at hand. [34] Mentioning the procession, Remigio commends it as a practice that increases devotion because, "as Augustine says in his *Letter to Proba*, 'From words and other signs, we stimulate our mind more keenly.'"[35] He also praises the participants, a mixed group of priests, religious, and lay people, who united as one to clamor loudly for peace. "And therefore it is to be hoped that peace will be achieved." Given his lament in "Omne regnum" that the laity was at odds with the city's clergy and religious, the friar must have been gratified to see the solidarity expressed in their procession for peace.

Nonetheless, Remigio uses his pulpit to warn Charles of Valois that the road to peace will not be without peril, because according to Augustine and (Pseudo-)Dionysius, while some intend true peace, others are interested merely in making a pretense at peace, especially those warmongers who only want to protect their honor, perhaps a subtle jab at the pro-Black *paciere*. In conclusion, however, Remigio exhorts his audience not to despair because peace can be attained through the power of God, through which "all discord can be made concordant and all enmity pacified."[36] He again pleads for concord as the means to outer peace.

His call went unheeded, however, as Charles's mission facilitated the Black party's ascendency and the downfall of their adversaries. Settling old scores with the Whites, in depressingly predictable fashion, the Blacks installed their own priors and sidelined their enemies through a combination of exile and the confiscation and destruction of property. They also emptied the prisons of Black party members who were being held as political prisoners. It was in this context that Remigio wrote *De bono comuni* (ca. 1302), his opus magnum on the common good.[37] Though composed in classic scholastic format that tends toward the theoretical, it was nonetheless written as a response to the contemporary social and political crisis in Florence. The Dominican preacher defends the proposition that the common good should take precedence over

34. Sermo I: "Fiat pax in virtute tua," in Panella, *Dal bene comune*, 348–52 (MS Conv. Soppr. G.4.936, fols. 357r-v). Compagni, *Chronicle*, 43.

35. Panella, ibid., 150.

36. Ibid.

37. *De bono comuni*, ed. Panella, *Dal bene comune*, 144–221 (MS Florence Bib. Nat. Conv. Soppr. C 4.940, fols. 97r-106r). On the dating, ibid., 48–49.

individual exigencies. It is noteworthy, however, that only in passing does Remigio identify the common good of the multitude with peace.[38] His pressing concern was to show how factionalism was destroying the city, and in the wake of the Black coup, Remigio paints a desolate picture. Using the same analogy he employed in his earlier sermons comparing the peace of the city to the health of the human body, he emphasizes that order governs every organism and is necessary if the whole is to function properly. This was the order of charity, the Augustinian metaphor that structured all of Remigio's thinking on the subject of peace and the common good. Following Aquinas and other scholastic thinkers, Remigio argues that the "common good is the manifestation of correctly ordered love." [39] When the order of charity is disturbed, so is the order of society, with the result that discord rules. According to Remigio, this was the cause of all Florence's problems.

The tract opens with an invocation of the Pauline prophesy (2 Tim. 3) that foresees dangerous times ahead when men will be self-centered and avaricious, boastful, arrogant, and proud. Those times are upon us, Remigio warns, "alas, especially among our fellow Italians," who neglect the common good by throwing into disorder whole regions of the peninsula and destroying the fortified towns, cities, and provinces.[40] Those "self-centered" individuals were upending the entire social order by putting themselves before the good of the community. The order of charity, he reminds his audience, dictates the order of the good, and the common good is to be favored over individual needs and desires. In other words, if concord is to defeat discord, citizens need to unite in aiming toward the common good of peace.

After establishing, through scholastic reasoning and proof texts, that the common good should be preferred to individual necessity, Remigio invokes the particular plight of Florence. And when he does, his usual workmanlike prose takes wing and soars off the page. In two famous laments, worth translating anew here in full, he paints a picture of Florence's wretched degradation, which, given the vengeance of the Black party on the Whites, may not have been an entirely rhetorical state of affairs:

> What delight can a citizen take seeing the wretched case of the Florentine city-state, all full of woe? Now are our public places empty spaces, our habitations desolations. A noble race has been debased, our families defamiliarized. Our solace is but seldom, our joys destroyed, all lost. The dignity of office undone, our podestariates, our captaincies are banished from the state; our officers, beguiled by bribes, have gone astray—I mean our priorates, our embassies, and all the rest.

38. *De bono comuni*, 150.

39. On this theme, see Kempshall, *The Common Good*, 297; and Teresa Rupp, "Damnation, Individual and Community in Remigio dei Girolami's *De bono comuni*," *History of Political Thought* 21.2 (2000): 217–36, at 223–26.

40. *De bono comuni*, 148.

Unfarmed our farms, the olives rooted out, the vineyards shorn, the structures deconstructed, there's no farmland where you can build a home or even roam without quaking and shaking.

The flower is flown; the sweet scent of its fair fame has become a frightful stench of deepest shame. So the prophetic doom in the name her citizens use has proven true. They call her not "Fiorenza," as foreigners do, but "Firenze." When fuming feces or something fetid is carried by, the French hold their noses and repeat with disgust, "Fie, Fie," as if to say "what a stinking stench!" And so, in this town, once flower-crowned, moans and groans resound. Now does each citizen's heart, which held its Florence-the-flourishing so dear, weep in torrents for this Florence of tears.[41]

In Remigio's despondent vision, the fabric of city and countryside has been destroyed, political institutions have broken down, and Florence has been despoiled. In the next chapter, Remigio continues his lament, but focusing now on the almost unimaginable economic and social consequences that civil disorder and discord produce.

What good is a Florentine citizen now? For business ventures have been dissolved, warehouses are, so to speak, are no-ware houses, shops are shuttered, idle and ailing, the guilds have lost their gilding, business deals have gone sour, medical practice has been made mendicant, laws are fettered, courts curtailed, public works work no more, nor do the workers, neighbors are estranged, agreements are gutless, friends are enemies, all trust has been abandoned, hearts are hardened and made cruel, good will is poisoned, compatriots are expatriates, so that now, as a result of the city's destruction, a citizen can be useful neither to himself nor to others, and indeed he can even be destructive. Appropriately,

---

41. *De bono comuni*, 184–86. On Fiorenza/ Firenze, see Panella, *Dal bene comune*, 184 n.26. One can only wonder whether Remigio witnessed this custom first-hand during his university days in Paris in 1267–1272. I again thank John Petruccione for his interventions. His deft hand has helped me to capture Remigio's wit and wordplay, which I cite in the original here: "Qualem enim delectationem poterit habere civis florentinus videns statum civitatis sue tristabilem et summo plenum merore? Nam platee sunt explatiate idest evacuate, domus exdomificate, casata sunt cassata, parentele sunt exparentate, solatia sunt insollita, ludi videntur lusi idest perditi, dignitates videntur indignate idest potestarie et capitanerie que egrediebantur de civitate, officia videntur affacturata idest fascinata, scilicet prioratus, ambascerie et huiusmodi, poderia videntur expoderata quia arbores evulse, vinee precise, palatia destructa, et non est iam podere, idest posse, ut in eis habitetur vel eatur ad ea, nisi cum timore et tremore. Denique flos exfloritus est et odor fame ipsius conversus est in horribilem fetorem infamie, iuxta prophetiam appellationis vulgaris civium: non enim 'Fiorença', ut persone extrane, sed 'Firençe' ipsam appellant. Gallici enim quando fimus vel aliquid aliud fetidum transit dicunt 'fi fi' obturantes nares suas, quasi dicant 'O quantus fetor est iste!' Et sic Florentia mutata est in Flerentiam. Quilibet ergo civis ex naturali amore ad Florentiam naturaliter habet flere."

but not for the better, "Florentia" has changed to "Firenze"; for just as once foreigners from distant parts once deposited their money here for utility and profit because of her good reputation, now, because of the stench of her infamy, even citizens try to withdraw their deposits, and worse yet they cannot reclaim what is theirs.[42]

Once a proud city with an economy built on trade and commerce, the Florence Remigio now sketches is a pitiful city brought to her knees by factional disputes. The chief point of the treatise, however, was not to enumerate the city's woes, but to argue that its welfare should take precedence over that of any individual, and that all must work together, united in concord, toward the common good of peace. By the order of charity, the will of the individual should yield to the common good and its end, civic peace.

In *De bono pacis*, his companion piece written two years later, Remigio returned to this theme, but now his goal was to answer a specific political question, posed at the beginning of the tract: namely, whether a polity, in its quest to establish the common good of peace, had the authority to set aside the claims of injured parties for damages to property and persons. He replied with a qualified affirmative: the common good of peace had to be elevated above all individual needs or claims.[43]

Likely written during the summer of 1304, this treatise, like *De bono comuni*, was composed in the midst of what would become another failed peace mission to Florence.[44] Pope Benedict XI, the short-lived successor to Boniface VIII, sent his envoy Cardinal Niccolò of Prato to the city in the hope that he could negotiate a peace settlement to end the on-going civil strife between the Whites and Blacks.[45] The mission began on a promising note,

42. Ibid., 188. "Qualem enim utilitatem potest modo habere civis florentinus? Sotietates enim sunt dissotiate, fundacha—ut ita dicam—sunt exfundata, apoteche sunt abortate idest otiose et apostemate, artes sunt artheticate, mercationes facte sunt marcide, medicine sunt facte mendice, leges sunt ligate, curie decurtate, opera exoperata, laboreria sunt libera idest defecerunt, vicini sunt exvicinati, concordes sunt excordati, amici sunt inimicati, omnes fides sunt exfidate, corda sunt accorata et facta crudelia, voluntates sunt facte venenate, concivantes sunt exconcivati, ut ex destructione civitatis iam unus civis nec sibi nec alteri civi possit esse utilis sed dampnosus. Et sic bene, immo male, 'Florentia' mutata est in 'Firençe' quia ubi ex odore fame extranei etiam de longinquis partibus suas pecunias propter utilitates temporales et lucra pecuniaria propria deponebant, nunc ex fetore infamie etiam cives inde auferre que posuerunt conantur et—quod miserabilius est—rehabere sua non possunt."

43. *De bono pacis* (MS Florence Bib. Nat. Conv. Soppr. C 4.940, fols. 106v–109r), ed. Panella, *Dal bene comune*, 222–47, at 222–24.

44. The tract was most likely written during Remigio's stay at the Dominican convent in Perugia, while Pope Benedict XI was also resident in the city. Panella, *Dal bene comune*, 25–26.

45. A former master-general of the Order of Preachers and mentor of Remigio, Benedict was as interested in pacifying Florence as were his predecessors.

but like its immediate predecessors ended in fiasco when, after a series of missteps, this cardinal also took flight, but not before launching an interdict against the recalcitrant Florentines. And that was not the worst of it. On the heels of the cardinal's hasty retreat, in a notorious act of vendetta, the Blacks set fire to the grain market at Orsanmichele, and in the process nearly burned the entire city to the ground.[46]

Remigio's *De bono pacis* has been read as a "practical application of his analysis of the common good."[47] The friar warns that the seeds of the city's destruction lie in discord—the result of disordered love. The teaching in this tract was meant to demonstrate above all that peace is the primary good of society, and that the order of charity—expressed in ordered love—promotes concord, the handmaiden of peace. The tract, as noted earlier, also had one further, practical objective, which was to suggest a solution to a vexing diplomatic question: Under what conditions could the White exiles return to the city? And if they did, should their confiscated goods and property be restored, or should they be declared forfeit?

The tract is predictably saturated in Aristotelian thought. Significantly, though, a tenet of canon law grounds Remigio's overarching argument about the subordination of the individual will to the highest good, here, finally, defined as peace. The preacher appeals to the notion of "public utility," or what we would call the legal theory of necessity, to undergird his argument that in extraordinary circumstances statute law or custom can be dispensed with for the sake of the common good, in this case peace. As a citizen of the city, he argues, one's obligation is to bow to the polity's necessity, here defined as peace or what other preachers called "outer peace."

As in any scholastic question, Remigio marshals all the relevant authorities to defend his proposition. In this case he draws on scriptural, patristic, and philosophical texts, as well as legal texts such as the *Decretum*. Augustinian and Aristotelian thought, as filtered through the lens of Aquinas to be sure, are employed to construct an argument about peace more explicit than the one advanced in *De bono comuni*. Adhering closely to Aristotle's *Nicomachean Ethics*, Remigio argues that the good of a people, a society, and the multitude is to be preferred to the good of a single individual. Continuing to cite "the Philosopher," he propounds that "the highest good of the multitude and its end is peace. Thus it follows that just as the entire body must take precedence over one body part, so the good of one individual should be set aside for the sake of the peace of the city."[48]

---

46. According to Compagni, he too was the victim of a half-hearted assassination attempt; see Compagni, *Chronicle of Florence*, 70. For the fire on 10 June 1304 in Orsanmichele and Via Calimala, see ibid. For the quotation, Villani, *Nuova Cronica*, vol. 2: Bk 9, chap. 69: 13; for his version of the fire, ibid., chap. 71: 132–35.

47. Kempshall, *The Common Good*, 316.

48. *De bono pacis*, 224. As Kempshall has observed, "the absence of the Aristotelian life of virtue [in this text] could not be more marked," *The Common Good*, 323.

We have already seen Remigio equate peace with the common good in *De bono comuni*. We have also seen him invoke the metaphor that likens the well-being of society to the health of the body in Sermon VIII. But we must not forget how influential Augustine's vision of peace as an ordered form of charity was to Remigio's thinking. In chapter three, he proceeds to lay out the similarities between the order of charity and the order of the good, indicating how he will eventually braid those strands of thought together into a new synthesis.[49] First, however, he has to return to Aristotle's *Ethics* and *Politics* to demonstrate that living in community is a natural condition for humankind because, as the Philosopher shows, man is a "political animal."[50] In chapter 4, then, Remigio applies the lessons drawn from Augustine to Aristotle. He teaches: "Society is ordered for the peace of society. Namely, each individual, while maintaining his own place, helps someone else who cannot provide for himself, in terms of body, intellect, or living in civic society. 'For the peace of the city is,' as Augustine says in *The City of God* (Book 19:13), 'the ordered harmony of the citizens for commanding and obeying.'"[51] Thus Remigio establishes that the Aristotelian polity, whose common good is peace, is ordered hierarchically through the Augustinian notion of love. In the sixth chapter, he continues to combine Aristotle and Augustine, along with other apposite scholarly citations, notably from (Pseudo-)Dionysius the Areopagite and Psalms, to show that peace is the final cause, the desired and perfect end. It is the perfect end because it is a divine good. "Therefore, for the good of peace, all other goods are to be passed over."[52]

Up to now, the aim of the treatise has been to prove that peace is tantamount to the common good and that good is divine. Now, having established that premise, his chapter seven answers the question posed at the outset—the crux of the matter—whether it is licit for a ruler to waive damages to private property for the sake of the common good. His answer, as we have noted, is a qualified yes. He cites the examples of a ruler's right to demand payment for travel, for the building of a bridge, to raise an army, or as a subvention for a daughter's wedding. If it is licit for him to requisition temporal goods for all those reasons, how much more justified is it, Remigio asks, for the common good of peace? Citing the lord's right to dispense justice by imposing financial penalties for such petty crimes as robbery and assault, how much more licit, Remigio asks, is his right to do so when the common good of peace is at stake?[53]

No doubt with an eye cast on the political question at hand—whether the exiled White Guelfs, whose property and goods had been seized by the Black party, should be able to reclaim the goods (or compensation) when they

49. *De bono pacis*, 230–32.
50. Ibid., 232–34.
51. Ibid.
52. Ibid., 240.
53. Ibid., 244.

returned—Remigio in the end somewhat tempers his conclusion. He argues that exceptions should no doubt be made to this policy if the confiscated goods are in the hands of those who seized them illicitly, or if the injured party is known to be poor. No doubt influenced by Cardinal Latino's peace of 1280, Remigio argues that if provisions cannot be made for these special cases, then damages should be paid from the city's treasury.[54] These few exceptions aside, Remigio has made his point. Individual wills have to align for the sake of establishing civic concord, after which outer peace, the common good of the city, can be achieved.

De bono pacis has been the subject of critique by modern political philosophers, who read it as a text that upholds the values of "extreme corporationalism." It is, they argue, a position that idealizes the commune in a dangerous way. Matthew Kempshall, however, makes an important corrective to this position by arguing that "to appeal to the responsibility of the individual Christian to love 'what is in common' in obedience to the *ordo caritatis* is not the same as being forced by factionalism and selfishness to express a political corporatism which left the individual no 'proper' function of his own beyond his obligation to the political community."[55] In this context we should remember that Remigio was first and foremost a theologian and preacher. He worked in a Christian tradition, attempting to construct a social and political ethic in which concord, the harmony and unanimity of wills in society, was both the necessary precondition and the means to establish outer peace, the definitive goal toward which the community was meant to strive. Though the peace of heaven (*pax patriae*) was the ultimate objective, Remigio reminds his readers that the outer peace of the here and now (*pax viae*) was an intermediary (and legitimate) goal that should not be neglected.[56]

Remigio's ideas supported the views of the popular government that held political power in Florence at the turn of the thirteenth century. That is, the Guelf priors of the guild government—be they either Whites or Blacks—were interested in promoting the common good of peace for three primary reasons: first, to protect themselves from the (real or imagined) predations of the magnates whose rights and political power they had circumscribed in the Ordinances of Justice; second, to create a stable environment of peace and security, where trade and commerce—the economic lifeblood of the city—could flow freely; and third, to safeguard their government from domestic enemies now banished or in exile. Remigio's vision of Florence bereft of the

---

54. Ibid., 246.

55. Kempshall, *The Common Good*, 293. He furthermore argues, that "Remigio's repeated use of the qualification *in quantum est pars*, his insistence on drawing a distinction between the individual qua individual and the individual qua part of a community, provides an important check on the characterization of his political thought as 'corporatist,'" ibid., 310.

56. *De bono pacis*, 240.

commodity and financial markets that had made it an economic powerhouse was calculated to strike terror into the heart of every citizen whose livelihood was tied to those lucrative activities. And, as he knew full well, that included most citizens of the city, as they were all in some way or another—directly or indirectly as Florentines—people of the "lamb." Both *De bono comuni* and *De bono pacis* demonstrate how scholastic thinking could be drafted into service for the benefit of the commune.[57] Both tracts provided the intellectual underpinnings for a civic ethic whose slogan could have been *pax et concordia.* Pax, however, was to be understood on at least two levels. On the spiritual level, Remigio equated peace with the eternity of heaven that would come after the Last Judgment, when the souls of the saved would reside in the peace and beatitude of God. It was nothing less than the fulfillment of the prophecy of Isaiah: "My people will sit in the beauty of peace" (Isaiah 26:3). On earth, however, peace had a different significance. In the here and now, Remigio envisioned outer peace as the delicate flower of the common good that could flourish only if nourished and cultivated in harmony and concord. Indeed, the entire health of the commonwealth—its peace, tranquility, and security— depended on the cultivation of concord and harmony among its citizens.

Remigio pictured *concordia,* on the other hand, as a union of hearts or wills striving toward the common good of civic peace. Extolling its benefits in a sermon given to the priors of the city, he lamented the discord that now infected the health of his city:

> By diabolical instigation or by divine judgment, it seems that there is very great discord in this city, a condition over which we ought to grieve deeply, because with discord "the good" cannot exist in the city; it comes with concord, which is nothing other than the union of hearts or wills striving for the highest good of the city.[58]

The conversion to charity through penance, as we have noted in chapter 1, was certainly one way to foster human concord; but another appropriate path to reach the *pax viae* was through the pursuit of justice, a path we have seen Brunetto Latini suggest. It was also the path that Remigio endorsed, as this

57. Kempshall, *The Common Good,* 292.

58. The sermons have been published in Giulio Salvadori and Vincenzo Federici, *I sermoni d'occasione, le sequenze e i ritmi di Remigio Girolami fiorentino* (Rome: Forzani, 1901), 481–84. In the 1290s Remigio also wrote an unfinished tract on justice, *De Iustitia.* It has been edited by Ovidio Capitani, "L'incompiuto 'Tractatus de iustitia' di fra' Remigio de' Girolami," *Bullettino dell'Istituto storico italiano per il Medio Evo* 72 (1960): 125–28. Unfortunately for us, the treatise on justice fades to black just as Remigio was about to take up the question of civil justice. For recent commentary on the tract and its relation to the sermons, see Teresa Rupp, "'Love justice, you who judge the Earth': Remigio dei Girolami's sermons to the Florentine Priors, 1295," in *Preaching and Political Society from Late Antiquity to the End of the Middle Ages* (Turnhout: Brepols, 2013): 251–63.

sermon further demonstrates. Preaching on a passage from the Book of Job (25:2), Remigio made the relationship between justice and concord his theme:

> Indeed without justice no city can be ruled well or remain in concord, just as a house built on an inferior foundation cannot stand for long without falling into ruin, for a curved line compromises all the quarters of the city. "Justice will strengthen the throne," however, as Proverbs 25 says, and thus all injustice ought to be removed from city statutes.[59]

For Remigio civic concord was the outcome of justice. Only through justice could concord, or the harmony of wills, obtain in the city. This, I think, explains his somewhat enigmatic reference to "a curved line" compromising the city, by which I understand Remigio to mean that the linear geometry of a city's quarters could not withstand the introduction of a curved line that would violate the symmetry of the urban plan, or its proportional harmony. Only the straight line, created by the proper administration of justice, could bring about civic harmony.

It has been suggested that this sermon was delivered in the summer of 1295, when discussions of revisions to the Ordinances of Justice were underway, and that the final line may be interpreted as Remigio's critique of the statutes as they were first drafted.[60] Remigio would hardly have been alone in thinking they were unjust; most of the magnates would no doubt have agreed.

But the first sentence of this passage is also of great interest. Here Remigio is making an argument similar to Brunetto's by suggesting that concord was the result of justice properly dispensed. Justice serves as the city's foundation, helping to maintain order in each of its municipal wards. Without justice, discord would reign. Or, to put it in contemporary terms: no justice, no peace.

As Remigio knew all too well, concord and harmony were scarce commodities in the marketplace of faction-riven Florence. Only a few years after penning this sermon, around the time the friar was writing *De bono pacis*, partisan violence dealt what was almost a mortal blow to his own family. His cousin Cardinale was attacked on the street and cut down in cold blood by one of the powerful Tornaquinci clan. He was left for dead in the Mercato Vecchio, but eventually recovered. Dino Compagni recorded this episode of bloodshed in his chronicle, remarking that it led to yet another episode of violence between the popolo and the magnates.[61] What he did not record, however, was that in the fullness of time, Cardinale settled this dispute. He did so by means of a peace agreement, an instrument of the Florentine judicial system

---

59. Rupp, "Love justice," 262. I include here a translation of the telling phrase about the curved line that Rupp omits.

60. Ibid., 260.

61. *Chronicle*, 65–66. Cardinale di Alberto dei Girolami, along with his brother Leoncino, were inscribed in the Arte del Cambio and were members of the Black Guelf party. For a discussion of this branch of the Girolami family tree, see Panella, *Del bene*, 71–73.

designed to achieve civic concord and peace. We find the evidence in a register
of the notary Matteo di Biliotto, who drafted the peace contract between the
Girolami and the Tornaquinci clan and associates in 1306.[62] It was sealed with
an *oris osculum* (a kiss on the mouth), a gesture meant to restore equilibrium
between the parties, which in turn would foster concord and peace. The peace
agreement was thus the civic junction where Justice and Peace were imagined
to kiss.

As we have seen throughout the last two chapters, the popular governments of central and northern Italy had both judicial and political remedies
at their disposal to establish peace. They included statutory reform, exile,
banishment, the confiscation of property, corporal punishment, and fines. But
these were blunt instruments. Significantly, notarial peace agreements, ratified with a ritual kiss, may have been better suited to produce external peace,
since, as bilateral agreements they frequently put the power to make peace
into the hands of the adversarial parties themselves. Moreover, the format,
method, and associated ritual of such agreements sounded some of the very
same notes as the penitential culture from which they emerged. In the next
two chapters we will see how Florentines employed these instruments to settle
almost every kind of violent dispute under the Tuscan sun, and in the process
achieved a version of Remigo's *pax viae.*

62. ASF, Not. Ant. 13364, fols. 88v–89r, and Panella's discussion of it, *Del bene*, 68–70.

CHAPTER THREE

Pax est Pactum

Justice and peace have kissed.

—PSALM 84:11

WHEN THE EMINENT jurist Bartolus of Sassoferrato (d. 1357) posed the rhetorical question "What is peace?" for a *consilium* he had been commissioned to draft, his initial response was the standard one: that peace was an end to discord.[1] But to give his definition legal utility, he clarified that peace should also be considered "a pact by which an end of discord or war is instituted through an agreement."[2] The peace treaty that brings an end to the hostilities of warfare is a well-known example of this genre. What is less well known is the *instrumentum pacis*—the peace agreement—which, when drawn up by a notary, was a flexible legal document that enabled adversaries to resolve their disputes and make peace. *Instrumenta pacis*, the pacts by which crimes and disputes were settled in medieval Florence, are the subject of this chapter, which argues that the social concord that they produced was the result of an alliance between two potent forces—religious and civic—which shared similar ideas about society. We see here the imprint of penitential ideas preached in the peace movements as they interacted with the legal culture of

1. This chapter draws on material from my articles, *"Pro bono pacis:* Crime and Dispute Resolution in Late Medieval Florence. The Evidence of Notarial Peace Contracts," *Speculum* 88.2 (April 2013): 427–56 and "Florentine Peacemaking: the Oltrarno, 1287–1297," in *Pope, Church and City: Essays in Honor of Brenda Bolton,* ed. Frances Andrews, Christoph Eggar, and Constance M. Rousseau (Leiden: Brill, 2004), 327–44. I am grateful to the Medieval Academy of America and Brill for permission to publish the material presented here in a revised and expanded form. Caveat lector: because I have added more notarial evidence since these articles were published, the numbers and statistical data have changed. My thinking about many of the issues considered here has also evolved.

2. Bartoli a Saxoferrato, *Consilia, quaestiones et tractatus* (Turin: [Compagnia della Stampa], 1589), Bk I: LXVI, 20: "Pax est pactum quo fit finis discordiae seu guerrae introductae per pactum." My thanks to Ken Pennington for first bringing the formulation of Bartolus to my attention.

the communes, particularly as manifested in the form of the notarial peace instrument. At this intersection we find the kiss of justice and peace.

The legal concept that equates peace to a pact has a long history in the scholarship on medieval Italian cities. Max Weber argued that the foundation stone of the communes, born in the late eleventh century, was the *conjuratio*, an "oath-bound association" or pact that promised mutual aid against the incursions of emperors, bishops, their vicars, or of any power that presumed to infringe on communal liberties. Though we tend to remember that the sworn oath entailed obligations of protection, it is often forgotten that protection included the safeguarding of judicial institutions, one such being the "peaceable settlement of disputes."[3] As Bartolus has already witnessed, the idea of peace as a pact is hardly a modern concept. Nor is the idea that a peace pact was the foundational moment in a city's history. It informed the thinking of a Bergamasque author of an encomium on his native city when, associating the two ideas, he wrote that it was a rare thing for people of his city to flee into their "towers in the air" or to be involved in violent conflict with each other, "for indeed golden peace ties citizens together in a secure knot: the pauper remains in peace as does the rich man bound in a pact of peace."[4]

Peace enshrined as a pact continued to play a crucial role in the Italian cities well into the fifteenth century, not least in Florence. In the previous

3. Max Weber, *The City*, trans. and ed. Don Martindale and Gertrud Neuwirth (Glencoe, Ill.: Free Press, 1958 [1921]), 110. He adds: "Not to be forgotten was the further aim of monopolizing the economic opportunities of the city." See also Paolo Prodi, *Il sacramento del potere: il giuramento politico nella storia costituzionale dell'Occidente* (Bologna: Il Mulino, 1992) and Diego Quaglioni, "*Civitas*: Appunti per una riflessione sull'idea di città nel pensiero politico dei giuristi medievali," in *Le ideologie della città europea dall'umanesimo al romanticismo*, ed. Vittorio Conti (Florence: Leo S. Olschki, 1993), 59–76. Founded in 980, the commune of Milan—one of the oldest in Italy—was established in this way. For a recent application of Weberian theory to the Italian communes, see Stephen J. Milner, "Rhetorics of Transcendence: Conflict and Intercession in Communal Italy, 1300–1500," in *Charisma and Religious Authority: Jewish, Christian and Muslim Preaching, 1200–1500*, ed. Katherine L. Jansen and Miri Rubin (Turnhout: Brepols, 2010), 235–51. Otto Gerhard Oexle, "Peace through Conspiracy," in *Ordering Medieval Society: Perspectives on Intellectual and Practical Modes of Shaping Social Relations*, ed. Bernhard Jussen, trans. Pamela E. Selwyn (Philadelphia: University of Pennsylvania Press, 2000), 285–322. Significantly, Charles Petit-Dutaillis observed that in the charters of the early French communes, the words *communia* and *pax* were used interchangeably to signify a sworn association. See *Les communes françaises. Caractères et evolution des origines au XVIIIe siècle* (Paris: Albin Michel, 1947), 91–92. This is not the view of Chris Wickham, *Sleepwalking into a New World: The Emergence of Italian City Communes in the Twelfth Century* (Princeton: Princeton University Press, 2015) who argues (as his title suggests) that the communal governments of central and northern Italy, governed by consular elites, were rather less aware of what they were engaged in than previous scholarship has suggested.

4. "Il *Liber Pergaminus* di Mosè de Brolo," ed. Guglielmo Gorni, *Studi Medievali*, 3rd series, XI.I (1970): 409–60, at 452.

chapter we saw how political divisions (which often manifested themselves as violent tumults) escalated to the point that mediators like Cardinal Latino were summoned to negotiate peace settlements, the terms of which were imposed by treaty. Hammered out by "neutral" parties, such accords between Guelfs and Ghibellines, or the White and Black parties, were diplomatic solutions to the civil wars that all too frequently plagued the city. But of course not all disputes and violence were the result of partisan strife involving the important families or grandees of Florence. Personal quarrels and enmities between members of the popolo needed resolution as well. Thus this chapter moves to the other end of the social spectrum to look at quotidian disputes and the ordinary people who were embroiled in them. Here we get a glimpse of how everyday folk went about settling their conflicts, a process, as it turns out, that bore hardly any resemble to chroniclers' descriptions of peacemaking ceremonies. Of the latter, Dino Compagni's account of Cardinal Niccolò of Prato's efforts is typical:

> On April 26, 1304, the popolo gathered in Piazza Santa Maria Novella in the presence of the signori and, having made many peace agreements, they kissed one another on the mouth as the sign of peace. They drew up peace contracts and set penalties for whoever contravened them. With olive branches in hand, the Gherardini made peace with the Amieri. Everyone was so pleased with this peacemaking that when a heavy rain fell that day, no one left, and they did not even seem to feel the downpour. Great bonfires were lit; the church bells sounded; everyone rejoiced. . . . The companies of the popolo went around making a great celebration in the name of the cardinal, bearing the banners, which they had received from him in Piazza Santa Croce.[5]

In Compagni's account the cardinal-peacemaker and the great families whom he reconciled, take center-stage as the protagonists of this particular drama, while the popolo are sidelined as mere witnesses and supernumeraries. This chapter shows that what Compagni and his fellow chroniclers have passed down to us are not portraits of everyday peacemaking as it existed on the streets of Florence, but present instead the exceptional spectacle, the tabloid headlines of the day, which have tended to obscure our view of what was typical practice. As we shall see, ordinary peacemaking rarely if ever involved an officiating go-between such as a priest, let alone a cardinal. And in place of the great lineages, it was most often members of the popolo, ranging from the most humble tradesmen to members of the rich *popolo grasso*, who were the protagonists in the majority of dispute resolutions.

The popolo used written peace instruments to restore social equilibrium after a crime or an act of violence had disturbed the tranquility of a given community.

5. *Dino Compagni's Chronicle of Florence*, ed. Daniel E. Bornstein (Philadelphia: University of Pennsylvania Press, 1986), 66–67.

They were an expedient and, like other documents of social practice—wills, betrothal contracts, loans, land conveyances, and the like—they are found in abundance in the notarial registers of Italian cities of the later Middle Ages. Thus, although the process of settling disputes rarely caught the chronicler's eye, it is clear that such resolutions occurred frequently, if not on a daily basis, in and around the city. And because a peace agreement was the culmination of a public process embedded in the legal system (though not necessarily the court room), we have available in the notarial casebooks snapshots of moments in time when disputes were settled and neighborhood harmony restored.

In this chapter, we will see that both men and women (and not just men representing political factions) appeared before Florentine notaries to resolve conflicts that had somehow degenerated into violence and enmity between neighbors. These were for the most part ordinary people, not unlike those who participated in the peace movements, who sometimes under legal pressure, undertook to restore concord between one another and tranquility to their neighborhoods. In Villani's terms, they were *piccola gente*. The peace instrument was drafted by a local notary and witnessed by two neighbors. The process encouraged face-to-face reconciliation, while providing the added benefit of allowing the parties to do away with financial penalties or suspend trials, avoiding all the attendant costs and risks. Peacemaking, then, was a local event for restoring harmony both to the disputing parties and the community. In Remigio dei Girolami's terms it allowed for the rebuilding of concord and a path forward on the *pax viae*, that intermediary peace on the way to Jerusalem.

Disputes and their settlements are but two sides to the same coin; therefore, to understand peacemaking agreements, we must first investigate the conflict—often a crime—that preceded the peace.[6] Following the lead of recent Italian scholarship, this chapter looks at dispute resolution as an integral part of the judicial system, or as modern terminology would have it, as part of the infra-judicial structure as it emerged in central Italy in the communal period.[7] But it follows the anthropological literature as well, by envisioning peacemaking as a dynamic process rather than a static act, one that ought not to be analyzed apart from the dispute itself.[8] Doing so allows us to

6. See the literature cited in the introduction, nn.40–43.

7. For two examples of this recent scholarship, see Andrea Zorzi, "Conflits et pratiques infrajudiciaires dans le formations politiques italiennes du XIIe au XVe siècle," in *L'infrajudiciaire du Moyen Age à l'epoque contemporaine: Actes du Colloque de Dijon 5–6 Octobre 1995* (Dijon: Publications de l'Université de Bourgogne, 1996), 19–36; and Massimo Vallerani, *Medieval Public Justice*, trans. Sarah Rubin Blanshei (Washington, D.C.: Catholic University Press, 2012), originally published as *La giustizia pubblica medievale* (Bologna: Il Mulino, 2005).

8. Max Gluckman, "The Peace in the Feud," *Past and Present* 8.1 (1955): 1–14. See also, among others, Sally Falk Moore, *Law as Process: An Anthropological Approach* (London: Routledge, 1978); Simon Roberts, *Order and Dispute: An Introduction to Legal Anthropology* (New York: Penguin, 1979); *Disputes and Settlements: Law and Human*

shed light on how this flexible legal document functioned in the settling of everything from tavern brawls to homicide, and it affords us a window, admittedly a rather grimy one, onto the grittier side of urban life in the later Middle Ages. [9] Through a study of peace instruments, this chapter presents then an

Relations in the West, ed. John Bossy (Cambridge: Cambridge University Press, 1983); and Anton Blok, Honour and Violence (Malden, MA: Blackwell, 2001).

9. For peacemaking, in addition to the literature mentioned in the introduction, there is an ever-increasing body of scholarship on late medieval Italy, beginning with Collectio chartarum pacis privatae medii aevii ad regionem Tusciae pertinentium, ed. Gino Masi (Milan: Vita e Pensiero, 1943); Antonio Padoa Schioppa, "Delitto e pace privata nel pensiero dei legisti bolognesi. Brevi note," Studia Gratiana 20 (1976): 271–87; Schioppa, "Delitto e pace privata nel diritto lombardo" in Diritto comune e diritti locali nella storia dell'Europa (Milan: Giuffrè, 1980), 555–78; Thomas Kuehn, "Dispute Processing in the Renaissance," in Law, Family, and Women: Towards a Legal Anthropology of Renaissance Italy (Chicago: University of Chicago Press, 1991), 75–100; Shona Kelly Wray, "Reconciliation after Violence: Peace Contracts in the Libri Memoriali of Fourteenth-Century Bologna" (conference paper delivered at Fordham University Conference on "Violence in the Middle Ages," 16 April 1994, which the author kindly shared with me); Massimo Vallerani, "Liti private e soluzioni legali: note sul libro di Th. Kuehn e sui sistemi di composizione di conflitti nella società tardomedievale," Quaderni Storici n.s. 89 (1995): 546–57; Ulrich Meier, "Pax et tranquillitas: Friedensidee, Friedenswahrung und Staatsbildung im spätmittelalterlichen Florenz," in Träger und Instrumentarien des Friedens im hohen und späten Mittelalter, ed. Johannes Fried (Sigmaringen: Jan Thorbecke, 1996), 489–523; Vallerani, "Pace e processo nel sistema giudiziario del comune di Perugia," Quaderni Storici n.s. 101 (1999): 315–53; Mario Sensi, "Per una inchiesta sulle 'paci private' alla fine del medio evo," in Studi sull'Umbria medievale e umanistica in ricordo di Olga Marinelli, Pier Lorenzo Meloni, Ugolino Nicolini, ed. Mauro Donnini and Enrico Menestò (Perugia: Centro italiano di studi sull'alto Medioevo, 2000), 526–58; Otto Gerhard Oexle, "Peace through Conspiracy," in Ordering Medieval Society, 285–322; Marco Bellabarba, "Pace pubblica e pace private," in Criminalità e giustizia in Germania e in Italia: Pratiche giudiziarie e linguaggi giuridici tra tardomedioevo ed età moderna, ed. Marco Bellabarba, Gerd Schwerhoff, and A. Zorzi (Bologna: Il Mulino, 2001), 189–213; Trevor Dean, "Violence, Vendetta and Peacemaking in Late Medieval Bologna," in Crime, Gender, and Sexuality in Criminal Prosecutions, ed. Louis A. Knafla (Westport, CT: Greenwood Press, 2002), 1–18; Chris Wickham, Courts and Conflict in Twelfth-Century Tuscany (Oxford: Oxford University Press, 2003); Katherine L. Jansen, "Peacemaking in the Oltrarno, 1287–1297," in Pope, Church, and Society; Glenn Kumhera, Making Peace in Medieval Siena: Instruments of Peace, 1280–1400 (Ph.D. dissertation, University of Chicago, 2005); Shona Kelly Wray, "Instruments of Concord: Making Peace and Settling Disputes through a Notary in the City and Contado of Late Medieval Bologna," Journal of Social History (Spring, 2009): 733–60; Emanuela Porta Casucci, "Le paci fra privati nelle parrocchie fiorentine di S. Felice in Piazza e S. Frediano: un regesto per gli anni 1335–1365," Annali di Storia di Firenze IV (2009): 195–241; Casucci, "La pacificazione dei conflitti a Firenze a metà Trecento nella pratica del notariato," in Conflitti, paci e vendetta nell'Italia comunale, ed. A. Zorzi (Florence: Reti medievali-Firenze University Press, 2009), 193–218. http://fermi.univr.it/rm/e-book/titoli/zorzi .htm 7–42 [consulted 6/21/17]; Alberto M. Onori, "Pace privata e regolamentazione della vendetta in Valdinievole," in ibid., 219–35; Kumhera, "Promoting Peace in Medieval Siena: Peacemaking Legislation and Its Effects," in War and Peace: Critical Issues in European Societies and Literature, 800–1800, ed. Albrecht Classen and Nadia Margolis (Berlin: de

overview—in the form of rough typologies—of crime and conflict resolution in late medieval Florence and its environs. It suggests that while in the religious context preachers maintained that penance produced an inner peace that promoted concord and the restoration of the order of charity; in the civic context, magistrates likewise held that enacting a peace agreement would foster concord and the restoration of social order. Both the order of charity and social order were tantamount to outer peace.

FLORENTINE MUNICIPAL INSTITUTIONS

Administrative Structure

In order to deepen our understanding of how peace agreements fit into the legal and administrative systems of late medieval Florence, I present here a short overview of the city's relevant municipal institutions.

From the thirteenth century until 1343, when the city was reorganized on the quarter system, the commune was divided into sixths (*sesti* or *sestieri*).[10] The sesti primarily took their names from the principal gates (*porta* sometimes shortened to *por*) in the late twelfth-century circuit walls.[11] In terms of sheer square kilometers covered, the largest sesto was the Oltrarno, the entire section of the city south of the River Arno. North of the river, on the eastern side of the city, were San Piero Scheraggio, the administrative center of the commune, and San Pier Maggiore, both about equal in size. The western side of the city, moving from south to north, was comprised of Borgo (less familiarly known as Santa Trinità), San Pancrazio, and Porta del Duomo, this last being the religious heart of the city where the cathedral and baptistery were located. (fig. 9).

The sesti unevenly incorporated the fifty-seven parishes or *popoli* of the city.[12] San Pier Maggiore boasted fourteen popoli; Oltrarno eleven; San Piero Scheraggio ten; Porta del Duomo and San Pancrazio each counted nine, while Borgo, the smallest sesto, claimed only four parishes.[13] At the center of every

Gruyter, 2011), 334–48 and James Palmer, "Piety and Social Distinction," *Speculum* 89.4 (2014): 974–1004. For a slightly later period, see *Stringere la pace: Teorie e pratiche della conciliazione nell'Europa moderna (secoli XV–XVIII)*, ed. Paolo Broggio and Maria Pia Paoli (Rome: Viella, 2011).

10. David Herlihy and Christiane Klapisch-Zuber, *Tuscans and Their Families: A Study of the Florentine Catasto of 1427* (New Haven: Yale University Press, 1985), 37–38.

11. For the dating of this set of walls to 1172–1175, not 1078 as the chroniclers suggest, see Franek Sznura, *L'Espansione urbana di Firenze nel Dugento* (Florence: La Nuova Italia, 1975), 44.

12. Herlihy and Klapisch-Zuber, *Tuscans*, 38. They give the figure of 57 for 1340, a number that remained stable for a century.

13. Robert Davidsohn, *Storia di Firenze*, trans. Giovanni Battista Klein, 8 vols. (Florence: Sansoni, 1962), 5: 278–79.

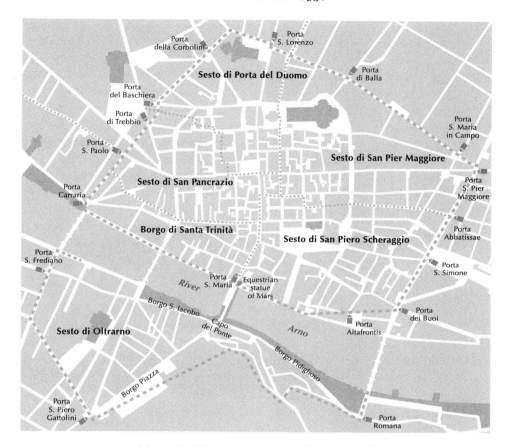

FIGURE 9. Map of the *sesti* of Florence prior to 1343. Map designed by Gaia Beltrame.

popolo stood the parish church, whose rhythms marked out the tempo of daily life. With the great exception of baptism, celebrated in the baptistery of San Giovanni, whose very image was synonymous with Florentine civic identity, the parish church was the center of local religious life, the place where parishioners observed religious feast-days and participated in the sacramental life of the Church. If the baptistery represented civic identity, the parish church provided neighborhood community of the most basic kind.[14] It also imparted one's legal identity when joined together with a patronymic. Notaries described their clients first as sons of father X, then as members of parish or popolo Y. Women, however, were identified as wives or daughters; thus one of the parties to a peace made in 1330 was one "Domina Francescha uxor Lippi Chelis populi Sancti Fridiani" (Signora Francesca, wife of Lippo Cheli of the parish of San Frediano).[15]

14. For a good synthesis of communal religion, see Augustine Thompson, *Cities of God: The Religion of the Italian Communes, 1125–1325* (University Park, PA: Pennsylvania State University Press, 2005).

15. Aldobrandino di Albizzo, ASF, Not. Ant. 251, fols. 95r-95v.

Each popolo took its name from its parish church, which also served as a locus for administrative functions. The *cappellano*, or rector, as he was known in the contado, oversaw public order in the parish. Despite the name, he was a secular official, who by statute law was elected by the council of the commune every six months.[16] Depending on its size, a parish could have anywhere from one to four cappellani. Among the prerequisites for holding office were homeownership, and having reached twenty years of age. One could not hold the same office elsewhere. Members of the twelve *Arti Maggiori* (the major guilds) were excluded from the ranks of the cappellani, confirming that this rather low-status office, was not one to which the upper echelons of society aspired.[17] A 1327 list of cappellani reveals more precisely the social origins of the officeholders; among them predominated bakers, unskilled workers in the wool industry, grocers, and fishmongers.[18]

The cappellano served his popolo in various capacities. During his tenure he was entrusted to inform his parish of new ordinances issued by the commune, either at Mass or some other fitting time. He also had oversight of neighborhood sanitation. In addition to seeing to it that roads were swept and kept clear of impediments such as rocks and building materials, he also had to ensure that wastewater was not disposed of in the streets. Most importantly for our purposes, he was entrusted to report to the podestà's judges disturbances of the peace or crimes committed within three days. If he failed to do so, he could face a fine up to 100 *fiorini piccoli* (f.p.)[19] An examination of peace agreements that contain information about how news of a crime initially reached the court, shows that the cappellani and rectors were responsible for reporting the majority of cases.[20] Piero Pucci, a rector of the contado, reported with great dispatch an altercation between Vanni and Tanino that took place in his parish, a case that will allow us to see sooner rather than later just what type of information peace agreements yield.

In the sultry days of August 1338, a violent scuffle erupted in the parish of San Marco al Mugnone between two paupers, called as such in the documents.[21] Perhaps Vanni of Pistoia, whose right foot had been amputated, and Tanino of Pescia, who suffered from some sort of paralysis, had been

16. "Rector" was the ancient name for this official, which in the commune was gradually replaced by the term *cappellano*, see Davidson, *Storia*, 5: 279. The parishes in the contado, however, retained the term rector.

17. *Statuti della Repubblica Fiorentina*, 2 vols., ed. Romolo Caggese; new edition editors: Giuliano Pinto, Francesco Salvestrini, Andrea Zorzi (Florence: Leo S. Olschki, 1999); hereafter *Statuti*, vol. 2: Podestà, Bk 1: XV–XVI, 47–48.

18. Davidson, *Storia*, 5: 279–81.

19. *Statuti*, vol. 2: Podestà, Bk 1: XV–XVI, 48.

20. Of 179 cases (drawn from the city and its contado) that record this information, 57 percent were reported by the cappellani; 22 percent were denounced by others; 13 percent were through accusation; and only 8 percent proceeded through judicial inquisition. For a comparison with the origins of court cases in Bologna in the year 1326, see Sarah Rubin Blanshei, *Politics and Justice in Late Medieval Bologna* (Leiden: Brill, 2010).

21. Andrea di Lapo, ASF, Not. Ant. 439, fols. 40v–41r. San Marco al Mugnone is located in Florence's northeastern territory near Fiesole, outside the Porta San Lorenzo.

competing for alms on the same street corner.[22] Tempers flared, insults were exchanged, and Tanino struck Vanni over the head with his walking stick. Vanni retaliated by shoving Tanino to the ground. Blood was shed. The news of this fracas reached Piero Pucci, the rector of San Marco, who then reported the incident to the criminal judge of the podestà at Por San Pier Maggiore. A few days later the two paupers appeared as parties to a peace instrument drawn up by the notary, Andrea di Lapo. A sanction clause threatened each of them with a fine of 100 f.p. should the agreement be broken. Among other things, this case shows clearly that peace agreements were not just the purview of the grandees of Florence. Everyone used them. They were part of a judicial system whose reach touched all, regardless of status or class—everyone from magnates to paupers. The case also demonstrates the limitations of these documents. As we shall see in depth below, they are formulaic texts that ordinarily present only the bare facts of the case. What they rarely include is evidence about what incited the dispute in the first place, or information on the deeper context that might shed light on the parties' relationship with each other.

PEACE INSTRUMENTS IN THE COURTS OF THE *SESTI* AND STATUTE LAW

San Marco al Mugnone, the site of Vanni and Tanino's altercation, was technically a parish in the Florentine contado, closer to Fiesole than to Florence but incorporated into the commune's juridical sphere in 1334, during the period of the city's territorial expansion.[23] Therefore it was subject to Florentine law and

22. An amputated foot was a judicial sentence mandated by statute law. It was, for example, the punishment for the crime of exporting grain from the contado to nearby territories; see Davidsohn, *Storia* 5: 612. It was also the punishment for assassins should their victims survive the attack with facial scarring or a permanent disability. If the fine of 2000 lire was not paid, it was decreed that the assailant's hand or foot be amputated as punishment. *Statuti*, vol. 2: Podestà, Bk 3: LXXXI, 193. It should also be noted that it is possible that these two paupers may not have been destitute beggars. Rather, they may have been deemed to have been paupers by the court after having made a plea of poverty that required that they have no more than 25 lire in goods and live solely by their labor. See n.25 below. Ordinarily, the statutory fine for breaking a peace agreement was severe: 500 lire. *Statuti*, vol. 2: Podestà, Bk 3: XXII, 176–77.

23. John Najemy gives a succinct version of Florentine expansion. By 1300 Florence's contado "extended roughly twenty-five miles north (to Barberino and Borgo San Lorenzo in the Mugello valley and beyond to Scarperia), a similar distance northeast (to Dicomano), fifteen miles east (beyond Pontessieve to the northern end of the Casentino), thirty miles southwest (to Castelfiorentino, Certaldo, and Poggibonsi in the Valdelsa), twenty miles down the lower Arno valley (to Empoli), but only some ten miles west by northwest (just beyond Signa and Campi). In the 1320s Florence pushed farther in this direction and took control of the Monte Albano, but not until 1350 was nearby Prato incorporated into the dominion. Later, when larger cities like Arezzo and Pisa came under Florentine rule, they were referred to as the district." *A History of Florence, 1200–1575* (Malden, Mass: Blackwell, 2006), 97.

its ever-expanding influence. Andrea di Lapo's peace instrument informs us that Piero Pucci reported the incident to a judge of one of the criminal courts whose jurisdiction comprised both Porta del Duomo and San Pier Maggiore.[24] The judge who heard the rector's complaint (*denuncia*) most likely advised Piero to have Vanni and Tanino make a peace agreement, a written dispute settlement, which was the form of resolution that in the majority of cases best served both the court and its clientele. The judge would not have to take up the court's precious time adjudicating a simple assault case, and Vanni and Tanino, who clearly could not have afforded it anyway, would be spared the fine of 200 f.p. required by statute law for bloody assault with a weapon, in this case Vanni's stick.[25]

Heavy fines, tariffed according to different degrees of assault, were incorporated into the statutes of the *podestà* (1325) and the *capitano del popolo* (1322–1325), our earliest extant body of Florentine law.[26] A simple fist fight carried a fine of 25 f.p.; if blood was spilled the fine was doubled; likewise if weapons prohibited by law were involved. If those arms (including rocks) produced bloody injuries, the fine shot up to 200 f.p. If the rock-throwing resulted in a feud, the fine escalated to a hefty 500 f.p. But woe to the aggressor who caused facial scarring or the disabling of a body part: those crimes were punished with a whopping fine of 1000 f.p. Such fines were meant to be punitive and they were, considering that in the 1340s the average daily wage for a mason, a skilled laborer, equaled 6.4 soldi.[27] If that mason had been charged with armed assault in which blood was shed, and for the sake of argument let us say that the case proceeded through the courts and he was ultimately

24. By 1290 there were three criminal courts with jurisdictions as follows: Oltrarno and Porta San Pancrazio; Borgo and San Piero Scheraggio; and Porta del Duomo and San Pier Maggiore. Flanked by their notaries, the judges sat at *banchi* located in the cortile of the Palazzo del Podestà (now the Bargello). Davidsohn, *Storia*, 5: 581–82. The matriculation list of 1338 reveals that there were sixty-three judges inscribed in the *Arte dei Giudici e Notai* (Guild of Judges and Notaries) in that year, twenty-four of them were inscribed in Porta del Duomo/San Pier Maggiore. Franek Sznura, "Per la storia del notariato fiorentino: i più antichi elenchi superstiti dei giudici e dei notai fiorentini (anni 1291 e 1338)" in *Tra libri e carte. Studi in onore di Luciana Mosiici*, ed. T. de Robertis and G. Savino (Florence: F. Cesati, 1998), 437–515.

25. *Statuti*, vol. 2: Podestà, Bk 3: XLV, 188–93. It is possible that these two made a "poverty plea" in court. Sarah Rubin Blanshei has tracked such pleas in Bologna in the mid-fourteenth century in "La procedura penale in età comunale e signorile," in *I costi della giustizia a Bologna in età moderna*, ed. Armando Antonelli (forthcoming). When successful they had their penalties reduced by one half. I thank the author for allowing me to read and cite her research prior to publication.

26. Ibid. Earlier statutes, such as those of 1285 and the Ordinances of Justice of 1295 were incorporated in Book II. By the end of the thirteenth century there was also an ample body of legal commentary on the statutes like that by the jurist Alberto Gandino, who had served as one of the foreign judges in the court of the podestà in Florence. See Davidson, *Storia*, 5: 130–31.

27. Charles-M. de la Roncière, *Prix et salaires à Florence au XIVe siècle (1280–1380)* (Rome: École française de Rome, 1982), 280.

sentenced, he would have been liable to pay almost three days' wages in fines alone. All this is to say nothing of court fees that could also mount up quickly. If we can import the court fees from Bologna of the same period, the court case itself would have cost 10 soldi in court fees, 2 soldi for every witness produced, and a few more for the preparation of a libellus, the official complaint. Already the fees would have more than tripled for the plaintiff, and this does not even include the 20 soldi one would have to pay if the accusation went unproven.[28] For the period running from 1295 to 1368, also in Bologna, Sarah Blanshei has uncovered fees for advocates (8 lire) and procurators (6 lire). It was even worse for the accused, as he would have been liable also for the financial penalty set by statute law for his particular crime. Moreover, if our mason had been accused and unlucky enough to be incarcerated while the trial was taking place, he would have incurred the cost of paying the prison guards (10 soldi), along with entrance/exit and lighting fees (3 s. 4 d.). Taverners would also have to be paid for victuals during the trial (23 lire) if the prisoner had no family to provide for him.[29] Clearly, fees associated with a court case could mount up quickly.

Alternatively, statute law provided that if a peace instrument was drawn up by a notary within fifteen days of the incident, all charges and fines would be dropped, even if one of the parties had previously been convicted in court for the same crime.[30] Given the costs of the court and prison systems, along with the fines and the risks one took in bringing cases to court, the low cost of a peace agreement would surely have seemed to offer the better option to those caught up in the legal system. Effectively, one could pay for a notarized peace agreement, settle the dispute, and exit the judicial system almost as quickly as one had entered it.

In addition to being spared the fines, Vanni and Tanino also saved on the court costs, which as paupers clearly neither one of them could afford to pay. Instead, in the company of two witnesses, they appeared before the notary, Andrea di Lapo, and agreed to make peace.[31] A simple contract such as this might cost no more than 5 soldi (60 f.p.), a price set by the *Arte dei Giudici e Notai* (Guild of Judges and Notaries). It was less than one day's wages for our mason, a bargain compared with the statutory fine for this type of assault, which would been almost three times more expensive. For consumers, notarial

28. Vallerani, *Medieval Public Justice*, 124–35, 162.

29. Blanshei, "La procedura penale." I quote from the English text that she shared with me.

30. *Statuti*, vol. 2: Podestà, Bk 3, XXII: 176–77. Peace agreements appear at least thirty times under various titles in the statutes. Not surprisingly we also find mentions of peace instruments in the rubrics that deal with punishing those who break the peace, private truces and putting an end to vendetta.

31. Even if the poverty plea was accepted in court, it remains unclear who assumed the costs of the notarial fee.

peace agreements were cost-effective, and this was just one of their numerous advantages, as we shall see.[32] They must have been regarded as a godsend for the court system too. If we can extrapolate from the Bolognese figures (always a risky business), in the 1290s in a city of about 60,000 the courts heard anywhere from 2,000 to 3,000 cases per year; in Florence, a city two times as large, the Florentine criminal courts were hearing perhaps double that number of cases.[33] The peace instrument allowed these busy courts to unburden themselves of simple dispute cases by handing them over to public notaries. In addition, as we will see in chapter 4, peace instruments helped alleviate the problems of contumacy and self-banishment that heavy fines and court costs would have aggravated.

All this is to say that it would be a grave mistake to regard notarial peace instruments as purely private remedies: they were incorporated into the public court system and must be considered an integral part of it. The courts benefitted as much from this solution as did the "consumers of justice." As legal historians spearheaded by Massimo Vallerani, Mario Sbriccoli, and Thomas Kuehn have been recently demonstrating, there was no bright red line dividing private and public systems; nor can we sustain any longer an evolutionary model which posits a progression from "private grievances to public prosecution of crimes."[34] The very existence and continued use of peace agreements in the age of the communal courts upends this model.[35] Indeed, peace instruments are now understood to be "infra-judicial" forms of dispute settlement instead of private resolutions. That is, ordinarily they intersected with legal processes already underway and were freighted with the authority of statute law and the judiciary.[36] Mario Sbriccoli even regards the pax as a form of procedure in itself, a third way alongside accusation and inquisition.[37] These revisionist scholars firmly reject an older master narrative of legal history that traced a straight line of development from accusatorial to inquisitional procedure. At the same time, they underscore the importance of the peace instrument in the

32. Due to the flooding of the Arno in 1557, which destroyed much of the archive of the Arte dei Giudici e Notai on Via del Proconsolo, we have no earlier statutes than 1344 for a guild that had certainly existed since at least the first quarter of the thirteenth century. The tariffed prices for documents are to be found in Santi Calleri, *L'Arte dei giudici e notai di Firenze nell'età comunale e nel suo statuto del 1344* (Milan: Giuffrè, 1966), 59–60.

33. Vallerani, *Medieval Public Justice*, 127.

34. Thomas Kuehn, quoting Vallerani, "Social and Legal Capital in Vendetta: A Fifteenth-Century Florentine Feud in and out of Court," in *Sociability and its Discontents: Civil Society, Social Capital, and Their Alternatives in Late Medieval and Early Modern Europe*, ed. Nicholas A. Eckstein and Nicholas Terpstra (Turnhout: Brepols, 2009), 51–72, and then Kuehn himself at 69.

35. Kuehn, "Social and Legal Capital," 62.

36. Vallerani, *Medieval Public Justice*, 6 and ibid.

37. Mario Sbriccoli, "'Vidi communiter observari': L'emersione di un ordine penale pubblico nelle città italiane del secolo XIII," *Quaderni fiorentini per la storia del pensiero giuridico moderno* 27 (1998): 231–68, at 236–37.

judicial system, a system, we must remember, that was sustained by the work of notaries.

NOTARIAL PRACTICE AND PEACE INSTRUMENTS

A medieval notary was much more than a mere scribe or copyist. His writing was known as *scriptura publica*, a practice one scholar has called "a legal fiction crafted by the jurists of medieval Europe."[38] In an act of sleuthing worthy of Sherlock Holmes, Ronald Witt tracked down an eleventh-century notary whom he suggests is the author of that legal fiction. He argues that a notary called Domenico, working in Bologna around 1060 or so, transformed charters into a new form of legal instrument by changing the way in which documents were subscribed. That is, Domenico omitted the *manufirmatio*, the witness signature, and replaced it with the new formula *hec instrumenta firmavi* (I have confirmed these documents) or *hiis instrumentis robur accomodavi* (I have given force to these documents) in place of *complevi et absolvi* (I have completed and released). Thus the authority of the document no longer depended on the signatures of the witnesses; now, instead, it was the notary's attestation that validated the contents of the agreement. By the next decade, "Bolognese notaries also appear to have been the first to separate clearly the juridical act itself from the document that proved it had been accomplished."[39] By the twelfth-century, Rogerius, a glossator commenting on a section of the *Digest* entitled *De fide instrumentorum et de amissione eorum*, observed that *scriptura publica* could take two forms: it could consist of *acta*, court records taken down in the presence of a judge; or, alternatively, it could be embodied in *instrumenta*, legal instruments enacted by a notary. Both counted as public writing invested with *publica fides*.[40] In Laurie Nussdorfer's apt formulation, notaries had become "brokers of public trust." They traded on it by earning private income from public writing.[41]

Inscribed by a trusted public hand, notarial documents were further invested with public trust because they were required to contain crucial data, in notarial jargon called *publicationes*.[42] That is, in addition to the substance of the contract arranged by the parties, the instrument had to list pieces of

38. Laurie Nussdorfer, *Brokers of Public Trust: Notaries in Early Modern Rome* (Baltimore: Johns Hopkins University Press, 2009), 9. This and much of what follows on the public character of the notary's output is indebted to her discussion, 11–12.

39. Ronald G. Witt, *The Two Latin Cultures and the Foundation of Renaissance Humanism in Medieval Italy* (Cambridge: Cambridge University Press, 2012), 173–74 and 236.

40. *Summa codicis* in *Biblioteca Iuridica Medii Aevi: Scripta Anecdota Glossatorum*, 3 vols., ed. Giovanni Battista Palmerio (Bologna: Societas Azzoguidianae, 1888), I: Bk 4: XXII: 7–174, at 66.

41. Nussdorfer, *Brokers of Public Trust*.

42. Ibid., 12.

information, which Rolandino dei Passaggieri, author of a popular *Summa* on the notarial arts (ca. 1255), numbered at six: in addition to the notary's name, the *publicationes* had to include the year, indiction, day, place, and names of witness, minimally two.

Unlike the work of their brother judges, who often adjudicated cases involving parties at least one of whom had been unwillingly brought before them, the clientele of the notariate was mostly voluntary, though sometimes coerced, directly or indirectly. Ordinarily the notary was neither negotiator nor advocate; instead he took down the salient facts of the transaction and formulated them into a binding legal agreement. But first he had to be asked to do so. Asking (*rogare*) the notary to draw up a contract gave rise to many variants in notarial usage: a notary was the *rogatorio*, while the requested instrument was "rogated," in notarial parlance. After having accepted his commission, the notary worked in stages to draw up the contracts. In the first stage, presumably in the presence of the contracting parties, the notary took notes (*notulae*) on the case. In the second stage, he produced a more formal redacted version of those notes, complete with *publicationes* and abbreviated formulas (*clausulae consuetae* or *ceteratae*). This document was called an *imbreviatura* (sometimes *abbreviatura*), and it was entered into the notary's register, called a protocol. The *imbreviatura* was all that was necessary for legal purposes, although parties could request and pay a separate fee for their own personal copies. If a client did so, the practice of Florentine notaries was to draw some sort of diagonal line through the original *imbreviatura* to signal that an individual parchment copy had been made. The method of archiving public instruments in notarial protocols further ensured public faith, as the temporal sequence of the registers made it difficult to change dates or indeed to add information on pages already so overgrown with *imbreviaturae* that often crept like untended vines into the margins of the folio pages.[43]

Although known in Florentine statute law and notarial protocols as *instrumenta pacis* (and only occasionally by the older terminology of *chartae pacis*), it was not uncommon for notaries to signal this genre of contract as a *pax* in the margins of their registers. Though the origins of this type of agreement remain unclear, some scholars suggest that it descends from the *compositiones* used to settle feud and vendetta in Germanic law. Others argue more specifically that *instrumenta pacis* bear a resemblance to the early medieval agreements used to settle disputes in Lombard law known as *convenientiae*.[44]

43. Ibid., 18–19.
44. Padoa Schioppa, "Delitto e pace privata nel pensiero dei legisti bolognese," 271–72; and Patrick Geary, "Extra-Judicial Means of Conflict Resolution," in *La giustizia nell'alto medioevo (secc. v–viii), Settimane di studio* 42 (Spoleto: Centro italiano di studi sull'alto medioevo, 1995), 569–605, at 575.

Whatever its origins, the pax was a bilateral agreement that brought settlement to a dispute between two quarreling parties. In theory, neither judge nor arbitrator intervened in this mutually binding agreement.[45] Nonetheless, having been drawn up and attested by a notary, a public authority of the commune, it carried the force of law. The peace contract contained four essential items: the names of the disputants; the formulaic promises exchanged to uphold the peace; the stipulated sanctions, financial and otherwise, should the peace be broken; and the formula documenting that the kiss of peace had been exchanged by the parties. As we have seen, in Italy public faith in the notary was such that by the twelfth century witness signatures had lost all import and were no longer necessary to authenticate a document. The presence of at least two witnesses—always named—was still required, but it was the signature and emblem of the notary in his register or *protocollum* that gave the document its public authority.

Those are the bare bones of the contract, which could be further elaborated with the addition of salient details according to local custom and notarial habit. As we shall see, Florentine notaries, though by no means prolix, inclined toward including some detail in a contract, especially if it shed light on how statute law had been broken or if the case had previously appeared in the dockets of the podestà's courts. All this suggests that a peace agreement was a rather pro forma document. And for the most part this was true because it depended on recognized legal formulae. Those formulae had been codified since at least the first quarter of the thirteenth century and characterized the *instrumentum pacis* that both Rolandino dei Passaggieri and Salatiele, Rolandino's competitor, included in their handbooks of formularies for the notarial arts.[46]

45. Arbitrators usually intervened in civil cases—mostly land disputes—from which a document called a *laudum* was produced. If a land dispute ended in violence, a peace act would also be warranted. For arbitration and *lauda*, see Thomas Kuehn, "Arbitration and Law in Renaissance Florence," *Renaissance and Reformation* n.s. 11 (1987): 289–319, repr. in his *Law, Family, and Women: Towards a Legal Anthropology of Renaissance Italy* (Chicago: University of Chicago Press, 1991), 19–74.

46. Rolandino dei Passaggieri, *Summa totius artis notariae* (Venice: Apud Iunctas, 1546), chap. VI: 158–59: *de compromissis: instrumentum pacis et concordiae* and Salatiele, *Ars notarie*, ed. Gianfranco Orlandelli, 2 vols. (Milan: Giuffrè, 1961), 2: *Instrumentum pacis et concordiae et treguae*, 305. See also, Ranieri da Perugia, *Ars Notaria* [sic] (1214), ed. Augusto Gaudenzi, in *Biblioteca Iuridica Medii Aevi: Scripta Anecdota Glossatorum*, 3 vols. (Bologna: In aedibus Petri Virano, 1892), 2: 37–73, Part I, chap. 121 at 55 *de pace*; and Ranieri da Perugia, *Ars notariae* in *Quellen zur Geschichte des römisch-kanonischen Prozesses*, 6 vols., ed. Ludwig Wahrmund (Aalen: Scientia Verlag, 1962), 3: 2, 54–55: rubr. LI *carta pacis concordie sive treugue; Il Formularium Florentinum artis notarie: 1220–42*, ed. Gino Masi (Milan: Vita e Pensiero, 1943–44), XX: *de tregua facta inter hodiales et inimicos; Summa notarie Aretii composita (1240–43)*, ed. Carlo Cicognario in *Biblioteca Iuridica Medii Aevi: Scripta Anecdota Glossatorum*, 3 vols. (Bologna: In aedibus successorum Monti, 1901), 3: 286–332, at 311–312 *carta pacis* and *instrumentum pacis*; and Bencivenne, *Ars notarie*, ed. Giovanni Bronzino (Bologna: Zanichelli, 1965), 68.

THE FLORENTINE NOTARIATE

In the age of the city republic, notaries were public officials enrolled in the *Arte dei Giudici e Notai,* one of the most prestigious of Florence's twelve major guilds. As we have seen, they drew up legal instruments: documents of social practice, such as wills, quittances, marriage contracts, dowry agreements, business and mortgage contracts, arbitrations, etc., which they then invested with public authority.[47]

The notary's agreements were written on parchment and preserved in thick notarial registers, comprised of multiple quires, inscribed with hundreds of acts, and preserved in a protective binding. They served as the foundation of Florentine public memory, and it was accordingly of the utmost importance that these casebooks be properly conserved. If a notary's practice had not been bequeathed to either another guild or family member, statutory regulations required that upon his death his registers be sealed and consigned to the guild consuls for preservation.[48]

The Florentine notariate probably emerged as a corporate body as early as the late twelfth century; records of a *consiglio generale* (general council) meeting in 1234 mark the first evidence of the guild, which in Lauro Martines's felicitous phrase was a "professional organization, a confraternity, and also an arm of the state."[49] Because of the untold damage that the floods of 1333 and 1557 wreaked on the guild archives located in Via del Proconsolo, the first documentation from the guild itself is rather late: a matriculation list of 1291. Franek Snzura's meticulous work on this water-damaged document has revealed that in that year 646 men were enrolled in the guild: 65 judges and 581 notaries.[50]

The first extant statutes—those of 1344—articulate the prerequisites for membership and distinguish between the office of judge and notary. In what follows the discussion pertains mostly to notaries, though some of the requirements applied also to judges. The notary had to have reached age twenty (or eighteen if he came from a notarial family), and be of Florentine birth. Further, the candidate's father had to have been a resident of Florence or the contado for at least twenty-five years.[51] Towncriers, undertakers, prison guards, actors,

---

47. In 1298, in the invocation that opens his register, the notary Biagio di Boccadibue records that his book contains imbreviaturae of contracts for "mutui, cessionum, finium, locationum, pacis, compromissorum, laudorum, depositorum, commandatorum, securitatum et sponsalitiarum, ac alias diversas imbreviatoras . . . ," *Biagio di Boccadibue (1298–1314),* ed. Laura De Angelis, Elisabetta Gigli, and Franek Sznura, 4 vols. (Pisa: Giardini, 1978–1986), 1:1.

48. Davidsohn, *Storia,* 6: 247.

49. Calleri, *L'arte dei giudici e notai,* 18 and Lauro Martines, *Lawyers and Statecraft in Renaissance Florence* (Princeton: Princeton University Press, 1968), 27.

50. Sznura, "Per la storia del notariato fiorentino, 6.

51. Martines, *Lawyers and Statecraft,* 26–40, at 28.

clowns, and elementary or music teachers were forbidden guild membership, as were bastards, heretics, vassals, clerics, and even physicians.[52] The prospective notary also had to have at least two years of training in the *ars notariae* at a university or the equivalent training as an apprentice in a notarial studio. Having presented all these qualifications, the candidate confronted a rigorous examination process. His handwriting and knowledge of Latin were tested, as was his moral character. If he passed this qualifying exam he went on to a public examination in front of a board consisting of at least one judge and four notaries. It was not unheard of for the guild's proconsul and consuls to participate in the oral portion of the exam. Here the candidate was questioned about various types of notarial formulae and then asked to render them into Latin. A two-thirds majority vote from the examining commission was required to pass the exam. After having satisfied all these requirements, a matriculation fee of 8 gold florins (close to a month's labor for our hypothetical mason) was required for enrollment in the guild. The privileges of guild membership entitled the notary to be addressed as Ser and to choose a visual emblem (*signum*), which like a coat of arms represented his public authority, invested originally by the imperial crown.[53]

A number of career paths were open to the notary. In public administration he could hold elected office, serving as a notary to a major guild. He could also serve the judiciary by appointment. Lastly he could work independently by developing a clientele in the city or countryside, or even abroad as did Brunetto Latini, who was exiled in France during Ghibelline rule and after his return to Florence in 1275 served as a consul of the *Arte dei Giudici e Notai* before becoming one of the city's priors, and eventually its chancellor.[54]

We have already seen that by the late thirteenth century, the guild had enrolled close to six hundred members. This is the figure that Villani reports and one that is quoted widely in the scholarly literature. Sznura, however, has shown that although that figure is more or less accurate for the 1291 matriculation list, the 1338 list is far more comprehensive. In that year 869 notaries were inscribed in the Guild of Judges and Notaries, an increase of 50 percent or 269 members.[55]

Our notary, who recorded the peace made between Vanni and Tanino, Andrea di Lapo (or andreas olim lapi de Florentia, as he appears in the membership roster of 1338), was one of 157 notaries inscribed in the Por San Pier

52. Ibid. Davidsohn, *Storia*, 6: 246 suggests that the ban on clerics must have been rather late, as he finds evidence for friar-notaries up until the early fourteenth century.

53. For a discussion of the link between Tuscan notaries, the imperial crown, and the counts palatine, a link that can be traced back to Henry VI's concessions confirmed by Frederick II; see Harry Bresslau, *Manuale di diplomatica per la Germania e l'Italia*, trans. Anna Maria Voci-Roth (Rome: Ministero per i beni culturali e ambientali, Ufficio centrale per i beni archivistici, 1998), 575–76.

54. Born in Porta di Duomo, Brunetto also matriculated there. Davidsohn, *Storia* 6: 237.

55. Sznura, "Per la storia del notariato fiorentino," 9.

Maggiore sesto of Florence. Por San Pier Maggiore ranked third in the number of notaries, after the Oltarno, which claimed 212 notaries and San Piero Scheraggio, which counted 205.[56]

THE EVIDENCE, APPROACH AND TIMEFRAME

Comprised of thousands of notarial protocols, the *Notarile Antecosimiano* of the Archivio di Stato of Florence is celebrated as one of the richest notarial archives in Europe. Perhaps less well known is the fact that the thousands of registers which make up its holdings represent only a mere fraction of what once existed in the thirteenth and fourteenth centuries. Snzura's comparison of the names inscribed in the thirteenth- and fourteenth-century matriculation lists to those indexed in the archive's own inventories reveals a stunning loss of material: the present holdings of the archive represent the work of only 8 to 9 percent of those named in the guild lists of the period.[57] Of course, just as Dante was inscribed in the *Arte dei Medici e Speziali* but never practiced medicine or the pharmaceutical arts, it is likely that many so-called notaries inscribed in the guild never actually practiced their profession either. And some may have practiced only on a part-time basis. Even taking those probabilities into account, Snzura's figures remain striking.

Whatever the loss, the amount of evidence that remains is abundant, indeed far too abundant for any researcher to master in one lifetime. I have read my way through all the notarial registers that are extant for the second half of the thirteenth century, and from them identified 110 peace acts. Doing so for the fourteenth century, however, when the documentary evidence grows exponentially, would not be humanly possible. [58] Given this documentary surfeit, I have perforce sampled the fourteenth-century registers, ensuring that I have included notarial evidence from all decades of the period under review

56. Ibid. The distribution for the other sesti was as follows: Porta del Duomo 119; San Pancrazio 97; Borgo 79. These figures of course exclude the thirty foreign notaries in the podestà's retinue distributed throughout the criminal and civil courts and in administrative offices under podestarial control. See Davidson, *Storia* 5: 148. With regard to the notaries' proportion of the population, on the basis of extant matriculation lists, Bartoli Langeli estimates for center-north Italian cities of the thirteenth and fourteenth centuries, the notariate averaged between 1.5 and 2 percent of the population, while at Treviso they figured at 5 percent. See Attilio Bartoli Langeli, *Notai: Scrivere documenti nell'Italia medievale* (Rome: Viella, 2006), 10.

57. Sznura, "Per la storia del notariato fiorentino," 11.

58. There are about forty notarial registers ("circa una quarantina") extant from the thirteenth century. See Luciana Mosiici, "Note sul più antico protocollo notarile del territorio fiorentino e su altri registri di imbreviature del secolo XIII," in *Il Notariato nella civiltà toscana. Atti di un convegno (maggio 1981)* (Rome: Consiglio nazionale del notariato, 1985), 174–238, at 178. My rough handlist, based on the ASF's indices, calculates that there are 629 names of fourteenth-century notaries whose imbreviaturae survive, some of whom have as many twelve casebooks indexed.

and all the sesti and their jurisdictional territories. All in all I have consulted the work of ninety notaries from whose registers I have gathered 526 peace agreements, which cover the period from 1257 to 1343, just under a century's worth of material.[59]

This study begins when the notarial records begin. The first notarial *imbreviatura* is dated 8 December 1237; our first extant peace agreement was drawn up two decades later in 1257.[60] The study concludes in 1343 not because peace instruments ceased to exist in that year. Far from it. But because the commune underwent administrative, judicial, and social changes that make it difficult to integrate evidence from the pre- and post-plague period. In August 1343, as we have already seen, the commune's sesto system was scrapped and replaced with the quarter system, with the result that the city's administrative and judicial boundaries were remapped. This new system may have streamlined Florentine justice and administration, but it causes problems for the historian who now has to generalize or draw conclusions from two systems that cannot be superimposed on each other without difficulty.[61]

One other consideration has compelled me to conclude my study of these documents in 1343. My interest in peacemaking is from the standpoint of a historian of social practice; consequently I have chosen to investigate this form of dispute settlement largely, but not exclusively, as it existed outside the "courtroom," while fully acknowledging that peace agreements were an essential part of the judicial system. My primary interest lies not in procedure, or in the cases that concluded in a formal court decision favoring one party over another, but in those cases that show peacemaking in practice and are probably typical of work-a-day conflict resolution as recorded in the notaries' studios and elsewhere around the city. Of course sometimes an appearance in court was inevitable to prod settlement forward. It should be noted, for example, that peace contracts were designed to settle disputes by avoiding

59. I have surveyed the protocols of ninety notaries, from which I have gathered 526 contracts. In addition to the (494) unpublished notarial contracts found in the Notarile Antecosimiano in the Archivio di Stato, my figure includes (8) Tuscan contracts from the fondo *diplomatico* published in *Collectio chartarum pacis*, ed. Gino Masi; (11) from the published protocols in *Biagio di Boccadibue (1298–1314)*; and (13) from Casucci, "Le paci fra privati nelle parrocchie fiorentine di S. Felice in Piazza e S. Frediano," 195–241.

60. The oldest notarial protocol housed in the archive—the register of Palmerio di Corbizio da Uglione—dates from 1237–1238. For the edition, see *Palmerio di Corbizo da Uglione, fl. 1213–1238. Imbreviature, 1237–1238* (Florence: Leo S. Olschki, 1982). Palmerio's register is the only exemplar that dates from the first half of the thirteenth century. It contains no peace contracts. Although it is striking that we have no exant peace acts for the decades between 1237 and 1257, it must be remembered that there are no surviving notarial records for this period either.

61. This was the approach taken by Samuel K. Cohn in *The Laboring Classes of Renaissance Florence* (New York: Academic Press, 1980). It should be noted, however, that most of his evidence was post-1343.

litigation altogether or putting an end to legal suits that had already begun, which were, as we have seen, both costly and risky. Though peace agreements may not have been designed with the cancellation of bans in mind, they were used for that purpose, a theme we will examine further in chapter 4. Since Florence's judicial records begin only in 1343, my study of peace in the communal age will make possible a basis for comparison should future scholars wish to further investigate this subject in the courts of the post-plague period.

CONFLICT, CRIMES, AND MISDEMEANORS

As noted earlier, peace contracts were flexible, they could cover a multitude of sins. And it is to those crimes that we now turn. We will take them up in order of the frequency with which they occurred: crimes of assault, theft, abduction, sex crimes, and domestic abuse. Though we find women involved in all of these categories, they are most frequently present as the victims in crimes of assault; consequently I discuss them at length in that section. All of these crimes and misdemeanors caused discord in the community. It was therefore one of the primary tasks of peace contracts to restore harmony and social order between disputing parties.

ASSAULT

Minor assault was the crime that most regularly disturbed the peace of the city and the one for which the majority of peace instruments were executed. Peace instruments thus became an essential means for restoring equilibrium and concord among neighbors. A good 57 percent of extant peace settlements were drawn up to reconcile parties who had been engaged in some sort of violent altercation. Of those, 76 percent are dispute resolutions for unarmed assault, typically a fistfight involving just two individuals.[62] Some of those quarrels may have taken place in public houses, or so noted Remigio dei Girolami, as we saw in a sermon examined in chapter 2. Good citizens should abstain from gaming and drinking in taverns, he warned, as it stirs people up against each other. But we do not need to take Remigio's word for it, as the tavern of Forte Piero in San Martino a Petroio is revealed as the site of brawl that took place in 1318. It was there that Duccino Zucca insulted, assaulted, and obstructed three *berrovarii* (policemen) from exercising their duties as officers of the law. It took him eighteen years, but Duccino finally settled his quarrel with the descendants of one of the three

---

62. Out of the total sample of peace agreements, 57 percent represent cases dealing with assault. Of those, 76 percent are cases of simple assault, here stipulated as a violent crime committed against another person with *manibus vacuibus*.

FIGURE 10. *A Tavern Brawl.* Fresco by Niccolò Miretto and Stefano da Ferrara,
ca. 1420. Palazzo della Ragione, Padua.
Photo reproduced by permission of Scala/Art Resource, New York.

officers when he came before the notary Bartolo Amici in 1336.[63] Though
not a common subject for medieval artists, an image of a violent tavern fight
from the Palazzo della Ragione in Padua gives us some idea of how these
scuffles were imagined[64] (fig. 10).

Many of these violent conflicts, like that of Duccino and the berrovarii,
were the result of arguments, insults, or threats caused by "assault speech."
Indeed, 13 percent of peace instruments mention some sort of assault
speech.[65] *Habuerunt verba simul* was the notary's stock phrase for an argument. While "injurious words" and "insults" were frequently cited as provoca-
tions or catalysts to violence, the offending words themselves were very rarely
recorded. Blasphemy is a rarity in these documents, but cursing with *malis
verbis* was not uncommon.[66]

63. Bartolo Amici, ASF, Not. Ant. 364, fol. 38r.

64. This scene, from a fresco cycle for the Palazzo della Ragione in Padua, was
commissioned ca. 1420 to replace one by Giotto lost in fire earlier that year. Enrico
Bellazzecca, "Miretto, Niccolò," DBI 75 (2011), 9–10.

65. The figure rises to 24 percent if we examine only the assault cases. Thus almost a
quarter of the peace contracts made for assault record some sort of assault speech.

66. There are rare mentions of assault by *verbo hostioso*. See, for example, Buonsignore
di Ser Rimberto da Rostolena, ASF, Not. Ant. 3792, fol. 31v. On the same folio, but in a
different case, he also mentions blasphemy.

An uncharacteristically vivid description of a dispute is recounted in the register of Ildebrandino d'Accatto in a pax made in 1275. We enter the scene in 1274, when Giuntino Jacobi of Quarrata (in the contado bordering Pistoia) arrived at the church of Santo Stefano, already fueled into a state of rage (*irato animo*). When he tried to enter the church, Donato (the priest) slammed the door in his face. Donato then raised a hue and cry by striking the alarm bell (*incepit pulsare campanam ad martellum*) and crying out for help. Meanwhile Giuntino, in a gesture portending Khrushchev's more famous act, took off his shoe and pounded on the church door until a group of local men arrived, subdued him, and carted him away. Donato lost no time in denouncing the shoe-thumping Giuntino to the court of the podestà. When Giuntino did not show up to defend himself, he was fined 200 f.p. and banned for contumacy.[67] Six months later, the two adversaries exchanged the kiss of fraternity, putting aside in the name of peace and tranquility any residual disagreements or animosity that they might have nurtured toward each other.[68]

It is not difficult to imagine Giuntino cursing and shouting out insults as he banged on the church door with his shoe. Because the exact nature of the insult was not legally necessary to give force to the peace contract, notaries rarely spelled it out. But if the judicial records of the Umbrian city of Todi can be our guide: "bastard" followed closely by "thief" and "liar" probably topped the list of slurs that frequently led to bared fists.[69] The capacity of verbal insults to unleash physical violence between parties is well documented.

We can also assume that threats played a role in escalating violence, though they too normally went unrecorded by the notary, unless bloodshed followed as in one such case recorded in the winter of 1294. It began when Guerruçço Danesi shoved Andrea, son of Maffeo Gennay, then threatened to cut off his

67. The process of banishment and its relation to peace contracts is discussed in chapter 4.

68. Ildebrandino d'Accatto, ASF, Not. Ant. 11252, fol. 37v. Quarrata (ancient Tizzano)—both names are used in the document—is in the contado of Pistoia bordering on that of Florence.

69. Daniel Lesnick, "Insults and Threats in Medieval Todi," *Journal of Medieval History* 17 (1991): 71–89, at 76. In Lesnick's study of Todi in the years between 1275 and 1280, four categories of insult are predominant in criminal condemnations: 1) those which impugn legitimacy and/or sexual fidelity, i.e., "bastard," "whore," "adulteress"; 2) "thief"; 3) "ass"; and 4) "shit." For a colorful list from fourteenth-century Savona, see Trevor Dean, *Crime and Justice in Late Medieval Italy* (Cambridge: Cambridge University Press, 2007), 113–32. For a comparative context see, R. H. Helmholz, *Select Cases on Defamation to 1600* (London: Seldon Society, 1985); Peter Burke, "Insult and Blasphemy in Early Modern Italy," in *The Historical Anthropology of Early Modern Italy: Essays on Perception and Communication* (Cambridge: Cambridge University Press, 1987), 95–109; Michael Toch, "Schimpfwörter im Dorf des Spätmittelalters," *Mitteilungen des Instituts für Österreichische Geschichtsforschung* 101 (1993): 310–27; and Daniel Lord Smail, "Hatred as a Social Institution in Late-Medieval Society," *Speculum* 76.1 (2001): 90–126.

nose or kill him should he pursue a legal case against him.[70] In another peace contract issued a year later, which reconciled Geri Cambi, a laborer, to Guccio of Arrigi, who had attacked him with a hatchet, Geri reported the graphic detail that Guccio had sworn to kill him and rip out his guts.[71] Similarly, in 1290, Giovannino Benvenuti was denounced for entering the home of Tura Raneri and, with a knife in hand, threatening to slit open Tura's veins.[72] Yet another settlement, this one from Acone in the contado's northeastern section, recorded that a group of assailants who attacked a farmhouse did so while crying out *moriantur!*—a threat that must have made the inhabitants' blood run cold. [73] Mostly, however, notaries supply rather stilted transcriptions such as the one recording a peace contract made between Matteo Tendi and Nero Pacini, both of Fiesole, and enacted in Florence on May 4, 1308. The notary, Giovanni di Buonaventura duly notes that Matteo and Nero exchanged *verba iniuriosa*, one saying to the other, "I am going to hit you."[74] This sounds, to say the least, a rather lifeless exchange that scarcely begins to capture the tenor of the argument, the threats, or the violent altercation that no doubt took place. It is a salutary reminder that notarial language describes an event; it is not itself an event.

Like these cases, the majority of assault settlements (72 percent) involved only two individuals. It is possible that many of these cases were the culmination of an escalating argument, or what scholars have now come to see as part of a "ritual of confrontation." That is, rather than seeing physical altercations as random episodes in which hot-headedness prevails and violence is the first response, historians have recently begun to look at violence as a culmination, the end of a ritual script in which each participant first enacted his part in various stages which could include disagreement, argument, insult, threat and then, finally, a resort to violence.[75] Giuntino and Donato's encounter at the church door seems to fit this mold as there appears to have been a history of bad blood between them, one unrecorded by the notary. This would account for Giuntino's initial state of rage and Donato's rapid response to it. An old

---

70. Peace was made months later, at the end of April 1295. Giovanni Cartepecchi, ASF, Not. Ant. 4111, fol. 155r: "Guerruçcus debuit spingere dictam Andream et sibi dicere quod amputaret sibi nasum vel quod occideret unde fuit facta quaedam inquisitio contra dictam Guerruçcum."

71. Ricevuto d'Andrea, ASF, Not. Ant. 17869, fol. 7r: "veniendo versus ipsum Guccium cum quadam açcetta in manu volendo eum percutere iurando eum interficere et ei extrahere coratam de corpore."

72. *Collectio chartarum pacis*, ed. Masi, 229: "ivit ad domum dicti Ture Ranerii populi Sancti Fridiani, et intravit ipsam domum enudo contra ipsum Turam, irato animo et malo modo, cum uno cultelo inlatus, minando eidem quod segaret ei venuas."

73. Bartolo Amici, ASF, Not. Ant. 363, fol. 18v. Likewise a contract in *Biagio di Boccadibue*, 3: 33–35.

74. Giovanni di Buonaventura, ASF, Not. Ant. 9483, fol. 20v: "Ego percutiam te."

75. Dean, *Crime and Justice*, 168.

grudge may also explain the following linked cases, recorded by the notary Matteo di Biliotto in January 1296. In the first, Neri, son of Nuzzo of the parish of Santa Maria Novella, and Benozio, a peddler from the shop of Pinuccio dei Tosinghi, were denounced for having entered the house of Pelliciano of San Piero Gattolino and assaulting him. In addition to sustaining blows to his chest and face, Pelliciano also suffered from a bloody bite to his thumb.[76] Interestingly, in the second case, recorded by the same notary on the same day and before the same witnesses, Neri (the assailant in the first case) was the victim of violence and was making peace with Borgese, a skinner, who with a couple of henchmen had seized Neri and thrown him down to the ground so forcefully that his head was smashed. They then grabbed him by the hair and dragged him through the street, all the while continuing to kick and punch him in the face and head.[77] One can only wonder if this was some sort of payback for the violence that Neri had visited on Pelliciano, but not having the deep context for the case, that intuition must remain in the realm of speculation. As Matteo di Biliotto records no further agreements between the two parties, it is perhaps safe to assume that the peace between them endured.

WOMEN

Engaging in violent conflict, it should be noted, was not a gender-specific crime; although men overwhelmingly outnumber women in this and all crimes for which peace contracts were made.[78] I have chosen to discuss some of the evidence of women in peace contracts here because—like men—they most often made peace contracts for incidents of assault. Women appear in 15 percent of the total peace contracts that I have examined, and of those 72 percent were made to resolve disputes that ended in assault. Of those assault cases, 37 percent show women as victims, 9 percent show them as perpetrators of violence, and 54 percent of the contracts are written so as not to assign fault

---

76. Matteo di Biliotto, ASF, Not. Ant. 13363, fol. 84v.

77. Andrea di Lapo, ASF, Not. Ant. 439, fol. 79r.

78. On women and crime in communal Italy, see Giovanna Casagrande and Michaela Pazzaglia, "'Bona mulier in domo': Donne nel giudizario nel Duecento," *Annali della Facoltà di Lettere e Filosofia. 2. Studi Storico-antropologici* 36 n.s. 12 (1998–99): 129–66. For comparison, see Barbara Hanawalt, "The Female Felon in Fourteenth-Century England," *Viator* 5 (1974): 253–68, repr. in *Women in Medieval Society*, ed. Susan Mosher Stuard (Philadelphia: University of Pennsylvania Press, 1976), 125–40; Lesnick, "Insults and Threats," 71–83; Samuel K. Cohn, "Women in the Streets, Women in the Courts, in Early Renaissance Florence," in *Women in the Streets: Essays on Sex and Power in Renaissance Italy* (Baltimore: Johns Hopkins University Press, 2008), 16–38; Ross Balzaretti, "'These Are Things That Men Do, Not Women': The Social Regulation of Female Violence in Langobard Italy," in *Violence and Society in the Early Medieval West*, ed. Guy Halsall (Woodbridge: Boydell, 1998), 175–92; and Garthine Walker, *Crime, Gender and Social Order in Early Modern England* (Cambridge: Cambridge University Press, 2003).

to either party. In those agreements where the victim can be distinguished from the aggressor, women are four times more likely to be victims of assault than the perpetrator of that crime. The case of Domina Bella, widow of Bernardo, is illustrative.

In the autumn of 1339, Buonocorso Lapi threw figs in Bella's face, little "settembrini" figs that he had grabbed from a fruit vendor, who happened to be in her company. The incident escalated when she demanded to know just what had provoked such an untoward outburst against her. Had she known what was in store for her, perhaps she would have held her tongue, as the worst was yet to come. Buonocorso responded by grabbing her hair, throwing her violently to the ground, and then finished off the job by punching her in the head, stomach, and chest, with the result that she was left battered, bloodied, and much the worse for wear. Notwithstanding her injuries, Bella lost no time in taking her complaint to the judge at San Pier Maggiore, and within a month the two parties had settled their dispute with a peace instrument.[79] It should be noted, however, that Bella, having no legal status in Florentine law, was represented by a *mundualdus*, a legal guardian.

As we have seen, in "no-fault" assault contracts, the most common type of peace agreement in which females participated, 54 percent show women as parties to peace. The case of Domina Lixa, wife of Lapo, and Giovanna of Prato is representative. On 3 November 1338, Lixa and Giovanna settled their dispute, which had ended in fisticuffs in the parish of San Lorenzo a few days earlier. [80] Neither of them was assigned fault and both were present for the drafting of the agreement, but like Bella they were represented by their mundualdi.

The mundualdus, a vestige of Lombard law, was usually appointed on the spot for the business at hand; he could be a brother, father, husband, or any available male body, so long as he had reached the age of majority, which in Florence was eighteen years of age.[81] It was a rather simple affair. The notary usually recited a legal formula such as this one: "Ghisola of Maffei de Luilla of the parish of San Giorgio, has come before me Giovanni, judge and notary undersigned, requesting me to bestow and confirm Lomo, son of Manovello of the aforesaid parish, who is present and wishes to be her true and legitimate mundualdus." The notary then took the woman by her right hand and handed her over—literally—into the *mundio* and power

79. Ibid., fol. 71r.

80. Andrea di Lapo, ASF, Not. Ant. 439, fol. 50r. Presumably Giovanna was unmarried, as she was not given the title Domina.

81. On *mundualdi*, see Thomas Kuehn, "*Cum consensu mundualdi*: Legal Guardianship of Women in Quattrocento Florence," *Viator* 13 (1982): 309–31; repr. in his *Law, Family, and Women*, 212–37. Note that the *mundualdus* was a Florentine, not a Tuscan institution. I have found women freely making contracts in San Gimignano and Prato, among other Tuscan cities.

of her representative while uttering these words: "You are the mundualdus for this woman."[82]

The weapon of choice in female assault cases was overwhelmingly "bare fists." There were, however, resourceful if improvised exceptions. In 1342 in the parish of San Lorenzo, Pina, daughter of Domina Bilia, launched a pear and a slice of bread against Margarita, wife of Gigletto. The ensuing ruckus caused such a disturbance that the cappellano was forced to make a complaint against the two of them.[83] They quickly settled their dispute with a peace instrument, which carried a sanction of 25 f.p.

The crime of armed assault was, however, rare among women. Occasionally we find them wielding weapons such as rocks or pieces of wood, but in one instance only have I found a woman armed with a knife. In that November 1329 case, Domina Francesca, wife of Donnino, used a knife with an iron blade (the most common type described in the documents) to attack Domina Francesca, wife of Lippo, who seems to have held her own in the fracas, aided by a wooden object. A month later the two Francescas wound up in court. Francesca of Donnino was convicted and sentenced to pay a fine of 200 f.p. for the knife attack and for a punch landed on Francesca of Lippo's nose, who herself had to pay a lesser fine for landing two bloody blows on her assailant's head. In January 1330 the two finally made peace through designated representatives. Francesca of Lippo had absented herself, nominating a procurator to represent her, while Francesca of Donnino acted through a mundualdus. Interestingly, she appointed her mundualdus at the Stinche, the municipal prison of Florence, suggesting that she may have been imprisoned there, awaiting a settlement.[84]

ARMED ASSAULT

Armed assault with a knife may have been an unusual crime for a woman to commit, but it was not so for men. Florentine statute law, like that of other cities, forbade carrying offensive arms such as swords and knives, but that does not mean that all Florentine men abided by the law.[85] Accordingly a veritable catalogue of medieval weaponry appears in notarial peace instruments, often cited merely as "offensive and defensive weapons" or as

82. ASF, Not. Ant. 4111, fols. 97r and 99v. In this case, I have combined language from two separate contracts. Though women did not exchange the kiss of peace with men, I have not seen anything in the agreements expressly forbidding women to exchange the kiss of peace with each other.

83. Andrea di Lapo, ASF, Not. Ant. 439, fol. 154r.

84. Aldobrandino di Albizzo, ASF, Not. Ant. 251, fol. 95v.

85. *Statuti*, vol. 2: Podestà, Bk 3: LX, 203: "de armis vetitis non portandis": "Nullus de civitate, comitatu vel districtu Florentie vel alia quecunque persona audeat vel presumat deferre vel tenere spatam, quaderlectum vel spuntonem seu cultellum vel aliquod aliud armorum offensibilium, eundo vel stando, eques vel pedes, in aliqua via vel platea seu per aliquam viam vel plateam civitatis Florentiae. . . ."

"forbidden arms."[86] Arms are mentioned in only about 14 percent of all peace agreements in this sample, a rather low figure that belies the common stereotype that all medieval men were armed and easily resorted to using their weapons.[87] However, when we drill down to examine the assault cases alone, we find that weapons were used in almost one quarter of those for which peace is being made. Knives, which statute law categorized as prohibited weapons, appear in about 40 percent of those cases.[88] As we have seen, most involved knives with iron blades, but in one case from October 1338, Piero, known as Albasito, attacked Bartolo Bonini with what was described as a bread knife, stabbing him in the shoulder and neck, presumably not a premeditated crime.[89]

Weapons, like clothing, were markers of social status. Though we can assume that most everyone had access to bread knives, mentions of swords, lances, *tabulacci* (or *tavolacci*, shields), *bracciauole* (armatures for the forearm), *quadraletti* (or *quadrelli*, daggers), and gauntlets all suggest that their owners were of a rather elevated socioeconomic status.[90] More modest weapons are evidenced in the documents as well. Pieces of wood—probably nothing more than sticks or firewood—became weapons when needed, as did the walking stick of Tanino, the pauper we encountered earlier making peace with Vanni after a row on a street corner. The notary Aldobrandino di Albizzo describes in unexpected detail a club made of beech wood that was used in a robbery in 1331.[91]

After fists and knives, rocks were the most popular weapon, and not only for the less affluent. Of the cases where arms are cited, rocks show up as weapons in 11 percent of the peace agreements made for resolving assault cases. In some they are the sole weapon; in others they appear alongside spears, knives, and swords, suggesting that they were not disdained by more well-off members of society. Domina Giovanna, wife of Jacopo Manzini, found herself on the wrong end of a hail of both lances and rocks when Lapo Credi and his men attacked her one night at a *podere* in Acone, over what seems to have begun as a property or perhaps a debt dispute. The unfortunate Giovanna was

86. The agreements made by Benintendi di Guittone (ASF, Not. Ant. 2354, fol. 148v) and Giovanni di Buoninsegna da Rignano (ASF, Not. Ant. 9491, fol. 105r) contain an arsenal of weapons.

87. This figure may reinforce indirectly one of the arguments of this chapter, that the elites—who presumably had more access to weapons—are not the predominant protagonists of peace agreements. For a discussion on misperceptions about the use of arms in medieval Italy, see Dean, *Crime and Justice*, 168.

88. Benintendi di Guittone, ASF, Not. Ant. 2354, fol. 148v.

89. Andrea di Lapo, ASF, Not. Ant. 439, fol. 52r.

90. The quadraletto, also know as a quadrello, is an arrow fitted with a particularly strong head, designed for piercing armor.

91. The assailant Piero was armed *cum legno de faggio squadrato ad modum conii*. Aldobrandino di Albizzo, ASF, Not. Ant. 251, fol. 148r.

evicted from the farmhouse and her property confiscated; she was also struck and injured by the rocks thrown at her. Four months after the event, in a series of contracts, she and her husband finally settled their dispute with Lapo in a peace agreement rogated by Bartolo Amici.[92]

In 1306, a shower of projectiles greeted Donato, son of Lord Martello, a member of the powerful Donati clan, when he was returning to Florence from San Cristoforo a Perticaia after participating in a cavalry action (*cavallata*). Lying in wait for him was Dino di Buonaguida, known as "Grasso," and his sons. They bore down on Donato letting loose on him a rain of arrows and quadrelli. During the assault they were heard to shout out, "Die! die!"[93] The pax noted that the attack on Donato had been against the "honor and institution of the Guelf Party, the commune of Florence, the Lords Podestà and Captain (of the people), the Lords Prior and the Standard-bearers." In other words, since Donato was a knight performing his civic obligation, the crime was not only against him as a private citizen, but was also considered a crime against the honor of the city and her institutions. The same held true for attacks on communal officials. In cases such as these, peace instruments not only restored concord and order between citizens, but between citizens and the body politic.

ARMED ASSAULT ON COMMUNAL OFFICIALS

The following three cases show how municipal officers—a *nunzio* and four berrovarii—could and did become victims of assault at the hands of enraged citizens. In early summer 1340, we find two individuals settling a dispute with one of Florence's heralds, Francesco Tura of the parish of San Procolo. It seems that Francesco, while trying to carry out his duties of office—in this case denouncing a public debtor and escorting him to prison—was attacked by a group of five, whose ringleader was Domina Bancha, wife of Cino Vanini of the parish of San Lorenzo. "With malice aforethought and seized by a diabolical spirit," they assaulted him, Bancha in the vanguard, beating the nunzio over the head and shoulders with a piece of wood, causing wounds that bled. Saginbene joined the fray by landing a blow to Francesco's upper body with the bracciauola that he wore on his wrist. They succeeded in freeing the debtor Guidone from the herald's grip, but the tumult escalated into an even graver crime when they tied up the herald Francesco and held him captive at the house of Bocchaccio dei Brunelleschi, where Domina Bancha lived. The report of the melée wound up in court, and in the ensuing case the judge ruled both the nunzio and Guidone's creditor harmed by the incident, to say nothing of the "great disrespect to the people and commune of Florence." Domina Bancha

92. Bartolo Amici, ASF, Not. Ant. 363, fol. 40v.
93. As if this was not enough, Donato's peace contract was doing double-duty: it was also making peace with the same group of malefactors for having stolen one of his horses, which was in the possession of his nephew Cionchino di Bartolo.

and Francesco Arrighi pled guilty to the charges, while the three others, who did not appear in court, were declared contumacious and banned.[94] Though we cannot be sure, perhaps we can infer that the debtor's friends and allies, led by Domina Bancha, offended at their friend's public humiliation, took out their anger on the unfortunate nunzio and the situation then proceeded to get out of hand. [95] Eventually, however, peace was made when the herald's brother, acting as his procurator (legal representative), made peace with Domina Bancha and one of her gang.

Like heralds, the berrovarii of the podestà's court were also at times at risk from the wrath of the popolo. We have already seen two officers insulted and assaulted in Forte Piero's tavern in San Martino a Petroio. In 1319 a dispute had to be settled when two berrovarii of the criminal court of Borgo were attacked violently while trying to escort the debtor Andrea of Piero Bernardi Mailis of the parish of Santa Felicità to the Bargello. It seems that Andrea was in debt to the tune of 500 gold florins to the knight Lord Nicholas Felli, and the brothers Anzolino and Giovanni helped Andrea resist arrest by assaulting the berrovarii with a sword and bracciauole. A series of contracts eventually settled their conflict, in which procurators acted for the injured berrovarii and Lord Nicholas.[96] In another instance, the brothers Tedaldo and Pepe assailed Matteo Grimaldi of Camerino and Cechone Venturelli of Osimo, two berrovarii in the retinue of the capitano del popolo. Tedaldo audaciously grabbed the weapon that the berrovarius Matteo wore at his side and knifed him with it while his brother Pepe threw rocks. The brothers' father Tendi aided and abetted them by giving counsel and helping them flee after the attack. The case wound up in court when the two policemen made a complaint against the brothers; it was, however, settled with a peace instrument that threatened a fine of 100 f.p. should they break the agreement. [97]

Whether an assault was committed against an officer of the commune or against a private citizen, it disturbed the tranquility of order in the city, and assaults did so more frequently than any other crime. As we have seen, 57 percent of *paci* were made to resolve disputes that had ended in violent altercations. There might have been other, better ways to restore social order, but this was the method that seemed best suited to meet the needs of the Florentine judicial system, and the one that cohered best with the message that citizens heard preached in their piazzas. A written peace agreement was analogous (but not equivalent) to sacramental confession insofar as it spelled

94. Andrea di Lapo, ASF, Not. Ant. 439, fols. 94v–95v.

95. On the recovery of debt and the violence that it could entail, see Daniel Lord Smail, "Violence and Predation in Late Medieval Europe," *Comparative Studies in History and Society* 54.1 (2012): 7–34; and now Smail, *Goods and Debts in Mediterranean Europe (1330–1450)* (Cambridge, MA: Harvard University Press, 2016).

96. Tano di Puccio di Guido, ASF, Not. Ant. 20546, fols. 78v–79r.

97. Andrea di Lapo, ASF, Not. Ant. 439, fols. 74r–74v.

out the crime for which peace was being made. It also relieved both the victim and perpetrator of the *culpa*, thereby cleansing their consciences, creating inner peace. And finally, it allowed for the restoration of outer peace and concord in the city.[98]

THEFT, ROBBERY, BURGLARY

The settlement of a dispute over a theft of private property or money could also be an occasion that elicited a pax; indeed after assault, feud, and vendetta (examined in chapter 4), theft was the category of crime most often represented as the source of conflict in these agreements. I have found a total of twenty-six settlements for theft (including robbery and burglary) of personal property, which represents 5 percent of total crimes for which peace was made, and 11 percent of the non-assault cases. I include under the category of theft all crimes in which private property was stolen, whether by force, violence, or intimidation, or by "breaking and entering."

Armed robbery was at the heart of a peace agreement made by the Fascelli brothers and Piero Nardi, who had used a wooden bat to assail the brothers Baldino and Jacopo and rob them of a sack of 150 gold florins, which they had just withdrawn from a cambio in the Mercato Vecchio. Piero followed the Fascelli brothers and just as they were about to enter their house, he hit Baldino over the head with the bat. As Baldino fell down the stairs, Piero snatched the sack out of his hands and fled.[99] Though the contract is silent on the issue, we must presume that Baldino's money was restored to him, as restitution of stolen property was ordinarily a prerequisite for making peace. The same held true in another case that we will examine in more depth below. For now it will suffice to note that as part of Salvatore Iunta's peace agreement he was ordered to return the five gold and silver rings set with emeralds, diamonds, and pearls and valued at 65 gold florins that he had stolen from Domina Tommasa and Simone.[100]

Tellingly, it was neither money nor jewels, but clothing that was most frequently stolen by Florentine thieves, at least by those thieves who were parties to peace contracts. Of all the cases involving theft, 58 percent list clothing or cloth as the stolen article at the heart of the dispute. The *mantello*, an outer cloak, often hooded, tops the list as the most frequently stolen article, but the tunic ran a close second, followed by the *guarnacchia*, a long overvest often lined and hooded, which, the documents report, was made in

98. It is worth noting that when confession of sin was visually represented, the sinner's confession was depicted as a written document, usually a parchment scroll.

99. Aldobrandino di Albizzo, ASF, Not. Ant. 251, fol. 148r. We can presume from the evidence of other contracts that Piero repaid the money before making peace; the contract, however is silent on this issue.

100. Pietro Nelli Corsi, ASF, Not. Ant. 5738, fols. 162r-162v.

a veritable rainbow of colors and variety of fabrics.[101] In a case from 1330, Donato Benincasa reported his tunic having been stolen off his back, which fortuitously for the thieves, also had a few denarii stashed in its pocket.[102] Certain pieces of clothing were markers or status, and this may have been a motive for their theft. The theft of a *gonella*, a long tunic usually made of leather and worn by knights, certainly suggests that its owner was a member of the elite, as does the description of a turquoise gown trimmed with vair and elaborate silver buttons pinched by Salvatore Iunta.[103] Other pieces of clothing were markers of civic office; they were uniforms, as it were. It was probably the case that Piccio, from whom assailants snatched a hat decorated with vermilion lilies (and a sky-blue mantello), was a nunzio, an officer of the commune whose position was announced by his distinctive headwear. Without the hat he could not discharge his official duties, which is just what the thief no doubt intended by committing this crime.[104]

Though it might be expected that the theft of weapons would rank high as a cause of disputes among medieval Florentines, they are in fact rarely enumerated in peace settlements for theft. When they are mentioned, they are catalogued in inventories, alongside other items, as was the case detailed in an act dating from the spring of 1308. Matteo Fortis Beççole exchanged the kiss of peace with Antonino Arrighi, who had been convicted five years earlier of stealing Matteo's iron gauntlet, mason's hammer, and a gold florin, a random collection of goods certainly, but with a defensive weapon ranked at the top of the list. In the original conviction, Antonino was ordered to return the stolen goods to Matteo and to pay a fine of 100 f.p. [105] Like others whom we shall meet, Antonino fled and became an outlaw. The peace agreement allowed him to return to Florence, a practice that we will examine in greater depth in the next chapter.

Thieves (or perhaps those who took the law into their own hands to recover private debt) also coveted household items, as a settlement from 1340 for breaking and entering demonstrates. Here Duccio Gaddi made peace with Ceccho Ghinazzi who, with a band of well-armed henchmen, forced his way into Duccio's farmhouse at Sant'Andrea a Candeli, a hamlet of Bagno a Ripoli in the contado of Florence. The gang robbed Duccio blind. Checco

---

101. See the list drawn up in Andrea di Lapo, ASF, Not. Ant. 439, fols. 121v-122v, cited at n.109 below.

102. Aldobrandino di Albizzo, ASF, Not. Ant. 251, fol. 117r.

103. See for example, Arrigho di Benintendi, ASF, Not. Ant. 950, fol. 67r and Pietro Nelli Corsi, ASF, Not. Ant. 5738, fols. 162r-162v.

104. Iacopo di Geri, ASF, Not. Ant. 11108, fol. 76r. The red lily of course was the symbol of Guelf-ruled Florence. I am grateful to Carol Lansing for pointing out that this was the hat of a *nunzio*, stipulated by statute law. The law demanded that nunzios wear a tall woolen hat with four large vermillion lilies appliquéd on it. *Statuti*, vol. 2 Podestà, Bk 1: XII, 40.

105. Giovanni di Buoninsegna da Rignano, ASF, Not. Ant. 9491, fols. 113v-114r.

and company made off with what may have been the entire contents of his well-stocked wardrobe and larder, to say nothing of a cartload of household objects.[106] With a Florentine merchant's eye for detail, the peace agreement listed the goods that Checco later confessed to stealing: "a light-weight woman's garment; five towels; four tablecloths; two napkins; five cloaks; three white garments; three linen headcloths; five canes of cloth; six silk cloths; one big brass pot; two tin flasks; one iron *staio* (measuring tub); three staia of grain; twelve empty sacks; twenty ounces of oil; one bit (for a bridle) worth 55 f.p.; seven pounds *panete*(?); one new white lining; a draped lining; a striped vest; a tunic; a guarnacchia of persian cloth; another tunic; one cane of persian twill fabric; a tunic and a guarnacchia lined with vermilion sendal; a cloak of yellow Irish cloth lined with blood-red sendal; a tunic and a yellow woolen guarnacchia; another tunic made of yellow linen; a yellow cloak; a bright red guarnacchia of mixed fabric; a guarnacchia of deep red cloth; a tunic of mixed cloth; two guarnacchie of romagnolo cloth (cheap, rough, natural color); a tunic of green and brown cloth and another new white one; two checked bedspreads, a striped mattress, a feather comforter; three sheets; a man's light-weight shirt; a woman's light-weight shirt; four salme of red wine; one salma of "vino cotto"; and one container full of vinegar." In addition to this comprehensive list, Ceccho confessed that he also helped one of his men pilfer four staia of grain, which he then had milled, and three salme of oil, which he subsequently sold to oil vendors. Ceccho was convicted of his crime, fined by the judge, and ordered to restore to Duccio all the goods that he had stolen as a precondition to his peace contract.[107]

In another case, also involving a break-in to private property and committed under the cover of night, Donatino Bertucci of San Leonardo della

106. Dean, *Crime and Justice*, see his chapter on theft in which these were the most frequently stolen objects.

107. Andrea di Lapo, ASF, Not. Ant. 439, fols. 121v-122v: "unum guarnellum ad usum muliere; quinque asciugatoio sive manutergia; quator tovagliole; duo tovaglie; quinque mantelli; tres guanarolli albi; tres bende de lino; quinque canelli [4 braccia] de panni; sex vele de seta; unum paiolum magnum de ramo; 2 fiaschi de stangno; unum starium de ferro; tria stari granii, 12 sacchi voti; 20 uncias oleii; unus frenum, 55 f.p.; 7 lb panete; unum foderum novum album; unum foderum de indisia; una gillecta dogata; una tunica et una guarnacchia de channo persa; una alia tunica; una saia de channo persa; una tunicha et una guarnacchia foderata de sindone vermiglio; unum mantellum de panno d'irlanda garofonato fodertatum de sindone sanguineo; una tunica et una guarnacchia panni lanii gharofonati; una alia tunica garofonata panni laney; unum mantellum garofonatum; una guarnacchia rossechina mistichiata; una guarnacchia vermiglia; una guarnacchia panni sanguineii; una tunica panni mistichiati; 2 guarnacchie panni romandioli; una tunica panni viridis bruni et una altera nova alba; duo copertaria de panno a schacchos; unum mattarazzum de bordo, unum piumaccium; tria pannas lintiamii; unum interule ad usum hominis; unum interule ad usum mulieris; 4 salme vini vermigli, una salma vini chotti; unum baule plenum de aceto." Dan Smail has suggested to me that this case could have been a "do-it-yourself" debt recovery. I thank him also for some of his suggested readings of these items.

Querciola illegally entered Bata's property and stole a pair of cows for which he was fined 100 f.p. and ordered to replace the cattle with others of the same value. It seems that Donatino did no such thing, at least not immediately, for in 1310 the court banished him from Florentine territory. He remained an outlaw for fourteen years, but in 1324 finally settled his dispute with Bata by drawing up a peace agreement with the notary Iacopo di Geri.[108]

Though of a rather different nature, we might also consider violations against the monopolies held by officers of the gabelle as a theft of sorts. I have found three such cases, each settled with a peace agreement. Decca, a servant from Acone was accused of selling wine on the black market because she had not submitted it for inspection. Nor had it been sealed or taxed by the current holder of the gabelle. Furthermore, she had committed this crime "many, many times" before she was prosecuted for it. It is unclear how her crime reached the court of the capitano del popolo, but when it did she was sentenced to pay a fine of 100 f.p. for so doing; but the officers of the gabelle of wine—the injured party—also had to make peace with Decca.[109] Similarly, Giovanni di Pacino's protocols report a case in which Guiduccio Ceni violated the gabelle of livestock for selling both retail and wholesale. Four years after his sentence, also levied by the capitano del popolo, he too made peace with the gabelle officers after paying a fine.[110] Offenses against the gabelle, however, were not always a question of selling on the black market. Sometimes the crime was not buying enough of a commodity or reneging on the amount contracted. Such was the issue at stake in a case that came to court when Benintendi Ughetti, rector of the parish of San Piero a Colognole in Acone, was accused of not buying all the salt that he had agreed to purchase. Benintendi was given a minimal and probably symbolic fine of 5 f.p. in May 1341; in October he settled his dispute with the officer of the gabelle by having Bartolo Amici draw up a pax.[111]

Theft ranked second only to assault of the crimes for which Florentines made peace settlements; i.e., 11 percent of the non-assault cases. Most of the time, the thieves had been convicted in the criminal court of the podestà, ordered to restore the stolen property, and pay a fine. But if they ignored the court summons and fled Florentine jurisdiction, only a peace agreement would allow them to return, a process we will examine more closely in chapter 4. For now let us note that money, jewels, clothing and cloth, household items, and

108. Iacopo di Geri, ASF, Not. Ant. 11108, fol. 57v. My thanks to Carol Lansing, who offered emergency paleographical assistance in the archive on the reading of "cows" in this document.

109. Bartolo Amici, ASF, Not. Ant. 364, fol. 77r: "contra formam pactorum dictorum emptorum debuit vendisse et vendi fecisse vinum ad minutum non singnatum [sic] et non gabellatum pluribus et pluribus vicibus."

110. Giovanni di Pacino, ASF, Not. Ant. 9692, fol. 3r. Although the courts of the podestà and the capitano del popolo often had overlapping jurisdictions, the cases of violation of the gabelle that I have found all went to the court of the capitano.

111. Bartolo Amici, ASF, Not. Ant. 364, fol. 151v.

livestock were all liable to fall prey to thieves and were protected under the jurisdiction of the criminal court; thefts against the gabelle—for which a peace contract could be employed—were the purview of the capitano del popolo.

ABDUCTION, KIDNAPPING, AND INVOLUNTARY DETENTION

Though theft or assault were frequently the primary offenses listed in peace contracts; sometimes they were only part of a larger crime spree, as witnessed in the following case. It began in 1302 when Gianuccio Biondi, along with his son Mino and some others, broke into Ubaldino di Paolo's house located near the fort of the villa of Acone.[112] First they cleaned him out of all his belongings and furnishings. Notably they also stole a pair of oxen, along with some linen and woolen cloth valued at 100 f.p. But that wasn't the end of it. The thieves then became abductors by taking Ubaldino captive and holding him at the fort of Monte Acuto, where he was tortured.[113] He was released upon payment of 50 f.p., but his ordeal did not end there. The kidnappers added arson to their list of crimes by burning Ubaldino's house to the ground. It will come as no surprise that the aggrieved victim brought the case to trial and Gianuccio was condemned for his crimes. In fact the judge threw the book at him: not only was Gianuccio given the death penalty, he was also ordered to pay damages to Ubaldino. [114] Predictably Gianuccio did not turn up for his sentencing, so the court declared him contumacious and he was banned accordingly. It took him decades, but thirty-six years later, Gianuccio returned to Acone, where we find him making peace in the house where Ubaldino now resided. *In bono animo et pura fide* Giannuccio made restitution to Ubaldino for the stolen items, the ransom money, and the cost of the destroyed house.[115] It will be remembered that statute law decreed that peace agreements had to be made within fifteen days of the crime—and the majority were—but many parties did not settle their dispute for years. Among the documents I have examined, the case of Ubaldino and Gianuccio sets the record for time elapsed between crime and peace settlement.

112. Acone was under the jurisdiction of Pontassieve in the contado of Florence.

113. Considering that the fort of Monte Acuto had traditionally been a Ghibelline stronghold, one wonders whether there was a political dimension to this crime and its resolution that remains veiled by the lacunae in the documentation. *Statuti*, vol. 2: *Podestà*, Bk 3: CXXVI, 251–52.

114. In ordinary circumstances none of these crimes warranted the death penalty, though the judge was allowed a certain amount of discretion in punishing crimes of abduction. See *Statuti*, vol. 2: Podestà, Bk 3: XXXIII, 181–82. One hypothesis is that this was a political crime, as the location of Monte Acuto suggests. Another theory is that Gianuccio's harsh sentence may have been for carrying out a vendetta against someone not deemed to be a principal in a given feud. A case such as this one reveals yet again the limitations of our sources.

115. Bartolo Amici, ASF, Not. Ant. 364, fol. 73r.

Another case of abduction, which might have had a political dimension (though this is obscured by the laconic character of the documentation), occurred when the brothers Dinuccio and Gherardo Cecchi began an altercation with Chellino by insulting him. Next they roughed him up, pocketed his money, and with *irato animo et malo modo* they attacked him, wounding him and drawing blood. He was then abducted and taken captive to the Castrum of Ancisa (modern Incisa in Val d'Arno), then in rebellion against Florence, where he was held prisoner in a dungeon until twenty-five gold florins were paid for his release. The peace contract was made in 1325, twelve years after the case had come to court. The case had never been concluded because the defendants fled after having been sentenced to death by hanging. Since the victim Chellino had since died, his next of (male) kin made peace with the Cecchi brothers, who had been in self-imposed exile all those years.[116]

Of the eight agreements that I have found making settlement for this crime, only one involves the abduction of a woman. The perpetrator was a member of the powerful Donati family: Tommaso, son of Lord Corso.[117] Recorded in the register of Aldobrandino di Albizzo, Tommaso's role is perfectly clear: he committed the crime with malice aforethought and with a "diabolical spirit."[118] His case went to court and he was sentenced for having forced his way into the house of Giovanni Bertini. The object of prey was Giovanni's wife, Veoma. Tommaso abducted her against her will, forcibly taking her off to his own house. As to what happened next, we are left in the dark, since the contract reveals neither the motive nor the outcome of the situation. What it does disclose, however, is that Giovanni, Veoma's husband, did not stand by idly; he made a formal accusation against Tommaso and the judge ruled that the accused had to pay a financial penalty of 200 f.p. within a month or be imprisoned. Apparently, the fine went unpaid and Tommaso was incarcerated: the contract making peace between the parties was enacted on 8 July 1327 at the Stinche, Florence's municipal prison, whose inmates were primarily debtors.[119]

SEX CRIMES: RAPE AND ADULTERY

The ambiguous nature of the case against Tommaso raises the question of sex crimes and whether they too could be settled with a peace contract. The answer is "yes," though I have found only three such cases in the archives, two for adultery and one for rape.

116. Benintendi di Guittone, ASF, Not. Ant. 2358, fol. 59v-60r.
117. Aldobrandino di Albizzo, ASF, Not. Ant. 251, fols. 12v-13r.
118. Ibid.: *pensate deliberate dyabolico spiritu instigate.*
119. For a study of medieval prisons, including *Le Stinche*, see Guy Geltner, *The Medieval Prison: A Social History* (Princeton: Princeton University Press, 2008), 51–52. He notes that debt was the most common reason for a stretch in prison.

The rape case comes from the Oltrarno ward of the city, from the register of Orlandino di Francesco.[120] In an inquisition that was initiated by the podestà on account of *mala fama*, which had reached his ears, Choccho of Toro of the parish of Santa Maria a Verzaia was found guilty of the rape of Martha, daughter of Pagno Guidingo of the parish of San Frediano in the Oltrarno ward. Extraordinarily, the notary provides a detailed description of this appalling crime. Because records of rape are such a rare occurrence in medieval documentation, I follow the lead of our notary and include the unusual if disturbing details needed for prosecution.[121]

It seems that Chocco, instigated by a diabolical spirit or "some enemy of mankind" and with *irato animo* and premeditation (*malo modo deliberate et pensante*) seized Martha, a young virgin, and tore off her clothing. He then beat her repeatedly with some kind of studded belt. Next, Chocco forced the naked girl into a thicket of reeds, where against her will, he "knew her carnally, violated, and deflowered her." Likely recapped from Martha's testimony, the notary includes the following information: the act of rape took place on top of her clothing strewn on the ground. It lasted for what seemed a long time. Indeed it was not until Martha's screams attracted the attention of a passerby that the whole dreadful episode came to an end. Lurid and gratuitous as the details are, especially in comparison to other agreements we have examined, in this case they were demanded by the inquisitio process, which called for the collection of as many facts as possible.

When the case came to court, the perpetrator was convicted and fined. The court divided the incident into three distinct crimes, each fined separately. Chocco was fined 40 f.p. for tearing off the girl's clothing, and 90 f.p. for the rape itself (*robatione pudicitie*), but the biggest fine of all—120 f.p.—was reserved for the beating the poor girl withstood, confirming that assault was considered a more serious crime than rape.[122] Chocco was not present to hear his sentence pronounced as he was already on the run. However, two years later in the neighborhood church of Sant'Agostino (Santo Spirito?) he exchanged the kiss of peace with Martha's father and the dispute was considered settled, at least according to the law.

Unlike the detailed rape case, the result of an inquisition, our first adultery case is recorded in a very short and terse contract drawn up by Giovanni di

120. Orlandino Francesco, ASF, Not. Ant. 15681, fols. 18v-19r.

121. Historical studies on rape are still scarce, but for medieval Perugia, see Giovanna Casagrande and Michaela Pazzaglia, "'Bona mulier in domo,'" at 146–49. For comparison, see now Caroline Dunn, *Stolen Women in Medieval England: Rape, Abduction and Adultery, 1100–1500* (Cambridge: Cambridge University Press, 2012). See also, Hanna Skoda, *Medieval Violence*, 68–80.

122. It is difficult to discern how this fine was determined, since the crime of rape usually carried a 500 f.p. fine if the woman was of age, or 100 f.p. if she was a minor, even less if she was a servant or prostitute. The statutes did, however, grant the judge discretion on the matter. *Statuti*, vol 2: Podestà: Bk 3, LXVIIII, 207–208.

Buto and enacted in the Pavanico Forum (Vicchio), in the northeastern part of the contado, on 8 January 1303. The contract made peace between the men acting on behalf of Domina Adalagia, daughter of Lapo Ferrari, and her cuckolded husband Drudino, son of Redolfo of Razzuolo, and his brother. Not having resulted from an *inquisitio*, the details of the case are alas lacking. We know only that Drudino had made a formal accusation against Adalagia. Both parties were threatened with a financial penalty of 500 f.p. should the peace be broken, a fine that echoed the sum that Adalagia would have had to pay for her crime of adultery had there been a conviction in court.[123]

The second case of adultery that emerges from the archives is one that we have already had cause to cite earlier, in reference to the theft of valuable jewelry. Though Salvatore Iunta of San Felice in Piazza had purloined some clothing and jewelry, theft was not the only reason that brought him to draw up a peace agreement in 1335. Using blandishments, it seems that he had seduced Domina Tommasa, described as being of *honeste vite* and convinced her to commit adultery "many, many times" on various days and at different hours. All this of course was against the will of her husband, Simone, and his family. The case had gone to court and the podestà had sentenced Salvatore to pay an enormous fine of 10,000 f.p., payable to the treasury of Florence within the month. He was also ordered to return the goods he had stolen. A little more than a month after he had been condemned, Salvatore's peace instrument absolved him of the court's fine but not of the requirement that he restore Simone's stolen property.[124]

Though these episodes are few and far between, it is notable that the peace instrument could be used to bring an end to the discord between families that sex crimes had caused. In both the case of rape and those of adultery, it should be clear by now that the women involved never made peace on their own behalf. In fact, the woman did not even need a mundualdus in such cases, because she was not a party to the peace. Either her father or husband made peace in his own name. It was the dishonor done to the family, not to the woman, that was at stake in such instances.

MARITAL DISCORD

Like the peace agreements for sex crimes, those made to resolve marital and family discord are scarce in the documentary evidence, presumably because it

123. Giovanni di Buto, ASF, Not. Ant. 9493, fol. 91v. *Statuti*, vol 2: Podestà: Bk 3, LXVIIII, 207–208. The financial sanction often mirrored the fine that would have been imposed if a conviction had been made in court. The judges did have discretion on this matter, however.

124. Piero Nelli Corsi, ASF, Not. Ant. 5738, fols. 162r-62v. I have not been able to ascertain why the fine was so high (a slip of the stylus?), nor can I discern why Salvatore Iunta is making peace with Bernardo Rossi, who is neither Domina Thommasa's husband nor a procurator so far as I can see.

was not considered a crime until it reached actionable proportions. Since our goal is to examine the wide range of disputes that instrumenta pacis resolved, it is worthwhile bringing these four lone contracts in this category to light as well.

In the first, a couple (and their families) used a peace agreement to settle an incident of domestic violence in the parish of San Lorenzo alle Rose in Santa Maria Impruneta. It seems that Bartolo, called Maçça, used a pruning hook to attack his wife Giovanna. The hapless Giovanna suffered serious damage to one of her eyes, such that it seems to have been dislodged from its socket, leaving a permanent and disfiguring scar. Giovanna brought the case before a criminal judge. Maçça, though summoned, did not appear at court and he was therefore banned for contumacy. Presumably there was some behind-the-scenes negotiation (unmentioned of course in the instrumentum), as a peace agreement dated 5 October 1330 reconciled the troubled couple, but under the threat of a fine of 500 f.p. should the contract be broken.[125]

Our second case of domestic violence, which sadly ended in homicide, comes from Prato, where an agreement was made in the spring of 1293 at the church of Sant'Agostino. The details are lacking. We know only that Domina Piubellina, guardian of Tessina, made peace on behalf of her ward with Gienovino, Tessina's father. In this distressing case Gienovino had killed his wife Finuccia, mother of his young daughter.[126]

Another pax for a similar crime comes from the Val di Pesa and was made in the church of Santo Stefano a Campoli in the fall of 1326.[127] Cinello Bonsegnoris and Vanni Corbiçci came together in "clear knowledge and not through error and with a pure, free, spontaneous will to give each other the kiss of peace on the mouth." Both were accompanied by their families and associates. Cinello was representing the interests of his deceased daughter Bene, while Vanni represented those of his son Guglielmo. Bene had been married to Guglielmo before her untimely death at the hands of her husband. He had beaten her so brutally that she died from her injuries. Now the families, in a clear effort to forestall the possibility of future vendetta and violence, were making peace not only for themselves but for their heirs, descendants, friends, relatives, and followers.

Our final case, which also may have been an attempt to prevent vendetta, produced an agreement of a different order. It dates from the autumn of 1298 and comes from the county of the Alberti near the Cerbaia bridge (Prato). In addition to the marital dispute, a homicide also seems to have occurred.

125. Benintendi di Guittone, ASF, Not. Ant. 2359, fols. 169r-69v. For domestic violence, see Skoda, *Medieval Violence*, 193–232.

126. *Collectio chartarum pacis*, ed. Masi, 254–55.

127. Benintendi di Guittone, ASF, Not. Ant. 2358, fols. 104r: "et certa scientia et non per errorem eorum pura et libera et spontanea voluntate horis ad hos hosculo pacis interveniente."

Coppia Parentis (along with a group of eight others) makes the usual promises to uphold the peace but, interestingly, he agrees also to a peace with his wife, Gina, and two others. Coppia is on one side, Gina on the other. Coppia promises to keep his marriage vows and to regard Gina as his lawful wife. Toward this end, he promises to keep her fed and nourished as far as he is able from the produce of his farm, provided that Gina comes to live with him. The case is inherently interesting, but it is also significant for another reason: although it states that the parties exchanged the kiss of peace, it notes specifically that Gina did not.[128] In imitation of the ritual in the Mass, women did not exchange the kiss of peace with men, because as William Durand, remarked, "Men and women do not exchange a kiss in church, so that nothing lascivious creeps in, because in that place, carnal embraces must be put to flight, and a chaste and spiritual comportment must be maintained; this is also why they are separated from each other in different parts of the church. Peace drives away hatred; peace nourishes a chaste love."[129] Presumably this rationale informed the kiss of peace in the civic context as well.

As is almost always the case, we do not know what transpired between the couple that brought them to the point that Coppia needed to stipulate that he would care for Gina in a peace contract. Had he been starving her to death? Had she run away? And who exactly had been the victim of homicide in this case? Like all other peace agreements we have seen, the parties looked to the future, not the past.[130] The aim was to establish a new relationship, a new reality in which concord—not discord—would become the defining element of the bond.

In this case, as in others we shall see, the threat of vendetta for a homicide committed loomed large and informed the circumstances of making peace. Indeed, peace contracts could be used in cases of homicide, especially when they were meant to preempt or put an end to feud, violence, and vendetta, the subject of the next chapter. Before we turn to those matters, however, it will be useful to draw some conclusions from the particulars of those peace instruments we have examined thus far.

As we have seen, peacemaking on an everyday level was not only a matter of reconciling feuding elites or political factions. It was about restoring public

---

128. Leggeri Riccobaldi, ASF, Not. Ant. 17856, fols. 101v-102r: "Ambe simul dicte partes et quilibet dictarum partium sibi adinvicem inter eos et unus alteri hosculo pacis interveniente excepta quam dicta domina Gina non intervenit obsculum."

129. *Rationale*, Book 4, trans. Timothy M. Thibodeau (Turnhout: Brepols, 2013), 465.

130. Padoa Schioppa, "Delitto e pace privata nel pensiero dei legisti bolognesi," 274. This is a point also suggested to me by Kim Scheppele, which may explain why fully one-quarter of the peace contracts in this sample do not specify the crime or offense for which settlement is being made.

order, tranquility, and concord to communities, neighborhoods, and families. It made possible a fresh start by restoring equilibrium to relationships that had somehow tipped over into violence and disorder. This was particularly important because most contending parties lived within close proximity to each other. By mapping the geography of violence, we find that violent conflicts, more often than not, took place in or very close to the parishes and wards where the disputing parties resided. If we can rely on the information drawn from the register of the neighborhood notary Giovanni Cartepecchi, which covers a decade (1287–1297) in the parish of San Giorgio alla Costa in the Oltrarno sesto, we find that about 70 percent of the individuals named as parties to peace came from the Contrada d'Oltrarno, and of those 38 percent came from the parish of San Giorgio itself. Moreover, fully 80 percent of the settled disputes began and ended in the Oltrarno ward. These figures suggest that the act of making a pax was a local affair, but one with wider implications for the commune's agenda of promoting civic peace. The outer peace of the community, as preachers rarely failed to mention, was built upon the inner peace of individuals, who could purge themselves of their crimes, recording them for posterity in peace instruments that rarely assigned blame to either party.

We have also seen the broad spectrum of crimes and misdemeanors—in granular particularity—peace instruments served to resolve. This spectrum ranged in gravity from tavern scuffles to armed assault, from theft to abduction, and from rape to homicide, but also included arson, giving false witness, breaking peace agreements, and other miscellaneous offenses. Ordinarily, peace agreements were used to resolve disputes that had ended in some form of violence. (If the dispute was of an economic nature, the remedy would have been found in a document called a *laudum*, the result of an arbitration.) Pacifications rarely stipulated financial damages to be paid as "their function was not to compensate the victim." To curtail further legal action, however, the courts did often demand as a condition of the settlement the restitution of any goods stolen.[131] It is also more than likely that financial compensation of the victims of crime is hidden from the historian's view because it was not part of the legal apparatus of making peace.

As for the social profile of the peacemakers, although we have seen that members of some of Florence's most important lineages—including the Bardi, Tornaquinci, Mannelli, and Donati—appear in peacemaking documents, they are a distinct minority. Out of well over a thousand names, I have found only twenty-two instances of Florence's most significant family names, a number that corresponds to their minority in the population of course, but also to their minority presence in the peace acts. Those who populate the documents as protagonists in quotidian peacemaking are for the most part ordinary folk, people who could not lay claim to the title of Lord.[132] Though our notaries

131. Trevor Dean, "Violence, Vendetta and Peacemaking," 10.

132. Although the title Domina is used to indicate a woman's marital status, Dominus, by contrast, is used to identify the social status of a lord.

were not required to list the professions of those using their services, on occasion they obliged, and from those scarce references we can discern that the clientele for peace contracts included paupers, laborers, and servants, hardly the grandees whom the chroniclers publicize as the peacemakers of Florence. Nor was age a limitation on making peace, as a family squabble in which Simona Bonazzini from San Miniato al Monte, who was "less than twelve but greater than eleven years old," attests. With her brother Andrea standing for her, she made peace with Francesca wife of Ceccho Bonazzini after an argument and a fistfight, which finally ended when Domina Francesca bit Simona's left hand so hard that it bled.[133]

As both women and men were parties to violence, so too were they both parties to peacemaking, even if women had to appear before the notary accompanied by a mundualdus who would assent to her peace. Following social and religious customs, they did not exchange the kiss with members of the opposite sex. Women were both the perpetrators and victims of assault, though not with the same frequency as men. In the peace agreements involving women, they are listed as the victims of crime in 37 percent of the cases and the perpetrators in only 9 percent of the instrumenta.[134] Rarely did they carry weapons—I have found only one case of a woman using a knife: Domina Francesca, whom we have met previously. If women were armed it was usually with rocks. As for perpetrating other crimes, though we find them at times as thieves, like Francesca, daughter of Tingho, who was denounced for petty theft in 1340, I have not found any cases of women committing homicide, though they certainly participated in aiding and abetting this crime, as we will see in the next chapter.[135]

Peace agreements—like other legal agreements—were not drawn up in any particular appointed setting. They were made wherever the notary had set up shop for the day. Most notaries record only that a contract was made in Florence: *Actum Florentiae* or in the contado. Sometimes, however, we find notaries moving around the city and countryside; then they will note that an agreement had been sealed in a church, at a specific person's home, or even at the Stinche, as we saw in the cases of Domina Francesca and Tommaso Donati. All this is to say that the statutes regulating peacemaking required no formal venue.

The law did, however, require a certain timeframe. As we have seen, the statute books stipulated that peace agreements had to be made within fifteen days from the time a crime was committed or a sentence handed down.[136] In a study of Cartepecchi's 1287–1297 register, I found that the majority of peace

---

133. Bartolo Amici, ASF, Not. Ant. 364, fol. 43v.

134. "No-fault" crimes account for the rest of the agreements (54 percent) for which women are parties to peace.

135. Andrea di Lapo, ASF, Not. Ant. 429, fol. 102v.

136. *Statuti*, vol. 2: Podestà, Bk 3: XLV, 188.

settlements were drawn up within seven days after a crime was committed, though in this chapter alone we have seen major exceptions to that rule, including a pax made thirty-six years after the incident in question.

It is also important to note that dispute resolution was generally a face-to-face affair. That it is, it was conceived as a bilateral pact in which the injured party consented to peace with his or her adversary. The two parties were imagined as the protagonists of the social drama; therefore, mediators and negotiators are never mentioned. And for good reason: they were not meant to be noticed. [137] In this scenario, the two quarreling parties were meant to "own" their pax: they were the protagonists to peace, restoring social equilibrium and concord to the community. Of course, not everyone was able to or wished to meet his assailant in this manner. Consequently, procurators served as legal delegates representing those who had appointed them. Many times they were representing those who had been banished, as we will see in the next chapter. In any event, procurators very likely served not only in their official capacity as legal representatives, but also as behind-the-scene mediators as well.

Finally, it should also be reiterated that day-to-day civic peacemaking, though not officially in the ecclesiastical purview, was nonetheless structured along the penitential religious lines we examined in chapter 1. The aim of peace agreements was, like that of sacramental confession, to wipe clean the slate, to recalibrate the relationship in question, and to create a new reality between contending parties, even after something as brutal as homicide had occurred. In the same way that confession—the central element of sacramental penance since 1215—allowed the contrite penitent to reconcile with the Lord, thereby reestablishing on a microcosmic level the equilibrium between God and humankind, the peace agreement was meant to serve a similar civic function between disputing parties. Now unburdened of the guilt of the crime committed, and blessed with a peaceful heart, a citizen could bind himself in the bonds of concord and contribute to the common good of the city, which as we have seen, was equated with peace. In the presence of a notary, the ritual kiss embodied reconciliation, a subject we will examine in depth in chapter 5. With interior peace established, civic concord and tranquility could then be restored in the parish.

In the event, the system of infra-judicial peacemaking institutionalized in the court system of Florence in the later thirteenth century, seems to have provided an efficient and familiarly comforting means of dispute resolution, one that well met the needs of a society saturated in penitential ideas.[138] In addition to that, it was on the whole a swift and cost-effective system. Finally, it had the capacity to settle disputes arising from the perennial challenge posed to medieval civic society by feud and vendetta, the subject of the next chapter.

137. I am grateful to Michael van Walt van Praag, conflict resolution specialist, for this observation.

138. Blanshei, foreword to Vallerani, *Medieval Public Justice*, ix.

CHAPTER FOUR

Feud, Vendetta, and the End of Exile

You will award life for life, eye for eye, tooth for tooth, hand for hand, foot for foot, burn for burn, wound for wound, stroke for stroke.

—EXODUS 21:23–25

You have heard how it was said: Eye for eye and tooth for tooth. But I say this to you: Offer no resistance to the wicked. On the contrary, if anyone hits you on the right check, offer him the other as well.

—MATTHEW 5:38–39

Just as contraries are cured by contraries by the physician, thus both in feud and vendetta and in other matters contraries are accustomed to be cured by contraries.

—ALBERTANUS DE BRESCIA, *LIBER CONSOLATIONIS ET CONCILII*[1]

DURING THE LENTEN season of 1424, Bernardino of Siena preached a sermon on forgiveness at the Franciscan church of Santa Croce in Florence. Celebrated for his colorful stories and exempla, which helped to animate the moral message that lay at the heart of all his preaching, Bernardino rose to this occasion. He captivated his audience with a riveting story about a young woman from Cremona who had forgiven the murderer of her father, but only after a miracle convinced her to do so. Having sworn that she would sooner die than forgive the killer, she was afflicted with a nosebleed so torrential that nothing could

1. *Albertani Brixiensis Liber Consolationis et Consilii, ex quo hausta est fabula gallica de Melibeo et Prudentia, quam, anglice redditam et 'The Tale of Melibe' inscriptam, Galfridus Chaucer inter 'Canterbury Tales' recepit*, ed. Thor Sundby (London: N. Trübner & Co., 1873), 7; hereafter *Liber consolationis*.

be done to staunch the bleeding and, with all other remedies exhausted, her relatives prevailed on her to go to church to pray for relief. Feeble from blood loss, and with family members propping her up on either side, she staggered into the sanctuary. And *mirabile dictu* the bleeding was staunched. Taking it as a sign from God, she hastened off to end her dispute with her sworn enemy.

Bernardino's stock of edifying stories was famously inexhaustible, and the *reportatio* of that sermon shows him hardly stopping for a breath before launching into another story, this one illustrating his theme of peace and reconciliation and featuring a local Florentine saint, Giovanni Gualberto (d. 1073). The preacher began as he usually did by recounting the episode of forgiveness that sparked the saint's conversion to the religious life. Always alive to audience response, and perhaps sensing some restlessness, Bernardino cut his tale short, acknowledging that his Florentine audience had probably already heard about that "stupendous miracle," which was so widely known that it hardly bore repeating in their presence, even if, he quickly justified, he had preached it many times in other places.[2]

Just what was that stupendous miracle? According to Atto of Vallombrosa, one of the saint's early hagiographers, it seems that during his youth one of Giovanni's near relatives was killed, an act that as a close kinsman he had an obligation to avenge. Events took an unforeseen turn sometime later when by chance the young man found himself in a narrow alleyway face to face with the killer. The assassin, seeing that Giovanni was fully armed, realized that he was cornered. With no way out, he dismounted his horse and prostrated himself on the ground in front of the impending saint. Hoping for mercy, he stretched his arms out so that his body took the form of a cross. Moved by the sight of the man splayed out on the ground before him, Giovanni interpreted this gesture as a sign from God. Accordingly, he immediately bade his adversary rise and fear no more. Giovanni then sent his erstwhile enemy on his way, while he himself took solace in the church of San Miniato to pray beneath a crucifix. There he was rewarded with a miracle: the Christ-figure on the cross inclined his head toward the supplicant as if to thank him for the great act of mercy he had just shown. [3] Later iterations of the vita embroidered the episode to include both the saint and his adversary beneath the cross, a scene especially beloved by Tuscan painters (fig. 11).

2. Bernardino da Siena, *Le prediche volgari*, ed. Ciro Cannarozzi, 5 vols. (Pistoia: Pacinotti, 1934), 2: Sermo 42: "Del perdonare," 2: 240–43.

3. Atto of Vallombrosa (aka Atto of Pistoia) in PL 146: 667–706, chap. 2: 672. One cannot help but wonder if this was the inspiration for the story Bernardino told in the same sermon examined in chapter 1, n. 91. According to recent research, the miraculous crucifix, translated in 1671 with great solemnity from San Miniato to the principal Vallombrosan church, Santissima Trinità in Florence, is datable no earlier than the thirteenth century. See Raffaello Volpini and Antonietta Cardinale, "Giovanni Gualberto, Iconography,'" *Bibliotheca Sanctorum* 6: 1029–32. For a description of the translation ceremony, see Emiliano Lucchesi, O.S.B., "Il crocifisso di S. Giovanni Gualberto e lo stendardo della Croce di S. Francesco di Sales," *Il faggio Vallombrosano* 10 (1937): 1–137, at 31–32.

FIGURE 11. *Giovanni Gualberto and the Assassin Pray beneath the Crucifix at San Miniato.* Attributed to Niccolò di Pietro Gerini, Florence, ca. 1410. Yale University Art Gallery, New Haven. Photo reproduced by permission of Yale University Art Gallery.

The episode was a powerful example of a revenge-killing averted—and one rooted in Florence—which Bernardino and doubtless many other preachers before him exploited to drive home their message of forgiveness and reconciliation in a city where vendetta, a traditional remedy of self-help, was legal, though highly regulated by Florentine statutory law.[4] Vendetta, it should be

4. A representative sample focusing on medieval Italy includes: Anna Maria Enriques, "La vendetta nella vita e nella legislazione fiorentina," *Archivio Storico Italiano* 19 (1933): 85–146, 181–223; Lauro Martines, *Violence and Civil Disorder in Italian Cities, 1200–1500* (Berkeley: University of California Press, 1972); Jacques Heers, *Parties and Political Life in the Medieval West*, trans. David Nicholas (Amsterdam: North Holland Publishing Co., 1977); Guido Ruggiero, *Violence in Early Renaissance Venice* (New Brunswick: Rutgers University Press, 1980); Andrea Zorzi, *Giustizia e società a Firenze in età comunale* (Naples: Edizioni Scientifiche Italiane, 1988); Osvaldo Raggio, *Faide e parentele: Lo stato genovese visto dalla Fontanabuona* (Turin: Einaudi, 1990); Daniel Waley, "A Blood-Feud with a Happy Ending: Siena 1285–1304," in *City and Countryside in Late Medieval and Renaissance Italy: Essays Presented to Philip Jones*, ed. Trevor Dean and Chris Wickham (London: Hambledon Press, 1990), 45–53; Edward Muir, *Mad Blood Stirring: Vendetta and Factions in Friuli during the Renaissance* (Baltimore: Johns Hopkins University Press, 1993); *Crime, Society and the Law in Renaissance Italy*, ed. Trevor Dean and K.J.P. Lowe (Cambridge: Cambridge University Press, 1994); Trevor Dean, "Marriage and Mutilation: Vendetta in Late Medieval Italy," *Past and Present* 157 (1997): 3–36; Christiane Klapisch-Zuber, "Les soupes de la vengeance: Les rites de l'alliance sociale," in *L'ogre historien. Autour de Jacques Le Goff*, ed. J. Revel and J.-C. Schmitt (Paris: Gallimard, 1998), 259–81; Trevor Dean, "Violence, Vendetta and Peacemaking in Late Medieval Bologna," in *Crime, Gender, and Sexuality in Criminal Prosecutions*, ed., Louis A. Knafla (Westport, CT: Greenwood Press, 2002): 1–17; Andrea Zorzi, "La cultura della vendetta nel conflitto politico in età comunale," in *Le storie e la memoria: In onore di Arnold Esch*, ed. Roberto

noted at the outset, was no mere atavistic vestige of Lombard society; it was, rather, as historians led by Andrea Zorzi have recently argued, an accepted form of dispute processing in which personal, social, or political tensions (in any combination) were acted out within a format structured by custom and tradition.[5] More specifically, it was a practice with tactical goals regulated by norms and law that provided Florentines with "a statutory right to redress grievances and seek revenge on their own."[6] Those engaged in infra-class discord, political factionalism between Guelfs and Ghibellines, or inter-class rivalries between magnates and popolo could undertake vendetta, which had its own internal logic and rules by which each side was expected to abide. Two of the most important norms—codified in law as of 1295—stipulated that

---

Delle Donne and Andrea Zorzi (Florence: Firenze University Press, 2002), 135–70, e-book Reading-1, http://fermi.univr.it/rm/ebook/festesch.html#Formati [consulted 6/21/2017]; Stefano Andres, "Oltre lo statuto: La vendetta nella letteratura toscana del Due-Trecento," *Laboratoire italien* 5 (2005): 57–83; online at: http://laboratoireitalien.revues.org/426 [consulted 6/21/2017]; Trevor Dean, *Crime and Justice in Late Medieval Italy* (Cambridge: Cambridge University Press, 2007), 123–32; and Thomas Kuehn, "Social and Legal Capital in Vendetta: A Fifteenth-Century Florentine Feud in and out of Court," in *Sociability and its Discontents: Civil Society, Social Capital, and Their Alternatives in Late Medieval and Early Modern Europe*, ed. Nicholas A. Eckstein and Nicholas Terpstra (Turnhout: Brepols, 2009), 51–72.

5. A. Zorzi, "La cultura della vendetta," 137. For almost two decades Andrea Zorzi has been enriching our understanding of feud and vendetta in the age of the commune. See particularly Zorzi, *"Ius erat in armis*: Faide e conflitti tra pratiche sociali e pratiche di governo," in *Origini dello stato: Processi di formazione statale in Italia fra medioevo ed età moderna*, ed. Giorgio Chittolini, Anthony Molho, and Pierangelo Schiera (Bologna: Il Mulino, 1994), 609–29; Zorzi, "Negoziazione penale, legittimazione giuridica e poteri urbani nell'Italia comunale," in *Criminalità e giustizia in Germania e in Italia: Pratiche giudiziarie e linguaggi giuridici tra tardomedioevo ed età moderna*, ed. M. Bellabarba, G. Schwerhoff, and A. Zorzi (Bologna: Il Mulino, 2001), 13–34; Zorzi, "La cultura della vendetta;" Zorzi, "Diritto e giustizia nelle città dell'Italia comunale (secoli XIII–XIV)," in *Stadt und Recht im Mittelalter/La ville et le droit au moyen âge*, ed. Pierre Monnet and Otto Gerhard Oexle (Göttingen: Vandenhoeck & Ruprecht, 2003), 197–214; Zorzi, "Pluralismo giudiziario e documentazione: Il caso di Firenze in età comunale," *Pratiques sociales et politiques judiciaires dans les villes de l'Occident à la fin du moyen âge*, ed. J. Chiffoleau, C. Gauvard, and A. Zorzi (Rome: École française de Rome, 2007), 125–87; Zorzi, "La legittimazione delle pratiche della vendetta nell'Italia comunale," in *Cultura, lenguaje y prácticas políticas en las sociedades medieval,"* ed. I. Alfonso, in *e-Spania: Revue électronique d'études hispaniques médiévales* 4 (2007), http://e-spania.revues.org/document2043. html [consulted 6/21/17]; Zorzi, "'Fracta est civitas magna in tres partes:' Conflitto e costituzione nell'Italia comunale," *Scienza e politica: Per una storia delle dottrine politiche* 39 (2008): 61–87, and most recently, Zorzi, "I conflitti nell'Italia comunale: Riflessioni sullo stato degli studi e sulle prospettive di ricerca," in *Conflitti, paci e vendetta nell'Italia comunale*, ed. A. Zorzi (Florence: Reti Medievali-Firenze University Press, 2009), 7–42 http://fermi.univr.it/rm/e-book/titoli/zorzi.htm [consulted 6/21/17].

6. Kuehn notes that it was not a legal practice in other central and northern communes, "Social and Legal Capital in Vendetta," 53.

death, facial disfiguring, or the infliction of a permanent handicap could be avenged by any male family member up to the fourth degree of consanguinity.[7] What this meant in practice was that serious blood crimes allowed sons, grandsons, great-great grandsons, first cousins, nephews, and great nephews to carry out vendetta on the principal perpetrator (or his male heirs) to restore parity between the parties. Vendetta against anyone who had made a legal peace agreement was forbidden.[8] As Zorzi makes clear, the logic of vendetta dictated that it should not exceed the initial offense and was expected to be proportionate to the original crime. It was a form of the *lex talionis*, the "eye for an eye" justice of the Hebrew Bible.[9] But it was also a way to level the playing field, so to speak. Reciprocity is one of the keys to understanding vendetta.[10] It was meant to resolve the dispute by reestablishing equilibrium between disputing parties. Problems arose when acts of reprisal continued, and sometimes escalated, after the initial vendetta had been carried out.

Following the lead of legal anthropologists of conflict resolution, historians now examine the "peace in the feud" as part of the structure of feuding, an integral stage of the disputing process, replete with its own choreography and script, which de-escalates conflict.[11] In this spirit, this chapter looks at the use of the pax from two standpoints: first as a legal and socially acceptable instrument to resolve feuds that had erupted into episodes of violence and vendetta, and second, as a tactic to forestall future acts of retaliation. Given that a number of our cases involve persons who had been judicially banned by the communal court, the chapter also includes a discussion of the peace agreement as a remedy for banishment and a tool for reintegration into the community. Finally, since our archival documents are laconic on so many issues bundled

7. *Statuti*, vol. 2: Podestà: Bk 3: XLV, 189–91: for vendetta *usque in quartum gradum*. Robert Bartlett makes the interesting point that "when the Church reduced the prohibited degrees [of consanguinity to four], so too enmity contracted," in "'Mortal Enmities': The Legal Aspect of Hostility in the Middle Ages," in *Feud, Violence and Practice: Essays in Medieval Studies in Honor of Stephen D. White*, ed. Belle S. Tuten and Tracey L. Billado (Burlington, VT: Ashgate, 2010), 197–212, at 208. The paper was originally given as the T. Jones Pierce Lecture, University of Wales (Aberystwyth, 1998).

8. *Statuti*, vol. 2: Podestà, Bk 3: XLV, 190.

9. Zorzi, "La cultura della vendetta," 168; and "'Ius erat in armis,'" 609–29.

10. Kuehn makes this point in "Social and Legal Capital in Vendetta," 52. See also, Anton Blok, *Honour and Violence* (Malden, MA: Blackwell, Press, 2001), 98–100.

11. Max Gluckman, "The Peace in the Feud," *Past and Present* 8.1 (1955): 1–14. For a useful historiographical discussion about the intersection of historical, legal, and anthropological work on violence and dispute processing, see Daniel Lord Smail, "Factions and Vengeance in Renaissance Italy: A Review Article," *Comparative Studies in Society and History* 38.4 (1996): 781–89. For some of the legal-anthropological studies on which this newer work is based, see among others, Sally Falk Moore, *Law as Process: An Anthropological Approach* (London: Routledge, 1978); Simon Roberts, *Order and Dispute: An Introduction to Legal Anthropology* (New York: Penguin, 1979); and *Disputes and Settlements: Law and Human Relations in the West*, ed. John Bossy (Cambridge: Cambridge University Press, 1983).

into the actual process of peacemaking, we conclude with an examination of Albertanus of Brescia's (ca. 1246) extraordinary anti-vendetta tract. In addition to providing clues as to how the practice of conflict resolution may have actually unfolded, the peace made between Albertanus's protagonist Melibeus and his adversaries was, as we shall see, steeped in the penitential culture in which the author himself was an active participant. Dedicated to his son, the *Liber consolationis et concilii* advocated substituting penance, reconciliation, and peace for vendetta. It seems that Albertanus was actively imagining a future for his son in which penance and forgiveness would supplant violence and vendetta as the means of resolving disputes.

Vendetta, as is well known, was so much a part of the social landscape of medieval Tuscany that for contemporary historians it has become almost a defining attribute of medieval Florentine identity.[12] Florentine historians of the period—everyone from Giovanni Villani to Leonardo Bruni—also recognized its centrality in the city's history by crediting the origins of the Guelf and Ghibelline parties in Florence to an act of vendetta that had become the stuff of legend.[13] Though the precise details differ from chronicle to chronicle, the outline of the story remains the same. Villani's version, memorialized in his *Nuova Cronica*, described that seminal event of 1215 as the result of the nobleman Buondelmonte dei Buondelmonti's having given offense to the honor of the Amidei lineage by breaking off his engagement to one of their daughters. To rub salt into the open wound, he had then betrothed himself to one of the Donati daughters, deeming her to be more attractive as a prospective bride. With shame brought down upon their house, the Amidei plotted revenge with the collusion of the Uberti, Fifanti, and Gangalandi families. The die was cast when Mosca dei Lamberti, a powerful ally of the Uberti, uttered the proverbial words: *cosa fatta capo ha*, loosely translated "what's done is done." It signified not only that Buondelmonte had signed his own death warrant, but more to the point that the social logic of the feud demanded vendetta, a fact that everyone including the culprit knew. Thus on his wedding day, which happened to fall on Easter Sunday, as Buondelmonte, resplendent astride a white palfrey, was crossing the Ponte Vecchio from the Oltrarno, a gang of conspirators led by Schiatta degli Uberti set upon him.

---

12. Kuehn argues that vendetta could contribute to "individual identity and lineage prestige" in "Social and Legal Capital in Vendetta," 54.

13. Villani, *Nuova Cronica*, vol. 1: Bk 6, chap. 38: 267. But see also Leonardo Bruni, *History of the Florentine People*, 3 vols., trans. James Hankins (Cambridge, MA: Harvard University Press, 2001), vol. 1: Bk 2: 217–21. The source of the account is Pseudo-Brunetto Latini, *Cronica fiorentina*, in *Testi fiorentini del Dugento dei primi del Trecento*, ed. Alfredo Schiaffini (Florence: Sansoni, 1954), 117–20. Enrico Faini has examined the various versions in "Il convito del 1216: La vendetta all'origine del fazionalismo fiorentino," *Annali di storia di Firenze* 1 (2006): 9–36.

Unhorsed beneath the statue of Mars at the foot of the bridge (and in front of the Amidei tower), glinting assassins' blades cut him down with a mortal blow delivered directly to his gullet (figs. 9 and 12). The ensuing tumult brought all of Florence into the streets, whereupon the city immediately divided into factions: those who supported the Buondelmonti and those who backed the Amidei. And this, says Villani, was "the cause and the origin of the cursed Guelf and Ghibelline parties in Florence."[14] By the fourteenth century what seems to have been a case of personal enmity avenged was understood to signify something much larger: the beginning of political factionalism in Florence.

The political implications of vendetta are also in evidence in the *Cronica* of Donato Velluti (d. 1370), who, like Villani, served Florence in the capacity of prior, but also as a standard-bearer of justice and an ambassador.[15] Begun in 1367, the first part of his text is a *ricordanza*—a family memoir—that traces his family's roots and deeds. One of those deeds consisted of a family member's involvement in a feud that began a century earlier in 1267, the year that the Guelfs took back control of Florence after their humiliating defeat at Montaperti.[16] The episode shows how a volatile combination of personal rancor, political factionalism, and inter-class rivalries coalesced to create a tinderbox set for explosion. The Velluti and the Mannelli were Florentine elites, but politics and class status divided them. The Ghibelline Mannelli were an old family of magnate status, while the Guelf Velluti were of the popolo grasso, the rich merchant elite that held political power in the city. They lived cheek by jowl—probably no more than two hundred meters apart at the head of the Ponte Vecchio in the Oltrarno ward of the city. As Christiane Klapisch-Zuber observes, they could scarcely have avoided seeing each other on a daily basis.[17] But, as noted in the previous chapter, physical proximity regularly bred acrimony.

Ostensibly, this dispute ignited because Ghino Velluti had had a hand in convincing the Guelf government to cancel the judicial ban on Fornaino Rossi, a magnate and enemy of the Mannelli lineage, causing outrage among them.[18]

14. *Nuova Cronica*, vol. 1: Bk 6, chap. 38: 268. Dante memorializes the phrase in *Inferno*, Canto 28, 96–102.

15. *La cronica domestica di Messer Donato Velluti*, ed. Isidoro del Lungo and Guglielmo Volpi (Florence: Sansoni, 1914). A portion of the chronicle is translated by Gene Brucker in *The Society of Renaissance Florence: A Documentary Study* (New York: Harper Torchbooks, 1971), 106–10.

16. The classic article on the subject is Isidoro del Lungo, "Una vendetta in Firenze il giorno di San Giovanni del 1295," *Istituto storico italiano*, series 4, 18 (1886): 355–409. See also, Charles de La Roncière, "Une famille florentine au XIVe siècle: les Velluti, " in *Famille et parenté dans L'Occident médiéval*, ed. Georges Duby and Jacques Le Goff (Rome: École française de Rome, 1977), 227–48; and Christiane Klapisch-Zuber, "Les soupes de la vengeance: les rite de l'alliance sociale," in *L'ogre historien: Autour de Jacques Le Goff*, ed. Jacques Revel and Jean-Claude Schmitt (Paris: Gallimard, 1999), 259–81.

17. Klapisch-Zuber, "Les soupes de la vengeance," 266.

18. Velluti does not name him, but del Lungo has deduced his identity from other sources, "Una vendetta," 365.

FIGURE 12. *Vendetta against Buondelmonte dei Buondelmonti.* Schiatta degli Uberti
delivers the mortal blow to Buondelmonte dei Buondelmonti at the foot of the
Ponte Vecchio under the statue of Mars. Manuscript miniature attributed to Pacino
di Bonaguida in Giovanni Villani, *Nuova Cronica*, ca. 1340–1348. MS BAV Chigi L
VIII 296, fol. 70r. Biblioteca Apostolica Vaticana, Vatican City. Photo reproduced by
permission of the Biblioteca Apostolica Vaticana. © 2018 Biblioteca Apostolica Vaticana

They were outraged at the temerity of the Guelf government for cancelling the
ban on one of their adversaries; they were outraged at the impertinence of the
upstart Velluti lineage for interfering in their affairs; and they were outraged
at the offense done to their family honor. In a defiant act of revenge against all
those who had dishonored them, they retaliated by murdering Ghino, thereby
creating formal enmity between the two houses. The choreographed assassination served as the opening salvo in the establishment of feud, "a physical
and memorable moment constituting a new status" between parties.[19] Con-
curring with John Najemy, let us note that this case also shows that "the pursuit of vendetta was a politically motivated rejection of the popolo's emerging
norms of the supremacy of law and the internalized discipline of the good
citizen."[20]

Though they had every legal right, the Velluti did not retaliate immediately; only in 1295, on the feast-day of John the Baptist, did they make their

19. Bartlett, "'Mortal Enmities,'" 202.
20. John M. Najemy, *A History of Florence* (Malden, MA: Blackwell, 2006), 17.

move on Lippo di Simone dei Mannelli (the nephew of Ghino's killer), who was riding out to compete in the palio, the signature event in the day's festivities honoring the city's patron saint. The statue of Mars at the foot of the Ponte Vecchio once again provided an appropriate public stage for vendetta when three of the Velluti clan, including the chronicler's father, Lamberto, ambushed and mortally wounded Lippo.

One can imagine that it was a vendetta such as this one that inspired Giordano of Pisa's condemnation of retaliatory violence when, in April of 1305, he preached at Santa Maria Novella:

> How many sins does he have, he who has been stewing for ten years and more in the hatred of his enemy; he who has thought of nothing else, day or night, except how to kill him? And he has been living in this hatred for all this time! How much guilt has he! How much punishment this villain deserves! His whole life is a sin![21]

In the case of the Velluti and Mannelli, the parties were brought together a short time after Lippo's murder to make peace. The Mannelli, however, came only grudgingly, under duress, and through a procurator, the notary Ser Viviano Aldobrandini. According to Donato, they submitted reluctantly because they were compelled to do so. But their rancor and hostility remained well alive, a troubling fact that did not fail to reach the ears of Guelf communal officials, who antagonized the Mannelli even further by passing a special measure, on July 17, 1295, that forced them to make yet another peace—in person—with the Velluti. On that same day, before representatives of the guild government, the two parties came together in the church of San Piero Scheraggio, exchanged the kiss of peace, and promised to uphold the peace on behalf of themselves and their male relatives.[22] In addition, both families provided *fideiussores* (guarantors) who pledged a substantial sum of money subject to forfeiture to the commune should either party violate the peace.

As we know from the preachers, these were not conditions under which a true peace could be made. Nor was this the first time that we have seen a peace imposed from above. It will be remembered that Cardinal Latino's peace of 1280 compelled members of the feuding Guelf and Ghibelline factions to reconcile. It also established the office of the Conservatore della Pace, which was empowered to enforce pacifications, a tactic that the popular government employed on occasion to curb violence when other means

21. Also known as Giordano da Rivalto: *Prediche del beato fr. Giordano da Rivalto dell'Ordine dei Predicatori*, ed. Domenico Maria Manni (Florence: Viviani, 1739), Sermon XXXVI, 280–81.

22. See the *provvisione* of 17 July 1295, published as appendix D in del Lungo "Una vendetta in Firenze," 398–99; participants: ibid., 400–409; kiss: ibid., 405.

failed.[23] Later, one of the primary purposes of the Ordinances of Justice was to restrict magnate violence—real and imagined—against the popolo. And though the vendetta carried out by the Velluti should have concluded matters between the two lineages, clearly the guild government of 1295 feared that the Mannelli, who were still seething over the murder of Lippo, would retaliate for his death. Therefore, a peace was forced upon them, even if the circumstances of it did not augur well.

Though peace contracts often pacified a volatile situation, they did not necessarily induce the desired concord. What they could do was establish a cooling-off period that laid the groundwork for concord to emerge, eventually, between the feuding parties. This is what happened between the Velluti and the Mannelli. It took more than half a century, but in 1349 Donato used his political influence to cancel the magnate status of Bertone Mannelli, and the two families then "became as close as brothers."[24] Concord came only when the families became fictive equals, even at the cost of at least one Mannelli family member sliding down a rung in the social hierarchy in order to have the magnate proscriptions lifted.[25] It is worth noting that the Velluti-Mannelli vendetta, a case of inter-class disputing, shows that the practice of vendetta was by no means restricted to the magnates, as is so often believed.

Another episode, this one again involving the Velluti, shows how vendetta was practiced between members of the popolo. Like Dante's encounter in hell with Geri del Bello in the *Divine Comedy*, it also shows how the obligation of vendetta could be bequeathed from one generation to the next.[26] In 1310 Velluto Velluti (a cousin of Donato's grandfather), in the company of another family member, Lorenzo di Dietaiuto Velluti, got mixed up in a conflict that resulted in twin homicides. It seems that Lorenzo had helped out a friend who was engaged in a dispute with Giovanni Berignalli, a cloth merchant. Giovanni lost the argument and was nursing a grudge when he encountered Lorenzo and his kinsman Velluto near the church of Santo Spirito in the Oltrarno. A scuffle ensued and Giovanni knifed Velluto in the side. His wounds appeared to be life threatening, so he was carried to his house, where he was persuaded to make a last will and testament. He did so and

23. Cardinal Latino's peacemaking tactics were preserved in subsequent statute law. See *Statuti*, vol. 2: Podestà: Bk 3: CXIII, 243–44.

24. *La cronica domestica di Messer Donato Velluti*, 66. Presumably Bertone became a *popolano* in order to have a voice in government and further his business interests.

25. Klapisch-Zuber, "Les soupes de la vengeance," 278–79.

26. It was not uncommon for the memory of injury committed to be more long-lived than the victim himself, so the obligation of vendetta was often transmitted to subsequent generations. In the *Inferno*, for example, Dante suffers a momentary pang of conscience when he hears that his ancestor Geri del Bello has fled his presence in a fit of high dudgeon because none of their common kinsmen had ever avenged his violent death with a revenge-killing. Canto 29: 18–36.

died shortly thereafter. A provision of that will stipulated that 500 florins should go to anyone who would avenge his death. And though Lamberto Velluti (Donato's father) warned his three sons against it, one of them, Piccio, eventually took up his kinsman's cause, enlisting his friend Giunta, a baker, to assist him. Twenty-three years later, "in 1333 or 1334," they encountered Niccolò Berignalli on the street, whereupon Giunta slit his throat, an act for which the family finally made peace ten years later during the lordship of the Duke of Athens.[27]

If we ask why peace contracts were needed in medieval Florence, vendetta is surely part of the multifaceted answer: peace agreements were an integral stage—often the symbolic culmination—of the disputing process. They could be forced on rebellious magnates at war with each other or on elites engaged in violence against the popular regimes. But they could also be a self-help remedy for anyone caught in a vicious cycle of feuding and vendetta and in need of an honorable and effective way out. As noted in chapter 3, at least 50 percent of peace instruments in medieval Florence record the settling of disputes by parties acting of their own volition. That is, the peace contracts make no mention of denunciation, accusation, or inquisitio; nor are third parties such as cappellani, rectors, judges, or procurators mentioned in them. They are written as bilateral pacts that recalibrate the relationship between parties, restoring social equilibrium without the loss of honor. If reconciliation was to be modeled on the prototype of Jesus's forgiveness of humankind, then peacemaking had to be an act of charity, not of weakness.

THE NOTARIAL EVIDENCE

After the crime of assault, feud and vendetta were the primary reasons for which peace agreements were made.[28] Anthropologists and historians have struggled to distinguish vendetta from feud, attempting to define those words precisely. Robert Bartlett usefully reminds us that "enmity was an institution . . . that is, it was a generally recognized relationship hedged by ritual, expectation and sanction."[29] I follow Trevor Dean in using the term feud (*faida*) to mean "continuous animosity" or conflict between parties. *Faida*, however, is a word that rarely shows up in the documents. In Tuscany, as in Lombardy, very early on the word *guerra*, or less frequently *briga*, was used to indicate a feud.[30]

27. *La cronica domestica di Messer Donato Velluti*, 72–74.
28. I have found thirty-four agreements that point to feud and vendetta, a number that represents 7 percent of the entire sample.
29. "'Mortal Enmities,'" 198.
30. Piero Brancoli Busdraghi, "Aspetti giuridici della faida in Italia nell'età precommunale," in *La Vengeance, 400–1200*, ed. Dominique Barthélemy, François Bougard and Régine Le Jan (Rome: École Française de Rome, 2006), 159–73, at 160.

Vendetta, on the other hand, refers to the obligation of kinsmen to retaliate for an injury done to a family member. As Dean has pointed out, vendetta "is an event or a response to an event, not a state of continuous animosity."[31] Zorzi's definition is even more precise. Vendetta, he argues, "is the moment of retaliation which re-establishes equilibrium" between parties and is the resolution of the dispute.[32]

Like the word faida, the term vendetta (*vindicta*) certainly existed—in fact, it is very much in evidence in Florentine statutory law, but it was rarely used in legal cases or notarial documents. Dean has argued that notaries used such words as *odium*, *guerra*, and *inimicitia* to signal ongoing enmity.[33] My work supports his conclusion: in no case have I found the word vindicta or faida used in peace contracts. What I have found in notarial pacifications are many examples of odium and inimicitia, along with one case of outright guerra.[34]

Even if the terms are not used, notarial formulae tend to signal when a case of feud or vendetta is at hand. That is, apart from the use of mundualdi and procurators, individuals, even if acting as part of a group making peace, ordinarily acted on their own behalf.[35] But in cases that appear to arise from vendetta or feuding, the parties do so on behalf of many others, besides themselves. For example, in a 1301 case from the protocols of the notary Giovanni di Buto, Guccio Baglioni and his brothers promised to keep peace with Duccio, son of Ser Gianni da Mucciano, on their own behalf and in the name of their "heirs, bloodkin, nephews, cousins, accomplices, followers, descendants, and relatives from both sides."[36] Similarly, in a 1343 case involving Franceschino

31. Dean, "Marriage and Mutilation," 15. In addition to the literature cited in the notes at the beginning of this chapter, see also the essays in *Vengeance in the Middle Ages: Emotion, Religion and Feud*, ed. Susanna A. Throop and Paul R. Hyams (Burlington, VT: Ashgate, 2009).

32. Zorzi, "La cultura," 147.

33. Dean, "Marriage and Mutilation," 15–16. For feud and vendetta in very different contexts, see Bartlett, "'Mortal Enmities,'" 200 and Daniel Lord Smail, "Hatred as a Social Institution in Late-Medieval Society," *Speculum* 76.1 (2001): 90–126, developed further in his *The Consumption of Justice: Emotions, Publicity, and Legal Culture in Marseille, 1264–1423* (Ithaca, NY: Cornell University Press, 2003).

34. Consequently, because the documents themselves do not distinguish between feud and vendetta, in what follows I have ordinarily chosen to pair the two together.

35. For *mundualdi*, see Thomas Kuehn, "*Cum consensu mundualdi*: Legal Guardianship of Women in Quattrocento Florence," *Viator* 13 (1982): 309–31, repr. in *Law, Family and Women: Toward a Legal Anthropology of Renaissance Italy* (Chicago: University of Chicago Press, 1991), 212–37.

36. Giovanni di Buto, ASF, Not. Ant. 9493, fol. 87r: "ipsorum et illorum heredibus, consanguineis, nepotibus, consobrinis, amicis, conplicibus, sequacibus, descendentibus et ascendentibus ex utraque linea." The penalty for breaking this agreement was 500 f.p., for which *fideiussores* were brought forward to swear to pay the penalty should the peace be broken.

di Tommaso dei Bardi and the Ugolini lineage, Franceschino and the others promised to maintain the peace on behalf of themselves for crimes and offenses that included injuries, aggressions, assault, and ill will. But heading the list were the evil twins, a sure tip-off to vendetta and feud: *hodium* and *homicidium*.[37] The pax committed the sons, heirs, descendants and consorteria, bloodkin and cousins of the Bardi and Ugolini to abide by the terms of the agreement to put an end to what clearly had turned into a brutal cycle of feuding and vendetta. The specificity of this wording was intentional: its goal was to identify all those who might be heirs to vendetta as it passed like a disease through the agnatic line. Since, as we have seen, Florentine statute law allowed vendetta up to the fourth degree of consanguinity, the listing of bloodkin and other sundry relationships attempted to be comprehensive so that no one might claim exemption from the agreement in order to exact a revenge killing.[38]

This was most certainly the situation described in a case, analyzed in chapter 3, from the register of Benintendi di Guittone in the year 1326. It will be recalled that in October a peace was made between Cinello Bonsengnori and his four sons, all from the parish of Santo Stefano a Campoli, and Vanni Corbiçci and his son, Monte. Vanni was making peace on behalf of his son Guilelmo, who had killed his wife in a case of domestic violence. It began when Guilelmo struck and wounded his wife Bene, daughter of Cinello. This domestic altercation turned into family tragedy when Bene subsequently died from her wounds. In the event, it was the fathers and brothers of Bene and Guilelmo who agreed to make peace. They came together *in pura et libera et spontanea voluntate* to exchange the kiss of peace on the mouth. A financial penalty of 500 f.p. threatened each of the parties should the peace be violated. It is telling that the notary's formula stipulated that both sides were also making peace on behalf of their *amicis, consanguinis, affinibus, consortibus et sequacibus*, evidence that vendetta was likely and that the contract meant to put an end to any thought of retaliation that Bene's family might have been nursing.[39]

Of the thirty-four cases in which peace was made to end or forestall vendetta and feud, a homicide had occurred in almost 30 percent of them,

37. Bartolo Amici, ASF, Not. Ant. 365, fol. 23r.

38. *Statuti*, vol. 2: Podestà: Bk 3: XLV, 190–93. When remembering in his *ricordanza* a peace that he had made with Pandolfo Ricasoli in 1422, Buonaccorso Pitti notes that both parties had done so in the name of their brothers, sons, grandsons. He recorded it in his diary so that those male relatives would abide by his wishes to observe it. *Two Memoirs of Renaissance Florence: the Diaries of Buonaccorso Pitti and Gregorio Dati*, trans. Julia Martines, ed. Gene Brucker (New York: Harper Torchbooks, 1967), 106.

39. Benintendi di Guittone, ASF, Not. Ant. 2358, fol. 104r-v. Santo Stefano a Campoli was a pieve in the commune of San Casciano in Val di Pesa, about 15 km south of Florence.

though (just as in the assault cases) we rarely learn the motive.[40] Most of our cases involve bands of brothers and cousins, some of them young men.[41] In a case where a father had been killed and his son was making peace with the killers, Monaldo (the son), who did not know his precise age but knew at least that he was older than fourteen and younger than twenty, had to swear on the gospel that he would observe all the provisions of the peace agreement and furthermore that he would not break it on account of his age.[42] The contract also named his future children and descendants as parties to peace in perpetuity.[43] The peace contract for feud and vendetta thus attempted to stipulate in detail all the family, relations, and followers who were obliged to uphold the peace. This had the effect of rounding up the usual male suspects and making them liable should the peace be broken. If nothing else, the peace contract was a prophylactic against the piling up of more corpses.

This surely is what an agreement drawn up by Giovanni Cartepecchi was meant to do. The contract aimed to pacify the warring factions from the *castelli* of Monte di Croce and Cuona, both at Pontassieve about fifteen kilometers east of Florence. They came together to make an "irrevocable pact" to put an end to the standard list of crimes frequently found in the *clausulae* of peace contracts. Tellingly, however, at the head of the list and again at its conclusion were two crimes, not the stuff of quotidian peace contracts, for which settlement was offered: feuds (*guerris*) and devastation caused by arson (*vastis per incendium*). On April 8, 1296, the two parties, led by Tingho, the emancipated son of Manetto of the commune of Monte di Croce, and Spaduccia of Cuona came together to assent to a peace that put an end to the escalating enmity, warfare, and devastation to property in which the feuding parties had recently been engaged.[44] The financial penalty was high: *fideiussores* guaranteed a payment of 1000 f.p., in the event that the peace was violated. The compact carefully spelled out that peace had been contracted not only for the signatories but also for *suis heredibus et descendentibus*, an indicator, as we have seen, that the document was concerned not just with the present feud but with quashing ideas of future vendetta. Finally, it should be noted that the parties had not been denounced by the rector of the territory, nor had a judge begun an inquest ex officio, no accusations or *denuncie* had been made: the Monte di

40. Of the total cases that I have identified as feud/vendetta, 70 percent use the telltale language of vendetta.

41. See for example, Arrigho di Benintendi, ASF Not. Ant. 950, fols. 161v-162r.

42. Matteo di Biliotto, ASF, Not. Ant. 13364, fol. 96r.

43. Ibid., fol. 95v: "pro se suisque futuris filiis et descendentibus in perpetum ex una parte."

44. Giovanni Cartepecchi, ASF, Not. Ant. 4111, fols. 174v-75r.

Croce-Cuona contract seems to have been a case of self-help, in which the parties themselves decided to forestall feuding and vendetta by employing the notarial services of Giovanni Cartepecchi. The disputing parties, perhaps wearied of the endless cycle of violence, had themselves initiated the process of dispute resolution.[45]

Such also seems to have been the case in 1344 when the communes of Santa Maria di Loro (now Loro Ciuffenna) drew up a peace contract with its neighbors, San Pietro a Gropina and Il Borro.[46] The towns were making peace for a long list of mutual injuries, headed by *odiis* (feuding), but including "killings, the taking of prisoners, horseback raids, arson, fires, vast damages, and plundering."[47] It is worth noting that a commune could also use the peace instrument to resolve a dispute with individuals, as happened in the summer of 1287 when the city of Volterra made peace with the nobleman Pepe of Sassoforte and his four sons. At the fort of Prata (near Massa Marittima) Lord Rodolfino of Catenaia, podestà of Volterra, along with his notary Matteo da Volterra, who were both acting on behalf of the interests of the commune, made peace with Foresino and Lungarello who represented themselves, their father Pepe, and their two other brothers. Among the many crimes and offenses for which the brothers and their heirs were making peace were *iniuriis, danpnis [sic], incendiis, arsuris et guastis, calvacatis et offensionibus realibus et personalibus et homicidiis et feritis* committed against the commune of Volterra and its district. Under a financial sanction of 500 silver marks, they also promised not to harbor or give aid or counsel to anyone who had been banned by the commune. They agreed to everything for themselves and their heirs and swore to uphold the agreement with their hands on the gospel.[48]

Although they are uncommon, these three contracts demonstrate the flexibility of the peace agreement. It could be used by individuals or factions, but so too could a polity such as a commune adopt this public instrument to pacify its enemies when necessary.

45. It is also possible that this may have been a peace imposed from above, perhaps by the priors of the commune of Florence, for which we do not have the documentation, but there is no evidence of that in the contract itself.

46. Florence took control of these towns in 1293. They are now part of the province of Arezzo.

47. Landino di Fortino, ASF, Not. Ant. 11383, fols. 2v-3r: "occisionibus, captoribus hominum, cavalcatis, combustionibus, incendiis, dampnis vastis, rapinis." The penalty for breaking the peace was steep, set at 2000 f.p.

48. As this was a vow, presumably no kiss was needed: "et insuper ad sancta Dei evangelia corpolariter [sic] tactis, predicti Foresinus et Lungarellus iuraverunt" 213. The case is from *Collectio chartarum pacis privatae medii aevii ad regionem Tusciae pertinentium,* ed. Gino Masi (Milan: Vita e Pensiero, 1943), 210–14, who also notes that on the dorso of this original parchment, a note in eighteenth-century hand says: "Carta pacis reddite comuni Vulterrarum a nobilibus de Prata et Sassoforte."

THE BAN AND REINTEGRATION

In these pages, we have already met many perpetrators of crimes—including the shoe-thumping Giuntino—who paid no heed to the charges or penalties awaiting them in court.[49] Instead, they took to their heels and fled to the safety of another jurisdiction or perhaps even went into hiding. But like time and tide, the judiciary waited for no man. If a summons to appear in court was disregarded, banishment for contumacy would inevitably follow.[50] It has been observed that contumacy rates were extraordinarily high in medieval Florence.[51]

Indeed, one historian has found that by the mid-fourteenth century more than half of those cited by a criminal judge chose to flee rather than make an appearance in court.[52] Historians have long interpreted the rates of sentencing for contumacy as a weakness in the judicial and political system. It has been argued that the courts did not have enough political power to enforce their sentences, so with predictable regularity, contumacy charges were decreed and Florentine citizens routinely banished. In accordance with recent scholarship on the subject, I would like to suggest an alternative reading of the evidence. It is likely that many Florentines were using the charge of contumacy to their advantage, opting for it as a lesser evil in a form of cost-risk analysis. That is, the ban for contumacy may have been a strategy for avoiding heavier sentencing and stiffer financial penalties. Moreover, seeing contumacy through this lens has the advantage of showing disputants not as pawns of the judicial system, but as actors making rational choices about how best to

49. See chapter 3.

50. For the ban in Florence, see Anthony M. C. Mooney, "The Legal Ban in Florentine Statutory Law and the *de Bannitis* of Nello da San Gemignano" PhD diss., U.C.L.A., 1976. The ban, exile, and confinement in Florence are discussed in Fabrizio Ricciardelli, *The Politics of Exclusion in Early Renaissance Florence* (Turnhout: Brepols, 2007). More generally, see Desiderio Cavalca, *Il bando nella prassi e nella dottrina giuridica medievale* (Milan: Giuffrè, 1978). For local studies, see Peter R. Pazzaglini, *The Criminal Ban of the Sienese Commune, 1225–1310* (Milan: Giuffrè, 1979); and Giuliano Milani, *L'esclusione dal comune. Conflitti e bandi politici a Bologna e in altre città italiane tra XII e XIV secolo* (Rome: Instituto storico italiano per il medio evo, 2003). For a comparative dimension on the subject, see Jason P. Coy, *Strangers and Misfits: Banishment, Social Control, and Authority in Early Modern Germany* (Leiden: Brill, 2008); and most recently, Joanna Carraway, "Contumacy, Defense Strategy, and Criminal Law in Late Medieval Italy," *Law and History Review* 29.1 (2011): 98–132.

51. Mooney, *"The Legal Ban,"* 173.

52. Laura Ikins Stern, *The Criminal Law System of Medieval and Renaissance Florence* (Baltimore: Johns Hopkins University Press, 1994), 229, 210. From 1352 to 1355 she notes a rate of 58.3 percent, and 55.6 percent from 1380 to 1383. In the first quarter of the fifteenth century (1425 to 1428), she notes a rate of 42 percent, a reduction that she attributes to a more effective criminal justice system and better policing. For the rates in late fourteenth-century Reggio Emilia (48 percent) and Bologna (52 percent in 1372 and 44 percent in 1393), see Carraway, "Contumacy," 101.

pursue resolution of their conflicts.[53] This vantage point helps to reveal yet again the relationship between peace agreements and institutions of public justice, such as the courts. The two were inextricably linked and not, as is commonly assumed, working in opposition to each other. Disputants could use peace instruments to their advantage every bit as much as they could use the courtrooms and trials, which many times served only as a stage in the processing of a dispute.[54] The ban and its cancellation through a peace accord was one such way that disputants could use the formal mechanisms of the judicial system to their own benefit.[55] Let us now take a closer look at the procedure for banishment.

Banishment entailed certain stages. First a court order was issued; a period for response was fixed; delay, disobedience, or contempt of the order (*contumacia*) followed; whereupon the court imposed a penalty.[56] The full procedure for criminal offenses ran as follows. Once charges had been made, the court summoned the accused to answer those charges. The summons was entrusted to one of six *bannitori* or town criers, civic officials who held the job for a year, knew how to read and write, and wore (at their own expense) a distinctive uniform. Each sesto had its own bannitore who rode out to the contado on his horse to break the news and make announcements. He was also equipped with a small silver trumpet that he sounded three times to attract a crowd to whom he would read out the summons.[57] A written citation was then affixed to the door of the accused. If the imputed was not a resident of Florence or its territories, the citation was sent to the city where he lived. Before being posted on the public notice board of the podestà's palace, it was also read out in the major piazze of the city; including San Giovanni, Orsanmichele, the Mercato Vecchio, and the Mercato Nuovo. If ignored, another announcement or ban was issued requiring the accused to appear within three days. When an additional fifteen days had passed and the accused still had failed to appear, the court would declare him to be a confessed criminal and therefore guilty

53. Carraway, ibid., 102.

54. Andrea Zorzi, "Conflits et pratiques infrajudiciaires dans le formations politiques italiennes du XIIe au XVe siècle," in *L'infrajudiciaire du Moyen Age a l'epoque contemporaine: Actes du Colloque de Dijon 5–6 Octobre 1995* (Dijon: Publications de l'Université de Bourgogne, 1996), 19–36, at 20. See also Smail, *The Consumption of Justice*.

55. Mario Sbriccoli, "Legislation, Justice and Political Power in Italian Cities, 1200–1400," in *Legislation and Justice*, ed. Antonio Padoa Schioppa (Oxford: Clarendon Press, 1997), 37–55, at 43 and Sbriccoli, "Giustizia negoziata, giustizia egemonica: riflessioni su una nuova fase degli studi di storia della giustizia criminale," in *Criminalità e giustizia in Germania e in Italia: pratiche giudiziarie e linguaggi giuridici tra tardo medioevo ed età moderna*, ed. Marco Bellabarba, Gerd Schwerhoff, and Andrea Zorzi (Bologna: Il Mulino, 2001), 345–64.

56. Mooney, "*The Legal Ban*," 22.

57. For a description of the *bannitori*, see Timothy J. McGee, *The Ceremonial Musicians of Late Medieval Florence* (Bloomington, IN: Indiana University Press, 2009), 53–55. See also *Statuti*, vol. 2: Podestà, Bk 1: XI, 37–39.

of the crime: *confessus propter contumaciam ergo convictus.* A penalty was then imposed, which was ordinarily equal to the one for which he would have been liable had he been found guilty of the crime. Now the *contumax* became a *bannitus* and was regarded as a convicted criminal.[58]

The legal state of bannitus was a judicially imposed liminal state; a condition that entailed the loss of civil, legal, and judicial rights. Those who had been banished forfeited their means of making a living and their rights as citizens, including public protection. They also lost the right to hold public office and plead in court. Registered in the commune's *Liber bannitorum*, those condemned to banishment could be assaulted with impunity by anyone, even killed.[59] Statute law further tightened the screws on the judicial outlaw by placing a bounty on his head. In a 1342 case from the parish of San Simone, a reward of 125 f.p. was offered to anyone who captured either of two assailants banned for contumacy, who stood accused of attacking a communal official.[60] But depending on his status and the type of crime he had committed, the reward for the capture of a bannitus could be as high as 500 f.p.[61] Those found harboring banniti were themselves subject to fines ranging from 100 to 1000 f.p.[62] Deprived of their homes, their livelihoods, and often their families, to say nothing of their legal rights, it is no surprise that many people wished to have their bans commuted. The peace instrument provided the legal means to do so. The presentation of a notarized peace agreement, along with payment of the assigned monetary fine, normally cancelled the ban for all but a few crimes.[63]

Reviewing all the settlements studied, I have found a total of seventy-six agreements (14 percent) in which a ban had been imposed on the offending party and the peace instrument was the remedy used to cancel it. But that figure is deceptive: when two-party, hand-to-hand brawls are eliminated from the calculation—cases that would have been remitted immediately to a notary for settlement—the percentage of reconciliations involving a judicial ban rises to 25 percent.[64] Thus a quarter of our remaining sample involves the use of

58. For procedure, see Mooney, *"The Legal Ban,"* 64–66.

59. Ibid., 114–20.

60. Emanuela Porta Casucci, "Le paci fra privati nelle parrocchie fiorentine di S. Felice in Piazza e S. Frediano: un regesto per gli anni 1335–1365," in *Annali di Storia di Firenze* IV (2009): 195–241, at 211. The case is from Pino di Vieri, ASF, Not. Ant. 17045, n.f.

61. Mooney, *"The Legal Ban,"* 119.

62. Ibid., 120.

63. Ibid., 172. Those crimes were "forging a notarized document, treason in the custody of any land, camp or location, sodomy, exacting tolls in Florentine territory without communal authority, highway robbery, damages to immoveable property, houses or goods, attacks on the food supplies to the city, being an assassin or hiring one, breaking a notarized peace settlement, practicing vendetta on any person other than the primary offender, corruption in public office (*baratteria*), and any offense from which the death of the victim resulted . . . ."

64. Of three hundred agreements (the total after simple assault contracts have been eliminated from the sample), there are seventy-six (25 percent) in which the sentence of the judicial ban plays a role.

peace instruments to cancel a ban. Only its use as a means to settle simple assault cases surpasses in frequency this use of the pax.[65]

It was the more complicated assault cases that were usually at the crux of the majority of ban cancellations.[66] The assailants were armed in over half of the cases. An imbreviatura recorded by Andrea di Lapo in March 1339 is typical of this type of agreement. A rector from the southwestern part of the contado denounced one Stefano Cianni of the parish of Santa Maria a Mantignano to the court. He was accused of kicking Jacopo Taddei of San Pietro a Solliciano in the chest. Jacopo countered by hurling his tavolaccio (shield), at Stefano's back.[67] Neither of the combatants showed up to answer the denuncia filed at the criminal court. After being summoned twice to answer the court's charges, they were declared contumacious and then judicially banished. They then made peace and paid the city's treasury 25 f.p., whereupon the ban was cancelled.[68]

Uncharacteristically, the notary failed to record the date of the podestà's original sentence, so we do not know how much time elapsed between the court's declaration of contumacia and when Stefano and Jacopo finally made peace. Ordinarily, however, settlements that involved banniti fleeing from assault penalties were concluded within a couple weeks to a few months. Another peace instrument, again from Florence's contado, this time from the Val di Sieve, may be typical of the time frame. In November 1336, Salimbene (called Ciambene) Rossi of San Martino a Farneto was banished due to assault charges brought against him, which presumably went unanswered. It seems that he had drawn blood when he struck Spigliato Guichini on the head with a lance, for which offence he had been sentenced to pay 150 f.p. In January 1337, Spigliato exchanged the kiss of peace with his one-time assailant, who by now had been in exile for two months, a period that seems to represent the mean time spent under the ban.[69] While the documents never disclose why those who ended up in contumacy absented themselves from the court in the first place, a plausible scenario suggests that there were a good many who could not afford to pay the financial penalties associated with a sentence. Public debtors were far from unknown in medieval Florence. Nor was arrest and incarceration for nonpayment of a judicially imposed fine. The fourteenth-century records from Le Stinche, Florence's communal prison, show that debt was the most frequent reason cited for imprisonment. Indeed, debt of some sort accounts for 64 percent of those arrested and imprisoned. Half of those debtors were public debtors, meaning anyone who owed money to the treasury, and

65. See chapter 3.

66. That is, if more than two people were involved and weapons are cited. These account for forty-one of seventy-six cases involving banniti (54 percent).

67. See fig. 21 for an image of a tavolaccio.

68. Andrea di Lapo, ASF, Not. Ant. 439, fol. 58r.

69. Bartolo Amici, ASF, Not. Ant. 364, fol. 41v.

those who had not paid their court-imposed fines were prominent among them.[70] It is likely that an extra month or two gave banniti time to raise the funds necessary to pay a reduced penalty once they had made peace. Statute law provided that one had only to pay three soldi on every lira of the original fine.[71] It was a risk, but a calculated risk that could be used as an effective strategy to avoid the terms of the original condemnation. One could enter into banishment, losing all legal rights, but if done with some care, the exile could hope to return home after negotiating a peace agreement with the offended party. Negotiations between parties were often carried out by relatives serving as procurators for their banished kinsmen, as we will see shortly in the case of Benci Bruni's brother who acted as his legal representative to make peace for a conflict in which Benci had been accused of homicide.

With or without procurators, some cases took years to resolve. In a pax from the protocols of Matteo di Beliotto, recorded in 1300, we find a settlement between Ser Gino, son of Lotto Formagio, a resident of San Miniato, and ten male members of the Camponsacchi family, a noted Ghibelline lineage, originally from Fiesole but whose tower now dominated the Mercato Vecchio in central Florence.[72] The case came before Lord Jacobino degli Amici, the criminal judge then presiding over the districts of Oltarno, San Pancrazio and Borgo. Gino's father Lotto accused Dardo, son of Neri Berlinghieri dei Camponsacchi, of being the "capo" of a gang of nine who assaulted his son with illegal weapons, specifically knives and quadraletti, particularly deadly arrows shot at close range from a crossbow. Gino's blood had been spilled: he suffered wounds to the head, side, and shoulder. The judge sentenced the Camponsacchi clan to pay the enormous fine of 3200 f.p., punishing them for their magnate status as much as for the use of illegal weapons that had spilled blood on the public streets of the city. A notary read out the sentence in public on 23 February 1282. Perhaps to avoid the financial hardship imposed by the penalty, the Camponsacchi fled. The peace agreement, made eighteen years later, annulled all legal suits, accusations, denunciations, and bans in effect against them.[73] Eighteen years, however, was an exceptionally long period of self-banishment; ordinarily, as we have seen, agreements cancelling bans followed within a few weeks to a few months of the original sentence or crime. In this case, we must remember that the intervening years saw many restrictions placed on old magnate lineages; thus it was perfectly possible that Neri Berlinghieri dei Camponsacchi and his gang waited in exile for the opportune moment to present their notarized pax, a passport for reentry into the city.

70. For a discussion of debt and imprisonment at *Le Stinche*, see Guy Geltner, *The Medieval Prison: A Social History* (Princeton: Princeton University Press, 2008), 51–52.

71. *Statuti*, vol. 2: Podestà: Bk 3: LXXXXIIII, 226.

72. Their ancient lineage and domination of the area are mentioned by Dante in *Paradiso*, Canto 16:121–22.

73. Matteo di Biliotto, ASF, Not. Ant. 13364, fol. 22r.

Although armed assault was the grounds of most cases that resulted in banishment, a peace agreement had the legal authority to cancel bans arising from other crimes as well. As we have seen, the notarized pax remitted bans for anything from violations against the gabelle to theft. In one of the latter instances, a case from 1303 that we saw earlier, Antonino Arrighi of Santa Felicità was fined and ordered to restore the possessions he had stolen from Matteo Fortis Beççole of San Salvatore. Apparently he did no such thing, at least not at first. Five years after the fact Antonino's procurator stood before the notary Giovanni di Buoninsegna da Rignano to settle his dispute with Matteo.[74] So long as Antonio paid the fine, restored the stolen goods, and made a pax, his status as bannitus was cancelled.

It is revealing of the Florentine legal system's reluctance to inflict corporal punishment upon its citizens that peace instruments could be used to cancel even bans that resulted from homicide charges.[75] In a case from 1332, the Bonarelli brothers, Tingho, Jacopo, and Pietro of San Felice in Piazza, made peace with another set of brothers, Megliorato and Gerolamo, sons of Dante of Careggi, who had killed their brother Simone. Armed to the hilt with lances and other deadly weapons, Megliorato and Gerolamo had killed Simone in cold blood. The sons of Dante were sentenced and banned for contumacy. Nonetheless, two months later a contract was drawn up between the Bonarelli procurator and their brother's killers, in which the parties rendered peace to each other.[76] The notarial instrument ended the ban and preempted any legal actions against the Bonarelli. A hefty fine of 500 gold florins threatened each and every one of them who at some future date might possibly violate the agreement.

In a pax dating a few decades earlier, we find the son of a victim of an assault (which subsequently became a homicide) composing a peace with the procurators who represented his father's killers. This agreement was probably meant to quell a potential vendetta. It seems that Ventura Fornari of the parish of San Pietro in Ciel d'Oro had been attacked late one September night (*post secundam penam*) in 1303, not fifty braccia from his home near Santa Reparata. Benci Bruni of the same parish and Guarnaccia Clavaroli of nearby San Tommaso had attacked poor Ventura with a knife and inflicted some very serious wounds on him, injuries from which he eventually died, but not before his two assailants were sentenced for the original assault. Their fines tripled because of the hour at which the crimes were committed and the proximity of the crime scene to Ventura's home: Guarnaccia, who had stabbed Ventura

74. Giovanni di Buoninsegna da Rignano, ASF, Not. Ant. 9491, fols. 113v-114r.

75. *Statuti*, vol. 2: Podestà: Bk 3: XLV, 192. Davidsohn indicates that peace instruments were the precondition "per ogni amnistia in caso di omicidi, ferimenti, percosse e offese verbali, si era che la parte lesa o i suoi eredi di diritto concedessero la 'pace,'" *Storia* 5: 590.

76. Bartolo di Giuntino, ASF, Not. Ant. 1712, fols. 105v-107r.

twice, was sentenced to pay 1200 f.p., while Benci Bruni was fined 1800 f.p. for the three bloody wounds he had inflicted. This was all by the book—the statute book, as it were. But matters were further complicated the following month when Ventura died of his wounds. Now the judge of the criminal court of the podestà had a homicide on his hands. Because they had not shown up to answer the charges, Benci and Guarnaccia were charged with contumacy, a charge that if not answered was considered tantamount to a confession of the crime. The two were sentenced accordingly for homicide. Florentine statute law decreed death by beheading and confiscation of property for this crime. Significantly, statute law also allowed for reconciliation by means of a notarized pax. In addition to a peace instrument, the law demanded payment to the treasury of a 2000 f.p. fine and incarceration in the municipal prison for six months. Only after all these requirements were fulfilled would the sentence and the ban be commuted.[77] Consequently, six years later, through their procurators, Benci and Guarnaccia made peace with Ventura's son, Monaldo. The agreement notes specifically that the peace, confirmed with a kiss on the mouth, released Benci and Guarnaccia from any legal suits, bans, and or sentences arising from the original case.[78] Presumably Benci and Guarnaccia, in fear for their lives, had escaped from Florence and had spent six years as fugitives from the law. It is possible that Giovanni, Benci's brother, who served as procurator in this agreement, had negotiated with Monaldo to resolve the dispute amicably, but we cannot know that with any certainty. These are details the documents do not yield. What they confirm is that peace agreements were a tool of legal accommodation. They enabled exiles to return home, even when, on occasion, the original crime in question was homicide.

Accomplices to homicide also had the right to use instrumenta pacis to have the charges against them dropped. In an agreement made to settle a feud between the Ricci and Orlandi clans, family members who had been participants in the original crime but had not been charged as killers themselves are found making peace with two of the descendants of the dead. Puccio, a son of Guazze (one of the six original killers who had been sentenced to death), had been at the scene of the crime that day and had even participated in it. However, unlike his six kinsmen, he and his brother Giovanni were sentenced only for assault against the three victims—not for killing them. After their condemnation was read out publicly in the General Council on 22 August 1327, they were placed under the ban. Eight years later, on the day after Christmas 1336, Puccio, his brother Santo, and his mother, Domina Lore, were found making peace with the sons of two of the victims. Domina Lore had also been fined for throwing rocks, aiding and abetting the assailants. On 30 September 1327,

77. *Statuti*, vol. 2: Podestà: Bk 3: XLV, 192.

78. Matteo di Biliotto, ASF, Not. Ant. 13364, fols. 95v-96r: "Et de omni processu banno et condempnationis ex inde secutis. Et de omni eo quod in dictis banno et condempnationibus continentur quam pacem oris osculo firmaverunt remictentes inter se vicissim et ad invicem omnia et singula supradicta."

she had been ordered to pay a fine of 200 f.p. to the treasury for her role in the crime, after which she seems to have gone on the lam. It is not difficult to imagine that after having witnessed her husband's death sentence decreed, she fled to safety outside communal jurisdiction. Now, wishing to return, the family employed procurators to make peace with the Orlandi brothers. A peace agreement was a return ticket of sorts, a safe passage back to their home in Santa Maria Impruneta.[79] Upon return from exile, the pax permitted the family to reintegrate into parish and civic life. The financial sanctions in the agreement attempted to guarantee that no personal reprisals would be made against them, while the cancellation of the ban ensured that no legal repercussions would encumber their reentry into community life. The reduced fines doubtless helped to ease the pain inflicted by reduced incomes. That 25 percent of our peace agreements include ban cancellations is important to understanding how these public instruments functioned in medieval Florence, or more precisely, how Florentines used peace contracts strategically, and to their own advantage. This figure also demonstrates that the commune had an interest in repatriating their outlaws, whose swelling numbers may have threatened the security and stability of the Florentine city-republic. Even more to the point, the greater the number of fugitives from justice there were outside Florentine jurisdiction, the greater was the loss of tax revenue that the city faced. In the event, the peace instrument functioned as an accommodation between the courts and their clientele—as a stealth initiative of sorts to resolve the problem of the increasing population of judicial exiles that statutory law had unwittingly created. Both the outlaw and the commune had an interest in reintegration. The peace instrument, in all its flexibility, thus served two masters. It allowed voluntary exiles to be restored to Florentine civic life, while at the same time ensuring that the commune itself legitimized its power, exercising what Zorzi has appositely termed "a politics of grace."[80] Not unlike the angel of peace we will meet in chapter 5, who spreads his wings open to shelter peacemakers, we might imagine the podestà, the chief magistrate of the commune, spreading his mantle wide to readmit the errant banniti into the protected enclave of the city.

ALBERTANUS DE BRESCIA AND VENDETTA

Banishment was intended to be a hardship. Cut off from friends, family, and worldly goods, and often stripped of one's means of financial support, to say nothing of legal identity, it was a condition calculated to make life

---

79. Benintendi di Guittone, ASF, Not. Ant. 2362, fols. 26v–28r. I have found a similar situation in a peace contract recorded in 1325, in which a homicide had been committed one and a half years earlier. The perpetrators of the homicide had been sentenced to death, but one of their henchmen was making peace with the relatives of the victim for his accessory role in the crime, see Jacopo Dandi, ASF, Not. Ant. 6019, fols. 32r–34r.

80. A. Zorzi, "Negoziazione penale," 13–34.

as tough as possible for the bannitus. It is a fate that the protagonist of a remarkable anti-vendetta tract from the pen of the *causidicus* (legal counselor), Albertanus da Brescia (d. ca. 1251) entertains but ultimately rejects as a penalty for his enemies.[81] Dedicated to his son Johannes, a surgeon, Albertanus wrote the *Liber consolationis et consilii* in 1246 in the form of a dialogue between his protagonist, Melibeus, and his wife, Prudence. Well known to literary scholars because it is the source for Chaucer's "Tale of Melibee," the *Liber* was even better known in the Middle Ages, as witnessed by over 160 extant Latin manuscripts, which are distributed in libraries from Philadelphia to St. Petersburg, and on the Italian peninsula from Milan to Naples.[82]

The dialogue is set in the aftermath of an attack on the unnamed daughter of Melibeus and Prudence. Though we never learn the motive, we do know that three assailants gained access to the house by scaling the walls with ladders and breaking in through unsecured windows. Upon entering, they assaulted the female members of the household with such force that Melibeus's daughter was left half-dead from her injuries. In the heat of the moment, her father's immediate response was to plot revenge against the assailants, as was his right by law. But all his rash plans for vendetta came to naught when his wife Prudence, the incarnation of her eponymous virtue, intervened and, in the cold light of day, led him to recognize the folly of his misbegotten plan. (It will be remembered that among "political theorists" of classical antiquity, as well as their medieval counterparts, Prudence was chief among the political virtues.[83]) With Prudence acting as the mediator between the parties, Melibeus reconciles with his enemies, and so the tale ends. Fortunately for us, it also paints a picture of the culminating ritual of peacemaking, which has many of the hallmarks of penitential peacemaking that we have seen already in chapter 1 and which we will examine further in chapter 5. What is also of interest is that the tract gives us a glimpse of behind-the-scenes negotiating that no other narrative or documentary source

---

81. I part ways with Zorzi on this question. He argues that this was not an anti-vendetta tract but rather a primer for citizens to reflect on the ways in which disputes could be resolved. Zorzi, "La cultura," 144–45. It may have been that too, but it was in the first place a firm condemnation of vendetta as a means to process disputes.

82. *Liber consolationis*, 7. Building on Angus Graham, "Albertanus of Brescia: A Supplementary Census of Latin Manuscripts," *Studi Medievali* 41 (2000): 891–924, is his 2004 census of both Latin and vernacular mss. The libraries of Florence have five Latin manuscripts and two vernacular texts. The tract was very quickly translated into Italian by two Tuscans, Andrea da Grosseto and the Pistoian Soffredi del Grazia; see Stefano Andres, "Oltre lo statuto," section 12. For an introduction to the work of Albertanus, see James M. Powell, *The Pursuit of Happiness in the Early Thirteenth Century* (Philadelphia: University of Pennsylvania Press, 2004).

83. Quentin Skinner, "The Artist as Political Philosopher," *Proceedings of the British Academy* 72 (1986): 1–56, at 26.

on peacemaking affords. Thus it is worth pausing for a moment to examine the text in some detail.

Let us pick up the story after the attack, when Prudence advises her shaken husband to convene a council of upstanding and faithful friends to counsel him on his best plan of action. This he does by gathering a large group professional men—physicians, surgeons, legal advisors—young men and old, neighbors and former enemies. Melibeus solicits each group in turn for advice about whether he should undertake vendetta immediately. Given the social diversity of his advisors, it is not surprising that he receives diverse and conflicting counsel.[84]

Having examined the protagonist's daughter, and having delivered a favorable prognosis for her recovery, one of the surgeons is the first to rise and counsel against vendetta.[85] He cites the Hippocratic oath that doctors should do no harm, and also the medical maxim *contraria contrariis curantur* to demonstrate that revenge is not the appropriate response to the situation. The causidicus, on the other hand, also skeptical of vendetta, warns Melibeus that if he must proceed, he should exercise due caution, leaving ample time for deliberation. Above all he should fortify his house to protect his family from further harm. The elders in the group add that though it is easy to initiate vendetta it is difficult to end the cycle once it has been set into motion.[86]

On the side of taking immediate action are his neighbors and erstwhile enemies. Shedding crocodile tears for what has transpired, they argue that Melibeus has the means to undertake vendetta: an ample vengeance group in the form of his blood relatives and in-laws and the required wealth to carry out such a plan. Naturally the hot-headed young men in the group concur whole-heartedly with this advice. For them, revenge is not a dish best served cold; instead, moving to the other end of the metaphoric thermometer, they urge Melibeus to strike while the iron is hot. And to drive home their point, they shout out in unison: "Yes! Yes! Let's do it! Let's do it!"[87]

Their enthusiasm wins the day and Melibeus decides on vendetta, much to the chagrin of Prudence, who asks him to delay his plan so that cooler heads may prevail. What follows is a remarkable defense of the integrity and rationality of women by Prudence, who defends her sex (and therefore her right to make an argument against vendetta) from an attack launched by Melibeus, who trots out just about every hoary, old chestnut from the venerable catalogue of medieval misogyny to denigrate the intelligence of women and silence his wife.[88] Prudence, however, methodically slashes her husband's

84. *Liber consolationis* II: 6.

85. Ibid., 6–7. Zorzi suggests that he is the first in the hierarchy of counselors to speak because of his expertise in blood-injuries, of great importance to medieval courts, "La Cultura," 147.

86. Ibid., 7–9.

87. Ibid., 9–10.

88. Ibid., III: 12–13.

arguments to ribbons before his very eyes. Citing scripture and the wisdom of the ancients, alongside a few more contemporary authorities, she wins the preliminary round, which allows her to plead her case against vendetta.[89] This she does by conducting a close forensic examination of what she has observed of her husband's handling of the matter thus far.

She opens her case by quoting from *De contemptu mundi* to cast aspersions on the judgment that Melibeus has shown up to now. Citing Innocent III's tract, she observes that "he who knows more is he who doubts . . . [and] therefore a part of wisdom is to know what you do not know."[90] She then goes on to denigrate the choice and credibility of her husband's consiglieri. She tells him that he has gathered too many, most of whom were inappropriate choices in the first place. He has sought the advice of yes-men and sycophants, the young and the witless, all of whom show him reverence out of fear, not love.[91]

Prudence then proceeds to examine their counsel. It is no surprise that she rejects the advice of the youth, the flatterers, and her husband's former enemies in favor of the guidance given by the men of the medical profession. Agreeing that contraries cure contraries, she argues that vengeance will beget only more vengeance, and that therefore "it is necessary to oppose discord with concord and war with peace."[92] She also agrees with the counsel of the sober causidici that caution should prevail and provisions and preparations should be made before any action is taken.[93] In an interesting aside, she excoriates the architectural fashion of building fortified towers, blaming them for turning friends and neighbors into enemies on account of the fear and hatred they generate.[94] (It will be remembered that our Bergamasque poet leveled a similar indictment against fortified towers when he noted that because of the peace pact by which the citizens of his town now abided, there was no longer any need for them to flee to their towers. Discord had been quelled.)

After running him through a gauntlet of arguments against feud and vendetta, Prudence finally arrives at the heart of the matter in the chapter entitled, "On Avoiding War through Reconciliation." Here she argues that wars are won only through reconciliation and concord, and, citing the *Sententiae* of the Roman moralist Publilius Syrus to make her point, she notes, "Where there is victory, there is concord." At which point, the embattled Melibeus justifiably inquires: "How can I reconcile with my enemies when they initiated the discord and they are not seeking reconciliation?" The essence of her lengthy response is "since your enemies have not initiated reconciliation, you ought to begin the process."[95]

89. Ibid., IV-VI: 13–20.
90. Ibid., X: 29; Innocent III, *Innocentii III. De contemptu mundi sive de miseria humanae conditionis libri tres*, ed. Johann Heinrich Achterfeldt (Bonn: E. Weber, 1855), 30.
91. Ibid., XXX: 64.
92. Ibid., XXXI: 67.
93. Ibid., 68.
94. Ibid., XXXIII: 72–73.
95. Ibid., XLVIII: 106–108.

Significantly, however, it is Prudence and not Melibeus who eventually opens negotiations with the enemy. In her husband's stead she serves as the facilitator and negotiator of the peace by privately summoning her assailants to lecture them on the benefits of peace and the evils of feud and vendetta. Struck by her words, the miscreants respond in tears, confessing that it was they who should have begun the work of reconciliation, but since she has done so they are willing to submit to her on bended knee. She assures them that her husband is a good and honorable man and will be merciful toward them. At that they commend themselves to her and await her command. Engaging in a premodern form of shuttle diplomacy, Prudence then sets off to Melibeus to recount the results of her negotiations. He is especially pleased with the "penance, heartfelt contrition, and confession of sins" of his enemies, whom he now deems worthy of forgiveness. And quoting Seneca, he remarks, "Ubi est confessio, ibi est remissio."[96]

This passage, in my view, is one of the keys to the text. In order for reconciliation to take place, Melibeus expects all the elements of the sacramental act of penance to be performed. Without contrition and confession, he will not grant absolution. The act of civic peacemaking Melibeus envisions is enacted using an entirely religious vocabulary. The author of this text, we should remind ourselves, was a member of the legal profession, one who knew well what the act of civic peacemaking entailed.

In what follows, Prudence advises that the terms of a peace agreement be hammered out at once. The couple immediately dispatches a delegation inviting their adversaries, accompanied by guarantors, to a meeting in order to help make peace and concord. Once all have been assembled at the house of Melibeus, he assumes the role of judge and father-confessor, adroitly joining together civic and sacred roles. He reminds the three assailants of the crimes they have committed against his family without just cause, crimes that are punishable by death. He then asks them to plead their case. They do so weeping, genuflecting, and finally prostrating themselves at Melibeus's feet, imploring him for mercy. Though he is pleased with this performance, he begs for time to consult yet again with his daughter's physicians and to deliberate on the punishment he will impose on her assailants. The "court" is recessed.[97]

The doctors deliver the welcome news that Melibeus's daughter will make a full recovery; and now it is time to decide on the penalty for the self-confessed culprits. Melibeus has decided not to request capital punishment, but he is in favor of confiscating all the possessions of his enemies and sending them into permanent exile across the sea, a punishment that, as William Jordan has shown, was very harsh indeed.[98] He consults Prudence who informs him that imposing such a punishment would be tantamount to an abuse of power and

96. Ibid., XLIX:115–16.

97. Ibid., 118–19.

98. Ibid., 119. William C. Jordan, *From England to France: Felony and Exile in the High Middle Ages* (Princeton: Princeton University Press, 2015).

would damage his reputation and honor.[99] After a discussion of clemency, piety, and mercy, and supported by all the learned authorities, Prudence wins Melibeus over to the side of righteousness. The court is adjourned once again and the three weeping criminals approach Melibeus on their knees asking his mercy. With the consent of Prudence, he decrees that their "devotion, heart-felt contrition, penance, and confession of sin" have guided him to "leniency, clemency, and piety." And in a line that could have been lifted directly from a notarial peace agreement, a type of document with which Albertanus was no doubt familiar, both parties agree to forgive mutual injuries, anger, indignities, and all rancor. The reconciliation ceremony concludes when Melibeus raises his three former adversaries up from their prostration on the ground and receives them in the kiss of peace. Finally, "following in the footsteps of the Lord, Melibeus bade them, 'Go in peace and sin no more.'"[100]

It is an extraordinary scene in an extraordinary treatise. This is neither the time nor place to comment at length on the breadth of learning Albertanus displays in this text, nor on his feminist defense of women, which may possibly have served as an inspiration for Christine de Pizan's *City of Ladies*.[101] What speaks to our purpose are two items. First, as we have seen, there is the ease with which Albertanus associates civic peacemaking with religious penance. In this Albertanus shows both his legal training and that he was very much a preacher manqué, steeped in the penitential mentality of the day. The second point to observe is how this text lifts the curtain to expose something of the goings-on behind the scenes of peace negotiations.

Significantly, Albertanus shows us the role of the intermediary or facilitator. In Giordano da Pisa's phrase, Prudence acted as a *tramezzatore*, opening the discussions that led to the peace agreement. And even after the first phase, she continued to advise her husband on the terms of that agree-ment. As the role of mediator is meant to be invisible, it is not surprising that frustratingly little is known about the function of intermediaries or facilitators in forging medieval peace agreements. Thus it is with great interest that we note that Albertanus cast a woman in this part. Here Prudence is not merely the personification of an allegorical figure gendered female; rather, Albertanus has written a female character who exemplifies the virtue after which she has been named. Does this mean that ordinary women undertook this responsi-bility as well? Unfortunately, it is difficult to say. But it may be a telling detail that Prudence summoned her husband's adversaries to approach her privately, since a public role for a female mediator would have been almost impossible

99. Ibid., L: 121–22.

100. Ibid., LI: 126–27.: "Et ita, sublevando illos per manus, recepti sunt in osculum pacis. Quibus Melibeus, sequens Domini vestigia, dixit: 'Ite in pace, et amplius nolite peccare.'"

101. Angus Graham, "Albertanus of Brescia: A Supplementary Census of Latin Manuscripts," 900–907 for the French manuscripts.

in late medieval Italy. There will of course be exceptions to any rule. Catherine of Siena is one. Called on to testify in her canonization process, one of her disciples, Stefano Maconi, describes how in 1376, Catherine mediated a peace between the Tolomei and the Rinaldini families.[102] Moreover, as we have seen, her diplomatic skills were so esteemed by the pope that he put them to work during the War of the Eight Saints, when Catherine shuttled between Siena, Pisa, and Lucca to prevent the progress of a Florentine-led Tuscan League united against the papacy.[103]

Catherine was an extraordinary woman who clearly cannot be made to represent "everywoman." But the very fact that the facilitator was almost always invisible suggests the possibility that ordinary women may have been working behind the scenes of at least some peace agreements, and the *Liber consolationis* shows us what they might have done: everything from initiating the dialogue between parties to advising on the terms of the settlement.

Finally, a word should be said about Albertanus of Brecia, a layman and legal advisor, and author of the *Liber consolationis et consilii*. In his capacity as a lawyer, he most certainly would have witnessed and likely even negotiated the terms of peace agreements. Although the clients whom he represented in his legal practice surely forgave each other for the crimes they had committed in the legal language of a notarial contract, in his fictional work, Albertanus nonetheless chose to cast his treatise's climactic moment of dispute resolution in terms of sacramental penance. The assailants made contrite confessions, humbled themselves in penance, and were forgiven their crimes by their victim. A Christian understanding of the ritual allowed for a shift in the power dynamics of the situation. Evoking Christ's reconciliation with humankind, Melibeus assumed the part of Jesus, and forgave those who had sinned against his family, bidding them go in peace. The victim whose honor had been compromised was now transformed into both the judge and active peacemaker, while his once-powerful aggressors were reduced to humble penitents seeking pardon. It is a powerful symbolic reversal, one we shall see at work again in chapter 5. The *Liber consolationis et consilii* demonstrates how a Christian framework of penance shaped representations and understandings of civic dispute resolution, even for those who had direct experience of it in the secular courts. Though vendetta would have allowed Melibeus to achieve equilibrium with his enemies, negotiating a peace settlement allowed him to advance to the moral high ground. Yet, he also restored his honor in so doing. Finally, through the character of Melibeus, Albertanus argued that penance, contrition and confession had a role in the civic peacemaking process.

102. F. Thomas Luongo, *The Saintly Politics of Catherine of Siena* (Ithaca, NY: Cornell University Press, 2006), 148. *Il Processo Castellano*, ed. M.-H. Laurent, *Fontes Vitae S. Catherinae Senensis Historici*, vol. 9 (Milan: Fratelli Bocca, 1942), 259: ". . . quia miraculose postmodum, ipsa mediante, pacem habuimus."

103. Luongo, *The Saintly Politics*, 148–49.

Though we do not know if there was a proximate catalyst that caused Albertanus of Brescia to compose this tract and dedicate it to his son, we do know from his sermons, and indeed from his entire career, that Albertanus the causidicus was interested in having a public voice and using it to shape the morals of society. It seems that toward that end he was crafting a social ethic for his peers, one that would show by example how men of power and influence like Melibeus could contribute to the common good by cultivating concord and peace rather than fanning the flames of discord and vendetta. And he did this by demonstrating, step by step, how Melibeus, acting on the advice and counsel of Prudence, settled his dispute with those who had wronged him. The conflict, which had the potential to explode into a cycle of retaliation and reprisals, was concluded with a peace, one that was informed by Christian teaching and ritual practice, including the kiss of peace. In the next chapter, through the examination of a wide range of evidence—including visual sources—we will investigate more deeply the elements of peacemaking that were integral to the ritual conclusion of the disputing process.

CHAPTER FIVE

Picturing Peace: Rituals and Remembrance

Greet one another with a kiss of love. Peace be to you all who are in Christ.

—1 PETER 5:14

Try to grow perfect; encourage one another; have a common mind and live in peace, and the God of love and peace will be with you. Greet one another with the holy kiss.

—II COR. 13:11–12

WE BEGIN WITH an infamous kiss, or rather a celebrated representation of it: the kiss of Judas, a scene from a wall mural of the life of Christ painted by Giotto for the Arena Chapel in Padua between 1303 and 1305.[1] (fig. 13) The emotional power that this image packs is arresting still today. Even the most casual viewer appreciates the painter's technique, skill as a colorist, and unparalleled eye for composition, all of which are pressed into service to animate the gospel passage that recounts the betrayal of Jesus in the Garden of Gethsemane (Mark 14:45). If, however, we look at this fresco with a "period eye," that is, taking into account the experiences and knowledge that a late medieval audience would have brought to viewing it, we gain yet another perspective to enhance our understanding of this iconic image.[2] From

1. Most recently, see Anne Derbes and Mark Sandona, *The Usurer's Heart: Giotto, Enrico Scrovegni and the Arena Chapel in Padua* (University Park, PA: Pennsylvania State University Press, 2008) and Franco Mormando, "'Just as your lips approach the lips of your brothers': Judas Iscariot and the Kiss of Betrayal," in *Saints and Sinners: Caravaggio and the Baroque Image*, ed. Franco Mormando (Chestnut Hill, MA: McMullen Museum of Art, Boston College, 1999), 179–90.

2. Michael Baxandall, *Painting and Experience in Fifteenth-Century Italy: A Primer in the Social History of Pictorial Style* (Oxford: Oxford University Press, 1988), 2nd ed., 29–108.

FIGURE 13. *Judas Kiss: The Betrayal of Christ*. Giotto, fresco, 1303–1305. Arena Chapel, Padua. Photo (post-2001 restoration) reproduced by permission of Alfredo Dagli Orti/Art Resource, New York.

the standpoint of an early Trecento viewer alive to the imagery and symbolism of contemporary peacemaking practices in which the kiss on the mouth stood as the culminating ritual of forgiveness and peace, this image would have radiated even more emotional shockwaves than it does today. It would have struck deeply at the foundations of belief, because it was the antithesis of everything the kiss was understood to represent. With one gesture Judas swept away the bonds of charity, fraternity, and community, all that the gesture had symbolized since the early days of the Christian church, epitomized in the words of Saints Peter and Paul that opened this chapter. As we have observed previously, by the late antique period and well into the later Middle Ages, the kiss had also come to represent reconciliation. To a late medieval audience, the kiss on the mouth was the sign par excellence of forgiveness and peace which, to use Remigio dei Girolami's terms, were the result of the correct ordering of charity. The Judas kiss turned all that upside down. Giotto's version, which portrays Judas poised to betray the Lord with a kiss on the mouth, shows how the ritual gesture, given in bad faith could be perverted.

And when it was, the results were calamitous: unity was shattered, community fractured, and a sacred pact was torn asunder.

This chapter brings full circle the argument made throughout this book that rituals of civic peacemaking must be understood in the religious context that informed them. In chapter 1 we examined the penitential aspect of peacemaking, which played such a large role in the peace movements of the later Middle Ages; here, we analyze its concluding ritual, the kiss on the mouth, in addition to other examples of late medieval rituals of reconciliation— each penitential in nature and each meant to seal and enact the peace. As in chapter 1, we will venture out from Florence to gather evidence from central and northern Italy, which suggests that the kiss of peace and other performative rituals were not peculiar to Tuscany, nor were efforts to memorialize peace so very different in other regions, as the visual evidence attests.

We begin with an examination of the meaning of the kiss of peace on the mouth, looking at its origins as a greeting in the early Christian community, its placement in the rite of the Mass, its religious significance as ritual in the Middle Ages, and finally its migration into civic practice as it became the symbolic culmination of a peace agreement. I have adopted Paul Connerton's distinctions of embodied rituals and inscribed rituals as the two pertain to social memory. In the case of the former, I argue that the ritual kiss was the embodiment of the civic act of peacemaking in that it served to enact the peace, thereby creating a new legal relationship between individuals.[3] As we shall see, the ritual kiss also had an especially important place in the repatriation of those citizens in exile under the ban. From an analysis of the ritual kiss, we travel to Rome and afterwards to San Gimignano to examine two quite elaborate rituals of peacemaking—penitential, performative, and embodied— developed to restore social order in those cities.

The case in San Gimignano then leads us to a discussion of how peace was commemorated or, in Conerton's terms, how its inscription shaped social memory, both through marriage agreements made *pro bono pacis* and through visual culture. From a corpus of visual evidence I have gathered, I advance a new iconography of peacemaking to argue that these images allow us a glimpse of how peace was envisioned, remembered, and memorialized by artists and their patrons in the later medieval period. Whether on the walls of churches, illuminated in books, carved on tomb sculpture, or in the form of ex-voto panel paintings, all these representations celebrated the holy kiss as the centerpiece of peacemaking.

THE KISS OF PEACE

In the early Christian period, the community was instructed to greet one another with a kiss. While the apostle Peter imagined the kiss as one of charity,

3. Paul Connerton, *How Societies Remember* (Cambridge: Cambridge University Press, 1989), 72–104, at 72–73. On social memory, see also James Fentress and Chris Wickham, *Social Memory* (Oxford: Blackwell, 1992).

"Greet one another with a kiss of love" (Pet. 5:14), in Paul's eyes, the fraternal kiss of the community was a sacred bond: "Greet one another with a holy kiss" (1 Cor. 16:20).[4] In the liturgy of the early church, the holy kiss was used as a greeting before the offertory, a position it continued to occupy in the rites of the Orthodox and Eastern churches.[5]

Thus, in the early Christian context, the meaning of the holy kiss was already twofold; by the late antique period, we find yet another meaning grafted onto the gesture. Our first evidence of this new meaning comes from Cyril of Jerusalem (d. 386) who, in his capacity as bishop, attempted to distinguish the sacred kiss of Saints Peter and Paul, exchanged before the offertory, from its profane incarnation. Cyril instructs his audience of post-baptism catechumens as follows:

> Then the deacon calls out: "Greet one another; let us kiss one another." Don't take this kiss to be like the kiss friends exchange when they meet in the marketplace. This is something different; this kiss expresses a union of souls and is a plea for complete reconciliation. The kiss then is a sign that our souls are united and all grudges banished. This is what our Lord meant when he said: "If you are offering your gift on the altar and remember that your brother has a complaint against you, leave your gift on the altar and go first and be reconciled with your brother and then come and offer your gift" (Matt 5:23–24). Thus the kiss is reconciliation, and so is holy, as blessed Paul implied when he proclaimed: "Greet one another with a holy kiss;" and Peter: "Greet one another with the kiss of charity"[6] [1 Cor. 16:20, 1 Pet. 5:14].

Theologians of the late antique period began to recognize the kiss as a sign of forgiveness and reconciliation, so much so that by the fifth century liturgists of the Roman rite Mass transferred the ritual kiss to a position before the Eucharistic

4. See also Rom. 16:16; 2 Cor. 13:12; 1 Thes. 5:26.

5. John Bossy, "The Mass as a Social Institution, 1200–1700," *Past and Present* 100 (1983): 29–61, at 52; Joseph A. Jungmann, *The Mass of the Roman Rite: Its Origins and Development*, 2 vols., trans. Francis A. Brunner (New York: Benzinger Brothers, 1951–1955; repr. Westminster, MD: Christian Classics, 1986), 2: 321–32. For studies on the kiss of peace in its wider cultural context, see Nicolas James Perella, *The Kiss Sacred and Profane* (Berkeley: University of California Press, 1969); Yannick Carré, *Le baiser sur la bouche au moyen âge: rites, symbols, mentalités à travers les texts et les images IXe–XVe siècles* (Paris: Le Léopard d'Or, 1992); Klaus Schreiner, "'Gerechtigkeit und Frieden haben sich geküßt' (Ps. 84:11): Friedensstiftung durch symbolische Handeln," in *Träger und Instrumentarien des Friedens im hohen und späten Mittelalter*, ed. Johannes Fried (Sigmaringen: Jan Thorbecke, 1996), 37–86; Kiril Petkov, *The Kiss of Peace: Ritual, Self and Society in the High and Late Medieval West* (Leiden: Brill, 2003); and Michael Philip Penn, *Kissing Christians: Ritual and Community in the Late Antique Church* (Philadelphia: University of Pennsylvania Press, 2005).

6. "Mystagogic Catechesis 5," in *Cyril of Jerusalem*, ed. and trans. Edward Yarnold, S.J. (London: Routledge, 2000), 182.

prayer and the congregation's reception of the host, where it remained through-out the Middle Ages.[7] Its new location signaled a ritual reenactment of forgive-ness prior to sharing communion.[8] Augustine supplies us with testimony regard-ing the new meaning and placement of the kiss when he tells us that before the consecration of the Eucharist, the priest says "*Pax vobiscum*," and the members of the congregation exchange the kiss on the mouth:

> After this, the "Peace be with you" is said, and Christians embrace one
> another with the holy kiss. This is a sign of peace; as the lips indicate,
> let peace be made in your conscience, that is, when your lips draw near
> to those of your brother, do not let your heart withdraw from his. [9]

For Augustine the kiss meant both reconciliation and peace, which were, as we have seen, predicated on inner tranquility and required that two hearts be aligned in unity. The Judas kiss provided a teachable moment for moralists and theologians like Augustine, for it illustrates the dire consequences that result when the kiss of peace is exchanged under false pretenses.

In a letter to the bishop of Gubbio, Pope Innocent I (d. 417) also witnesses the new position of the kiss in the liturgy, and offers a justification for the change. He explains that the placement of the kiss before the consecration of the host was to emphasize that the congregation has given its consent to the celebration of the mysteries of the church. The kiss was a sign of this consent. Even in the thirteenth century, Pope Innocent III (d. 1216), his successor and namesake, continued to cite his predecessor's explanation for the reposition-ing of the kiss in the Roman rite mass.[10]

In his *Rationale,* a treatise explicating the Mass in each of its elements, written in 1286, William Durand (d. 1296), one of the preeminent scholars of liturgy of the later Middle Ages (who also happened to have been a paciere in the papal territories of the Romagna for Pope Boniface VIII), gives a lengthy exegesis of the kiss of peace. Durand duly notes that the kiss of peace rep-resents reconciliation, suggesting that the Church had decreed the kiss in the Mass in memory of Christ's sacrifice for the community's sins. "Therefore, men give each other a kiss, that is, a sign of peace, so that they can show that they are joined together in the Body of Christ, through which peace has been made

7. Jungmann, *The Mass* 2: 322. Significantly, Penn also argues that there are very few Greco-Roman antecedents for this meaning of the kiss: *Kissing Christians*, 43.

8. Jungmann, ibid.; Penn, ibid., 45; and Bossy, "The Mass," 52.

9. Sermon 227 (Easter Sunday), in Saint Augustine, *Sermons on the Liturgical Seasons*, trans. Sister Mary Sarah Muldowney [*The Fathers of the Church*, vol. 38] (Washington, D.C.: Catholic University of America Press, 1959), 197–98.

10. *Mysteriorum evangelicae legis et sacramenti eucharistiae*, PL 217: col. 909c. Jungmann notes that this justification came as a reply to the Bishop of Gubbio in 416. *The Mass* 2: 322. For more on peace in the medieval liturgy, see Luisella Cabrini Chiesa, "Gesti e formule di pace: note in margine all'età medievale," in *La pace fra realtà e utopia* in *Quaderni di Storia Religiosa* 12 (2005): 47–97.

between heaven and earth."[11] For Durand, the kiss is first and foremost the Christian community's sign of unity and reconciliation with Christ.

But Durand, like any good medieval theologian, noted that the kiss of peace in the Mass had multiple senses, in this case five, the first of which we have just seen. The second sense, he adduces, is that ascribed to it by Innocent I, which we have also noted. The third reason why Christians kiss during the Mass, Durand argues, is on account of the immense gratitude they feel for having been deemed worthy of God's grace. The fourth reason is of particular interest to us as it lends support (though in different terminology) to the peace envisioned by his contemporary in Florence, Remigio dei Girolami and adds credence to our reading of the Judas kiss as the antithesis of the kiss of peace, which opened this chapter. Durand remarks: "Those who kiss one another in hatred, imitate the kiss of the traitor, Judas." Giordano da Pisa was also concerned with the false kiss. In a sermon dating from 1305, at the same time as Giotto was working on his Judas kiss in Padua, Giordano was preaching on the subject in Florence, telling his audience that they could pay lip service to peace by exchanging a kiss on the mouth, but if the kiss was not given from the heart then it was not a true kiss of peace.[12] Or as Durand noted: "In the kiss, flesh is united with flesh, and spirit with spirit, and we, who are joined in the flesh by our descent from Adam, will be connected by the bond of charity" (Hos. 11:4).[13]

For Durand the unity of spirit—inner peace—expressed itself in the flesh by means of the embodied kiss of peace, a sign of outer peace. What Durand calls the bond of charity, Remigio might have called the bond of concord, a sign that the order of charity was operative and had thus arranged everything in its proper place. The kiss joined heaven and earth.

Durand's fifth meaning issued from Saint Paul's precept to the Christian community to greet each other in the kiss of peace. He concludes this section by noting, "Before we receive communion, we give the peace, so that we might show harmony among us, without which, our gifts will not be received by God."[14] Here, then, the kiss of peace expresses concord in the community.

Durand opens his chapter on the kiss of peace with a vivid description of how the peace descends hierarchically from the altar. The priest receives the peace after he has completed the Eucharistic prayer and shares it with his deacon by offering a kiss on the mouth. "The deacon gives the peace to those around him, and they do this [kiss] among themselves as a sign that all must be given the peace." In an interesting postscript to this paragraph, he describes a local practice of some churches in which "the priest spreads his chasuble, so

11. William Durand, *Rationale on the Mass and Each Action Pertaining to It*, Book 4, trans. Timothy M. Thibodeau (Turnhout: Brepols, 2013) [CCCM, vol. CXL], 463. Carré gives an extended treatment of Durand's *Rationale*, see *Le baiser sur la bouche*, 227–37.

12. Sermo XXX, *Prediche del Beato G. Giordano da Rivalto dell'ordine dei Predicatori*, ed. Domenico Maria Manni (Florence: Viviani, 1739), 134.

13. Durand, ibid.

14. Ibid., 464.

FIGURE 14. *The Kiss of Peace Exchanged between a Priest and Deacon in the Mass*. Miniature, Roman Rite Missal, possibly from Abruzzo or Bologna, 14th c. MS G.16, fol.129r, the Morgan Library & Museum, New York. Gift of the Trustees of the William S. Glazier Collection, 1984. Photo reproduced by permission from the Morgan Library & Museum.

that through the kiss of peace and the extension of his chasuble, the extension of charity will be shown." [15] His image evokes the gesture of the Madonna della Misericordia, a visual type that originated in this period, in which the Virgin Mary opens wide her cloak, like a mother hen protecting her chicks, to receive her supplicants in all-encompassing mercy.

The Roman *Ordo* for the mass specifies that the kiss of peace descends from the altar when the priest accepts the kiss from the bishop, after which it is passed along in a chain reaction to the people, "like a gift which comes from the Sacrament." [16] An illustration of the descent of the kiss from the altar appears in a richly illustrated Roman rite *Ordo*, now in the Morgan Library (fig. 14).[17]

From the altar to the people, the kiss of peace then descended into legal practice, particularly, as we have seen, as the enacting gesture of a peace instrument. It will be remembered that the ritual kiss was a *sine qua non* of Rolandino dei Passaggieri's model instrumentum pacis. Indeed, over 80 percent of Florentine contracts note its presence. The contracts ordinarily use the term *oris osculum*, or more precisely, given the Florentine dialect's characteristic aspiration, the *horis hosculum*, or alternatively, the *hosculum pacis*. A typical formula for expressing the exchange of the kiss runs like this one taken from the case book of Ildebrandino di Benvenuto: *Fecerunt et*

15. Ibid., 461–65

16. Jungmann, *The Mass* 2: 326.

17. I thank Colum Hourihane for bringing this image to my attention. The Morgan catalogue suggests that the manuscript dates between 1375 and 1399; however, after a brief examination of the codex, I would backdate it to the later thirteenth century and argue that it may well be a product of the Roman chancery. The incipit reads, *Ordo Missalis secundum consuetudinem romane curie.*

reddiderunt simul sibi invicem inter se uno alteri perpetuam pacem, finem et remissionem cum oris obsculo [sic].[18] The formula stresses that *both* parties actively exchanged the kiss, a ritual that sealed the peace, ended the dispute, and offered reconciliation. As anthropologists have shown, reciprocity is central to both feuding and peacemaking.[19] As neither party submits or dominates in this gesture, it would seem that the reciprocity of the kiss was meant to embody both the restoration of equilibrium between the disputants and the transmission of the gift from the sacrament.

I would suggest that this is one meaning of the kiss underscored in an extraordinary tomb sculpture executed in the early years of the fourteenth century for the funerary monument of Berardo Maggi (d. 1308), bishop of Brescia (fig. 15). While occupying the episcopal see, his great achievement, analogous to Cardinal Latino's in Florence, was to have pacified the Guelf and Ghibelline factions, whose decades-long internecine wars had brought the Lombard city to its knees.[20] In 1298 the chief magistrates of Brescia granted the bishop full authority to negotiate peace between the factions. Berardo was successful in that mission, and he—or his brother Matteo, who succeeded him as "perpetual Lord" of Brescia—touted that triumph in the design of the bishop's ammonite tomb, sculpted with deeds from his life, including a pacification Mass.[21] Present in the crowd at that ceremony are not one, but three pairs of Guelfs and Ghibellines, poised to exchange the kiss of peace on the mouth.[22] The leading pair of peacemakers, who attract our eye because they occupy the privileged central space of the composition, are shown on their knees in genuflection, a posture of supplication. They cross their arms on their chests in another gesture from the Virgin Mary's gestural repertoire, this one from Annunciation iconography. In both cases the gesture indicates obedience and submission. It is important to note that in none of the three pairs of figures offering the kiss on Maggi's sarcophagus does one individual dominate over the other. The artist or patron envisioned the actors on an equal plane and thus readied to exchange the ritual kiss.

18. Ildebrandino di Benvenuto, ASF, Not. Ant. 11250, fol. 134v.

19. Thomas Kuehn makes this point in "Social and Legal Capital in Vendetta: A Fifteenth-Century Florentine Feud in and out of Court," in *Sociability and its Discontents: Civil Society, Social Capital, and Their Alternatives in Late Medieval and Early Modern Europe*, ed. Nicholas A. Eckstein and Nicholas Terpstra, (Turnhout: Brepols, 2009), 51–72, at 52. See also Anton Blok, *Honour and Violence* (Malden, MA: Blackwell, 2001), 15.

20. Matteo Ferrari, "I Maggi a Brescia: politica e immagine di una 'signoria' (1275–1316)," *Opera · Nomina · Historiae* 4 (2011): 19–66; online http://onh.giornale.sns.it [consulted 6/21/17] and Marco Rossi, "L'immagine della pace nel monumento funerario di Berardo Maggi, vescovo e signore di Brescia" in *Medioevo: immagini e ideologie. Atti del convegno internazionale di studi Parma, 23–27 settembre 2002*, ed. Arturo Carlo Quintavalle (Milan: Mondadori Electa, 2005), 588–96.

21. Ferrari, "I Maggi a Brescia," 33.

22. For detailed versions of the other exchanges of the kiss on the tomb, see: http://commons.wikimedia.org/wiki/Category:Kiss_of_peace#mediaviewer/File:Sarcofago_Berardo_Maggi_by_Stefano_Bolognini_particolare14.JPG [consulted 6/21/17].

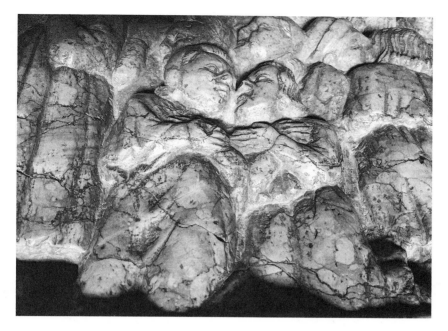

FIGURE 15. *Kiss of Peace between Guelf and Ghibelline Factions in Brescia.* Tomb of Berardo Maggi, 14th c. Duomo Vecchio, Brescia. Photo credit: author.

It is worthwhile at this point to underscore the important meanings ascribed to bodily gestures, particularly as they relate to the ritual analysis of the kiss of peace. And notwithstanding a rather recent critique of medieval historians' use of ritual analysis, I would argue that just such an analysis should be applied to the ratifying kiss of late medieval peace agreements.[23] If, following Catherine Bell, we regard ritual as "above all, an assertion of difference,"[24] the ritual kiss, as distinguished from its mundane incarnation was, as we have seen, differentiated, codified, and defined as an *oris osculum*. It was emphatically *not* an everyday peck on the cheek or an "air kiss." And contrary to the wisdom of an old standard, in a peace agreement, a kiss was not "just a kiss." Moreover, in the medieval lexicon, different words distinguished different types of kisses. Following a distinction made by Isidore of Seville

23. Philippe Buc, *The Dangers of Ritual* (Princeton: Princeton University Press, 2001). It should be noted that Buc's critique is centered mainly on ritual as a narrative construct in sources of the early and central Middle Ages. He argues that authors could frame the ritual as effective or not, depending on the writer's point of view. It is important to note that our notarial sources record only the formula without commentary on it, thus rendering it as an act without judgment. For further critique of Buc, see Geoffrey Koziol, "The Dangers of Polemic: Is Ritual Still an Interesting Topic of Historical Study?" *Early Medieval Europe* 11.4 (2002): 367–88.

24. Catherine Bell, *Ritual Theory, Ritual Practice* (Oxford: Oxford University Press, 1992), 74–90, 204–205 and Penn, *Kissing Christians*, 17.

in his *De differentiis verborum*, friends exchanged *oscula*, spouses *basia*, and lovers *suavia*.[25] Used in Florentine dispute settlements, the *osculum* was a kiss planted fully on the mouth and specified as such. It served to transform enemies into friends, hatred into friendship, discord into concord. Deriving as it did from the pax in the Mass, the kiss in the civic peacemaking process imbued that ritual with something of the nature of a sacred rite. Transmitting an aura of sacrality through its lineal descent from the mass, the kiss tinged the grey legal formulas of the notarial contract with the golden hues of holiness. As a gift from the sacrament, the embodied kiss on the mouth in the context of civic peacemaking doubtless fixed it as the sacred culmination of the process.

The body language of gesture frequently rivals words in its power to convey meaning. As Connerton reminds us, "memory is sedimented, or amassed, in the body" by what he calls the "incorporating practice" of ritual.[26] The body takes center stage in a ritual performance, providing what has been called "gestural discourse."[27] If, for example, we look at lay participation in the liturgy, it is ordinarily the gestural discourse of the body that produces meaning. Think, for example, of any of the most important rites of the Catholic Church. The defining moment of the rite of baptism is when the child's head is immersed at the font, of the Mass when communion is taken by mouth, of marriage when the ring is slipped on the finger, followed by the kiss. Language is almost supplementary, though the two work together in most ritual performances. Lay participation, however, is primarily though the human body, supplemented by the officiant's ritual formulae. Gestures are the moments of power and significance for both enactors and audience alike.[28] And as Connerton argues, ritual gestures both preserve and "convey conviction by incorporating it."[29]

Similarly, I would argue that the embodied kiss of peace conveyed meaning for both the peacemaking parties and their publics. By foregrounding the body and ritual we recognize that, as one historian reminds us, "the deepest human memories are buried in the body. . . . Humans first learn to think with their skins and remember with their bodies."[30] And this I think is the importance of the performance of the ritual kiss: muscle memory of the gesture incorporated

25. No. 398 "Inter osculum et pacem," Bk II of *Differentiarum* in PL 5: col. 51.

26. Connerton, *How Societies Remember*, 72–73.

27. Nathan D. Mitchell, *The Mystery of the Rosary: Marian Devotion and the Reinvention of Catholicism* (New York: New York University Press, 2009), 88. The term is Mitchell's but it should be noted that much of his discussion is based on the historical material presented by Virginia Reinburg, "Liturgy and the Laity in Late Medieval and Reformation France," *The Sixteenth-Century Journal* 23. 3 (1992): 526–47.

28. For gestural discourse in the medieval world, see Jean-Claude Schmitt, *La raison des gestes dans l'Occident médiéval* (Paris: Gallimard, 1990).

29. Connerton, *How Societies Remember*, 70.

30. Mitchell, *The Mystery of the Rosary*, 222.

itself into the bodies of the participants, while the performance imprinted itself into the memories of the witnesses to the event. It is worth remembering that while the peace instrument recorded the legal details of the transaction, it was not the transaction itself. Even the jurists agreed on that point. Baldus de Ubaldis (d. 1400), commenting on the *Digest*, argued: "The point of writing is to prove the transaction more easily, but the transaction, if proved, is valid without it."[31] And that I believe is the work that the kiss was meant to perform.

Theorists have taught us that ritual enactments can in themselves construct or constitute social reality. The sociologist Joachim Knuf argues for the efficacy of ritual performances by its enactors thus:

> From the point of view of the enactor of a ritual, a ritual has a distinctively performative character and serves to bring about changes in the world. . . . Participation in a ritual is tantamount to a subjection of its intent; implementation of the ritual action plan therefore involves participants in behavior that not only symbolizes a certain order of things (or of the world), it executes this order. Many elements of ritualized communication can hence be regarded as signs that create the state they signify.[32]

I take this passage to mean that the outcome of a ritual performance or enactment is to create a "certain order of things" or an intended social reality. On the most basic level, the kiss of peace brought an end to conflict between individuals or groups. From the moment the kiss was exchanged the dispute was considered settled, and a new social reality of peace and concord was constituted between formerly hostile parties. The kiss, as the concluding rite of the agreement between parties was meant to perform three principal functions: first, on a legal level the kiss as a performative gesture enacted the peace; second, on a social level, its action was meant to reset the relationship between antagonists by creating a new social equilibrium; and third, on a civic level, the action of the kiss was meant to transform discord into concord.[33] Therefore, the kiss embodied the moment when the bonds of concord were reestablished and the social relationship, governed by the order of charity, was rebalanced in harmony.

The ability of ritual, in this case the ritual kiss, to enact a new social order or "to assert that what is culturally created and man-made is as undoubtable as physical reality" was an important precondition to reintegrating into the

31. Baldus de Ubaldis, *Commentaria*, 8 vols. (Venice: Giunti, 1599), 7:55v, as cited by Laurie Nussdorfer, *Brokers of Public Trust: Notaries in Early Modern Rome.* (Baltimore: Johns Hopkins University Press, 2009), 15.

32. Joachim Knuf, "Where Cultures Meet: Ritual Code and Organizational Boundary Management," *Research on Language and Social Interaction* 23 (1989/90): 109–38, at 115.

33. Here a gesture is similar in its efficacy to J. L. Austin's concept of speech acts described in *How to Do Things with Words* (Cambridge, MA: Harvard University Press, 1962; repr. 1975), 7, 109, 117.

city those Florentine citizens who, as we saw in chapter 4, had been judicially banished.[34] Anthropologists long ago demonstrated the important role of ritual in reintegrating liminal members of society into their communities.[35] The banniti were among Florence's liminal members, and the ritual was critical to their reintegration into civic society.[36] In this context, the performance of the kiss of peace, a ritual of consensus, unlocked the gates of the city and allowed for the repatriation of the commune's outlaws. The exchange of the kiss of peace, an act saturated with Christian notions of forgiveness and reconciliation, allowed reincorporation of the outlaw into the body social of the late medieval Italian commune. Moreover, it restored Florentine identity to the bannitus, enabling him to participate fully in civic life. Especially where banishment was concerned, the ritual kiss served also to create a new legal reality, ushering in the desired civil state of concord, peace, and security between the commune and its once wayward citizen, reflecting on earth the peace established in heaven. For the sake of peace and security, it was better to repatriate errant citizens than to have them establish what Randolph Starn has termed a "contrary commonwealth" outside the city limits.[37] In this regard the peace instrument served to accommodate both the needs of city and citizen, reestablishing social order through the charity or mercy dispensed by the communal judicial system.

TWO PENITENTIAL PERFORMANCES

Roman Peacemaking

Sometimes, however, one gesture was not deemed sufficient to restore equilibrium and concord between parties. Certain special situations demanded more elaborate penitential rituals if the terms of the peace agreement were to be enacted. Such cases entailed the design of costumes, scripts, and intricate choreography. This section examines two types of performative peace agreements, which combined all these elements. The first case I present is comprised of a few snapshots of Roman peacemaking drawn from scattered protocols in the few notarial registers that survive from the age of Cola di Rienzo.[38] The second is found in one Tuscan notarial casebook. Let us first make the journey to fourteenth-century Rome.

34. *Secular Ritual*, ed. Sally F. Moore and Barbara Myerhoff (Amsterdam: Van Gorcum, 1977), 24.

35. Victor Turner, *The Ritual Process: Structure and Anti-Structure* (Chicago: Aldine, 1969).

36. See chapter 4.

37. Randolph Starn, *Contrary Commonwealth: The Theme of Exile in Medieval and Renaissance Italy* (Berkeley: University of California, 1982). His book, however, deals with the theme of political exile, a punishment—not the judicial ban—which resulted from *contumacia* on the part of the imputed.

38. Glenn Kumhera and James Palmer have both recently analyzed these agreements. See Glenn Kumhera, "Making Peace in Medieval Siena: Instruments of Peace, 1280–1400," PhD diss., University of Chicago, 2005, 147–52; and James Palmer, "Piety and Social

In the mid-fourteenth century Roman peacemaking efforts were sometimes performed following a script prepared by arbiters. In that script, one
party confessed his guilt for the offense given, while the injured party offered
forgiveness to the perpetrator. Often the parties spoke their lines while
reenacting the crime with props and gestures. The script ingeniously rewrote
the original problematic conclusion of the episode. Scenes that had previously
ended in violence and enmity now concluded on a harmonious note, as feuding parties forgave each other and made peace, restoring equilibrium between
the aggrieved disputants.

The earliest penitential peace agreement dates to 1348, the second year
of the operatic Cola di Rienzo's tribuneship of Rome. One year earlier he had
established the Buono Stato for the commune of Rome, a variation on the
"good governments" that ruled central Italy. Among his innovations were a set
of new ordinances and the establishment of the House of Justice and Peace,
an office dedicated to law and order. According to the chronicler known as the
Anonimo Romano, that office mandated a new form of conflict resolution:

> Two enemies came and gave vows of making peace; then, according
> to the nature of the injury, he who had committed the injury suffered
> exactly what he had done to the victim. Then they kissed each other on
> the mouth, and the injured party granted full peace. [For example],
> one man had blinded another in the eye; he came and was accompa-
> nied up the steps of the Campidoglio where he knelt. The man who had
> been blinded came; the malefactor wept and prayed to God that he be
> forgiven. Then he turned up his face to have his eye gouged out, should
> his victim so wish. [But] because he was moved by pity, the victim did
> not blind his assailant. Instead he forgave him his injury.[39]

This new type of Roman dispute settlement was a brilliant admixture of
traditions that drew from both the Hebrew Bible and the New Testament. It
gave the aggrieved party a chance to act out a bloodless version of "an eye
for eye" justice, but in the end he resolved the dispute by turning the other
cheek and offering forgiveness to his assailant. A number of Roman peace

Distinction," *Speculum* 89.4 (2014): 974–1004, whom I thank for sharing the article with
me prior to its publication. Palmer has counted thirty-seven peace agreements of this
type in the years between 1348 through the 1420s. As Massimo Miglio notes, the notarial
records for Rome are completely absent until 1348. It might be worth adding that this
situation results primarily from the sack of Rome in 1527 by the troops of the Holy Roman
Emperor. See his "Gli ideali di pace e giustizia a Roma a metà del Trecento," in *La pace nel
pensiero*, 177–97, at 177.

39. Anonimo Romano, *Cronica*, ed. Giuseppe Porta (Milan: Adelphi, 1979), 159–60.
Identified by Giuseppe Billanovich as Bartolomeo di Iacovo da Valmontone (d. 1357
/1358). G. Billanovich, *Come nacque un capolavoro: la Cronica del non Anonimo romano.
Il vescovo Ildebrandino Conti, Francesco Petrarca e Bartolomeo di Iacovo da Valmontone*
(Rome: Accademia Nazionale dei Lincei, 1995).

contracts appear to follow the spirit if not the letter of the script described by the Anonimo Romano. In August 1360, Lello di Lorenzo di Benedetto, who seems to have been the victim of an assault perpetrated by Nuccio Mangia, made peace with his attacker. Nuccio was directed to approach Lello, whom he would find standing outside the church of Sts. Sergius and Bacchus, and confess his crime according to a prepared text: "Lello, I am guilty of what I've done. Since you didn't defend yourself against me, here is a rod; take whatever vengeance on me that you please." Lello's response—both in word and deed— was equally scripted: "Since I didn't protect myself against you, and because you are guilty, I want to give you a penance." He then struck Nuccio with the rod twice on the shoulder (without blood) before making peace with him.[40] The crime-drama had been rewritten so that now Lello responded with an act of vengeance of his own, albeit a symbolic and bloodless one. In the subsequent contract, Lello and Nuccio exchanged the kiss on the mouth and promised to observe the peace. All this had the effect of reestablishing the social order, as it were. And now that Lello's honor was restored, the two could resolve their conflict. In penitential terms, Nuccio confessed his sin contritely, made satisfaction, and was forgiven by Lello. In secular terms they resolved their dispute. The exchange of the kiss both offered reconciliation and enacted the peace.

In another case, this one from the fourth quarter of the century, the arbiter had the two protagonists reenact the scene of the original offense, but with strategic changes. After exchanging confessions and words of forgiveness, the two quarreling parties had to switch places in a restaged version of the crime. This time Nardolo di Silvestro became the victim and Paolo di Nuzio Cocoli, the aggressor. The stage directions read: "Nardolo ought to move and flee Paolo at a steady pace until reaching the said intersection, and Paolo should approach him at the aforesaid place with his sword sheathed in his hand. When both parties arrive, [Paolo], with a certain rod that we will place in his hands, ought to strike Nardolo two times on the shoulder, below the neck, without blood."[41]

Such ritualized performances satisfied the demands of penance and pardon, honor and justice. Guilt and contrition were offered up in a confession. Retributive justice of the "eye for an eye" sort prescribed by Mosaic law, or what the participants would have recognized as the *lex talionis*, was administered symbolically with the rod, thereby restoring honor to the injured party. The ritual kiss then brought reconciliation. The net effect of these scripted penitential rituals was to reset the clock so that social order was restored to the community and honor to the aggrieved parties. Tellingly, the peace agreement from San Gimignano had other intentions as well.

40. This took place on 25 August 1360. See *I Protocolli di Iohannes Nicolai Pauli, un notaio romano del '300 (1348–1379)*, ed. Renzo Mosti (Roma: École Française de Rome, 1982), 145–46. Cited in Palmer, "Piety and Social Distinction," 982.

41. A case from 13 September 1380, *Un notaio romano del Trecento: I protocolli di Francesco di Stefano de Caputgallis (1374–1386)*, ed. Renzo Mosti (Rome: Viella, 1994), 332.

PEACE, PENANCE, AND PERFORMANCE
IN SAN GIMIGNANO[42]

On 10 April 1258, the four brothers of the Salvucci lineage—Maso, Abate, Palmerio and Michele—came together "to seek peace humbly with members of the Mangeri family: namely, Mangerio, along with his sons Ranuccio, Rainaldo, Offreduccio, Forciore, Orlandino (all commonly known as the sons of Mangerio) and Ranieri, son of Ildebrandino della Torre."[43] The Salvucci men were seeking peace because they had violated the city statute of 1255 that had placed height restrictions on San Gimignano's towers.[44]

San Gimignano is well known as the archetypal city of medieval towers. Taddeo di Bartolo's panel painting captured that city's skyline in 1381 (fig. 16), but tower construction had begun at least two centuries earlier at the beginning of the communal period. Only sixteen towers remain of the medieval seventy-two, or the twenty-five noted in the sixteenth century,[45] the most imposing of which was "la Rognosa," the tower of the Palazzo del Podestà, which rose to a vertiginous 85 braccia, almost 51 meters tall. A building code written into the statutes protected its dominance on the skyline, prohibiting the height of any tower in any quarter of the city to surpass that of la Rognosa.[46]

42. This section, here slightly revised, was originally published by Brill as "Peacemaking, Performance, and Power in Thirteenth-Century San Gimignano," in *Center and Periphery: Studies on Power in the Medieval World in Honor of William Chester Jordan*, ed. Katherine L. Jansen, Guy Geltner, and Anne E. Lester (Leiden: Brill, 2013), 93–106.

43. Arrigo di Ianni, ASF, Not. Ant. 956, fols. 1r–1v. This contract is among those published in *Collectio chartarum paci private Medii Aevi ad regionem Tusciae pertinentium*, ed. Gino Masi, (Milan: Vita e Pensiero, 1943), 293–301. Note that Salvi and Salvucci are one and the same family. See Giovanni Coppi, *Annali, memorie et huomini illustri di San Gimignano* (Florence: Cesare & Francesco Bindi, 1695), avviso, n. p. The Salvucci towers still define the skyline of San Gimignano. The town had fallen to Florentine domination by the mid-thirteenth century, which may explain why the contract is dated with reference to the term of Aliotto Contenacci as podestà of Florence, and why Arrigo di Ianni's register is among the holdings of the ASF. For the Salvucci, Mangeri, and della Torre, see Enrico Fiumi, *Storia economica e sociale di San Gimignano* (Florence: Leo S. Olschki, 1961), 261–62, 274–75, 277–78.

44. On the statute law of 1255, see now *Lo Statuto di San Gimignano del 1255*, ed. Silvia Diacciati and Lorenzo Tanzini, with contributions from Enrico Faini and Tomaso Perani (Florence: Leo S. Olschki, 2016). For the judicial system in San Gimignano in a slightly later period, see now Tamara Graziotti, *Giustizia penale a San Gimignano, 1300–1350* (Florence: Leo S. Olschki, 2015).

45. Luigi Pecori, *Storia della terra di San Gimignano* (Florence: Tipografia Galileiana, 1853), 581.

46. "Statuti del commune di San Gimignano compilati nel 1255," ed. Luigi Pecori, in *Storia della terra di San Gimignano*, Lib. IV, Rub. 12, 721–22: "Item omnia hedificia in S. Gem. ulterius construenda, vel altius elevanda, tantum construi et altius elevari possint, quantum est aer turris roniose, et non plus aliquo modo; in quacumque contrada sunt vel fuerint a campanile inferius, et ipsa turris roniosa non altius elevetur, quam modo est."

FIGURE 16. *The Rognosa Tower* (detail). Taddeo di Bartolo, panel painting of
San Gimignano, 1381. A flag waves atop the tower, which is located
in the rear center. Museo Civico, San Gimignano.
Photo reproduced by permission of Scala/Art Resource, New York.

Here we examine the case of a family who ignored that law to their own
detriment. They were forced to submit to an act of penitential peacemaking,
punished, and brought low as much for their pretensions of grandeur as for
their politics. Significantly, it was the peace agreement through which the penalty or penance—in this case the two were indistinguishable—was imposed.

At issue was the Salvucci family's fortified tower that had already been the
object of the podestà's concern ten years earlier. In 1248 the tower had reached
such an alarming altitude that Lord Lanfranchino Bocci, then podestà of the
city, warned Salvuccio, under a stiff penalty of 1000 silver marks, that his
tower had better not surpass the height of la Rognosa.

The Mangeri enter the picture one year later, in 1249, when the first piece
of evidence documenting enmity between the families surfaces: a truce had
been arranged between their warring factions.[47] It must be remembered that
this was a period of heated unrest between the Guelfs and Ghibellines in all of
Tuscany, and San Gimignano offered a microcosm of that unrest. There, the
Guelf Party, led by Guido Ardinghelli, had fomented a rebellion against the
Ghibelline sons of Salvuccio three years earlier.[48] The Mangeri lineage, Guelfs
to the bone, staunchly supported the Ardinghelli family against their enemies,
and most particularly against the Salvucci.

The Salvucci-Mangeri pax stipulated as part of the settlement that ten
braccia had to be removed from the principal tower—there were two—of the
Salvucci clan's palazzo.[49] But the tower was not the only issue at stake. The

47. See *Collectio chartarum*, ed. Gino Masi, 434–38.
48. Pecori, *Storia della terra di San Gimignano*, 68.
49. Arrigo di Ianni, ASF, Not. Ant. 956, fols. 1r–1v: "ipsi filii quondam Salvii debeant
destruere de summitate turris eorum maioris .x. brachia." The phrasing confirms that Salvi
had more than one tower. One braccio was equal to the "length of the two arms extended

architecture of the Salvucci palace itself also caused offense to the Mangeri, presumably because of the addition of some defensive constructions. The palace architecture featured a crenellated parapet, a type of defensive wall on the roof. It also had lower exits that could be accessed by a back passageway, perhaps installed for quick getaways or easy provisioning in the event of a siege.

The peace agreement compelled the Salvucci to destroy the crenellations and parapets on the upper story of the palace. They also agreed to wall up with brick and plaster all the offending entrances at the rear of the building, which opened onto the passageway. [50] The Mangeri further demanded that the Salvucci not buy any property within a radius of 20 braccia (10 meters) of their own family tower, which most likely soared heavenward from the southern end of the Piazza del Duomo, near their Guelf allies, the Ardinghelli. Together their towers stood tall in fierce opposition to the Salvucci compound on the northern end of the square.[51] The location of all these towers was notable as it was at the heart of both the religious and secular power in the city, where the Collegiata and the Palazzo Vecchio del Podestà were also located (fig. 17).[52]

As noted earlier, it is important to place the Mangeri complaint against the Salvucci palace and tower in the partisan context of seemingly endless and bitter Guelf and Ghibelline strife. In 1251, after the death of Frederick II, when Ghibelline influence was temporarily on the wane, the Guelfs were able to seize power in the city. And it is in this framework—of Guelf ascendency and temporary Ghibelline retreat—that we must understand the peace agreement of 1258 that settled the dispute between the Salvucci and the Mangeri.

In addition to the architectural sanctions, there is another set of provisions in the contract which are initially a bit more puzzling. They stipulate:

> The aforesaid Maso and Abate shall wear black clothing, lined in black, and they shall not have their beards shaved with a razor for fewer than

---

when measured from the tips of the middle fingers and was reckoned generally between 5 and 6 piedi." Ronald Edward Zupko, *Italian Weights and Measures from the Middle Ages to the Nineteenth Century* (Philadelphia: American Philosophical Society, 1981), 40.

50. Ibid., "item merlos et pectoralia de ipsorum palatio a volta superius; item quod murent ostia omnia inferiora eorum palatii ex parte anteriori, iuxta carrariam, ad mattones et calcinam."

51. Although all traces of the Mangeri palazzo and tower have since disappeared, we do have some evidence that it was located in the vicinity of the Ardinghelli family complex. Giovanna Casali notes that Piazza del Duomo was widened in the thirteenth century and that a new road was made on land bought from the Mangeri where their *claustrum* had once stood. See her *L'evoluzione della città tra XIV e XVI secolo* (Florence: Leo S. Olschki, 1998), 13. In addition, Fiumi cites a document of 1250 that notes that the Mangeri had a tower behind the baptismal church, which confirms their southern position on the piazza. See his *Storia economica*, 262.

52. The Palazzo del Popolo (or Palazzo del Comune) had not yet been built. It was begun in 1288 and became the new seat of the podestà in 1337.

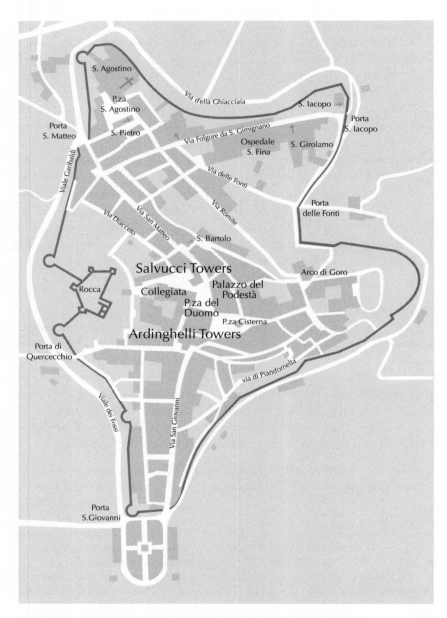

FIGURE 17. Piazza del Duomo, San Gimignano. The Salvucci Towers
are on the northern end of the piazza, those of the Mangeri (no longer
extant) and the Ardinghelli were on the southern end. For the purposes of
orientation, modern street names are given. Map by Gaia Beltrame.

ten years, at the discretion of the Mangeri. And all these things shall begin when it pleases the aforesaid Mangerio and Ranuccio.[53]

It appears that we have now left the world of secular pecuniary fines and entered into the realm of religiously inspired penance, somewhat akin to that received by Melibeus from his enemies in Albertanus da Brescia's *Liber conciliationis et consilii*, examined in the previous chapter. The agreed-upon penalty seems to have been borrowed from the bishop's court and was imposed by Lord Niccolò di Andrea, an expert in law, mentioned in the agreement and most likely the mediator or broker of the peace.[54] In this case, satisfaction was imposed and imbued with penitential overtones drawn from Christian tradition, but it was not expressed through spoken word or gesture; rather, it was displayed through costume. Through penitential clothing and unkempt hair, penance was performed and publicly enacted.

The imposition of the color black on the Salvucci men was without doubt a form of penance.[55] The wardrobes of the fashionable elite in thirteenth and fourteenth-century Italy were splashed with color, as is revealed by the spectrum of bold colors in which the leading citizens of Siena are arrayed in Ambrogio Lorenzetti's allegory of Good Government (fig. 18).[56]

Sartorial splendor, flaunted in colorful textiles, was a mark of status. Vivid color announced to the world that your income allowed for expensively dyed and finished fabrics. Significantly, this was true not only for women, but for men as well. If clothing made the man, it was richly colored and textured clothing that made the elite, powerful, and fashionable man of the thirteenth century.[57] Inventories of wardrobes often take pains to distinguish colors and textiles, as does a Florentine peace agreement, already examined in chapter 3, which listed articles of clothing declared stolen. Among other things it listed two vermilion overvests, two more scarlet garments, and a tunic colored green

53. Arrigo di Ianni, ASF, Not. Ant. 956, fols. 1r-1v: "Item quod dicti Masus et Abate induant pannos nigros et fodera nigra et sibi barbas cum rasorio radi non faciant per decem annos vel minus ad voluntatem ipsorum. Et quod huius omnia incipiant quando placuerit dicto domino Mangerio et Ranuccio."

54. "Et ipsorum preceptis omnibus parere publice statim dicendis per dominum Nicholaum quondam Andree iuris peritum nomine predictorum . . . ." He may have even been an arbiter or arbitrator but is never referred to as such.

55. For the clothing of male religious, see Cordelia Warr, *Dressing for Heaven: Religious Clothing in Italy, 1215–1545* (Manchester: Manchester University Press, 2010), 57–129; and Maureen Miller, *Clothing the Clergy: Virtue and Power in Medieval Europe, c. 800–1200* (Ithaca, NY: Cornell University Press, 2014).

56. Literature on this wall mural is cited in chapter 1, n. 1.

57. Susan Mosher Stuard, *Gilding the Market: Luxury and Fashion in Fourteenth-Century Italy* (Philadelphia: University of Pennsylvania Press, 2006), 60. See also Maria Giuseppina Muzzarelli, *Guardaroba medievale: vesti e società dal XIII al XVI secolo* (Bologna: Il Mulino, 1999).

FIGURE 18. *Citizens of Siena* (detail). *Allegory of the Bonds of Concord.* Ambrogio
Lorenzetti, "Buon Governo," fresco, 1338–1339. Sala dei Nove, Palazzo Pubblico,
Siena. Photo reproduced by permission of Alinari/Art Resource, New York.

and brown.[58] Herman Pleij, historian of color, tells us that shades of red, such
as scarlet, crimson, and vermilion "were especially coveted, as these costly red
dyestuffs were extracted from snails that were difficult to obtain."[59]

The association of vibrant color with luxury and fashion would per-
sist until the mid-fourteenth century, when black and blue became the
somber colors favored by princes and the urban aristocracy.[60] But here in
mid-thirteenth-century San Gimignano, black was the antithesis to the
rainbow hues worn in the world. The rich intensity that would characterize the
color in subsequent centuries was not possible given thirteenth-century dying
techniques. Black in the Duecento was likely rather dull, since even black wool
tended to yellow in the sunlight.[61] Its dull sobriety would suggest a state of
contrition comprised of equal parts self-abnegation, repentance, and humility.[62]
Not coincidentally, earlier in the century, in explicating the meanings of liturgical colors worn by the clergy, Pope Innocent III had noted that "black
clothing is used on days of affliction and abstinence, for sins, and for the dead;
namely, from Advent up to Christmas Eve and from Septuagesima until Holy

58. See chapter 3, n. 109 for the Latin description. Andrea di Lapo, ASF, Not. Ant. 439,
fols. 121v–122v.

59. Herman Pleij, *Colors Demonic and Divine: Shades of Meaning in the Middle Ages
and After*, trans. Diane Webb (New York: Columbia University Press, 2004), 6.

60. See Pleij, *Colors Demonic*, 6 and 33; Stuard, *Gilding the Market*, 42.

61. Michel Pastoureau, *Black: the History of a Color* (Princeton: Princeton University
Press, 2008), 90.

62. Pleij, *Colors Demonic*, 6.

Saturday."[63] For all these reasons, it was an appropriate color for penance.[64] Obligating the Salvucci men to wear it every day would compel them to reflect daily—and with compunction—on the crime they had committed. That the color black was stipulated down to the lining of their garments shows that this was meant not only as a penance, but as a secular punishment as well: it was a symbolic demotion in the social hierarchy. To don black forced a renunciation of the Salvucci men's privilege of wearing sumptuous, expensively dyed, and fur-lined clothing, a marker of birth and status in status-conscious medieval Italy.[65] It put them in the same category, at least sartorially, as Fra Benedetto that trumpet-blasting penitent, who, it will be remembered, wore a tunic of black sackcloth. It was, moreover, a particularly pointed punishment given the social origins of the Salvucci lineage, a family that could not claim ancient magnate status like the Mangeri knights, whose roots reached back to one of the city's original consuls.[66] Indeed, the *Cronichetta of San Gimignano*, written in verse by a Franciscan friar a century later, describes the Mangeri as "men of arms and very wise."[67] By contrast, the Salvucci, born of *piccola gente* according to the chronicler, had raised themselves up by their bootstraps to become the richest family in San Gimignano.[68] Himself the son of a merchant moneylender, Salvuccio had a shop that traded in saffron, a commodity precious to San Gimignano's economy.[69] He used his profits to earn an even greater income by lending money at profit to both individuals and the communal government. The term usurer is not out of place. In a legal case brought against him for overcharging on saffron, Salvuccio was described in accurate if unflattering terms: "Salvuccius est usurarius et cotidie extorquet usuras."[70]

One is reminded of another better known but equally contrite usurer memorialized by Giotto about 45 years after the Salvucci-Ranieri peace agreement was made. Enrico Scrovegni, the founder of the Arena Chapel in Padua,

63. "Nigris autem indumentis utendum est in die afflictionis et abstinentiae, pro peccatis et pro defunctis. Ab adventu scilicet usque ad Natalis vigiliam, et a Septuagesima usque ad Sabbatum Paschae." *Mysteriorum evangelicae legis et sacramenti eucharistiae*, Lib. I: 65 ("De quatuor coloribus principalibus, quibus secundum proprietates dierum vestes sunt distinguenda"), PL 217:802A.

64. For the changing significance of the color black, see Pastoureau, *Black: The History of a Color*.

65. Among other studies that consider male fashion in communal Italy, see Stuard, *Gilding the Market* and Catherine Kovesi Killerby, *Sumptuary Law in Italy, 1200–1500* (Oxford: Clarendon Press, 2002).

66. Fiumi, *Storia economica e sociale*, 261–62.

67. "Uomini furon d'armi, e ben sagagi." Fra Matteo Chiaccheri, "Cronichetta di San Gimignano (1353)" and the "Libro d'oro sangimignanese," ed. Carlo Talei in *Miscellanea storica della Valdelsa*, n.s. 160 (1865): 125–46.

68. "Cronichetta," 128.

69. The "Cronichetta's" description of the family's origins is less flattering: "Attorno andavano col panier vendendo agora, anella e cotai cose lievi," 28.

70. Fiumi, *Storia economica e sociale*, 93.

FIGURE 19. *Enrico Scrovegni Dressed in Penitential Violet*. Giotto, donor
portrait fresco, 1305. Arena Chapel, Padua. Photo: Mauro Magliani.
Reproduced by permission of Alinari/Art Resource, New York.

is portrayed in his donor portrait in what art historians have recently come to
call a garb of "penitential violet" (fig. 19).[71] And not without reason: at least
as early as Innocent III, as we have seen, violet and black were regarded as
interchangeable colors of penance.[72]

71. Derbes and Sandona, *The Usurer's Heart*, 7.
72. "Ad hos quatuor caeteri referuntur. Ad rubeum colorem coccineus, ad nigrum vio-
laceus, ad viridem croceus." *Mysteriorum evangelicae legis et sacramenti eucharistiae*, Lib.
I: 65 ("De quatuor coloribus principalibus"), PL 217:802C.

Like Scrovegni, Salvuccio had amassed a great fortune. Therefore it is not without reason that Enrico Fiumi has called the Salvucci clan *i più grossi capitalisti della terra*.[73] In the *estimo* (tax assessment) of forty-three hearths of 1277, the Salvucci clan topped the list of the commune's wealthiest citizens, while the Mangeri ranked twenty-second on the same list. The disparity in income between the two families is striking: the Mangeri claimed only 468 lire, while the Salvucci declared 5,379 lire, an income more than eleven times that of their Guelf rivals, and certainly enough to afford the golden spurs that the *Cronichetta* claimed the Salvucci men wore on their heels![74] One can only imagine that the cash-strapped but noble Mangeri were only too happy to agree to a punishment for the nouveau-riche Salvucci that would take them down a rung in the city's social hierarchy. The peace agreement, then, served to curb the Salvucci's showy displays of power and wealth. It put them in their place—at least figuratively speaking.

The punishment of wearing long beards and hair complicates the picture even further.[75] Big bushy beards would have set the brothers apart from properly "civilized" and clean-shaven male society. But here too, there is a penitential aspect to their punishment as John Beleth, a twelfth-century Parisian master, suggested when he observed, "Those who perform penance let their hair and beard grow in order to show the abundance of crimes with which the head, that is, the mind of the sinner, is burdened."[76] According to G. G. Meersseman, the eminent scholar of religious confraternities, long-bearded penitents were not an uncommon sight in the piazze of late medieval urban Italy, and one need only recall the wild and wooly Fra Benedetto da Cornetta to confirm this assertion.[77]

Leaving their hair untamed as punishment may also have had a gendered dimension to it. By the thirteenth century, most pundits and moralists agreed that long hair was a female attribute; men's hair was generally worn closely cropped and covered by a *cuffia*, a sheer white cap tied under the chin. Ten years growth of hair—untouched by scissors—no doubt would have resulted in the long, unruly hair more generally associated with women, particularly

73. *Storia economica e sociale*, 93.

74. *Storia economica e sociale*, 116–17. "E calzati hanno poi gli spron dell'oro, perchè venuti sono in gran ricchezza," "*Cronichetta*," 129.

75. Robert Bartlett, "Symbolic Meaning of Hair in the Middle Ages," in *Transactions of the Royal Historical Society*, 6th series, 4 (1994): 43–60; and Giles Constable, "Introduction" (on beards in the Middle Ages) to Burchard of Bellevaux, *Apologiae de Barbis*, ed. R.B.C. Huygens, in *Apologia duae*, CCCM 62 (Turnhout: Brepols, 1985), 47–130. Many thanks go to Bill Jordan for these references. See now Christopher Oldstone-Moore, *Of Beards and Men: The Revealing History of Facial Hair* (Chicago: Chicago University Press, 2016).

76. Quoted in Constable, "Introduction," 67.

77. "I penitenti nei secoli XI e XII," in *I laici nella 'Societas Christiana' dei secoli XI e XII. Atti della terza settimana internazionale di studio. Mendola, 21–27 agosto 1965* (Milan: Vita e Pensiero, 1968), 306–45, at 323.

young women or those in mourning. By playing with the signification of hair, it is possible that the penance was meant to demote the Salvucci brothers symbolically to the status of women—repentant women—figured most prominently in medieval art by the penitent-saint Mary Magdalen clothed in nothing but her mane of abundant hair.[78] According to legend, this great mane of hair was the result of thirty years of expiation in the desert. Only in the fourteenth century would images of Saint Onuphrius, wild and hairy, offer a complementary vision of a male penitent in the wilderness.

With its focus on color and hair, the Salvucci men's punishment for breaking the law and overstepping their social position, experimented with the categories of social status and gender: in the first case, degrading it—or unmasking it—and in the second inverting it. And just as distinguishing signs marked out Jews and prostitutes from the rest of medieval society, so too did somber black clothing and unkempt beards identify the Salvucci men as penitents who were making amends for a crime.[79] In agreeing to dress themselves in black and grow out their beards, Maso and Abate donned the costume of those atoning for sins in order to perform an act of public penance for the wrongs they had committed. Their unadorned wardrobe had the effect of transforming them from belligerents into humble penitents on the stage of communal social life. Each morning, for a decade, they would be required to enact or act out their penance, replacing what could have been the social drama of vendetta with a penitential performance. Embodying penance was thus perhaps a sentence far more effective than any pecuniary penalty could have been. The Mangeri succeeded in imposing (at least contractually) a harsh penance—essentially a targeted sumptuary law—on their arriviste Ghibelline rivals, and they would be obligated to perform it for ten long years. Stripped visually of their power and status, the Salvucci men were humbled daily in the central square of San Gimignano. One can only wonder if the repetition of this penitential performance might have had an actual transformative effect, bringing about self-reformation in the Salvucci men. Today's cognitive neuroscience suggests that this is possible when a subject adheres to such emotional scripts.

We noted earlier that this was not an ordinary, *pro forma* peace agreement. Nor were these ordinary, just-plain folks. They were among the most important families of the city, each representing feuding factions on either side of the political divide. Their disputes and their ensuing vendettas

---

78. It was common belief by the twelfth century that as a sign of her penitence, Mary Magdalen's already long mane of hair had grown out to cover her entire body. See Katherine L. Jansen, *The Making of the Magdalen: Preaching and Popular Devotion in the Later Middle Ages* (Princeton: Princeton University Press, 2000), 130–34.

79. The classic article showing the link between Jews and prostitutes is Diane Owen Hughes, "Distinguishing Signs: Earrings, Jews, and Franciscan Rhetoric in the Italian Renaissance City," *Past and Present* 112 (1986): 3–59.

inevitably embroiled and disrupted the entire city. Consequently, the provisions of the Mangeri-Salvucci peace agreement almost by necessity had to be a public affair. The city needed to see that the contract was in force and its terms respected. On the political plane it demonstrated daily that the Guelfs were in power and the Ghibellines had submitted to their authority. It was an unusual, extraordinary settlement, one that is not representative of ordinary Tuscan peacemaking practices. Though informed by penitential ideas and practice, its aim was a bit different from the others we have seen. In this case, restoring equilibrium meant restoring the social hierarchy, with each family in its proper place, as the Mangeri wished things to be. Or as Giordano da Pisa encapsulated the problem and its solution in a sermon he would later preach in Florence on the theme of *Pax vobis*: "If people were humble, and remained in their places, there would be peace and prosperity."[80] One can imagine that the Mangeri could not have agreed more with this sentiment.

The San Gimignano peace sought to humble the Salvucci men through public penance, while simultaneously restoring the honor of the Mangeri family by bringing down their political enemies. At the outset, the contract specified that the Salvucci men had sought peace humbly from Lord Mangerio. Tellingly, only the Salvucci had to vow on the gospel to abide by the terms of Lord Niccolo's judgment in the case, accepting their ritual punishment and humiliation for the good of peace. As Keith Brown notes in regard to a very different set of circumstances in sixteenth-century Scotland, "The honour lost in the failure to attain blood vengeance was regained in the public humiliation of one's enemies." [81] Paradoxically, however, the agreement contains signs of reciprocity as well: in addition to the exchange of the kiss of peace on the mouth, appended to the pax were five separate agreements that recorded events meant to strengthen relations between the families. These were marriage contracts aimed to secure the peace between the two lineages and bind them into a future friendly rapport (*pro ipsa pace firma reddenda et inter se amicitia copulanda*). If peace contracts aspired to create a new social reality, transforming enmity into concord, marriage alliances went a step further, attempting to construct a new emotional reality where hatred would be converted into friendship. In this case it may not have been the sort of friendship between social equals imagined by Cicero, but it may have had a

80. Sermo LII, *Prediche del Beato Giordano da Rivalto*, 316.

81. Quotation: Keith M. Brown, *Bloodfeud in Scotland, 1573–1625: Violence, Justice and Politics in an Early Modern Society* (Edinburgh: John Donald, 1986), 54. Ethnographical studies have revealed ritual humiliation as part of the peacemaking process in diverse cultures. See, for example, among many, the rituals described in Montenegro and Morocco in Christopher Boehm, *Blood Revenge: The Anthropology of Feuding in Montenegro and Other Tribal Societies* (Lawrence, KS: University Press of Kansas, 1984), 135–36; and Raymond Jamous, "From the Death of Men to the Peace of God: Violence and Peacemaking in the Rif," in *Honor and Grace in Anthropology*, ed. J.G. Peristiany and Julian Pitt-Rivers (Cambridge: Cambridge University Press, 1992), 167–91, at 181–82.

Ciceronian dimension in that there was reciprocity, as good will was meant to be "reciprocated in equal measure."[82]

MARRIAGES: *PRO BONO PACIS*

Marital alliances in the Middle Ages, especially between elites, were rarely based on ties of affection; they were a reciprocal means to an end, instruments for establishing harmonious political relationships or stabilizing relations between warring factions.[83] In the latter case, as Anton Blok and other anthropologists studying peacemaking practices in Mediterranean societies have observed, such practice has "homeopathic implications." That is, on the same principle as the old adage that declared "like things are cured by like," so, in marriage agreements. The blood of enemies shed in violence would be symbolically remedied by the blood of the virgin-bride shed in the marriage bed.[84]

In 1239, however, the bloodshed inflicted in one particular act of vengeance could not wait for the nuptial bed. Blood had been spilled in Campo di Valdarno, at the wedding feast celebrating the marriage of Neri Piccolino degli Uberti and the daughter of Ranieri "lo Zingaro" Buondelmonte, an alliance forged to establish peace between those two important lineages. Those family names should set bells ringing. It will be recalled that in an act of vendetta in 1215, Schiatta degli Uberti killed Buondelmonte dei Buondelmonti for

82. On the history of emotions, see Barbara H. Rosenwein, "Worrying about Emotions in History," *AHR* 109 (2002): 821–45 and Rosenwein, *Generations of Feeling: A History of Emotions, 600–1700* (Cambridge: Cambridge University Press, 2015). The bibliography on Ciceronian friendship is vast, therefore I limit myself to citing one recent article with up-to-date bibliography: Constant J. Mews, "Cicero on Friendship," in *Friendship: A History*, ed. Barbara Caine (New York: Routledge, 2014), 65–73, at 66.

83. On marriage, family and kinship in medieval Italy, see Giovanni Tabacco, "Le rapport de parenté comme instrument de domination consortiale: Quelques exemples piemontais," in *Famille et parenté dans l'Occident medieval. Actes du Colloque de Paris (6–8 juin 1974): organisé par l'École pratique des hautes études (VIe section) en collaboration avec le Collège de France et L'École française de Rome: communication et débats*, ed. Georges Duby and Jacques Le Goff (Rome: l'École française de Rome, 1977), 153–58; Christiane Klapisch-Zuber, *Women, Family, and Ritual in Renaissance Italy*, trans. Lydia Cochrane (Chicago: University of Chicago Press, 1985); David Herlihy and Christiane Kapisch-Zuber, *Tuscans and Their Families: A Study of the Florentine Catasto of 1427* (New Haven: Yale University Press, 1985); Carol Lansing, *The Florentine Magnates: Lineage and Faction in a Medieval Commune* (Princeton: Princeton University Press, 1991); Christiane Klapish-Zuber, "Kinship and Politics in Fourteenth-Century Florence," in *The Family in Italy from Antiquity to the Present*, ed. David L. Kertzer and Richard P. Saller (New Haven: Yale University Press, 1991), 208–228; *Marriage in Italy, 1300–1650*, ed. Trevor Dean and K.J.P. Lowe (Cambridge: Cambridge University Press, 1998); and Diana C. Silverman, "Marriage and Political Violence in the Chronicles of the Medieval Veneto," *Speculum* 86 (2011): 652–87.

84. Blok, *Honour and Violence*, 94–95.

breaking off his engagement to the daughter of an Uberti ally, a grave offense to the family honor. With this new wedding, a generation later, it appeared that the two families were about to lay those enmities to rest. Or were they? At the wedding feast all such pacific plans (if ever they had existed) were scuttled when Simone Donati killed Jacopo, son of Schiatta degli Uberti, in vendetta for Buondelmonte's killing twenty-four years earlier. Neri Piccolino degli Uberti, the bridegroom, lost no time in taking retaliation on the Buondelmonti, repudiating his newly wedded wife by proclaiming publicly: "I don't want to sire children from a race of traitors!"[85]

Notwithstanding this spectacularly unsuccessful example of an arranged marriage intended to secure peace in medieval Florence, the practice continued. The marriages made between the Strinati and the della Tosa in 1267 were of this sort, as were those that we have already seen arranged by Cardinal Latino to promote the peace of 1280. The commune borrowed a leaf from the cardinal's playbook when ten years later the priors resorted to the same tactic to bring peace between the della Tosa and Lamberti families, even supplying generous dowries for the brides.[86]

Dowries of course were economic transactions. In the San Gimignano case we have been considering, they provided the economic basis for the five marriage and betrothal contracts intended to cement the peace between the Salvucci and the Mangeri.[87] The first contract—about a month after the peace—saw Ventriglio, son of Mangeri, married to Ammirata, daughter of Salvuccio. The ceremony took place in the Salvucci palace before two judges and three witnesses. The ritual formula recorded in the notarial contract notes that the marriage was contracted when Ventriglio put a ring on Ammirata's "fourth finger of her right hand as a sign of the true marital bond" (*contraxerunt immisso anulo ab ipso viro in quarto digito dextre manus ipsius mulieris, in signum vere copule coniugalis*).[88] Seven months later the young couple declared that they had received the generous dowry assigned to them by Ammirata's brothers and agreed to the disposition of it should the marriage dissolve. This marriage (and the others made between the Salvucci women and the Mangeri men) produced another added benefit that would not have gone unnoticed by the Mangeri family. A portion of Ammirata's not insubstantial

85. Lansing, *The Florentine Magnates*, 125–26. The episode is also described in Massimo Tarassi, "Buondelmonti, Ranieri, detto lo Zingaro," in DBI 15 (1972): 219–20.

86. Lansing, ibid., 27.

87. On the dowry system, see Diane Owen Hughes, "From Brideprice to Dowry in Mediterranean Europe," *Journal of Family History* 3 (1978): 262–96; Julius Kirshner, *Pursuing Honor While Avoiding Sin: The Monte delle doti of Florence* (Milan: Giuffrè, 1978); Anthony Molho, *Marriage Alliance in Late Medieval Florence* (Cambridge, MA: Harvard University Press, 1994); and among her many articles on the subject, Isabelle Chabot, "La beneficenza dotale nei testamenti del tardo Medioevo," in *Povertà e innovazioni istituzionali in Italia dal Medioevo ad oggi*, ed. Vera Zamagni (Milan: Il Mulino, 2000), 55–76.

88. *Collectio chartarum*, ed. Gino Masi, 304.

dowry would likely have been used to relieve the financial pressure caused by the declining fortunes of the Mangeri.

The subsequent contracts made on the same day and in the same place were betrothal agreements, because in each of them at least one of the parties was still underage. In the first, *pro bono pacis*, with the dowry stipulated, Ranerio of Ildebrandino della Torre contracted with Maso Salvucci to marry Ghisluccia, his daughter, when she reached puberty. In the second, Forciore, son of Forciore, promised in the name of his son Ugolino (called Ghino) to marry Nese, another daughter of Maso Salvucci. Because both were underage their fathers pledged betrothal on their behalf. And in the final contract made that day for the good of peace, Palmerio Salvucci made a promise to Rainaldo of Ildebrandino that his son Bonacurso (called Pelliccione) would marry Migliuça, daughter of Rainaldo. In this case Palmerio received a dowry of 200 Pisan denarii, a sum he promised to return two-fold if Pelliccione failed to marry Migliuça.

A few days later, on the ides of May, and again *pro bono pacis*, the two lineages contracted one final marriage, this time uniting Salvuccio's grandson Upizino, son of Ranuccio Pantalei, with Suffredingha daughter of Offreduccio Mangeri. It would be nice to think that the Mangeri daughters flourished in their marriages to the Salvucci, because after 1332 the noble house of Mangeri disappeared from the tax records of San Gimignano, while the Salvucci continued to prosper well into the seventeenth century.[89]

I have found only two further examples of notarial betrothals made as a result of a peace agreement, and both come from the register of Ser Boldrone of Civitella, who worked deep in the Florentine contado as a notary at the Abbey of Santa Maria di Trivio a Monte Cornaro, located in the Tosco-Romagnoli Apennines. Neither contract appears to involve particularly important lineages.[90] Enacted in the fall of 1326 in Cameragia at the house of Nutio, the three sons of Zuardo—Cuito, Ducio and Giovannutio—made peace with Nutio and Cambino, sons of Santino. As was standard, both parties promised to maintain the peace; unusually, they also promised to Federico, abbot of the monastery of Cornaro, that they would do so. Each side then brought forward six *fideiussores* who promised to pay the fine should the peace be broken. The scene then shifts to Cambino's house where a second contract was drawn up. Here Cambino arranges to betroth his daughter Vanna to Giovannutio. Cambino promises that when she reaches legal age Vanna will marry Giovannutio; for his part, the future bridegroom promises to accept her when she does. To seal this contract Cambino advances more than two-thirds of the dowry, the other part payable when, at a future date, they actually tie the knot.

The other agreement, enacted in Mercatale di Trivio in the dead of winter 1330, was made to bring peace to two parties for various offenses, including

---

89. Arrigo di Ianni, ASF, Not. Ant. 956, fols. 11r-11v. For the conclusion of the story, see Jansen, "Peacemaking, Performance and Power in Thirteenth-Century San Gimignano," 106.
90. Boldrone de Civitella, ASF, Not. Ant. 3830, fols. 195r-195v.

homicide. Though we do not know who was killed or why, we do know that Caso and Pelegrino, sons of Banfeltro, who made up one of the parties to peace, promised to marry their niece, Iohanna, to Gianotto of Balze, one of the ten men comprising the other party settling the dispute that day. The precise dowry was not stipulated but when it was (sometime in the future), Gianotto would promise to accept Iohanna as his wife; he was bound by a financial penalty if he reneged on his word.[91]

Though the documentary evidence is too scant to draw any sweeping conclusions, what can be said for now is that, like dispute resolutions themselves, marriage alliances for the good of peace were not restricted to the elites. Members of the popolo also used marriages strategically to fortify their resolutions to end conflict. And like elites, the popolani used peace instruments in an effort to transform relationships, converting hatred into friendship and discord into concord.

Such marriages, we should note, became living embodiments of peace. The bride was possibly considered a paciere of sorts, charged with defending the peace between lineages. If children were born from such alliances, they too were destined to become living memorials to peace. One can imagine parents whose marriages had been arranged *pro bono pacis* spinning out tales for their children about how they were the fruits of peace; stories that, in turn, would have been passed on in an oral tradition recounting, preserving, and memorializing family history. That is only one way peace may have been commemorated. It could also have been embodied through naming practices. Though my database reveals only three men called "Pace," we might speculate that the name was sometimes given to embody and memorialize the peace made between families.

The kiss of peace, the pentitential rituals of Rome and San Gimignano, marriages made *pro bono pacis*, and (possibly) naming practices, each used the body to communicate an act of peacemaking. The social memory of peace was embodied in these practices; it is what Connerton refers to as "incorporating practice." But, as he also notes, social memory can be accomplished through "inscribing practice" as well.[92] And one way to inscribe peace was to note the occasions on which peace agreements were made in *ricordanze*, the journal-cum-account books kept by many Florentine families. In these daybooks peace agreements became written memorials for future generations. Notwithstanding the Velluti and Pitti diary entries commemorating peace that we examined in earlier chapters, most of those reports are laconic, mimicking notarial contracts in content and form.[93]

91. Boldrone da Civitella, ASF, Not. Ant. 3830, fol. 243v.

92. Connerton, *How Societies Remember*, 72–73.

93. For example Luca da Panzano's entry: "Memoria che a ddi ***di dicembre 1350 Filippo fratello charnale di Lulloci rende pacie qui in Firenze, al Piovano, Bandino e a tutti noi altri, charta per mano di ser Jacopo da Arfoli a chapo Chasscia, e poi detto ser Jacopo fu piovanno di Santa Maria Novella dal chastello di Chianti" in *'Brighe, affanni, volgimenti di stato:' Le ricordanze quattrocentesche di Luca di Matteo di Messer Luca dei Firidolfi da Panzano*, ed. Anthony Molho and Franek Sznura (Florence: Sismel, 2010), 469.

Visual evidence, however, helps us to form a more complete picture of how peacemaking practices were envisioned and memorialized, or in Connerton's terms "inscribed," in the later Middle Ages. I have collected a repertoire of images made largely for sacred usage, a fact that italicizes the notion that civic peacemaking rituals were suffused with ideas and iconography of the holy. The evidence ranges from frescoes to manuscript illuminations, to a votive panel painting. Let us turn first to the panel, which serendipitously conjoins matrimonial imagery to a striking image of the kiss of peace. It is a fitting launch for our discussion of picturing peace.[94]

PICTURING PEACE

Long misattributed to a nonexistent painter known as Barna da Siena, the panel, now in the Museum of Fine Arts in Boston, has been reattributed to Tederigo Memmi, an associate of Simone Martini.[95] (fig. 20) Painted in the 1340s, the main subject is the "Mystic Marriage of Saint Catherine of Alexandria," which shows Jesus in the act of contracting marriage to Saint Catherine. The Lord dutifully follows the medieval notarial formula as he slips a ring on the "fourth finger of her right hand as a sign of the true marital bond." In a domestic scene at their feet, we see Mary, her mother Saint Anne, and the baby Jesus, comprising a depiction of the bridegroom's lineage, the one that counted in medieval Italy. Machtelt Israëls observes that the theme of Saint Catherine's mystic marriage suggests "an original provenance of the panel from a convent, church, chapel, or altar dedicated to Catherine."[96] Given the work's enormous size this proposal makes good sense, for the panel was neither por-

94. It is noteworthy that the kiss of peace depicted in the predella of this panel, here exchanged under the guardianship of an angel, seems to be a prototype of this image. It should also be noted that the iconography of the kiss, like the embodied act itself, perhaps descended from iconography of the "Concordia apostolorum," the kiss Saints Peter and Paul were imagined to have exchanged in Rome. See Herbert Kessler, "The Meeting of Peter and Paul in Rome: An Emblematic Narrative of Spiritual Brotherhood," *Dumbarton Oaks Papers: Studies on Art and Archeology in Honor of Ernst Kitzinger on His Seventy-Fifth Birthday* 41 (1987): 265–75.

95. I would like to thank Machtelt Israëls for sharing her observations and research on this panel with me via an email exchange. The remarks here revise and expand my thinking on the panel published in *"Pro bono pacis*: Crime, Conflict, and Dispute Resolution. The Evidence of Notarial Peace Contracts in Late Medieval Florence," *Speculum* 88.2 (2013): 427–56. I also thank Austin Powell for bringing her work on the panel to my attention. On the iconography of the panel, see Lois Drewer, "Margaret of Antioch the Demon-Slayer, East and West: the Iconography of the Predella of the Boston Mystic Marriage of St. Catherine," *Gesta* 32. 1 (1993): 11–20. For the iconography of peace in general, see Enzo Carli, "La pace nella pittura senese," *La pace nel pensiero nella politica negli ideali del trecento, Convegno XV del centro di studi sulla spiritualità medievale* (Todi: L'Accademia Tudertina, 1975), 227–42; Adriano Prandi, "La pace nei temi iconografici del trecento," ibid., 245–59; Klaus Arnold, "Bilder des Krieges—Bilder des Friedens," in *Träger und Instrumentarien des Friedens*, 561–86.

96. Private email correspondence (2/12/2014).

FIGURE 20. *Mystic Marriage of St. Catherine.* Workshop of Tederigo Memmi,
panel painting, 1340s. Museum of Fine Arts, Boston. Sarah Wyman
Whitman Fund. Photograph © 2018 Museum of Fine Arts, Boston.
Reproduced by permission of Museum of Fine Arts, Boston.

table nor likely to have been used for private devotion in a domestic space.[97] As
we have seen, marriages sometimes issued from peace agreements, a fact which
may suggest that the nuptial imagery at the center of the panel points beyond
the mystic marriage of Saint Catherine. That is, the panel's commissioner may
have been commemorating an actual marriage, one that cemented peaceful relations between former adversaries, a subject to which we now turn.[98]

97. According to the Museum of Fine Arts, it measures 138.7 × 111.1 cm (54⅝ × 43¾ in.)
98. For marital imagery in the early and central Middle Ages, see Chiara Frugoni,
"L'iconografia del matrimonio e della coppia nel Medioevo," in *Il matrimonio nella società
altomedievale. Settimane di Studio del Centro Italiano di studi sull'alto medievo 24*
(Spoleto: Centro italiano di studi sull'alto medioevo, 1977), 901–66.

In the predella, beneath the central marriage scene, a visual record of a pax is captured at its ritual climax, as the two parties embrace and offer the kiss of peace (fig. 21). Commissioned most likely to memorialize a peace between two erstwhile enemies who have now discarded their weapons, the panel brings them together under the auspices of an angel whose own embrace guides them toward the kiss of peace on the mouth. Like the Madonna della Misericordia's mantle (or indeed the priest's cope that Durand describes), the angel's wings are spread wide to protect and dispense charity, but also, I would suggest, to delimit a sacred space for the ritual act. The inscription, prominently positioned above the peacemaking scene, tells us that Arico di Neri Arighetti commissioned the panel. Scholarly consensus holds that Arico is one of the two figures depicted. The coats of arms in the upper corners of the panel confirm that identification. They represent the Arrighetti family, natives of Prato, who for the most part resided in Florence by the mid-fourteenth century, when the panel was commissioned.[99]

Though at first glance the images that flank the ritual kiss do not seem of a piece with the iconography of concord and union that characterizes the two scenes discussed thus far, Lois Drewer nevertheless has made a convincing argument that both scenes represent the conquest of discord and chaos.[100] On the left, Saint Margaret defeats Beelzebub, prince of demons, by grabbing him vigorously by his hair and battering him over the head with a mallet; on the right, brandishing a cross in front of him, the Archangel Michael slays a dragon that rears up on his hind legs. Minions of the devil, both the demon and dragon were symbols of evil, disorder and conflict authored by Old Nick himself. In a sermon we have already had cause to cite, Giordano da Pisa put it this way when he preached on 20 April 1305:

You want to rule over your neighbor: why? This is a great evil. Why do you want to boss your neighbor around, since he's equal to you? Such was the pride of Lucifer, who wanted to lord it over others, and therefore he disturbed the peace of heaven, from whence he was ejected and chased out. And from that battle, and that root, all battles, fights, tensions, and divisions between people were born; that is on account of this pride, that says I want to dominate you and you me: one against the other. But if people were humble, and remained in their places, there would be peace and prosperity.[101]

99. Israëls notes: "The coat of arms (azure semé-de-lys argent, on a bend or three wreaths vert tied gules) is documented both in the ASF (Raccolta Ceramelli Papiani, Famiglia Arrighetti, fasc. 202) and the shield on Palazzo Arrighetti-Gaddi in via del Giglio in Florence." Private email correspondence (2/12/2014). On the palazzo, see *I Palazzi: arte e storia degli edifici civili di Firenze*, ed. Sandra Carlini, Lara Mercanti, and Giovanni Straffi, 2 vols. (Florence: Alinea, 2001–2004), vol. 2: 8–9. In the medieval period Arighetti was spelled with one r. Modern spelling convention adds the second r to Arrighetti.

100. Drewer, "Margaret of Antioch the Demon-Slayer," 18.

101. Sermo LII, *Prediche del Beato Giordano da Rivalto*, 316.

FIGURE 21. *The Kiss of Peace.* Predella detail of the *Mystic Marriage of St. Catherine.*
Workshop of Tederigo Memmi, panel painting, 1340s. The inscription reads: "Arico di Neri
Arighetti fece fare questa tavola." (Arico di Neri Arrighetti had this panel made.) Sarah
Wyman Whitman Fund. Museum of Fine Arts, Boston. Photograph © 2018 Museum
of Fine Arts, Boston. Reproduced by permission of Museum of Fine Arts, Boston.

Good student of Remigio dei Girolami that he was, Giordano was arguing
that Lucifer is the sower of the seeds of all discord. If sin were renounced, the
order of charity could be established. Only then could the bonds of concord
lead people to peace. The "Mystic Marriage" panel, in the event, is a beautifully
realized and psychologically sophisticated homage to the processional nature
of peacemaking as envisioned by medieval preachers. As Federico Visconti
preached, one must first slay one's own inner demons before turning outward
into the world to compose peace.[102] And though his ordering of events differed,
William Durand's sentiment lined up with his contemporaries when he observed that "we pass from earthly peace, to peace of heart, to peace of eternity."[103] The narrative of the predella suggests that with the intercession of Saints
Margaret and Michael, Arico di Neri Arrighetti had passed from the peace of the

102. See chapter 1.
103. William Durand, *Rationale*, Book 4, 319.

heart to exterior peace. This suggestion is also supported by the composition of the subjects of the predella paintings. The two outer images depict unbridled action and rapid movement suggestive of discord and violence. Demonic talons thrash wildly in the air, devilish haunches are coiled, ready to spring, and saintly arms slash upwards, equipped with weapons that will rain down mortal blows on the heads of their enemies. The composition of the central image, on the other hand, which features the Archangel, radiates the tranquility of angelic order. The angel's frontal positioning, in the Byzantine style suggests the immobile calm of eternity, the heavenly Jerusalem. His wings, as suggested earlier, define a timeless sacred space, one in which the order of charity and mercy reign. The lesson for the viewer is that interior peace can be achieved but only after inner demons are vanquished. Outer peace, which includes the forgiveness of enemies, is the result of inner peace emanating outward from within.

THE ANGEL OF PEACE

In the "Mystic Marriage" panel a monumental archangel facilitates the kiss of peace between Arrighetti and his adversary, a prototype for things to come when angels will begin to play an important role in the iconography of peacemaking. [104] The New Testament is alive with the flutter of angels' wings; by one scholar's count they alight in those hallowed pages 179 times.[105] They are ubiquitous as intermediaries between God and man. To understand the importance of angels in the gospel, one need only remember that the herald of the annunciation to Mary was the archangel Gabriel (Luke 1:26–38), and that an angel announced the good news of the birth of the Lord to shepherds, proclaiming "peace on earth to men of good will" (Luke 2:8–14). In the Book of Revelation angels are everywhere, sounding the trumpets of the apocalypse of course, but also at Michael's side as champions of the Lord, battling and defeating Satan (Rev. 12:7–9). Indeed, medieval theologians taught that at the end of time Saint Michael would slay the Antichrist on Mount Olivet, at which point Christ would return to rule the world for a thousand years before the Last Judgment. Given the presence of angels in the iconography of peacemaking, it will be at this point useful to take a brief look at the theology of angels as formulated in the thirteenth century. One of our best guides to the popular expression of angelology is Jacobus de Voragine's *Golden Legend*, a collection of saints' lives that had an enormous diffusion throughout the medieval world

104. Drewer has identified him as Michael the Archangel in "Margaret of Antioch the Demon-Slayer," 11.

105. Steven Epstein, *Purity Lost: Transgressing Boundaries in the Eastern Mediterranean, 1000–1400* (Baltimore: Johns Hopkins University Press, 2007), 183 n. 88. For the choirs of angels, see Barbara Bruderer Eichberg, *Les neuf choeurs angéliques: Origine et évolution du theme dans l'art du Moyen Age*. Thèse de doctorat, l'Université de Genève. (Poitiers: Civilisation Médiévale, 1998).

beginning around 1260. Jacobus took the opportunity of Saint Michael's feast-day to discuss the role of angels in salvation history.[106]

Medieval theologians constructed elaborate hierarchies of angelic beings, but it was the order of archangels and their lesser associates, angels, who were believed to interact most frequently with humankind. Thus they will attract our attention here. In their relations with humans, they took on a number of roles, of which three are relevant to peacemaking iconography: they served as God's champions against the devil and his demons, they helped in the administration of justice, and in perhaps their least known capacity, they acted as guides to penance.

An important aspect of the angel's persona (and iconography) was as a van-quisher of the devil and his minions. Jacobus notes that the archangel Michael and his army of angels ejected Satan from heaven, "for when Lucifer wanted to be equal to God, the archangel Michael, standard-bearer of the celestial host, marched up and expelled Lucifer and his followers out of heaven, and shut them up in this dark air until the Day of Judgment." [107] For that reason "the angels win over the demons every day, when they fight for us and save us from the demons' efforts to tempt us."[108] They do that by leading sinners from temptation to penance, and by showing them that discord can be transformed into concord, yet another reason why the angel was a fitting intermediary in visual scenes of peacemaking. That of course is the theme of the peacemaking scenes in the predella of the "Mystic Marriage" panel.

Angels were also arbiters of justice. Saint Michael, as is well known, was believed to have an important role awaiting him at the end of time when he would wield his scales, weighing the merit of each individual, soul by soul. On a secular plane, we might think of his role as something akin to a judge in the podestà's court, weighing evidence in his scales and dispensing justice, the *sine qua non* of concord and peace, as we saw in chapter 2. Alternatively, we might envision him as Bishop Berardo, who brought peace to Brescia, or even more fittingly, as Cardinal Latino Malabranca, who brought peace to Florence. It is useful to recall that by the thirteenth century, the expression "angel of peace" was already a figure of speech. Pope Nicholas III, as we have seen, re-ferred to his peacemaking envoy, Cardinal Latino, whose second name was Angelo, as *tamquam pacis angelus*, an angel of peace, so to speak.

The role of guardian angel is familiar even today. Jacobus de Voragine notes that honor is due to angels for performing this role, for in it they

106. Jacobus de Voragine, *The Golden Legend*, trans. William Granger Ryan (Princeton: Princeton University Press, 1993), 2 vols. The entry on Michael is vol. 2: 201–11. For a good account of angelology in the later Middle Ages, see David Keck, *Angels and Angelology in the Middle Ages* (Oxford: Oxford University Press, 1998). There is an enormous bibliogra-phy on the *Golden Legend*; most recently see Jacques Le Goff, *In Search of Sacred Time: Jacobus de Voragine and the Golden Legend* (Princeton: Princeton University Press, 2014).

107. *Golden Legend*, 205.

108. Ibid.

remove obstacles, and more to the point move sinners to penance, "and we see this in Tobias, when Tobias, instructed by the angel anoints his father's eyes, i.e., his heart, with the gall of the fish, which represents repentance."[109] The heart, it will be recalled, was the corporeal site in the human person where theologians suggested penitential transformation first occurs. The Book of Tobit identified the angel in this episode as the Archangel Raphael, the healer. (Tobit 6:2–11:15). In the Middle Ages, theologians and preachers considered the healing medicaments destined for the body akin to the penitential balm that was appropriate to soothe the soul. As further proof of the angel's role as a guide to penance, Jacobus notes that an angel cleansed Isaiah's lips in preparation for confession. And finally, the angels rejoice when penance is done, for "we read in Luke that there will be more joy in heaven over one sinner who repents than over ninety-nine righteous [men] who need no repentance."[110] What we have seen in chapter 1 of the relationship of penance to peacemaking, and now too of the angel's association with penance, puts us in a better position to understand the meaning of the angel's sacral presence presiding over the peacemaking ritual. This association also helps to explain why he is present in the visual mementos connected particularly with the Bianchi's penitential peace movement, to which we now turn.

AN ICONOGRAPHY OF PEACEMAKING

Monumental iconography of the angel of peace first appears in central Italy at the turn of the fourteenth century and is associated with the Bianchi as they processed throughout Umbria into Lazio in 1399. Three images emerged more or less contemporaneously in Terni and Rieti. In Terni the angels are found in frescoes in the churches of Sant'Alò and San Pietro, in Rieti at Sant'Eusanio. At Sant' Alò, the fresco is at eye level in the nave, to the right of the sacristy (fig. 22). In it an archangel mediates a dispute by lightly touching the shoulders of the two antagonists, joining them together for the exchange of the kiss of peace on the mouth.[111] Framed by their discarded swords, the two embrace and genuflect at the feet of the angelic mediator in a gesture of submission that affirms the solemnity of the moment. The painter depicts the peacemakers as they prepare to exchange the kiss.

109. Ibid., 208.

110. Ibid.

111. *La chiesa di Sant'Alò in Terni*, ed. Maria Cristina Marinozzi (Arrone: Edizioni Thyrus, 2010), catalogue no. 18, at 119. Located in the nave to the right of the sacristy, Marinozzi identifies the fresco as fifteenth century. Paolo Renzi, "La Devozione dei Bianchi a Terni negli affreschi di S. Maria del Monumento," in *Sulle orme dei Bianchi dalla Liguria all'Italia centrale. Atti del convegno storico internazionale Assisi-Vallo di Nera-Terni-Rieti-Leonessa (18–19 June 1999)*, ed. Francesco Santucci (Assisi: Accademia Properziana del Subasio, 2001), 273–307, publishes these images in black and white.

FIGURE 22. *Monumental Angel Facilitating the Kiss of Peace*. Fresco, early 15th c., Church of Sant'Alò, Terni, Umbria. Photo: author.

In a similar but damaged image from the church of San Pietro, also in Terni, the angel performs the same function for two kneeling peacemakers.[112]

112. Giuseppe Cassio, "La chiesa agostiniana di San Pietro apostolo in Terni e i suoi dipinti ritrovati," in *Arte sacra nell'Umbria meridionale. Atti del 1° corso per la formazione di volontari dell'animazione culturale promosso dall'Associazione Volontari per L'Arte e la Cultura*, ed. Giuseppe Cassio (Terni: Ufficio per i beni culturali ecclesiastici, 2007), 101–10. The church was given to the Augustinian friars in the thirteenth century; the interior decoration began after 1310, at 106. Though Cassio does not mention our angel of peace, he does reproduce another fragmentary angel as fig. 35, at 146.

FIGURE 23. *Monumental Angel Facilitating the Kiss of Peace.* Fresco,
early 15th c., Church of San Pietro, Terni, Umbria. Photo: author.

(fig. 23) Again located at eye-level, to the right of the entrance on the vestibule
wall, the angel practically looks the viewer in the eye as he brings peace to a
pair of supplicants. Instead of their shoulders, the angel lays hands on their
heads, which are the only parts of them that have survived the ravages of time.
It is a gesture that since the early Christian period has signified the invocation
of the Holy Spirit, yet another indication that peacemaking was regarded as "a
gift that comes from the sacrament." Tellingly, at both Sant'Alò and San Pietro,
the frescoes make up part of a diptych with a "Madonna del latte" image. Such
a pairing links the angel of peace with the Virgin Mary's mercy and charity

toward mankind, poured out in her mother's milk. While the angel is restoring the order of charity, the Virgin nurses her son at her breast, the quintessential symbol of charity in the Middle Ages, and well beyond.

At Rieti, on the other hand, in the church of Sant'Eusanio, the fresco of the monumental angel, located on the right wall of the nave (fig. 24), is

FIGURE 24. *Monumental Angel Facilitating the Kiss of Peace.* Fresco, early 15th c., Church of Sant'Eusanio, Rieti, Lazio. Photo: author.

again placed just above eye level and underneath a scene depicting one of the
Bianchi origin stories, the "Legend of the Three Loaves". To the right of the angel
stands a bishop, and next to him a "Man of Sorrows."[113] The monumental angel
mediates between the two antagonists, whose genuflection this time seems
suspended in midair. Knights, whose faces are covered by nasal helmets, ac-
company them, and they too seem to levitate in a kneeling position. Like the
peacemakers on Berardo Maggi's tomb, the protagonists in this scene cross
their arms over their chests in a gesture of humility and submission. Their
simple tunics suggest that they have come in penance. The "Man of Sorrows"
scene adjacent to the peacemaking scene further suggests a penitential theme,
binding the two images together thematically. The Christ figure is surrounded
by the instruments of his passion (including the column of his flagellation
and the whip), an image especially dear to penitents, especially Bianchi penitents, who identified so closely with Christ's passion. It also recalls William
Durand's explication of the kiss of peace in the Mass, which he grounded in
salvation history. Jesus had sacrificed himself for humanity's sins; therefore,
the kiss in the Mass is a sign of peace to show that the community is joined
in the Body of Christ, "through which peace has been made between heaven
and earth."[114]

In nearby Terni, as in Rieti, we see at the turn of the fourteenth century,
in the church of Santa Maria del Monumento, the iconography of the angel
of peace, along with imagery of Bianchi peace processions. The right wall of
the church records two miracle stories, one a foundation legend, the other
associated with the Bianchi after they passed through Assisi in the summer
of 1399.[115] Yet another monumental angel of peace stands this time on the
interior wall of the façade.[116]

In the Assisi legend known as the "Madonna of the Olive Grove," the Virgin
Mary appears to a boy and exhorts him to encourage the citizens of Assisi to
do penance, a theme we have seen previously associated with the Bianchi.
What draws our attention here, however, is that at the center of the fresco, in
a scene outside of the city walls, the Bianchi are shown making peace (fig. 25).
Two white-clad Bianchi kneel face-to-face in profile outside of the basilica of
San Francesco, their arms crossed over their chests, ready to exchange the
kiss on the mouth. In this case the role of the angel-intermediary appears to
be filled by one of the confrères to the left of the scene. His right hand rests

113. See also Elisabeth Bliersbach, "I Bianchi nell'arte Umbro-Laziale," in *Sulle orme
dei Bianchi*, 363–405 and fig. 1, 409.

114. Durand, *Rationale*, Book 4, 463.

115. The "Madonna of the Olive Grove" recorded an apparition that was supposed to
have occurred in the olive grove of the convent of Santa Chiara when the Virgin Mary
appeared to a young peasant boy. It is to be distinguished from the "Madonna of the Three
Loaves," the foundation story of the Bianchi (see chapter 1). For the "Madonna of the Olive
Grove," see Arnaldo Fortini, *La Madonna dell'oliva* (Venice: Nuova Editoriale, 1956).

116. Renzi, "La Devozione dei Bianchi a Terni," 280.

FIGURE 25. *The Kiss of Peace*. Detail from the *Madonna of the Olive Grove*. Fresco, early 15th c., Church of S. Maria del Monumento, Terni, Umbria. Photo: author.

on one of the principal's shoulders, guiding him to lean in to the kiss. If we follow the narrative to the left of the peacemaking group, in the subsequent scene we see the backs of two white-clad Bianchi walking side by side into the basilica, recalling Venturino's pilgrimage in which former adversaries walked in pairs, united in peace and penance. Presumably they are our two protagonists entering the sanctuary to give thanks for their peace. Paolo Renzi has suggested that this scene is a commemoration of an actual peace made in Assisi on 13 August 1399.[117]

On the adjacent wall (the interior façade) of the same church, we find a heavily restored late fifteenth-century angel whose laying-on-of-hands to heads gesture seems to have been modeled on his heavenly brother at San Pietro, also in Terni (fig. 26). Like his confrères in the scenes we have examined, the angel's outstretched wings serve both as a mantle of charity and as a demarcation of sacred space for the ritual performance of the kiss. The angel confers peace on two young men who have cast aside their shields to kneel and embrace in the kiss of peace.[118] Like the examples from San Pietro and Sant'Alò, it is notable that the angel of peace at Santa Maria del Monumento is part of a diptych that includes the Madonna and child.

117. Ibid.

118. Renzi suggests that this was not its original location; rather, it was moved from a wall of the original church now destroyed: "La Devozione dei Bianchi a Terni," 291.

FIGURE 26. *Monumental Angel Facilitating the Kiss of Peace*. Fresco, 15th c., Church of S. Maria del Monumento, Terni, Umbria. Photo: author.

This iconography continued to develop throughout the Middle Ages, and in our final examples we find that although the angel is still central to the composition, he is very much diminished in size (fig. 27). In a miniature decorating a folio page of a Mass for peace from a Paduan gospel lectionary dated 1436, the central imagery of the knights is not dissimilar to Arico di Neri Arrighetti's votive panel, or indeed to Suor Sara's ex-voto, which we examined in chapter 1, but in this case the angel's wings spread out above two armor-clad knights, whose swords lie abandoned at their feet. And like others we have seen, this

FIGURE 27. *Two Knights Exchange the Kiss of Peace*. Miniature from the lectionary
made for Bishop Donato of Padua in 1436. MS M. 180, fol. 104r, the Morgan
Library & Museum, New York. Purchased by J. Pierpont Morgan (1837–1913) in
1902. Photo reproduced by permission of the Morgan Library & Museum.

angel is engaged in the laying on of hands. It is a gesture that indicates the
angel's role as mediator, who in this case both summons the Holy Spirit and
blesses the ritual.[119] In a strange twist of fate, this representation of the kiss, a
gesture that was initially borrowed from the Christian Mass and inserted into
civic ceremonies, has now returned to a sacred setting—a lectionary—but as
an image of the secular ritual embodied.

The final image of the kiss on our iconographical journey returns us to
Umbria, to the church of San Francesco (now Santa Maria Assunta), which
recorded on its walls, again at eye level, the presence of a Bianchi procession
in Vallo di Nera in 1399.[120] Though we discussed this "newsreel" fresco in

119. Iohannes Monterchio copied the manuscript for Bishop Donato in 1436.
120. See chapter 1 for the series of images from this cycle (figs. 5–8).

chapter 1, we should recall at this juncture that to the right of the crucifix supported by one of the Bianchi, a banderole unfurls, containing precious information about the patron: *Hoc opus fe*(cit fieri) *Iuvannoni a* (Vallo et Dio). *Li dia pace.*[121] That is, "Giovannone of Vallo (di Nera) and God commissioned the fresco to bring peace".[122] (ch. 1, fig. 7)

At the center of that fresco is an image of the by now familiar peacemaking ritual in which the two protagonists kneel while a small-scale angel hovers above them, laying on hands.[123] (fig. 28) In this case the Bianchi—both men and women—surround the enactors of the peace; however, a central group of three is directly involved in the ritual itself. Read from the left, a bearded male figure gestures with his hands raised and open at his chest, inviting the spectator to stop, look, and reflect upon the scene. A *flagellum* is draped over his left arm reminding us that though it was a peace movement, the Bianchi practiced penance to achieve their goal. The central figure, just behind the peacemakers, holds his hands clasped in a gesture of prayer, underscoring the sacred nature of the act. The figure at the right, identified by Mario Sensi as the paciere, places her right hand over her heart. The heart of course was the repository of charity, but it was also the place where the inner transformation necessary for peace first had to ignite. With her left hand she gently prods one of the ritual participants forward to facilitate the kiss of peace. Though no other commentator has raised the issue, I would like to suggest that perhaps at last we catch a glimpse here of a female intermediary in the process of making peace. Our fine-featured, white-cowled peacemaker just may be the visual analogue to Albertanus of Brescia's Prudence.[124]

And just as Arico di Neri Arrighetti commissioned his "Mystic Marriage" panel as a souvenir of peace, and is likely represented as one of the protagonists of peace in that painting, so we can just as easily imagine Giovannone as one of the enactors of peace in this scene.[125] It may be that Giovannone hoped, by representing an act of peace on the walls of the Church of San Francesco, and furnishing the date of that particular act of peacemaking, to inscribe that signal moment into the social memory of the community of Vallo di Nera. But the mural was meant to serve as a memorial for future generations as well.

121. Mario Sensi, "Le paci private nella predicazione, nelle immagini di propaganda e nella prassi fra Tre e Quattrocento," in *La pace fra realtà e utopia. Quaderni di Storia Religiosa* 12 (2005): 159–200, at 168.

122. Sandro Ceccaroni, "Testimonianze del movimento dei Bianchi a Vallo di Nera agli inizi del XV secolo," in *Spoletium: Rivista di Arte Storia Cultura* 27 (1982): 39–44, at 41.

123. The angel was misidentified as the Baby Jesus both by Piero Pirri, "Una pittura storica di Cola di Pietro da Camerino" (Perugia: Unione Tipografica Cooperativa, 1918): 1–15, at 12 and by Ceccaroni, "Testamonianze," 41.

124. All commentators assume this paciere is male. See, for example, Mario Sensi, "Le paci private nella predicazione," 171.

125. Piero Pirri was first to make this suggestion (and Ceccaroni follows him), though Pirri misidentifies the angel. See his "Una pittura storica di Cola di Pietro da Camerino," 12; and Ceccaroni, "Testamonianze," 41.

FIGURE 28. *The Kiss of Peace.* Fresco of Bianchi Procession, 1401. A female facilitator on the right helps to make the peace, while an angel hovering above the central figures lays on hands, sanctifying the peace. Church of S. Maria Assunta (formerly San Francesco), Vallo di Nera, Umbria. Photo: author.

With the ritual kiss presented at eye level, the painter and his patron reminded spectators that the prospect of peace was always present; indeed it was right in front of their eyes.

In the event, Giovannone in collaboration with the painter Cola di Pietro da Camerino, produced an enduring monument to peace. It served to imprint into social memory how penitential practice brought about peace of the heart, the precondition, as we have seen throughout this study, for civic peacemaking.

CONCLUSION

THE RITUAL KISS was the performative gesture that enacted a new social and legal reality, one in which concord and harmony were expected to reign. Concord between neighbors, as we have seen, was considered by all contemporary theologians and political theorists to be an essential ingredient of the *bene comune*. It was the means by which civil society attained its end, conceived as the common good of peace. The commune itself was a self-created sphere of law and peace, bound together by the bonds of concord, which according to Thomas Aquinas signified a union of wills.[1]

There is no better visual representation of concord from the mid-fourteenth century than Ambrogio Lorenzetti's vision of the *buon governo* in the Sala dei Nove of Siena's Palazzo Pubblico (fig. 29). Here the allegorical figure of Concord receives the cords of harmony from the scales of Justice and hands them on to the twenty-four citizen-representatives of the Sienese popolo, who in turn deliver them to the personification of the commune of Siena, the embodiment of the idea of "good government." Concord holds a carpenter's plane, which has been interpreted in various ways. One reading holds that she is using the plane to smooth away discord among Siena's citizens. We might say that peace agreements functioned similarly in the judicial system: they served as tools of accommodation to bring about concord.[2]

In a twist on this theme, a recently discovered fifteenth-century fresco, a painted frieze atop the wall elevation enclosing a loggia of the Palazzo Trinci in Foligno, shows Concord (in this case substituting for the angel of peace) mediating a peace between two adversaries who earlier in the narrative sequence are shown *in flagrante delicto*, pushing and shoving, their fists flying (fig. 30). Depicted as two infants—often the material representation of immaterial souls—the two adversaries are shown drinking the milk of human kindness at the breasts of Charity (fig. 31) where, presumably, their animosity will be transformed into friendship. They are then delivered to the personification of Clemency (an aspect of Justice), who instead of inflicting punishment upon them gathers them into her abundant embrace, while prodding them forward to exchange the ritual kiss on the mouth[3] (fig. 32). This vision of civic peace draws on a repertoire of pastoral, political, and legal ideas to

1. *Summa Theologiae*, IIa, IIae, Q. 29.
2. For a selected bibliography on the frescoes, see chapter 1, n. 1.
3. *Il Palazzo Trinci di Foligno*, ed. Giordana Benazzi and Francesco Federico Mancini (Perugia: Quattroemme, 2001). See especially the essay by Mancini, "La Loggia delle Virtù, allegoria di un governo illuminato," 299–336, in which he identifies this figure as Clemency and proposes Corrado Trinci as the patron, ca. 1424–1428.

FIGURE 29. *Allegory of Concord*. Ambrogio Lorenzetti, detail from "Buon Governo," fresco, 1338–1339. Holding the carpenter's plane, the allegory of Concord dispenses her bonds, which bind the Sienese citizens in harmony to each other and ultimately to the good government of the commune. Sala dei Nove, Palazzo Pubblico, Siena. Photo reproduced by permission of Scala/Art Resource, New York.

suggest that when the order of charity is operative, justice prevails, the bonds of concord are forged, and the common good of peace can be achieved. These ideas informed the conceptualization of the peace instrument and contributed to its success as a legal solution for settling disputes in the urban centers of central Italy in the later medieval period.

FIGURE 30. *A Fist Fight*. Fresco, "La Loggia delle Virtù,"
1424–1428. Palazzo Trinci, Foligno. Photo: author.

FIGURE 31. *Allegory of Charity Nursing*. Fresco, "La Loggia delle
Virtù," 1424–1428. Palazzo Trinci, Foligno. Photo: author.

It is necessary to investigate the pedigree of those ideas in order to answer
the question of why the peace instrument emerged in this form, in this place,
and at this time in the middle of the thirteenth century. To do so, we must
examine the ideas as they coalesced in three university disciplines, all of which
were formulated only in the twelfth century, but had matured and borne
ample fruit by the Duecento. And although philosophy, theology, and law

FIGURE 32. *Charity Fosters the Kiss of Peace.* Fresco, "La Loggia delle Virtù," 1424–1428. Palazzo Trinci, Foligno. Photo: author.

would each develop into discrete disciplines, we must not forget that it was not until the mid-thirteenth century that distinct faculties emerged to claim them and enforce disciplinary boundaries. In the twelfth century, and even at the beginning of the thirteenth, each of them participated in a "multidisciplinary" intellectual culture nourished by the cross-fertilization of ideas. For that reason we turn now to the Universities of Paris and Bologna to understand first the social implications of their curricula, and second, how these ideas, when forged together in the crucible of the communes of central Italy, shaped the political, religious, and legal cultures that were emerging in tandem with the republican regimes of the thirteenth century. We will begin by examining the three disciplines, taking particular note of the ideas and particular forms of knowledge they were advancing that were relevant to the rapidly developing communes of the period.

We begin in Paris by looking first at philosophy, at what today we distinguish as the fields of logic and ethics, where a transformation in critical modes of thinking had already begun in the twelfth century. This transformation gave rise to the university, as charismatic teachers such as Peter Abelard drew students from all parts of the Latin-speaking world who were eager to learn the dialectical methods he had pioneered and on which he had established his reputation. Much of the content and method of this new learning was based upon the work of translators working in Toledo, who had begun the slow process of recovering "lost" Greek texts, many of them preserved only in Arabic. And although some elements of the Aristotelian corpus, already translated from Greek into Latin, had been preserved in western curricula since the early medieval period, it was not until the twelfth century that fragmentary versions of the philosopher's *Nicomachean Ethics* were translated from Arabic into Latin. The *Ethics* introduced politics as a field of study and a practice worthy in its own right. As we have seen, when writing the *Tresor*, Brunetto Latini had a version of the *Ethics* at hand. Around 1246–47, the Oxford master Robert Grosseteste (d. 1253) made a full translation from the Greek, preparing the way for a translation of the *Politics* a few years later when, in about 1260, the Dominican William of Moerbeke (d. circa 1286) translated it into Latin.[4] Together the *Politics* and the *Ethics* provided the foundation on which a new western political philosophy was to emerge.

Aquinas would have reckoned with the *Politics* while in Italy in the 1260s, between his first and second regencies in Paris. He wrote an unfinished commentary on the tract during his second regency (1269–1272), and he incorporated its political philosophy into his teaching, which his student Remigio dei Girolami imbibed and eventually carried home to Santa Maria Novella, where he then taught as lector for more than forty years. The Thomistic thought that so structures Remigio's thinking about the common good and its end—peace— was the result of the new Aristotelian philosophy infused into the curriculum in Paris in the late 1260s and early 1270s. From there the students of Aquinas transmitted it widely. The particular case of Remigio, and his student Giordano da Pisa in Florence, is a prime example of this mode of transmission. As we have seen, Remigio preached on numerous political occasions, where his ideas may have had some influence on the political leaders of the city. It should also be remembered that Remigio had the ear of the priorate as well, as a number of his family members served that magistracy. Giordano da Pisa, on the other hand, took this new political philosophy directly to the streets, where the popolo would have received his message, preached in the vernacular, about the relationship of peace to the common good.

This period of course coincides with the emergence of the new popular political regimes of medieval Italy, which began wielding the reigns of power in the mid-thirteenth century. Though the first popular government in Florence had already been toppled by 1260, the intervening period between the Primo Popolo and the Secondo Popolo in 1293 saw similar iterations, all meant to curb the factionalism and its attendant violence that continued to disturb the public order of the city. It was a period of diverse experiments in institution-building, which finally produced the guild government in 1282, along with its legislation, the *Ordinances of Justice*. It

---

4. C. J. Nederman, "Aristotelianism and the Origins of 'Political Science' in the Twelfth Century," *Journal of the History of Ideas* 52 (1991): 179–94. For a good account of the background, introduction, and reception of Aristotle's *Politics* in Italy, see Grace Allen, *Vernacular Encounters with Aristotle's* Politics *in Italy, 1260–1600*. PhD diss., The Warburg Institute, University of London, 2015.

was hoped that this would bring some measure of peace to the city, even as guild rule demonized its enemies and excluded them from holding civic office. It was a government, moreover, in search of an ideology, and Remigio dei Girolami's *De bono comuni* and *De bono pacis* filled that need, arguing in Aristotelian terms that the end of good government was peace. It was political philosophy wrapped in penitential thought. The new regimes now had a political philosophy to justify their actions. And—in the name of peace and security—they sought to suppress both the political violence of the factions and everyday interpersonal violence, much of it due to the unprecedented demographic growth of the commune, which introduced waves of new immigrants from the contado into the old established neighborhoods of the city.

The University of Paris, by way of the University of Bologna, shaped Remigio's views on penance as well. Beginning in the late twelfth century, pastoral theology, the practical expression of speculative theology, came into its own, and a rethinking of penance was at its core. The idea was a venerable one in the Christian tradition. Already in the late antique period, penitent Christians had both performed public penance and participated in penitential processions. Beginning in the early medieval period, priests began to dole out penances to the laity that would enable them to atone for their sins, and handbooks called "penitentials" circulated widely, which advocated tariffed penalties according to the severity of the sin committed.[5] By the twelfth century, however, theologians began to treat the subject of penance in a more systematic manner. It has recently been argued that Gratian, the monk and master who taught canon law at the University of Bologna in the mid-twelfth century, was among the very first to do so. Embedded in his *Concordia discordantium canonum*, now known as the *Decretum*, is a treatise entitled *Tractatus de penitentia*. Unlike the rest of the *Decretum*, this was a theological treatise, one of the first to give the subject of penance systematic treatment. Significantly, it was inserted into one of the most widely circulated "textbooks" used by teachers of canon law, and thus would have had the potential to impact not only canon lawyers, but also theologians, even as far away as Paris. And it seems that its impact was indeed enormous.[6]

At the turn of the twelfth century, the masters of theology at Paris began to think anew about penitential theology and to tie it to pastoral care (the *cura animarum*). Masters like Peter the Chanter (d. 1197) gathered around him some of the best and brightest minds of the period, and they turned their attention toward answering the challenging moral questions posed by a rapidly

5. For the early period, see Rob Meens, *Penance in Medieval Europe, 600–1200* (Cambridge: Cambridge University Press, 2014).
6. Atria A. Larson traces this history in *Master of Penance: Gratian and the Development of Penitential Thought and Law in the Twelfth Century* (Washington, D.C.: Catholic University of America Press, 2014).

changing society that was in large part the product of the new merchant economy. His *Verbum abbreviatum*, a tract on applied ethics, written in the form of a treatise on the virtues and vices, is the apogee of Peter's work. His thinking had enormous influence, and was diffused widely by his students who included, among others, Robert of Sorbonne, Jacques de Vitry, and possibly Lothario dei Conti, the future Pope Innocent III.[7] At the same time, Peter the Chanter's colleague Alain of Lille (d. 1202/3), who was also interested in contemporary social issues, produced an influential handbook for preachers, alongside a *Liber poenitentialis*, which became the progenitor of a new generation of penitential handbooks produced in the wake of Innocent III's Fourth Lateran Council (1215), which reformulated the sacrament of penance. There, as we have seen, confession was folded into the sacrament as an annual obligation before communion, the ultimate symbol of participation and fraternity in the Christian community. These handbooks, which often took the form of *summae confessorum*, were guides that provided detailed advice for confessors and parish priests to prepare them for pastoral work.[8] Among the most important ideas that these works conveyed was that the priest, in confession, had to examine the circumstances of sin to ascertain whether or not the penitent exhibited true remorse or contrition. Before the thirteenth century, penitential practice emphasized the penances imposed by the priest as a satisfaction for sin; now inner contrition was considered tantamount to satisfaction. Joseph Goering has summed up this important reconceptualization thus: "The single most important change distinguishing the new directions in penitential teaching and practice in the twelfth and thirteenth centuries was the gradual shift of emphasis from satisfaction for sins toward a pastoral concern with the penitent's contrition and confession of sins."[9]

These ideas informed the theology and practice of penance. Though they were already percolating in the early thirteenth century, they were disseminated even more widely after 1215, when the friars received their mandate to preach to the laity. And, as we have seen, the cities were their targets, particularly the urbanized centers of central and northern Italy, where both mendicant orders established themselves, in Florence before 1225. They urged the examination of conscience, confession of sin, and reconciliation with the Lord as the means to inner peace. From that spiritual center, peace could radiate outward into the world. For medieval preachers, inner

7. John W. Baldwin, *Masters, Princes and Merchants: The Social Views of Peter the Chanter and His Circle* (Princeton: Princeton University Press, 1970).

8. Leonard E. Boyle, O.P. did the groundbreaking work in this field. See his collected essays in *Pastoral Care, Clerical Education and Canon Law, 1200–1400* (London: Variorum, 1981).

9. For the quotation, see Joseph Goering, "The Summa of Master Serlo and Thirteenth-Century Penitential Literature," *Mediaeval Studies* 40 (1978): 290–311, at 296. For an excellent overview of the literature of penance, see his "The Internal Forum and the Literature of Penance and Confession," *Traditio* 59 (2004): 175–227.

peace—established through the court of inner self-examination, contrition, and confession—was the *sine qua non* for the tranquility of the social order and the common good.

This penitential court of self-examination, with confession as its center-piece, emerged side-by-side with the communal legal system and was surely a factor in shaping some aspects of legal culture—including the institution-alization of peace agreements. In a similar manner to how confession, made in contrition, mitigated the *culpa* of sin and allowed for forgiveness and rec-onciliation with the Lord, peace agreements spelled out the circumstances of the crimes committed and relieved both the victim and perpetrator of guilt, allowing forgiveness and reconciliation to take place between adversarial par-ties. Both systems demanded that the details of the crime or sin committed be made known in granular particularity. And in both cases, once this was provided, the slate was wiped clean and equilibrium restored to the relation-ship. In the case of sacramental confession, the penitent was then admitted into communion with the body of Christ and the Christian community; in the case of the civic peace instrument, the peacemaker, after having committed his crimes to the peace instrument and exchanged the ritual kiss, was readmitted into the bonds of civic society. Our first Florentine peace agreement dates to the mid-thirteenth century, allowing for the sedimentation of a few decades of penitential preaching to prepare a context for it.

The documentary form the peace instrument took was, as we have seen, the product of an emerging legal culture that originated in the schools that shaped both the judicial institutions and bodies of statutory law as they developed in Italy in the central Middle Ages. Consequently, we must return momentarily to Bologna, where in addition to the *Decretum*, two other developments are of significance for this discussion; the first predating Gratian in the late eleventh century, the second postdating him, beginning around 1200.

By the 1070s, a master called Irnerius had begun to teach Roman civil law, founded on the *Corpus Iuris Civilis*, the compilation of civil law produced by the jurists in the court of Justinian (d. 565). Gathering students around him, as Parisian masters would do a generation later, Irnerius and others like him taught the basis of what would become the new law curriculum at the University of Bologna, where judges and notaries, the personnel of the com-munal courts, received their training. Though Florence was not a "Roman-law city," it is likely that the city's judges, members of the podestà's retinue, were trained there from early on.[10]

The same holds true for its notaries. Indeed, the grandfather of the notarial arts was himself a Florentine, who studied at Bologna before becoming a mas-ter there. Buoncompagno of Signa (d. circa 1240) probably audited at least some of the law curriculum before becoming a master of rhetoric and grammar

---

10. For "Roman-law city" and training, see Chris Wickham, *Courts and Conflict in Twelfth-Century Tuscany* (Oxford: Oxford University Press, 2003), 171–72, n. 8.

at the university by the late twelfth century. Likely taught by the master Azo, Buoncompagno's legal training informed his textbooks, which were used for the training of notaries. In his *Oliva* he tackles legal questions on such matters as privileges and confirmations; in his *Cedrus*, statutes; and last wills and testaments in both the *Mirra* and *X Tabule*.[11] Rolandino dei Passaggieri, a jurist himself, dates from a subsequent generation of Bolognese masters who taught the notarial arts. As we have seen, his *Summa Artis Notariae*, published in 1255, ultimately surpassed Buoncompagno's work as the handbook of choice for notaries. He codified his teachings in the *Summa*, which became the predominant handbook of notarial formularies by the mid-thirteenth century. Divided in three parts: contracts, testaments, and juridical acts, it outstripped all others because of its clarity of presentation.[12]

Only after 1160 do we have a handful of scattered evidence of Florentine notaries recording juridical acts—a late start in comparison to other communes. Two consular tribunals associated with Orsanmichele and San Martino issued these acts.[13] The development of judicial institutions in Florence was also rather late in coming. Only in the early thirteenth century do we begin to see evidence of the growth of communal courts. By about 1230, the city may have had seven in operation. All this has led Chris Wickham to remark that "there was not much legal business going through the Florentine courts until well into the thirteenth century."[14]

It will be remembered that it is not until 1234 that we have our first evidence of the Guild of Judges and Notaries, and not until 1237 that our first notarial casebook appears. The first peace instrument appears in 1257. By 1290 three criminal courts had been established, though we have no court records until the mid-fourteenth century. So far as the codification of normative law is concerned, there are "*ordinamenta* first referred to in 1159; a *constitutum* that is routinely cited in courts from 1183, that can determine court procedure by 1219; and the beginnings of fragmentary citations of Roman law in 1197."[15] As for the thirteenth century, although some of the earlier statutes were incorporated into the Ordinances of Justice, a full

11. For Buoncompagno, see Enrico Artifoni, "Boncompagno da Signa, i maestri di retorica e le città comunali nella prima metà del Duecento," in *Il pensiero e l'opera di Boncompagno da Signa*, ed. Enrico Artifoni and Massimo Baldini (n.p., 2002), 23–36.

12. For Rolandino, see *Rolandino e l'ars notaria da Bologna all'Europa: atti del convegno internazionale di studi storici sulla figura e l'opera di Rolandino: Bologna, città europea della cultura, 9–10 ottobre 2000*, ed. Giorgio Tamba (Milan: Giuffrè, 2002).

13. The documents were edited and published by Pietro Santini, *Documenti dell'antica costituzione del comune di Firenze* (Florence, G.P. Vieusseux, 1895). For a discussion of the early Florentine courts, see Daniela De Rosa, *Alle origini della Repubblica fiorentina: dai consoli al "primo popolo" (1172–1260)* (Florence: Arnaud, 1995), 32–66.

14. For the number of courts, Wickham, *Courts and Conflict*, 169; for the quotation, ibid., 171.

15. Wickham, *Courts and Conflict*, 171–72.

codification of Florentine statutory law had to wait until the years between 1322 and 1325.[16]

All these institutional developments and innovative ideas, which grew out of the new learning fostered by the universities of the twelfth century, and which had matured by the turn of the century, converged in the communal laboratories of the mid-thirteenth century, informing their often overlapping legal, political, and religious spheres. University educated jurists and judges, along with notaries and statesmen such as Brunetto Latini, and friar-preachers such as Remigio dei Girolami and Giordano da Pisa, to say nothing of learned laymen such as Albertanus of Brescia (also a lawyer), conveyed these ideas eloquently, and often braided them together, producing what we might call a "confessional mentality." This mindset was now brought to bear on the lives of those who inhabited the crowded Italian urban centers, where partisan and interpersonal violence—often indistinguishable—routinely disturbed the peace and public order.

The animating force of peace instruments, sealed with a ritual kiss of reconciliation, drew from this suggestive admixture of ideas, so richly developed first in the university curricula, then preached by the friars, and subsequently applied in the republican cities of central Italy. It is what made them attractive to Florentine consumers of justice. They appealed also because, as we have seen, they enshrined an old ethos of mutual cooperation and consent, making it *appear* at least that the parties to peace were taking matters into their own hands, as frequently they were. My data reveal that out of 526 notarial peace instruments, 266 settlements seem to have been self-initiated. That is, fully one half of these agreements bear no imprint of the court or its functionaries having initiated the case by denunciation or inquisition; nor do we find any evidence of accusation in these particular settlements. Acting according to statutory law, the disputing parties themselves initiated and enacted the peace. And even if at their inception many communes were "sleepwalking" while creating a new form of government; nonetheless, some of their subsequent propagandists, as we have seen, may have believed they were founded on the associative principles of peace.[17] The use of instrumenta pacis continued to evoke

16. For a new edition of the Ordinances of Justice, see *La legislazione antimagnatizia a Firenze*, ed. Silvia Diacciati and Andrea Zorzi (Rome: Istituto Storico Italiano per il Medio Evo, 2013); for the statutes, *Statuti della Repubblica Fiorentina*, 2 vols., ed. Romolo Caggese; new ed. Giuliano Pinto, Francesco Salvestrini, and Andrea Zorzi (Florence: Leo S. Olschki, 1999).

17. For the importance of peace and protection in very different contexts, see *Peace and Protection in the Middle Ages*, ed. T.B. Lambert and David Rollason (Toronto: Pontifical Institute of Mediaeval Studies, 2009). As noted earlier, in *Sleepwalking into a New World: The Emergence of Italian City Communes in the Twelfth Century* (Princeton: Princeton University Press, 2015), Chris Wickham argues against the view that collective peace oaths were the foundations of the communes. Instead he suggests that the communes at their inception "were most likely making it up as they went along," 19. This does not mean

that ethos in their formulae. As written texts, peace instruments continued to enshrine an origin myth of medieval communes that suggested that they were founded on shared principles of civic peace. The vast majority note that the agreement had been made in *bona voluntate* or even in *pura, libera et spontanea voluntate*,[18] formulaic phrases, of course, but ones carefully chosen to suggest the voluntary and non-coercive nature of the agreement, even if at least half of the time, peace was imposed from above by the commune, compelled by the judicial system, or coerced from outside by other pressure groups. No matter how the end result was achieved, the peace agreements themselves evoked a spirit of voluntary lateral associations, solidarity and common cause.

The paradox was that peace instruments were embedded in the legal system. They were not private remedies between individual citizens. If you committed a crime that violated the civic peace of the city and it reached the ears of the court, you were obligated by statute law to settle that dispute with a pax. The peace agreement was a swift and cost-effective solution, one that enabled its holder to avoid the risks and costs of a protracted court case whose outcome could never be predicted in advance.[19] Moreover, the act of drawing up a peace contract frequently served as your exit visa from the judicial court system, but not from justice itself. Justice and peace were not diametrical opposites: they coexisted, and as legal anthropologists have shown, they cooperated in the settlement of disputes. For this reason, justice was so often thought to be a facilitator of civic peace.[20]

At the same time, peace agreements and their attendant rituals captured something of the new and contemporary spirit of the popular regimes, which,

---

that subsequent generations of patriotric urban publicists were not cultivating or indeed commemorating a myth that the communes had been founded as peace associations.

18. This formula comes from the protocols of Benintendi di Guittone, ASF, Not. Ant. 234, fol. 168r-169v. Other phrases such as *in bona voluntate, pax et concordia, amiciter amicitia*, and *amor pacis* punctuate the otherwise "legalese" language in which the documents are written. Perhaps suggesting a connection with Lombard *convenientiae*, the *instrumenta pacis* are suffused in the language of concord, good will, love, and friendship. See Patrick Geary, "Extra-Judicial Means of Conflict Resolution," in *La giustizia nell'alto medioevo (secc. v–viii), Settimane di studio 42* (Spoleto: Centro italiano di studi sull'alto medioevo, 1995), 569–605, at 577.

19. Andrea Zorzi has examined one very unusual notarial register that covered all the peace settlements made in Florence in the year 1342–1343. It shows that about 5,800 people in all were parties to peace, amounting to about one-sixth of the population. These figures assume that at least half of the "signatories" to peace had committed some sort of crime, while the other half were victims of that crime. "Conflits et pratiques infrajudiciaires dans les formations politiques italiennes du XIIIe au XVe siècle," in *L'infrajudiciaire du Moyen Age à l'époque contemporaine. Actes du colloque organisé par le Centre d'études historiques sur la criminalité et les déviances de l'Université de Bourgogne, Dijon, 5-6 Octobre 1995*, ed. B. Garnot (Dijon: Publications de l'Université de Bourgogne, 1996), 9–36, at 27.

20. Wickham, *Courts and Conflict*, 7.

as we have seen, were waging peace on all fronts. Peace instruments served their purposes too, which was to discipline violence in order to promote the common good of peace. Political treatises, popular literature, sermons, and wall murals all promoted ideals of peace as part of an ideological platform of the republican governments determined to usher in an age of peace, one built on the idea of peace of the heart, even if—in the case of the Ordinances of Justice—that meant suppressing and demonizing one's enemies. In this, they were aided immeasurably by the preaching of laymen and friars alike, who propounded the message that penance was a necessary medicine for the body politic. Only through the purgation of sin could inner peace produce the outer peace equated with the common good.

It should be noted, however, that this penitential regime, disciplinary in nature, and based on the order of charity, was not necessarily charitable to all. The order of charity after all was a Christian idea of social order, one that was not particularly tolerant of those who did not comply with its teachings or believe the tenets of its faith. Only the Christian faithful were imagined to be true citizens of this peaceful social order. Nor were those who dissented from it always left to live in peace. Sometimes they were coerced into making peace. On one occasion, they fared far worse. In July 1233, John of Vicenza, the demagogue-preacher who so captivated audiences in the Veneto and Lombard regions during the Great Devotion, consigned to the fire sixty "heretics" of Verona, who refused to swear the oath endorsing him as *dux et rector* of the city, empowered to arbitrate disputes in the region. Were they Cathars, who refused to swear the oath, because oath-taking was against their beliefs? Or were they political dissenters? Or were they both, as most likely was the case?[21] These questions remain open; what we need to underscore here is that peacemaking was a not always a peaceful affair.

21. See Augustine Thompson, *Revival Preachers and Politics in Thirteenth-Century Italy: The Great Devotion of 1233* (Oxford: Clarendon Press, 1992), 71, and for further analysis of the event, Malcom Barber, *The Cathars: Dualist Heretics in Languedoc in the High Middle Ages* (New York: Longman: 2000), 175–76. On Catharism and politics in medieval Italy, see Carol Lansing, *Power and Purity: Cathar Heresy in Medieval Italy* (Oxford: Oxford University Press, 1998). In the newly restored Aula Gotica at the Santi Quattro Coronati complex in Rome, there is an interesting mid-thirteenth-century image that represents the link between heresy and discord. It is found on the north wall of the great hall decorated with the virtues and vices in the *torre maggiore*, commissioned by Stefano Conti, the *vicarius urbis*, the pope's representative in Rome. In one of its many scenes, St. Paul is portrayed as the living embodiment of the virtue Concord, with whom he is pictured. Arius, the arch-heretic of the late antique period, is represented as the sower of discord, whose works are shown in the depiction of a brawl at the feet of the central figures. For this recently recovered masterpiece of thirteenth-century Roman painting, see Andreina Draghi et al., *Gli Affreschi dell'aula gotica del monastero dei Santi Quattro Coronati: una storia ritrovata* (Milan: Skira, 2006).

Ultimately we must pose the question of whether peace agreements made to create social order and restore equilibrium actually worked, especially when, as we have seen, it was sometimes external pacieri or the commune itself that imposed them. Neither the initial Velluti–Mannelli agreement, to say nothing of the "sentence" of peace imposed by Cardinal Latino in 1280 seems to have held up for long. However, if we return to one of our notarial casebooks—the one from the Oltrarno district that covers a twenty-year period (1287–1297) in a single crowded neighborhood of the Oltrarno sesto of the city—we find more positive news, if we can judge by cases of repeated offenses. Of the seventy-three signatories to peace commemorated in Giovanni Cartepecchi's register, only three appear as repeat offenders. Pacino Buoni of San Giorgio made three separate peace contracts in one six-month period in 1294. Despite his name, he seems to have been a rabble-rouser. In one case he seems to have engaged in a violent confrontation with an entire family (not his own), including a husband, wife, and three children.[22] In all three cases he was accused of assault. In two he added insult to injury—literally: not only was he denounced for physical violence, but for insulting words as well.[23] Another repeat offender was Dosso di Lapo Delbene who was involved in two violent melees in less than two weeks; while Ormannozzio, son of Cionis Mannelli, spread his two offenses out over a period of three years.[24] This means that only 4 percent of those who made peace in this ten-year period were documented as repeat offenders, and this in a period when the Oltrarno sesto was experiencing extraordinary population growth due, as we have seen, to successive waves of migration from the contado. Thus, notwithstanding our repeat offenders, the expedient of the pax seems to have been an effective infra-judicial remedy for the needs of late medieval Florentines, who, imbued as they were in the culture of penance preached by friars and laymen alike, found that the peace instrument, with its comforting similarities to confession and religious reconciliation, accorded well with their understanding of peacemaking as a penitential practice.[25]

22. ASF, Not. Ant. 4111, fols., 150r-v.

23. Ibid., fols., 141r; 143r.

24. Ibid., fols., 104r; 149v; 157v; 158r.

25. I have also found a few repeat offenders in the casebook of Andrea di Lapo, ASF, Not. Ant. 439, fols. 21r-v, 43v, 47v. For example, one Spagnolo Zenobi of San Lorenzo made four agreements with different parties over a fifteen-month period.

BY THE SECOND HALF of the Trecento, Florence was on the cusp of a political transition, which, by the end of the century would transform the city into a territorial state. The second half of the century marked a period in which the associative forms of communal government—characterized especially by local parish and neighborhood organs—slowly disappeared and were replaced by state apparatus, most notably the Otto di Guardia, a magistracy charged with maintaining public order.[1] A marker of this change was the demise of the cappellani, whose primary function, as we have seen, was to report ruptures of the peace in their parishes. Andrea Zorzi has closely tracked their demise: in 1343 over 60 percent of the sentences issuing from the podestà's court were based on reports made by the cappellani; after the Black Death this percentage declined to 25 percent; in 1368 it fell to 11 percent, and by 1400 complaints made by the cappellani had disappeared altogether. The office of the cappellano was virtually extinct by 1415, the Otto di Guardia having absorbed this function.[2] Such evidence suggests a crisis in the local, parish-based administrative system, a suspicion that is further strengthened by the increase in fines levied on entire parishes that neglected to control public order, an example being the popolo of San Pier Maggiore, fined by the court of the podestà because its citizens had failed to raise a hue and cry, ring the church bells, or capture the perpetrator of an assault.[3]

Though the cappellani disappeared, peace instruments perdured in an age in which the city-state and its courts were consolidating their power. Peace agreements existed side by side with inquisition and accusation, better-known forms of legal procedure in the courts. All of these modes of conflict resolution operated simultaneously in the late medieval communes. Mario Sbriccoli has argued that the peace instrument was in fact so firmly entrenched in the

1. The Otto di Guardia was a committee formed by the Signoria of the city in 1378, after the Ciompi rebellion, for the purpose of maintaining public order. Neighborhood watches and militias had been discredited after many of them sided with the rebels. In essence, the Otto di Guardia was a summary court presided over by noble Florentine citizens; by the mid-fifteenth century it had become the dominant criminal tribunal in Florence, and its surveillance apparatus replaced the parish watch of the cappellani. See A. Zorzi, "The Judicial System in Renaissance Florence," in *Crime, Society and the Law in Renaissance Italy*, 40–58 at 50. For the later period, see John K. Brackett, *Criminal Justice and Crime in Late Renaissance Florence, 1537–1609* (Cambridge: Cambridge University Press, 1992). It endured well into the sixteenth century.

2. Zorzi, "The Judicial System," 45–46.

3. Cohn's dating for this is a rough one: 1374–1375. Samuel Kline Cohn, Jr., *The Laboring Classes in Renaissance Florence* (New York: Academic Press, 1980), 199.

communal legal system that it catalyzed judicial developments in the Italian
city-republics to the point that the pax was poised between the accusatory
and the inquisitional as a third type of procedure.[4] And as a number of other
prominent scholars on the subject have recently argued, such infra-judicial
solutions witness "jural diversity" or plurality, evidence of a fluid system that
permitted an array of options for dispute resolution that interacted with both
legal and political institutions.[5]

In the event, peace instruments continued to be a popular solution for
dispute settlement well into the regime of the Otto di Guardia. And here, in
conclusion, we might consider one final reason. The raison d'être of the *bene
comune* was to promote peace in all senses of the word: to maintain public
order, to control violence, to foster civic harmony, and to provide security. In
the thirteenth century, the Ordinances of Justice were predicated on circumscribing real and imagined magnate violence and promoting the security of
the popolo. The city statutes, codified in 1325, also did their share of the work
of prescribing and fostering the common good of peace, but the communal
government's message was conveyed as well through a diversified set of public
media platforms, all playing variations on a theme.

Ambrogio Lorenzetti's celebrated wall mural of "Buon Governo" is a visual
representation of this political ideology (fig. 33). And just as Lorenzetti's fresco
directs the eye toward the figure of Peace reclining languidly in a diaphanous
white gown in the Sala dei Nove, so too, contemporary theorists put peace
front and center in their discussions of good government, as did Remigio dei
Girolami in his treatise, *De bono pacis*.[6] Referring to Aristotle in his discussion, Remigio wrote: "As the Philosopher says in the *Ethics* Book 3, 'the highest good of the multitude, and its end, is peace.'" The *pax publica* was at the
forefront of all political ideology promulgated by the popular governments of
the communal era, a position that Remigio, one of Florence's great political
theorists, helped to promote.[7]

4. Massimo Vallerani, *The Medieval Public Justice System*, trans. Sarah Rubin
Blanshei (Washington, D.C.: Catholic University of America Press), 12–72 et passim. Mario
Sbriccoli, "'Vidi communiter observari': L'emersione di un ordine penale pubblico nelle
città italiane del secolo XIII," *Quaderni fiorentini per la storia del pensiero giuridico moderno* 27 (1998): 231–68, at 236.

5. Robert Bartlett, "'Mortal Enmities': The Legal Aspect of Hostility in the Middle
Ages," in *Feud, Violence and Practice: Essays in Medieval Studies in Honor of Stephen D.
White*, ed. Belle S. Tuten and Tracey L. Billado (Burlington, VT: Ashgate, 2010), 197–212,
at 198.

6. In *Dal bene comune al bene del comune: I trattati politici di Remigio dei Girolami
(†1319) nella Firenze dei bianchi-neri*, ed. Emilio Panella (Florence: Nerbini, 2014),
169–183.

7. Massimo Vallerani, "Mouvements de paix dans une commune de *Popolo*: les
Flagellants à Pérouse en 1260," in *Prêcher la paix et discipliner la société: Italie, France,
Angleterre (XIIIe-XVe siècles)*, ed. Rosa Maria Dessì (Turnhout: Brepols, 2005), 313–55.

FIGURE 33. *Peace as the Centerpiece of Good Government.* Ambrogio Lorenzetti, "Buon Governo" fresco, 1338–1339. Vested in a white gown and holding an olive branch, the allegorical figure of Peace reclines upon a cache of arms. She is positioned between Justice and Good Government. Concord, the result of Justice, Peace, and Good Government sits below them. Siena, Sala dei Nove, Palazzo Pubblico. Photo reproduced by permission of Scala/Art Resource, New York.

In the end, the settlement of disputes, the restoration of civic harmony, and the achievement of a more secure state were elements of the civic practice of peacemaking, institutionalized as the notarial peace instrument and enacted with a ritual kiss on the mouth.

Paradoxically, however, just as the kiss on the mouth had become the sign and seal of civic peacemaking rituals in Florence and its territories, it began to slip out of the Roman rite Mass, which dominated the liturgical practice of Latin Christendom. Its slow decline began in thirteenth-century England, where a bloodlessly chaste substitute replaced the mouth-to-mouth kiss. The "pax board," an object that came in various shapes and sizes—also called an *oculatorium* or sometimes even an *instrumentum pacis*—was passed between individuals before the Eucharistic prayer. The priest kissed the pax board after first kissing the altar, then handed it to an acolyte who passed in on to the congregation, where it was circulated among the parishioners, each kissing it in turn. Protocols of social hierarchy dictated that the parish elites kiss the pax first, followed by the middling classes, and finally by the women in the congregation.[8] A rare and radiant painted example from Florence

8. Virginia Reinburg, "Liturgy and the Laity in Late Medieval and Reformation France," *The Sixteenth Century Journal* 23. 3 (1992): 526–47, at 539–40 and John Bossy, "The Mass as a Social Institution," 1200–1700," *Past and Present* 100 (1983): 29–61, at 48–59 and 56–58.

Figure 34. *Pax Board Painted with the Face of Christ*. Panel Painting, Master of the Orcagnesque Misericordia, late 14th c. The inscription reads: *Pacem meam do vobis* (I give you my peace). Gift of the Jack and Belle Linsky Foundation, 1981. The Metropolitan Museum of Art, New York. Photo: by permission of ©The Metropolitan Museum of Art; reproduced by Art Resource.

shows two angels of peace presenting an imprint of Christ's face known as the Veronica (fig. 34). The inscription at its base reads: *Pacem meam do vobis* (My peace I give you [John 14:27]).[9] This new gesture, employing a mediating object, modulated the traditional sense of the kiss, and brought to the fore yet another meaning; one, it will be remembered, that William Durand had adduced. Now, instead of kissing each other in a sign of charity and concord, members of the Christian community kissed an image of Christ, emphasizing

9. It dates from the latter part of the fourteenth century. For a description of the panel, see Millard Meiss, *Painting in Florence and Siena after the Black Death: The Arts, Religion, and Society in the Mid-Fourteenth Century* (Princeton: Princeton University Press, 1951; repr. 1978), 35–38. Osculatoria are not rare but they are usually made of metal. For other examples, see Giuseppe Bergamini, "Instrumenta Pacis," in *Ori e tesori d'Europa: Atti del Convegno di Studio, Castello di Udine 3-4-5 dicembre 1991*, ed. G. Bergamini (Udine: Arti Grafiche Friulane, 1992), 85–108.

not the community's fraternal relationship with each other, but each individual's love for and reconciliation with the Lord.

By about 1500 the pax board had become a commonplace throughout Europe, though its days in Protestant countries were now numbered. Eventually Reformers eliminated it from the Eucharistic rites "because of its suggestion of a contractual element in the salvation of Christians," a purge that tellingly illustrates how closely the religious kiss of peace had become associated with the civic gesture. In Catholic Italy, however, its decline was not so precipitous. Not until the mid-twentieth century did the kiss (on the pax board) fall entirely out of use, replaced by the business-like handshake.[10]

In the civic realm, however, the kiss on the mouth nevertheless continued to be the ritual act associated with dispute settlements throughout the Middle Ages and well beyond.[11] And peace agreements were long-lived in certain parts of Italy, particularly those isolated areas that clung to traditional ways of life. Although peace instruments, products of a medieval penitential mentality, gradually fell into desuetude in Florence, elsewhere they endured into the twentieth century. In Sardinia, for example, three cases of medieval-style peacemaking were reported between the mid-nineteenth and the first quarter of the twentieth century. The last was celebrated at Tempio (now Tempio-Pausania), a town in the Gallura region of Northern Sardinia, which in the later Middle Ages had fallen under Pisan domination. Reported on October 8, 1920, in the *Corriere della Sera*, one of Italy's newspapers of record, five families representing about two hundred individuals (one of whom was over 90), made peace for hostilities and homicides they had committed against each other. Witnessed by the bishop and a crowd of townspeople, the parties came together and exchanged the kiss of peace. It was a scene that would not have looked out of place in late medieval Florence.[12]

10. Bossy, "The Mass," 58. For an interesting article that traces the fortunes of the placement of the kiss of peace in the Mass up to recent times, see Thomas J. Reese, "A Kiss Is Never Just a Kiss," *America: The National Catholic Review* (April 15, 1995) at http://americamagazine.org/issue/100/kiss-never-just-kiss [consulted 6/21/17].

11. For the post-medieval life of peace instruments, see *Stringere la pace: teorie e pratiche della conciliazione nell'Europa moderna, secoli XV-XVII*, ed. Paolo Broggio, Maria Pia Paoli, Marco Cavina (Rome: Viella, 2011).

12. As reported in Robert Davidsohn, *Storia di Firenze*, trans. Giovanni Battista Klein, 8 vols. (Florence: Sansoni, 1962), 5: 592.

Unpublished Archival Sources: Archivio di Stato di Firenze

ARCHIVIO NOTARILE ANTECOSIMIANO

Not. Ant. 251	Aldobrandino di Albizzo
Not. Ant. 363	Bartolo Amici
Not. Ant. 364	Bartolo Amici
Not. Ant. 365	Bartolo Amici
Not. Ant. 439	Andrea di Lapo
Not. Ant. 950	Arrigho di Benintendi
Not. Ant. 956	Arrigo di Ianni
Not. Ant. 1712	Bartolo di Giuntino
Not. Ant. 2354	Benintendi di Guittone
Not. Ant. 2358	Benintendi di Giuttone
Not. Ant. 2359	Benintendi di Guittone
Not. Ant. 2362	Benintendi di Guittone
Not. Ant. 3792	Buonsignore di Ser Rimberto da Rostolena
Not. Ant. 3830	Boldrone da Civitella
Not. Ant. 4111	Giovanni Cartepecchi
Not. Ant. 5738	Pietro Nelli Corsi
Not. Ant. 6019	Jacopo Dandi
Not. Ant. 9483	Giovanni di Buonaventura
Not. Ant. 9491	Giovanni di Buoninsegna da Rignano
Not. Ant. 9493	Giovanni di Buto
Not. Ant. 9692	Giovanni di Pacino
Not. Ant. 11108	Iacopo di Geri
Not. Ant. 11250	Ildebrandino di Benvenuto
Not. Ant. 11252	Ildebrandino d'Accatto
Not. Ant. 11383	Landino di Fortino
Not. Ant. 13363	Matteo di Biliotto
Not. Ant. 13364	Matteo di Biliotto
Not. Ant. 15681	Orlandino di Francesco
Not. Ant. 17045	Pino di Vieri
Not. Ant. 17856	Leggeri Riccobaldi
Not. Ant. 17869	Ricevuto d'Andrea
Not. Ant. 20546	Tano di Puccio di Guido

The preceding list follows the ASF's more recent numbering system as found in the indices to the Archivio Notarile Antecosimiano, *Inventario alfabetico dei notai*, N/37, vols. 1–2 and N/38, vols. 1–2.

Unpublished Manuscript Sources

ASSISI, SACRO CONVENTO
MS 470

NEW YORK, PIERPONT MORGAN LIBRARY
MS G.16
MS M.180

ROME, BIBLIOTECA CASANATENSE
MS 17

ROME, BIBLIOTECA ANGELICA
MS 151

VATICAN CITY, BIBLIOTECA APOSTOLICA VATICANA
MS Borgh. 175
MS Chigi L. VIII. 296

Published Primary Sources

Albertanus of Brescia. *Albertani Brixiensis Liber Consolationis et Consilii, ex quo hausta est fabula gallica de Melibeo et Prudentia, quam, anglice redditam et "The Tale of Melibe" inscriptam, Galfridus Chaucer inter "Canterbury Tales" recepit.* Ed. Thor Sundby. London: N. Trübner & Co., 1873.

Alighieri, Dante. *De monarchia.* Ed. E. Moore. Oxford: Clarendon, 1916.

———.*Inferno.* Trans. Mark Musa. New York: Penguin, 1971.

———.*Paradise.* Trans. Mark Musa. New York: Penguin, 1986.

Anonimo Romano. *Cronica.* Ed. Giuseppe Porta. Milan: Adelphi, 1979.

Aquinas, Thomas. *Summa Theologica.* Trans. Fathers of the English Dominican Province. 3 vols. New York: Benzinger Bros., 1947–48.

Atto Pistoriensis, episcopus. *Vita S. Ioannis Gualberti.* PL 146: 667–706.

Augustine of Hippo. *The City of God.* Trans. Marcus Dods. New York: Random House, 1950.

———. Sermon 227 (Easter Sunday). In *Sermons on the Liturgical Seasons.* Trans. Sister Mary Sarah Muldowney. Vol. 38. The Fathers of the Church. Washington, D.C.: Catholic University of America Press, 1959.

Baldus de Ubaldis. *Commentaria.* 8 vols. Venice: Giunti, 1599.

Bartolus de Sassoferrato. *Consilia, quaestiones et tractatus.* Turin: [Compagnia della Stampa], 1589.

Bencivenne. *Ars notarie.* Ed. Giovanni Bronzino. Bologna: Zanichelli, 1965.

Bernardino of Siena. *Le prediche volgari.* Ed. Ciro Cannarozzi. 5 vols. Pistoia: Pacinotti, 1934.

———.*Le prediche volgari.* Predicazione del 1425 Siena. Ed. Ciro Cannarozzi. 2 vols. Florence: Rinaldi, 1958.

———. *Prediche volgari sul Campo di Siena 1427*. Ed. Carlo Delcorno. 2 vols. Milan: Rusconi, 1989.

Biagio di Boccadibue. *Biagio di Boccadibue (1298–1314)*. Ed. Laura De Angelis, Elisabetta Gigli, and Franek Sznura. 4 vols. Pisa: Giardini, 1978–1986.

Bruni, Leonardo. *History of the Florentine People*. 3 vols. Trans. James Hankins. Cambridge, MA: Harvard University Press, 2001.

Cavalca, Domenico. *Frutti della lingua*. Rome: Antonio de' Rossi, 1754.

Chiaccheri, Matteo. "'Cronichetta di San Gimignano' (1353) ed il 'Libro d'oro sangimignanese.'" Ed. Carlo Talei. *Miscellanea storica della Valdelsa* n.s. 160 (1865), 125–46.

Collectio chartarum pacis privatae medii aevii ad regionem Tusciae pertinentium. Ed. Gino Masi. Milan: Vita e Pensiero, 1943.

Compagni, Dino. *Dino Compagni's Chronicle of Florence*. Trans. Daniel E. Bornstein. Philadelphia: University of Pennsylvania, 1986.

Compilatio Assisiensis dagli scritti di fr. Leone e compagni su S. Francesco d'Assisi dal MS 1043 di Perugia. Ed. Marino Bigarmi. Assisi: Tipografia Porziuncula, 1975.

Cronaca B. In *Corpus chronicorum Bononiensium*. Ed. Albano Sorbelli. RIS2: 18 Part I (vol. 2 of text).

Cronica fiorentina compilata nel secolo XIII. In *Testi fiorentini del Dugento e dei primi del Trecento*. Ed. A. Schiaffini. Florence: G. C. Sansoni, 1926, 82–150.

Cronaca fiorentina di Marchionne di Coppo Stefani. Ed. Niccolò Rodolico. RIS2: 30 Part I.

Cronica volgare di anonimo fiorentino dall'anno 1385 al 1409 già attribuita a Piero di Giovanni Minerbetti. Ed. Elina Bellondi. RIS2: 27.2 Part II.

Cyril of Jerusalem. "Mystagogic Catechesis 5." In *Cyril of Jerusalem*. Ed. and trans. Edward Yarnold, S.J. London: Routledge, 2000, 182–87.

Documenti dell'antica costituzione del comune di Firenze. Ed. Pietro Santini. Florence, G.P. Vieusseux, 1895.

Dominici, Luca. *Cronaca della venuta dei Bianchi e della morìa, 1399–1400*. 2 vols. Ed. Giovan Carlo Gigliotti. Pistoia: Alberto Pacinotti, 1933.

Durand, William. *Iuris Speculum*. 3 vols. Venice: Società dell'Aquila che si rinnova, 1585.

———. *Rationale on the the Mass and Each Action Pertaining to It*. Book 4. Trans. Timothy M. Thibodeau. CCCM 140. Turnhout: Brepols, 2013.

I Fioretti di San Francesco. Ed. Cesare Segre and Luigina Morini. Milan: Rizzoli, 1979.

Il Formularium Florentinum artis notarie: 1220–42. Ed. Gino Masi. Milan: Vita e Pensiero, 1943–44.

Francesco di Stefano de Caputgallis. *Un notaio romano del Trecento: I protocolli di Francesco di Stefano de Caputgallis (1374–1386)*. Ed. Renzo Mosti. Rome: Viella, 1994.

Giacomo delle Marche. (S. Iacobus de Marchia). *Sermones Dominicales*. 3 vols. Ed. Renato Lioi, O.F.M. Falconara Marittima: Biblioteca Francescana, 1978.

Giordano da Pisa. (Giordano da Rivalto). *Prediche del Beato fr. Giordano da Rivalto dell'Ordine dei Predicatori*. Ed. Domenico Maria Manni. Florence: Viviani, 1739.

Innocent III. *Innocentii III. De contemptu mundi sive de miseria humanae conditionis libri tres*. Ed. Johann Heinrich Achterfeldt. Bonn: E. Weber, 1855.

———. *Mysteriorum evangelicae legis et sacramenti eucharistiae*. PL: 217.

Iohannes Nicolai Pauli. *I Protocolli di Iohannes Nicolai Pauli, un notaio romano del '300 (1348–1379)*. Ed. Renzo Mosti. Rome: École Française de Rome, 1982.

Iuncta Bevegnatis. *Legenda de vita et miraculis beatae Margaritae de Cortona*. Ed. Fortunato Iozzelli, O.F.M. Bibliotheca Franciscana Ascetica medii aevi. Vol. 13. Grottaferrata: Editiones Collegii S. Bonaventurae ad Claras Aquas, 1997.

———. *The Life and Miracles of Saint Margaret of Cortona, 1247–1297*. Trans. Thomas Renna. St. Bonaventure, NY: Franciscan Institute Publications, 2012.

Latini, Brunetto. *Li livres dou Tresor*. Ed. Francis J. Carmody. Berkeley: University of California Press, 1948.

———. *The Book of the Treasure (Li Livres dou Tresor)*. Trans. Paul Barrette and Spurgeon Baldwin. New York: Garland, 1993.

"Legenda Beati Fratris Venturini, O.P." Ed. P. A. Grion, O.P. *Bergomum*, n.s. 30.4 (1956): 38–110.

"La Lezenda de Fra Raniero Faxano." Ed. G. Mazzatinti. *Bollettino di Società Umbra di Storia Patria* 2 (1896): 561–63.

"Il Liber Pergaminus di Mosè de Brolo." Ed. Guglielmo Gorni. *Studi Medievali*, 3rd series, XI.I (1970): 409–60.

Luca da Panzano. *'Brighe, affanni, volgimenti di stato:' Le ricordanze quattrocentesche di Luca di Matteo di Messer Luca dei Firidolfi da Panzano*. Ed. Anthony Molho and Franek Sznura. Florence: Sismel, 2010.

Marsilius of Padua. *Defensor pacis*. Ed. C.W. Previté-Orton. Cambridge: Cambridge University Press, 1928.

Ordinamenta. Ordinances of Justice. In *La legislazione antimagnatizia a Firenze*. Ed. Silvia Diacciati and Andrea Zorzi. Rome: Istituto Storico Italiano per il Medio Evo, 2013.

Ordinamenta. Ordinances of Justice. In *Magnati e popolani in Firenze dal 1280–1295*. Ed. Gaetano Salvemini. Florence: Carnesecchi, 1899, 384–432.

Palmerio di Corbizo da Uglione. *Palmerio di Corbizo da Uglione, fl. 1213–1238. Imbreviature, 1237–1238*. Ed. Luciana Mosiici and Franek Sznura. Florence: Leo S. Olschki, 1982.

Il Processo Castellano. In *Fontes Vitae S. Catherinae Senensis Historici*. Ed. M.-H. Laurent. Vol. 9. Milan: Fratelli Bocca, 1942.

Pseudo-Brunetto Latini. Cronica fiorentina. In *Testi fiorentini del Dugento dei primi del Trecento*. Ed. Alfredo Schiaffini. Florence: Sansoni, 1954.

Ranieri da Perugia. *Ars Notaria*. Ed. Augusto Gaudenzi. In *Biblioteca Iuridica Medii Aevi: Scripta Anecdota Glossatorum*. 3 vols. Bologna: In aedibus Petri Virano, 1892.

———. *Ars notariae*. In *Quellen zur Geschichte des römisch-kanonischen Prozesses*. 6 vols. Ed. Ludwig Wahrmund. Aalen: Scientia Verlag, 1962.

Raymond of Capua. *The Life of St Catherine of Siena*. Trans. George Lamb. London: Harvill Press, 1960.

Remigio dei Girolami. *De bono comuni*. In *Dal bene comune al bene del comune: I trattati politici di Remigio dei Girolami (†1319) nella Firenze dei bianchi-neri*. Ed. Emilio Panella, O.P. In *Memorie domenicane* 16 (1985): 123–68; 2nd. ed. Florence: Nerbini, 2014, 146–221.

———. *De bono pacis*. In *Dal bene comune al bene del comune: I trattati politici di Remigio dei Girolami (†1319) nella Firenze dei bianchi-neri*. Ed. Emilio Panella, O.P. In *Memorie domenicane* 16 (1985):169–83; 2nd. ed. Florence: Nerbini, 2014, 222–47.

———. *De iustitia*. "L'incompiuto "Tractatus de iustitia" di fra' Remigio de' Girolami," *Bullettino dell'Istituto storico italiano per il Medio Evo* 72 (1960): 125–28.

———. Sermo: "De domino Carolo. Accingere gladio tuo." In *Dal bene comune al bene del comune: I trattati politici di Remigio dei Girolami (†1319) nella Firenze dei bianchi-neri*. Ed. Emilio Panella, O.P. In *Memorie domenicane* 16 (1985): 41–42; 2nd. ed. Florence: Nerbini, 2014, 55–56.

———. Sermo: "Omne regnum." In *Dal bene comune al bene del comune: I trattati politici di Remigio dei Girolami (†1319) nella Firenze dei bianchi-neri*. Ed. Emilio Panella, O.P. In *Memorie domenicane* 16 (1985): 116–17; 2nd. ed. Florence: Nerbini, 2014, 138–39.

———. Sermo I *De pace*: "Fiat pax in virtute tua." In *Dal bene comune al bene del comune: I trattati politici di Remigio dei Girolami (†1319) nella Firenze dei bianchi-neri*. Ed. Emilio Panella, O.P. In *Memorie domenicane* 16 (1985): 187–88; 2nd. ed. Florence: Nerbini, 2014, 248–52.

———.Sermo VIII *De pace*: "Vade in pace." In *Dal bene comune al bene del comune: I trattati politici di Remigio dei Girolami (†1319) nella Firenze dei bianchi-neri*. Ed. Emilio Panella, O.P. In *Memorie domenicane* 16 (1985): 193–95; 2nd. ed. Florence: Nerbini, 2014, 264–66.

———. Sermo: "Si linguis." In *Dal bene comune al bene del comune: I trattati politici di Remigio dei Girolami (†1319) nella Firenze dei bianchi-neri*. Ed. Emilio Panella, O.P. In *Memorie domenicane* 16 (1985): 115; 2nd. ed. Florence: Nerbini, 2014, 137.

———. *Sermons to the Priors*. In *I sermoni d'occasione, le sequenze e i ritmi di Remigio dei Girolami fiorentino*. Ed. Giulio Salvadori and Vincenzo Federici. Rome: Forzani, 1901, 481–84.

Rogerius. *Summa codicis*. In *Biblioteca Iuridica Medii Aevi: Scripta Anecdota Glossatorum*. 3 vols. Ed. Giovanni Battista Palmerio. Bologna: Societas Azzoguidianae, 1888.

Rolandino dei Passaggieri. *Summa totius artis notariae*. Venice: Apud Iunctas, 1546.

Rufino. "Life of Raymond 'the Palmer' of Piacenza (1212)." Ed. Kenneth Baxter Wolf. In *Medieval Italy: Texts in Translation*. Ed. Katherine L. Jansen, Frances Andrews, and Joanna Drell. Philadelphia: University of Pennsylvania Press, 2009, 357–76.

Rufinus of Sorrento. *De bono pacis*. Ed. Roman Deutinger. MGH Studien und Texte, 17 (1997).

Salatiele. *Ars notarie*. Ed. Gianfranco Orlandelli. 2 vols. Milan: Giuffrè, 1961.

Salimbene de Adam. *Cronica*. In CCCM 125.

Salutati, Coluccio. *Epistolario*. Ed. Francesco Novati. 4 vols. Rome: Istituto Storico Italiano, 1891–1911.

Savonarola, Girolamo. *Prediche sopra i Salmi*. Ed. Vincenzo Romano. 2 vols. Rome: A. Belardetti, 1969–1974.

Speeches from the Oculus Pastoralis. Ed. Terence O. Tunberg. Toronto: PIMS, 1990.

Statuti del commune di San Gimignano compilati nel 1255. Ed. Luigi Pecori. In *Storia della terra di San Gimignano*. Florence: Tipografia Galileiana, 1853.

Statuti della Repubblica Fiorentina. 2 vols. Ed. Romolo Caggese. New edition ed. Giuliano Pinto, Francesco Salvestrini, Andrea Zorzi. Florence: Leo S. Olschki, 1999.

Lo Statuto di San Gimignano del 1255. Ed. Silvia Diacciati, Lorenzo Tanzini with contributions from Enrico Faini and Tomaso Perani. Florence: Leo S. Olschki, 2016.

Summa notarie Aretii composita (1240–43). Ed. Carlo Cicognario. In *Biblioteca Iuridica Medii Aevi: Scripta Anecdota Glossatorum*. 3 vols. Bologna: In aedibus successorum Monti, 1901.

Thomas de Spalato. *Historia Salonitarum*. Ed. P. A. Lemmens. "Testimonia minora saec. XIII de sancto Francisco." *AFH* 1 (1908): 69–84. Trans. by John R.H. Moorman, "St. Francis preaches at Bologna." In *St. Francis of Assisi: Writings and Early Biographies: English Omnibus of the Sources for the Life of St. Francis*. Ed. Marion A. Habig. Chicago: Franciscan Herald Press, 1983, 1877.

Two Memoirs of Renaissance Florence: The Diaries of Buonaccorso Pitti and Gregorio Dati. Ed. Gene Brucker. Trans. Julia Martines. New York: Waveland Press, 1967.

Velluti, Donato. *La cronica domestica di Messer Donato Velluti*. Ed. Isidoro del Lungo and Guglielmo Volpi. Florence: Sansoni, 1914. Excerpts in *The Society of Renaissance Florence: A Documentary Study*. Trans. Gene Brucker. New York: Harper Torchbooks, 1971, 106–10.

Villani, Giovanni. *Nuova Cronica*. Ed. Giovanni Porta. 3 vols. Parma: Ugo Guanda, 1991. On line at: http://www.classicitaliani.it/villani/cronica_09.htm.

Il Villani illustrato: Firenze e l'Italia medievale nelle 253 immagini del ms. Chigiano L VIII 296 della Biblioteca vaticana. Ed. Chiara Frugoni, Alessandro Barbero, et al. Vatican City: Biblioteca Apostolica Vaticana, 2005.

Visconti, Federico. *Les sermons et la visite pastorale de Federico Visconti archevêque de Pise (1253–1277)*. Ed. Nicole Bériou and Isabelle le Masne de Chermont et al. Rome: École Française de Rome, 2001.

Secondary Sources

Allen, Grace. "Vernacular Encounters with Aristotle's *Politics* in Italy, 1260–1600." Ph.D. diss. The Warburg Institute, University of London, 2015.

Andres, Stefano. "Oltre lo statuto: La vendetta nella letteratura toscana del Due-Trecento." *Laboratoire italien* 5 (2005): 57–83. Online at: http://laboratoireitalien.revues .org/426

Andrews, Frances. "Le voci della *Legenda beati fratris Venturini*: tra santità e condanna." *Cristianesimo nella storia* 34.2 (2013): 507–41.

———. "Preacher and Audience: Friar Venturino da Bergamo and 'Popular Voices.'" In *The Voices of the People in Late Medieval Europe. Communication and Popular Politics*. Ed. Jan Dumolyn, Jelle Haemers, Hipólito Rafael, Oliva Herrer and Vincent Challet. Turnhout: Brepols, 2014, 185–204.

Arnold, Klaus. "Bilder des Krieges—Bilder des Friedens." In *Träger und Instrumentarien des Friedens*. Ed. Johannes Fried. Sigmaringen: Jan Thorbecke, 1996, 561–86.

Artifoni, Enrico. "Boncompagno da Signa, i maestri di retorica e le città comunali nella prima metà del Duecento." In *Il pensiero e l'opera di Boncompagno da Signa*. Ed. Enrico Artifoni and Massimo Baldini (n.p., 2002), 23–36.

Ascheri, Mario. *The Laws of Late Medieval Italy (1000–1500): Foundations for a European Legal System*. Leiden: Brill, 2013.

Austin, J. L. *How to Do Things with Words*. Cambridge, MA: Harvard University Press, 1962; Repr. 1975.

Baldwin, John W. *Masters, Princes and Merchants: The Social Views of Peter the Chanter and His Circle*. Princeton: Princeton University Press, 1970.

Balzaretti, Ross. "'These are things that men do, not women': The Social Regulation of Female Violence in Langobard Italy." In *Violence and Society in the Early Medieval West*. Ed. Guy Halsall. Woodbridge: Boydell, 1998, 175–92.

Barber, Malcolm. *The Cathars: Dualist Heretics In Languedoc In The High Middle Ages*. New York: Longman, 2000.

Barthélemy, Dominique. *L'an mil et la paix de Dieu: La France chrétienne et féodale, 980–1060*. Paris: Fayard, 1999.

Bartlett, Robert. "Symbolic Meaning of Hair in the Middle Ages." In *Transactions of the Royal Historical Society* 6th series 4 (1994): 43–60.

———. "'Mortal Enmities:' The Legal Aspect of Hostility in the Middle Ages." In *Feud, Violence and Practice: Essays in Medieval Studies in Honor of Stephen D. White*. Ed. Belle S. Tuten and Tracey L. Billado. Burlington, VT: Ashgate, 2010, 197–212.

Bartoli Langeli, Attilio. *Notai: Scrivere documenti nell'Italia medievale*. Rome: Viella, 2006.

Baxandall, Michael. *Painting and Experience in Fifteenth-Century Italy: A Primer in the Social History of Pictorial Style*. Oxford: Oxford University Press, 1988; 2nd ed.

Bell, Catherine. *Ritual Theory, Ritual Practice*. Oxford: Oxford University Press, 1992.

Bellabarba, Marco. "Pace pubblica e pace privata." In *Criminalità e giustizia in Germania e in Italia: Pratiche giudiziarie e linguaggi giuridici tra tardomedioevo ed età moderna*. Ed. Marco Bellabarba, Gerd Schwerhoff, and A. Zorzi. Bologna: Il Mulino, 2001, 189–213.

Bellazzecca, Enrico. "Miretto, Niccolò." DBI 75 (2011), 9–10.

Bergamini, Giuseppe. "Instrumenta Pacis." In *Ori e tesori d'Europa. Atti del Convegno di Studio, Castello di Udine 3-4-5 dicembre 1991*. Ed. G. Bergamini. Udine: Arti Grafiche Friulane, 1992, 85–108.

Billanovich, Giuseppe. *Come nacque un capolavoro: la Cronica del non Anonimo romano. Il vescovo Ildebrandino Conti, Francesco Petrarca e Bartolomeo di Iacovo da Valmontone*. Rome: Accademia Nazionale dei Lincei, 1995.

Blanshei, Sarah Rubin. *Politics and Justice in Late Medieval Bologna*. Leiden: Brill, 2010.
———. Foreword. Massimo Vallerani, *Medieval Public Justice*. Trans. Sarah Rubin Blanshei. Washington, D.C.: Catholic University of America Press, 2012.
———. "La procedura penale in età comunale e signorile." In *I costi della giustizia a Bologna in età moderna*. Ed. Armando Antonelli (forthcoming).
Bliersbach, Elisabeth. "I Bianchi nell'arte Umbro-Laziale." *Sulle orme dei Bianchi dalla Liguria all'Italia centrale. Atti del convegno internazionale Assisi -Vallo di Nera -Terni -Rieti-Leonessa (18-19-20 giugno 1999)*. Ed. Francesco Santucci. Assisi: Accademia Properziana del Subasio, 2001, 363–405.
Blok, Anton. *Honour and Violence*. Malden, MA: Blackwell, 2001.
Boehm, Christopher. *Blood Revenge: The Anthropology of Feuding in Montenegro and Other Tribal Societies*. Lawrence, KS: University Press of Kansas, 1984.
Bornstein, Daniel. *The Bianchi of 1399: Popular Devotion in Late Medieval Italy*. Ithaca, NY: Cornell University Press, 1993.
Bossy, John. "The Mass as Social Institution, 1200–1700." *Past and Present* 100 (1983): 29–61.
———. *Christianity in the West*. Oxford: Oxford University Press, 1985.
———. *Peace in the Post-Reformation*. Cambridge: Cambridge University Press, 1998.
Boyle, Leonard E. *Pastoral Care, Clerical Education and Canon Law, 1200–1400*. London: Variorum, 1981.
Brackett, John K. *Criminal Justice and Crime in Late Renaissance Florence, 1537–1609*. Cambridge: Cambridge University Press, 1992.
Brancoli Busdraghi, Piero. "Aspetti giuridici della faida in Italia nell'età precommunale." In *La Vengeance, 400-1200*. Ed. Dominique Barthélemy, François Bougard and Régine Le Jan. Rome: École Française de Rome, 2006, 159–73.
Bresslau, Harry. *Manuale di diplomatica per la Germania e l'Italia*. Trans. Anna Maria Voci-Roth. Rome: Ministero per i beni culturali e ambientali, Ufficio centrale per i beni archivistici, 1998.
Brown, Daniel A. "The Alleluia: A Thirteenth Century Peace Movement." *AFH* 81 (1988): 3–16.
Brown, Keith M. *Bloodfeud in Scotland 1573-1625: Violence, Justice and Politics in an Early Modern Society*. Edinburgh: John Donald, 1986.
Brown, Peter. *The Body and Society: Men, Women, and Sexual Renunciation in Early Christianity*. New York: Columbia University Press, 1988.
Brown, Warren. *Violence in Medieval Europe*. London: Routledge, 2010.
Bruderer Eichberg, Barbara. *Les neuf choeurs angéliques: Origine et évolution du theme dans l'art du Moyen Age*. PhD diss., l'Université de Genève. Poitiers: Civilisation Médiévale, 1998.
Buc, Philippe. *The Dangers of Ritual: Between Early Medieval Texts and Social Scientific Theory*. Princeton: Princeton University Press, 2001.
Burke, Peter. "Insult and Blasphemy in Early Modern Italy." In *The Historical Anthropology of Early Modern Italy: Essays on Perception and Communication*. Cambridge: Cambridge University Press, 1987, 95–109.
Calleri, Santi. *L'Arte dei giudici e notai di Firenze nell'età comunale e nel suo statuto del 1344*. Milan: Giuffrè, 1966.
Carli, Enzo. "La pace nella pittura senese." In *La pace nel pensiero nella politica negli ideali del trecento. Convegno XV del centro di studi sulla spiritualità medievale*. Todi: L'Accademia Tudertina, 1975, 227–42.
Carraway, Joanna. "Contumacy, Defense Strategy, and Criminal Law in Late Medieval Italy." *Law and History Review* 29.1 (2011): 98–132.
Carré, Yannick. *Le baiser sur la bouche au moyen âge: rites, symbols, mentalités à travers les texts et les images IXe-XVe siècles*. Paris: Le Léopard d'Or, 1992.

Casagrande, Giovanna and Michaela Pazzaglia. "'Bona mulier in domo': Donne nel giudizario nel Duecento." *Annali della Facoltà di Lettere e Filosofia* 2. *Studi Storico-antropologici* 36 n.s. 12 (1998–99): 129–66.

Casali, Giovanna. *L'evoluzione della città tra XIV e XVI secolo*. Florence: Leo S. Olschki, 1998.

Cassio, Giuseppe. "La chiesa agostiniana di San Pietro apostolo in Terni e i suoi dipinti ritrovati." In *Arte sacra nell'Umbria meridionale. Atti del 1° corso per la formazione di volontari dell'animazione culturale promosso dall'Associazione Volontari per L'Arte e la Cultura*. Ed. Giuseppe Cassio. Terni: Ufficio per i beni culturali ecclesiastici, 2007, 101–110.

Cavalca, Desiderio. *Il bando nella prassi e nella dottrina giuridica medievale*. Milan: Giuffrè, 1978.

Ceccaroni, Sandro. "Testimonianze del movimento dei Bianchi a Vallo di Nera agli inizi del XV secolo." *Spoletium: Rivista di Arte Storia Cultura* 27 (1982): 39–44.

Chabot, Isabelle. "La beneficenza dotale nei testamenti del tardo Medioevo." In *Povertà e innovazioni istituzionali in Italia dal Medioevo ad oggi*. Ed. Vera Zamagni. Milan: Il Mulino, 2000, 55–76.

Chiesa, Luisella Cabrini. "Gesti e formule di pace: note in margine all'età medievale." In *La pace fra realtà e utopia* [*Quaderni di Storia Religiosa* 12]. Verona: Cierre, 2005: 47–97.

La chiesa di Sant'Alò in Terni. Ed. Maria Cristina Marinozzi. Arrone: Edizioni Thyrus, 2010.

Cipolla, Carlo. *The Monetary Policy of Fourteenth Century Florence*. Berkeley: University of California Press, 1982.

Cobianchi, Roberto. "Franciscan Legislation, Patronage Practice, and New Iconography in Sassetta's Commission at Borgo San Sepolcro." In *Sassetta: The Borgo San Sepolcro Altarpiece*. Ed. Machtelt Israëls. 2 vols. Florence: Villa I Tatti, 2009, 1: 107–19.

Cohen, Jeremy. *The Friars and the Jews: The Evolution of Medieval Anti-Judaism*. Ithaca, NY: Cornell University Press, 1982.

Cohn, Samuel Kline. *The Laboring Classes of Renaissance Florence*. New York: Academic Press, 1980.

———. "Women in the Streets, Women in the Courts, in Early Renaissance Florence." In *Women in the Streets: Essays on Sex and Power in Renaissance Italy*. Baltimore: Johns Hopkins University Press, 2008, 16–38.

The Compact Oxford English Dictionary. Oxford: Clarendon Press, 1991; 2nd ed.

Connerton, Paul. *How Societies Remember*. Cambridge: Cambridge University Press, 1989.

Constable, Giles. "Introduction" (on beards in the Middle Ages) to Burchard of Bellevaux, *Apologiae de Barbis*. Ed. R.B.C. Huygens. In *Apologia duae*, CCCM 62.

Coppi, Giovanni. *Annali, memorie et huomini illustri di San Gimignano*. Florence: Cesare & Francesco Bindi, 1695.

Corsi, Dinora. "La 'crociata' di Venturino da Bergamo nella crisi spirituale di metà Trecento." In *Archivio Storico Italiano* 4 (1989): 697–747.

Coy, Jason P. *Strangers and Misfits: Banishment, Social Control, and Authority in Early Modern Germany*. Leiden: Brill, 2008.

Crime, Society and the Law in Renaissance Italy. Ed. Trevor Dean and K.J.P. Lowe. Cambridge: Cambridge University Press, 1994.

Cursi, Marco. "Un nuovo codice appartenuto della famiglia Mannelli: la cronica figurata di Giovanni Villani (Vat. Chigi L.VIII. 296)." In *Segni: per Armando Petrucci*. Rome: Bagatto, 2002, 141–58.

Davidsohn, Robert. *Storia di Firenze*. Trans. Giovanni Battista Klein. 8 vols. Florence: Sansoni, 1962.

Davis, Charles T. "An Early Florentine Political Theorist: Fra Remigio de' Girolami." *Proceedings of the American Philosophical Society* 104.6 (1960): 662–76. Repr. in Davis, Charles T., *Dante's Italy and Other Essays*. Philadelphia: University of Pennsylvania Press, 1984, 198–223.

d'Avray, D. L. *The Preaching of the Friars: Sermons Diffused from Paris before 1300*. Oxford: Oxford University Press, 1985.

Dean, Trevor. "Marriage and Mutilation: Vendetta in Late Medieval Italy." *Past and Present* 157 (1997): 3–36.

———. *Crime in Medieval Europe*. New York: Longman, 2001.

———. "Violence, Vendetta and Peacemaking in Late Medieval Bologna." *Crime, Gender, and Sexuality in Criminal Prosecutions*. Ed. Louis A. Knafla. Westport, CT: Greenwood Press, 2002, 1–18.

———. *Crime and Justice in Late Medieval Italy*. Cambridge: Cambridge University Press, 2007.

de la Roncière, Charles-M. "Une famille florentine au XIVe siècle: les Velluti." In *Famille et parenté dans L'Occident médièval*. Ed. Georges Duby and Jacques Le Goff. Rome: École française de Rome, 1977, 227–48.

———. *Prix et salaires à Florence au XIVe siècle (1280–1380)*. Rome: École française de Rome, 1982.

Delcorno, Carlo. *Giordano da Pisa e l'antica predicazione volgare*. Florence: Leo S. Olschki, 1975.

———. "Professionisti della parola: predicatori, giullari, concionatori." In *Tra storia e simbolo: Studi dedicati a Ezio Raimondi, dai direttori, redattori e dall'editore di Lettere italiane*. Ed. Ezio Raimondi and Carlo Delcorno. Florence: Leo S. Olschki, 1994, 1–21.

Del Lungo, Isidoro. "Una vendetta in Firenze il giorno di San Giovanni del 1295." *Istituto storico italiano*, series 4, 18 (1886): 355–409.

Derbes, Anne and Mark Sandona. *The Usurer's Heart: Giotto, Enrico Scrovegni and the Arena Chapel in Padua*. University Park, PA: Pennsylvania State University Press, 2008.

de Riquer, Martín. *Cavalleria fra realtà e letteratura nel Quattrocento*. Trans. M. Rostaing and V. Minervini. Bari: Adriatica, 1970.

De Rosa, Daniela. *Alle origini della Repubblica fiorentina: dai consoli al "primo popolo" (1172–1260)*. Florence: Arnaud, 1995.

Dessì, Rosa Maria. "Predicare e governare nelle città dello Stato della Chiesa alla fine del medioevo: Giacomo della Marca a Fermo." In *Studi sul Medioevo per Girolamo Arnaldi*. Ed. Giulia Barone, Lidia Capo, and Stefano Gasparri. Rome: Viella, 2001, 125–59.

———. "Pratiche della parola di pace nella storia dell'Italia urbana." In *Pace e guerra nel basso medioevo. Atti del XL Convegno storico internazionale, Todi, 12–14 ottobre 2003*. Spoleto: Centro italiano di studi sull'alto medioevo, 2004, 270–312.

———. "Pratiques de la parole de paix dans l'histoire de l'Italie urbaine. " In *Prêcher la paix et discipliner la société: Italie, France, Angleterre (XIIIe–XVe siècles)*. Ed. Rosa Maria Dessì. Turnhout: Brepols, 2005, 245–78.

d'Hiver, C. S. "Ex voto de San Francisco de Asis." In *A la búsqueda del Toisón de oro. La Europa de los principles, la Europa de las ciudades*. Ed. Eduard Mira and An Blocksman-Delva. Valencia: Generalitat, 2007, 100–101 and 459–60.

Diacciati, Silvia. *Popolani e magnati: società e politica nella Firenze del Duecento*. Spoleto: Fondazione Centro italiano di studi sull'alto Medioevo, 2011.

Disputes and Settlements: Law and Human Relations in the West. Ed. John Bossy. Cambridge: Cambridge University Press, 1983.

Draghi, Andreina et al. *Gli Affreschi dell'aula gotica del monastero dei Santi Quattro Coronati: una storia ritrovata*. Milan: Skira, 2006.

Drewer, Lois. "Margaret of Antioch the Demon-Slayer, East and West: The Iconography of the Predella of the Boston Mystic Marriage of St. Catherine." *Gesta* 32. 1 (1993): 11–20.

Dunn, Caroline. *Stolen Women in Medieval England: Rape, Abduction and Adultery, 1100–1500*. Cambridge: Cambridge University Press, 2012.

Enriques, Anna Maria. "La vendetta nella vita e nella legislazione fiorentina." *Archivio Storico Italiano* 19 (1933): 85–146 and 181–223.

Epstein, Steven. *Purity Lost: Transgressing Boundaries in the Eastern Mediterranean, 1000–1400.* Baltimore: Johns Hopkins University Press, 2007.

Faini, Enrico. "Il convito del 1216: La vendetta all'origine del fazionalismo fiorentino." *Annali di storia di Firenze* 1 (2006): 9–36.

———. *Firenze nell'età romanica (1000–1211): l'espansione urbana, lo sviluppo istituzionale, il rapporto con il territorio.* Florence: Leo S. Olschki, 2010.

Fentress, James and Chris Wickham. *Social Memory.* Oxford: Blackwell, 1992.

Ferrari, Matteo. "I Maggi a Brescia: politica e immagine di una 'signoria' (1275–1316)." *Opera · Nomina · Historiae* 4 (2011): 19–66. Online: http://onh.giornale.sns.it

Feud, Violence and Practice: Essays in Medieval Studies in Honor of Stephen D. White. Ed. Belle S. Tuten and Tracey L. Billado. Burlington, VT: Ashgate, 2010.

Fiumi, Enrico. *Storia economica e sociale di San Gimignano.* Florence: Leo S. Olschki, 1961.

Fortini, Arnaldo. *La Madonna dell'oliva.* Venice: Nuova Editoriale, 1956.

———. *La lauda in Assisi e le origini del teatro italiano.* Assisi: Edizioni Assisi, 1961.

Frugoni, Arsenio. "La devozione dei Bianchi nel 1399." In *L'attesa dell'età nuova nella spiritualità della fine del medioevo. Atti del III convegno del centro di studi sulla spiritualità medievale.* Todi: Accademia Tudertina, 1960, 232–48.

Frugoni, Chiara. "L'iconografia del matrimonio e della coppia nel Medioevo." In *Il matrimonio nella società altomedievale. Settimane di studio del centro Italiano di studi sull'alto medievo* 24. Spoleto: Centro italiano di studi sull'alto medioevo, 1977, 901–66.

Gatti, Daniela. "Religiosità popolare e movimento di pace nel'Emilia del secolo XIII." *Itinerari storici: il medioevo in Emilia.* Modena: Mucchi, 1983, 79–107.

Geary, Patrick J. "Living with Conflicts in Stateless France: A Typology of Conflict Management Mechanisms, 1050–1200." In *Living with the Dead in the Middle Ages* (Ithaca, NY: Cornell University Press, 1994), 125–60. Originally published as "Vivre en conflit dans un France sans état: Typologie des mechanismes de règlement des conflits, 1050–1200." *Annales ESC* 41 (1986): 1107–33.

———. "Extra-Judicial Means of Conflict Resolution." In *La giustizia nell'alto medioevo (secc. v–viii). Settimane di studio* 42. Spoleto: Centro italiano di studi sull'alto medioevo, 1995, 569–605.

Geltner, Guy. *The Medieval Prison: A Social History.* Princeton: Princeton University Press, 2008.

Gennaro, Clara. "Venturino da Bergamo e la Peregrinatio Romana del 1335. " In *Studi sul medioevo cristiano offerti a Raffaello Morghen: per il 90° anniversario dell'Istituto storico italiano (1883–1973).* 2 vols. Rome: Istituto Storico per il Medio Evo, 1974, 374–406.

———. "Movimenti religiosi e pace nel XIV secolo." In *La pace nel pensiero nella politica negli ideali del Trecento, 13–17 Ottobre, 1974. Centro degli Studi sulla spiritualità medievale* 15. Todi: L'Accademia Tudertina, 1975, 93–112.

Gentili, Sonia. "Girolami, Remigio de'." DBI 56 (2001): 531–41.

Ghinato, Alberto. "Apostolato religioso e sociale di Giacomo delle Marche in Terni." *AFH* 49 (1956): 106–42.

Gibbs, Robert. "In Search of Ambrogio Lorenzetti's Allegory of Justice: Changes to the Frescoes in the Palazzo Pubblico." *Apollo* 149, no. 477 (1999): 11–16.

Giraldi, Maria Cecilia. "Il passaggio dei Bianchi a Rieti nelle testimonianze iconografiche." *Sulle orme dei Bianchi dalla Liguria all'Italia centrale. Atti del convegno internazionale Assisi -Vallo di Nera -Terni -Rieti -Leonessa (18-19-20 giugno 1999).* Ed. Francesco Santucci. Assisi: Accademia Properziana del Subasio, 2001, 25–37.

Gluckman, Max. "Peace in the Feud." *Past and Present* 8.1 (1955): 1–14.

Goering, Joseph. "The Summa of Master Serlo and Thirteenth-Century Penitential Literature," *Mediaeval Studies* 40 (1978): 290–311.

——. "The Internal Forum and the Literature of Penance and Confession." *Traditio* 59 (2004): 175–227.

Graham, Angus. "Albertanus of Brescia: A Supplementary Census of Latin Manuscripts." *Studi Medievali* 41 (2000): 891–924.

Graziotti, Tamara. *Giustizia penale a San Gimignano (1300–1350)*. Florence: Leo S. Olschki, 2015.

Greenstein, Jack. "The Vision of Peace: Meaning and Representation in Ambrogio Lorenzetti's Sala della Pace Cityscapes." *Art History* 11.4 (1988): 492–510.

Hanawalt, Barbara. "The Female Felon in Fourteenth-Century England. " *Viator* 5 (1974): 253–68. Repr. *Women in Medieval Society*. Ed. Susan Mosher Stuard. Philadelphia: University of Pennsylvania Press, 1976, 125–40.

——. *Crime and Conflict in English Communities, 1300–1348*. Cambridge: Harvard University Press, 1979.

—— and David Wallace. *Medieval Crime and Social Control*. Minneapolis: University of Minnesota Press, 1999.

Heers, Jacques. *Parties and Political Life in the Medieval West*. Trans. David Nicholas. Amsterdam: North Holland Publishing Co., 1977.

Helmholz, R. H. *Select Cases on Defamation to 1600*. London: Seldon Society, 1985.

Henderson, John. "The Flagellant Movement and Flagellant Confraternities in Central Italy, 1260–1400." In *Studies in Church History* 15 (1978), 147–60.

Herlihy, David and Christiane Klapisch-Zuber. *Tuscans and Their Families: A Study of the Florentine Catasto of 1427*. New Haven: Yale University Press, 1985.

Hocedez, E. "La légende latine du B. Venturino de Bergamo." *Analecta Bollandiana* 25 (1906): 298–303.

Hughes, Diane Owen. "From Brideprice to Dowry in Mediterranean Europe." *Journal of Family History* 3 (1978): 262–96.

——. "Distinguishing Signs: Earrings, Jews and Franciscan Rhetoric in the Italian Renaissance City." *Past and Present* 112 (1986): 3–59.

Hyams, Paul. *Rancor and Reconciliation in Medieval England*. Ithaca, NY: Cornell University Press, 2003.

Iannella, Cecilia. *Giordano da Pisa: etica urbana e forme della società*. Pisa: ETS, 1999.

——. "Predicazione domenicana ed etica urbana tra due e tre trecento." In *Predicazione e società nel medioevo: riflessione etica, valori e modelli di comportamento/ Preaching and Society in the Middle Ages: Ethics, Values and Social Behaviour. Atti/Proceedings of the XII Medieval Sermon Studies Symposium Padova, 14–18 luglio 2000*. Ed. Laura Gaffuri and Riccardo Quinto. Padua: Centro Studi Antoniani, 2002, 171–85.

——. "La paix dans la prédication de Giordano de Pisa (vers 1260–1310). In *Prêcher la paix et discipliner la société: Italie, France, Angleterre (XIIIe-XVe siècles)*. Ed. Rosa Maria Dessì. Turnhout: Brepols, 2005, 367–82.

Inglese, G. "Latini, Brunetto," DBI 64 (2005), 4–12.

Kimura, Yoko. "Preaching Peace in Fifteenth-Century Italian Cities: Bernardino da Feltre." In *From Words to Deeds: The Effectiveness of Preaching in the Late Middle Ages*. Ed. Maria Giuseppina Muzzarelli. Brepols: Turnhout, 2014, 171–83.

Jamous, Raymond. "From the Death of Men to the Peace of God: Violence and Peacemaking in the Rif." In *Honor and Grace in Anthropology*. Ed. J. G. Peristiany and Julian Pitt-Rivers. Cambridge: Cambridge University Press, 1992, 167–91.

Jansen, Katherine Ludwig. *Making of the Magdalen: Preaching and Popular Religion in the Later Middle Ages*. Princeton: Princeton University Press, 2000.

Jansen, Katherine Ludwig. "Florentine Peacemaking: the Oltrarno, 1287–1297." In *Pope, Church and City: Essays in Honor of Brenda Bolton*. Ed. Frances Andrews, Christoph Egger, and Constance M. Rousseau. Leiden: Brill, 2004, 327–44.

———. *"Pro bono pacis*: Crime and Dispute Resolution in Late Medieval Florence. The Evidence of Notarial Peace Contracts." *Speculum* 88.2 (April 2013): 427–56.

———. "Peacemaking, Performance and Power in Thirteenth-Century San Gimignano." In *Center and Periphery: Studies on Power in the Medieval World in Honor of William Chester Jordan*. Ed. Katherine L. Jansen, Guy Geltner, and Anne E. Lester. Leiden: Brill, 2013, 93–106.

Jordan, William C. *From England to France: Felony and Exile in the High Middle Ages*. Princeton: Princeton University Press, 2015.

Jungmann, Joseph A. *The Mass of the Roman Rite: Its Origins and Development*. 2 vols. Trans. Francis A. Brunner. New York: Benzinger Brothers, 1951–1955. Repr. Westminster, MD: Christian Classics, 1986.

Keck, David. *Angels and Angelology in the Middle Ages*. Oxford: Oxford University Press, 1998.

Kempshall, M.S. *The Common Good in Late Medieval Political Thought*. Oxford: Clarendon Press, 1999.

Kessler, Herbert. "The Meeting of Peter and Paul in Rome: An Emblematic Narrative of Spiritual Brotherhood." *Dumbarton Oaks Papers: Studies on Art and Archeology in Honor of Ernst Kitzinger on His Seventy-Fifth Birthday* 41 (1987): 265–75.

Kirshner, Julius. *Pursuing Honor While Avoiding Sin: The Monte delle doti of Florence*. Milan: Giuffrè, 1978.

Klapisch-Zuber, Christiane. *Women, Family, and Ritual in Renaissance Italy*. Trans. Lydia Cochrane. Chicago: University of Chicago Press, 1985.

———. "Kinship and Politics in Fourteenth-Century Florence." In *The Family in Italy from Antiquity to the Present*. Ed. David L. Kertzer and Richard P. Saller. New Haven: Yale University Press, 1991, 208–28

———. "Les soupes de la vengeance: Les rites de l'alliance sociale." In *L'ogre historien: Autour de Jacques Le Goff*. Ed. J. Revel and Jean-Claude Schmitt. Paris: Gallimard, 1998, 259–81.

———. "Kinship and Politics in Fourteenth-Century Florence." In *The Family in Italy from Antiquity to the Present*. Ed. David L. Kertzer and Richard P. Saller. New Haven: Yale University Press, 1991, 208–28

Kovesi Killerby, Catherine. *Sumptuary Law in Italy, 1200–150*. Oxford: Clarendon Press, 2002.

Koziol, Geoffrey. "The Dangers of Polemic: Is Ritual Still an Interesting Topic of Historical Study?" *Early Medieval Europe*. 11.4 (2002): 367–88.

Knuf, Joachim. "Where Cultures Meet: Ritual Code and Organizational Boundary Management." *Research on Language and Social Interaction* 23 (1989/90): 109–38.

Kuehn, Thomas. *"Cum consensu mundualdi*: Legal Guardianship of Women in Quattrocento Florence." *Viator* 13 (1982): 309–31. Repr. *Law, Family, and Women: Towards a Legal Anthropology of Renaissance Italy*. Chicago: University of Chicago Press, 1991, 212–37.

———. "Arbitration and Law in Renaissance Florence." *Renaissance and Reformation* n.s. 11 (1987): 289–319. Repr. *Law, Family, and Women: Towards a Legal Anthropology of Renaissance Italy*. Chicago: University of Chicago Press, 1991, 19–74.

———. "Dispute Processing in the Renaissance: Some Florentine Examples." In *Law, Family, and Women: Towards a Legal Anthropology of Renaissance Italy*. Chicago: University of Chicago Press, 1991, 75–100.

———. "Social and Legal Capital in Vendetta: A Fifteenth-Century Florentine Feud In and Out of Court." In *Sociability and Its Discontents: Civil Society, Social Capital, and Their Alternatives in Late Medieval and Early Modern Europe*. Ed. Nicholas A. Eckstein and Nicholas Terpstra. Turnhout: Brepols, 2009, 51–72.

Kumhera, Glenn. "Making Peace in Medieval Siena: Instruments of Peace, 1280–1400." Ph.D. diss. University of Chicago, 2005.

——."Promoting Peace in Medieval Siena: Peacemaking Legislation and Its Effects." In *War and Peace: Critical Issues in European Societies and Literature, 800–1800*. Ed. Albrecht Classen and Nadia Margolis. Berlin: de Gruyter, 2011, 334–48.

Labriola, Alda. "Pacino di Bonaguida." In *Dizionario biografico dei miniatori italiani, secoli IX-XVI*. Ed. Milvia Bollati and Miklós Boskovits. Milan: Sylvestre Bonnard, 2004, 841–43.

Lansing, Carol. *The Florentine Magnates: Lineage and Faction in a Medieval Commune*. Princeton: Princeton University Press, 1991.

——.*Power and Purity: Cathar Heresy in Medieval Italy*. Oxford: Oxford University Press, 1998.

Larson, Atria A. *Master of Penance: Gratian and the Development of Penitential Thought and Law in the Twelfth Century*. Washington, D.C.: Catholic University of America Press, 2014.

Late Medieval and Early Modern Ritual: Studies in Italian Urban Culture. Ed. Samuel Cohn, Jr., Marcello Fantoni, Franco Franceschi, and Fabrizio Ricciardelli (Brepols: Turnhout, 2012).

Lea, Henry Charles. *A History of Auricular Confession and Indulgences in the Latin Church*. 3 vols. Philadelphia: Lea Bros. & Co., 1896.

Le Goff, Jacques. *In Search of Sacred Time: Jacobus de Voragine and the Golden Legend*. Princeton: Princeton University Press, 2014.

Lerner, Robert. "Medieval Millenarianism and Violence." In *Pace e guerra nel basso medioevo: Atti del XL Convegno storico internazionale, Todi, 12–14 ottobre 2003*. Spoleto: Accademia Tudertina, 2004, 37–35.

Lesnick, Daniel. "Insults and Threats in Medieval Todi." *Journal of Medieval History* 17 (1991): 71–89.

Lucchesi, Emiliano. "Il crocifisso di S. Giovanni Gualberto e lo stendardo della Croce di S. Francesco di Sales." *Il faggio Vallombrosano* 10 (1937): 1–137.

Luongo, F. Thomas. *The Saintly Politics of Catherine of Siena*. Ithaca, NY: Cornell University Press, 2006.

Maire Vigeur, Jean-Claude. "Il problema storiografico: Firenze come modello (e mito) di regime popolare." In *Magnati e popolani nell'Italia comunale*. Pistoia: Centro italiano di studi di storia d'arte, 1997, 1–16.

Malegam, Jehangir Yezdi. *The Sleep of the Behemoth: Disputing Peace and Violence in Medieval Europe, 1000–1200*. Ithaca, NY: Cornell University Press, 2013.

Mancini, Francesco Federico. "La Loggia delle Virtù, allegoria di un governo illuminato." *Il Palazzo Trinci di Foligno*. Ed. Giordana Benazzi and Francesco Federico Mancini. Perugia: Quattroemme, 2001, 299–336.

Marmursztejn, Elsa. "Guerre juste et paix chez les scolastiques." In *Prêcher la paix et discipliner la société: Italie, France, Angleterre (XIIIe-XVe siècles)*. Ed. Rosa Maria Dessì. Turnhout: Brepols, 2005.

Marriage in Italy, 1300–1650. Ed. Trevor Dean and K.J.P. Lowe. Cambridge: Cambridge University Press, 1998.

Martines, Lauro. *Lawyers and Statecraft in Renaissance Florence*. Princeton: Princeton University Press, 1968.

——. *Violence and Civil Disorder in Italian Cities, 1200–1500*. Berkeley: University of California Press, 1972.

McGee, Timothy J. *The Ceremonial Musicians of Late Medieval Florence*. Bloomington, IN: Indiana University Press, 2009.

Meens, Rob. *Penance in Medieval Europe, 600–1200*. Cambridge: Cambridge University Press, 2014.

Meersseman, G. G. "I penitenti nei secoli XI e XII." In *I laici nella 'Societas Christiana' dei secoli XI e XII. Atti della terza settimana internazionale di studio. Mendola, 21–27 agosto 1965*. Milan: Vita e Pensiero, 1968, 306–45.

Meier, Ulrich. "*Pax et tranquillitas:* Friedensidee, Friedenswahrung und Staatsbildung im spätmittelalterlichen Florenz." In *Träger und Instrumentarien des Friedens im hohen und späten Mittelalter*. Ed. Johannes Fried. Sigmaringen: Jan Thorbecke, 1996, 489–523.

Meiss, Millard. *Painting in Florence and Siena after the Black Death: The Arts, Religion, and Society in the Mid-Fourteenth Century*. Princeton: Princeton University Press, 1951; repr. 1978.

Mews, Constant J. "Cicero on Friendship." In *Friendship: A History*. Ed. Barbara Caine. New York: Routledge, 2014, 65–73.

Miglio, Massimo. "Gli ideali di pace e giustizia a Roma a metà del Trecento." In *La pace nel pensiero nella politica negli ideali del Trecento, 13–17 ottobre, 1974. Centro degli studi sulla spiritualità medievale* 15. "Todi: L'Accademia Tudertina," 1975, 177–97.

Milani, Giuliano. *L'esclusione dal comune. Conflitti e bandi politici a Bologna e in altre città italiane tra XII e XIV secolo*. Rome: Instituto storico italiano per il medio evo, 2003.

Miller, Maureen. *Clothing the Clergy: Virtue and Power in Medieval Europe, c. 800–1200*. Ithaca, NY: Cornell University Press, 2014.

Miller, William. *Bloodtaking and Peacemaking: Feud, Society, and Law in Saga Iceland*. Chicago: University of Chicago Press, 1990.

Milner, Stephen J. "Rhetorics of Transcendence: Conflict and Intercession in Communal Italy, 1300–1500." In *Charisma and Religious Authority: Jewish, Christian and Muslim Preaching, 1200–1500*. Ed. Katherine L. Jansen and Miri Rubin. Turnhout: Brepols, 2010. 235–51.

Mitchell, Nathan D. *The Mystery of the Rosary: Marian Devotion and the Reinvention of Catholicism*. New York: New York University Press, 2009.

Molho, Anthony. *Marriage Alliance in Late Medieval Florence*. Cambridge, MA: Harvard University Press, 1994.

Mooney, Anthony M. C. "The Legal Ban in Florentine Statutory Law and the *de Bannitis* of Nello da San Gemignano." Ph.D. diss. U.C.L.A., 1976.

Moore, Sally F. and Barbara Myerhoff. *Secular Ritual*. Amsterdam: Van Gorcum, 1977.

———. *Law as Process: An Anthropological Approach*. London: Routledge, 1978.

Mormando, Franco. "'Just as your lips approach the lips of your brothers': Judas Iscariot and the Kiss of Betrayal." In *Saints and Sinners: Caravaggio and the Baroque Image*. Ed. Franco Mormando. Chestnut Hill, MA: McMullen Museum of Art, Boston College, 1999, 179–90.

———. *The Preacher's Demons: Bernardino of Siena and the Social Underworld of Renaissance Italy*. Chicago: University of Chicago Press, 1999.

Mosiici, Luciana. "Note sul più antico protocollo notarile del territorio fiorentino e su altri registri di imbreviature del secolo XIII." In *Il Notariato nella civiltà toscana. Atti di un convegno (maggio 1981)*. Rome: Consiglio nazionale del notariato, 1985, 174–238.

Muir, Edward. *Mad Blood Stirring: Vendetta and Factions in Friuli during the Renaissance*. Baltimore: Johns Hopkins University Press, 1993.

Musto, Ronald G. *Catholic Peacemakers: A Documentary History*. 2 vols. New York: Garland, 1993.

Murray, Alexander. *Conscience and Authority in the Medieval Church*. Oxford: Oxford University Press, 2015.

Muzzarelli, Maria Giuseppina. *Guardaroba medievale: vesti e società dal XIII al XVI secolo*. Bologna: Il Mulino, 1999.

Najemy, John. *A History of Florence 1200–1575*. Malden, MA: Blackwell, 2006.

Nederman, C. J., "Aristotelianism and the Origins of 'Political Science' in the Twelfth Century." *Journal of the History of Ideas* 52 (1991): 179–94.

Niccoli, Ottavia. "Rinuncia, pace, perdono. Rituali di pacificazione della prima età moderna." *Studi Storici* 40.1 (1999): 219–61.

Nussdorfer, Laurie. *Brokers of Public Trust: Notaries in Early Modern Rome.* Baltimore: Johns Hopkins University Press, 2009.

Oexle, Otto Gerhard. "Pax und Pactum: Rufinus von Sorrent und sein Traktat über den Frieden." In *Italia et Germania: Liber Amicorum Arnold Esch.* Ed. Hagen Keller, Werner Paravicini, and Wolfgang Schieder. Tübingen: Walter de Gruyter, 2001, 539–55.

———. "Peace through Conspiracy." In *Ordering Medieval Society: Perspectives on Intellectual and Practical Modes of Shaping Social Relations.* Ed. Bernhard Jussen. Philadelphia: University of Pennsylvania Press, 2001, 285–322.

Oldstone-Moore, Christopher. *Of Beards and Men: The Revealing History of Facial Hair.* Chicago: Chicago University Press, 2016.

Onori, Alberto M. "Pace privata e regolamentazione della vendetta in Valdinievole." In *Conflitti, paci e vendetta nell'Italia comunale.* Ed. A. Zorzi. Florence: Reti medievali-Firenze University Press, 2009, 219–35. http://fermi.univr.it/rm/e-book/titoli/zorzi.htm.

Ottokar, Nicola. *Il comune di Firenze alla fine del Dugento.* Turin: Einaudi, 1962.

Padoa Schioppa, Antonio. "Delitto e pace privata nel pensiero dei legisti bolognesi. Brevi note." *Studia Gratiana* 20 (1976): 271–87.

———. "Delitto e pace privata nel diritto lombardo." In *Diritto comune e diritti locali nella storia dell'Europa.* Milan: Giuffrè, 1980, 555–78.

Il Palazzo Trinci di Foligno. Ed. Giordana Benazzi and Francesco Federico Mancini. Perugia: Quattroemme, 2001.

I Palazzi: arte e storia degli edifici civili di Firenze. Ed. Sandra Carlini, Lara Mercanti, and Giovanni Straffi. 2 vols. Florence: Alinea, 2001–2004.

Palmer, James. "Piety and Social Distinction." *Speculum* 89.4 (2014): 974–1004.

Panella, Emilio. *Dal bene comune al bene del comune. I trattati politici di Remigio dei Girolami (†1319) nella Firenze dei bianchi-neri.* In *Memorie domenicane* 16 (1985), 1–198; 2nd. ed. Florence: Nerbini, 2014.

Pastoureau, Michel. *Black: The History of a Color.* Princeton: Princeton University Press, 2008.

Pazzaglini, Peter R. *The Criminal Ban of the Sienese Commune, 1225–1310.* Milan: Giuffrè 1979.

Peace and Protection in the Middle Ages. Ed. T. B. Lambert and David Rollason. Toronto: Pontifical Institute of Mediaeval Studies, 2009.

The Peace of God: Social Violence and Religious Response around 1000. Ed. Thomas Head and Richard Landes. Ithaca, NY: Cornell University Press, 1992.

Pecori, Luigi. *Storia della terra di San Gimignano.* Florence: Tipografia Galileiana,1853.

Penn, Michael Philip. *Kissing Christians: Ritual and Community in the Late Ancient Church.* Philadelphia: University of Pennsylvania Press, 2005.

Perella, Nicolas James. *The Kiss Sacred and Profane.* Berkeley: University of California Press, 1969.

Petit-Dutaillis, Charles. *Les communes françaises. Caractères et evolution des origines au XVIIIe siècle.* Paris: Albin Michel, 1947.

Petkov, Kiril. *The Kiss of Peace: Ritual, Self and Society in the High and Late Medieval West.* Leiden: Brill, 2003.

Piana, Celestino O.F.M. "I processi di canonizzazione su la vita di S. Bernardino di Siena." *AFH* 44 (1951): 87–160 and 383–435.

Pirri, Piero. "Una pittura storica di Cola di Pietro da Camerino." Perugia: Unione Tipografica Cooperativa, 1918.

Pleij, Herman. *Colors Demonic and Divine: Shades of Meaning in the Middle Ages and After.* Trans. Diane Webb. New York: Columbia University Press, 2004.

I podestà dell'Italia comunale. Ed. Jean-Claude Maire Vigueur. Rome: École Française, 2000.

Polecritti, Cynthia L. *Preaching Peace in Renaissance Italy: Bernardino of Siena and His Audience.* Washington, D.C.: Catholic University of America Press, 2000.

Porta Casucci, Emanuela. "Le paci fra privati nelle parrocchie fiorentine di S. Felice in Piazza e S. Frediano: un regesto per gli anni 1335–1365." *Annali di Storia di Firenze* IV (2009): 195–241.

———. "La pacificazione dei conflitti a Firenze a metà Trecento nella pratica del notariato." In *Conflitti, paci e vendetta nell'Italia comunale.* Ed. A. Zorzi. Florence: Reti medievali-Firenze University Press, 2009, 193–218.

Post, Gaines. "*Ratio publicae utilitatis, ratio status,* and 'Reason of State,' 1100–1300." In *Studies in Medieval Legal Thought: Public Law and the State, 1100–1322.* Princeton: Princeton University Press, 1964, 241–309.

Powell, James M. *The Pursuit of Happiness in the Early Thirteenth Century.* Philadelphia: University of Pennsylvania Press, 2004.

Prandi, Adriano. "La pace nei temi iconografici del trecento." In *La pace nel pensiero nella politica negli ideali del trecento. Convegno XV del centro di studi sulla spiritualità medievale.* Todi: L'Accademia Tudertina, 1975, 245–59.

Prêcher la paix et discipliner la société: Italie, France, Angleterre (XIIIe-XVe siècles). Ed. Rosa Maria Dessì. Turnhout: Brepols, 2005.

Prodi, Paolo. *Il sacramento del potere: il giuramento politico nella storia costituzionale dell'Occidente.* Bologna: Il Mulino, 1992.

Quaglioni, Diego. "*Civitas*: Appunti per una riflessione sull'idea di città nel pensiero politico dei giuristi medievali." In *Le ideologie della città europea dall'umanesimo al romanticismo.* Ed. Vittorio Conti. Florence: Leo S. Olschki, 1993, 59–76.

Raggio, Osvaldo. *Faide e parentele: Lo stato genovese visto dalla Fontanabuona.* Turin: Einaudi, 1990.

Raveggi, Sergio et al. *Ghibellini, Guelfi e popolo grasso: i detentori del potere politico a Firenze nella seconda metà del Dugento.* Florence: La Nuova Italia, 1978.

Reese, Thomas J. "A Kiss is Never Just a Kiss." *America: The National Catholic Review* April 15 1995. http://americamagazine.org/issue/100/kiss-never-just-kiss

Reinburg, Virginia. "Liturgy and the Laity in Late Medieval and Reformation France." *The Sixteenth-Century Journal* 23. 3 (1992): 526–47.

Renzi, Paolo. "La devozione dei Bianchi a Terni negli affreschi di S. Maria al Monumento." *Sulle orme dei Bianchi dalla Liguria all'Italia centrale. Atti del convegno internazionale Assisi -Vallo di Nera -Terni -Rieti-Leonessa (18-19-20 giugno 1999).* Ed. Francesco Santucci. Assisi: Accademia Properziana del Subasio, 2001, 273–306.

Ricciardelli, Fabrizio. *The Politics of Exclusion in Early Renaissance Florence.* Turnhout: Brepols, 2007.

Roberts, Simon. *Order and Dispute: An Introduction to Legal Anthropology.* New York: Penguin, 1979.

Rolandino e l'ars notaria da Bologna all'Europa: atti del convegno internazionale di studi storici sulla figura e l'opera di Rolandino: Bologna, città europea della cultura, 9-10 ottobre 2000. Ed. Giorgio Tamba. Milan: Giuffrè, 2002.

Rosenwein, Barbara H. "Worrying about Emotions in History." *AHR* 109 (2002): 821–45.

———. *Generations of Feeling: A History of Emotions, 600-1700.* Cambridge: Cambridge University Press, 2015.

Rossi, Marco. "L'immagine della pace nel monumento funerario di Berardo Maggi, vescovo e signore di Brescia." In *Medioevo: immagini e ideologie. Atti del convegno internazionale di studi Parma, 23-27 settembre 2002.* Ed. Arturo Carlo Quintavalle. Milan: Mondadori Electa, 2005, 588–96.

Rossi, Mariaclara. "Polisemia di un concetto: la pace nel basso medioevo: Note di lettura." In *La pace fra realtà e utopia* [*Quaderni di Storia Religiosa* 12]. Verona: Cierre, 2005: 9–45.

Rubinstein, Nicolai. "Le allegorie di Ambrogio Lorenzetti nella Sala della Pace e il pensiero politico del suo tempo." *Rivista Storica Italiana* 109 (1997): 781–802.

Ruggiero, Guido. *Violence in Early Renaissance Venice.* New Brunswick: Rutgers University Press, 1980.

Rupp, Teresa. "Damnation, Individual and Community in Remigio dei Girolami's *De bono comuni.*" *History of Political Thought* 21.2 (2000): 217–36.

———. "'Love justice, you who judge the Earth': Remigio dei Girolami's sermons to the Florentine Priors, 1295," in *Preaching and Political Society from Late Antiquity to the End of the Middle Ages.* Turnhout: Brepols, 2013, 251–63.

Sacchetti Sassetti, Angelo. "Giacomo delle Marche paciere a Rieti." *AFH* 50 (1957): 75–82.

Sanfilippo, Isa Lori. "La pace del cardinale Latino a Firenze nel 1290. La sentenza e gli atti complementari." *Bullettino dell'istituto storico italiano per il medio evo e Archivio Muratoriano* 89 (2001): 193–259.

Sanfilippo, Mario. "Guelfi e Ghibellini a Firenze: la 'pace' del Cardinal Latino (1280)." *Nuova Rivista Storica* 64 (1980): 1–24.

Santucci, Francesco. "Il passaggio dei Bianchi in Assisi." *Sulle orme dei Bianchi dalla Liguria all'Italia centrale. Atti del convegno internazionale Assisi -Vallo di Nera -Terni -Rieti–Leonessa (18-19-20 giugno 1999).* Ed. Francesco Santucci. Assisi: Accademia Properziana del Subasio, 2001, 155–71.

Sassetta: The Borgo San Sepolcro Altarpiece. Ed. Machtelt Israëls. 2 vols. Florence: Villa I Tatti, 2009.

Sbriccoli, Mario. "Legislation, Justice and Political Power in Italian Cities, 1200–1400." In *Legislation and Justice.* Ed. Antonio Padoa Schioppa. Oxford: Clarendon Press, 1997, 37–55.

———. "'Vidi communiter observari': L'emersione di un ordine penale pubblico nelle città italiane del secolo XIII." *Quaderni fiorentini per la storia del pensiero giuridico moderno* 27 (1998): 231–68.

———. "Giustizia negoziata, giustizia egemonica: riflessioni su una nuova fase degli studi di storia della giustizia criminale." In *Criminalità e giustizia in Germania e in Italia: pratiche giudiziarie e linguaggi giuridici tra tardo medioevo ed età moderna.* Ed. Marco Bellabarba, Gerd Schwerhoff, and Andrea Zorzi. Bologna: Il Mulino, 2001, 345–64.

Schmitt, Jean-Claude. *La raison des gestes dans l'Occident médiéval.* Paris: Gallimard, 1990.

Schreiner, Klaus. "'Gerechtigkeit und Frieden haben sich geküßt' (Ps. 84: 11): Friedensstiftung durch symbolisches Handeln." In *Träger und Instrumentarien des Friedens im hohen und späten Mittelalter.* Ed. Johannes Fried. Sigmaringen: Jan Thorbecke, 1996, 37–86.

Sensi, Mario. "Per una inchiesta sulle 'paci private' alla fine del Medio Evo." In *Studi sull'Umbria medievale e umanistica in ricordo di Olga Marinelli, Pier Lorenzo Meloni, Ugolino Nicolini.* Ed. Mauro Donnini and Enrico Menestò. Spoleto: Centro italiano di studi sull'alto medioevo, 2000, 527–59.

———. "Le paci private nella predicazione, nelle immagini di propaganda e nella prassi fra Tre e Quattrocento." In *La pace fra realtà e utopia. Quaderni di Storia Religiosa* 12. Verona: Cierre, 2005: 159–200.

Silverman, Diana C. "Marriage and Political Violence in the Chronicles of the Medieval Veneto." *Speculum* 86 (2011): 652–87.

Skinner, Quentin. "Ambrogio Lorenzetti: The Artist as Political Philosopher." *Proceedings of the British Academy* 72 (1986): 1–56.

———. "Ambrogio Lorenzetti's *Buon Governo* Frescoes: Two Old Questions, Two New Answers." *Journal of the Warburg and Courtauld Institutes* 62 (1999): 1–28.

Smail, Daniel Lord. "Common Violence: Vengeance and Inquisition in Fourteenth-Century Marseille." *Past and Present* 151 (1996): 28–59.

——. "Factions and Vengeance in Renaissance Italy: A Review Article." *Comparative Studies in Society and History* 38.4 (1996): 781–89.

——. "Hatred as a Social Institution in Late-Medieval Society." *Speculum* 76.1 (2001): 90–126.

——. *The Consumption of Justice: Emotions, Publicity, and Legal Culture in Marseille, 1264–1423*. Ithaca, NY: Cornell University Press, 2003.

——. "Violence and Predation in Late Medieval Europe." *Comparative Studies in History and Society* 54.1 (2012): 7–34.

——. *Goods and Debts in Mediterranean Europe (1330–1450)*. Cambridge, MA: Harvard University Press, 2016.

Starn, Randolph. *Contrary Commonwealth: The Theme of Exile in Medieval and Renaissance Italy*. Berkeley: University of California Press, 1982.

——. "The Republican Regime of the 'Room of Peace' in Siena, 1338–40." *Representations* 18 (1987): 1–33.

—— and Loren Partridge. *Arts of Power: Three Halls of State in Italy, 1300–1600*. Berkeley: University of California Press, 1992.

——. *Ambrogio Lorenzetti: The Palazzo Pubblico, Siena*. New York: George Braziller, 1994.

Stern, Laura Ikins. *The Criminal Law System of Medieval and Renaissance Florence*. Baltimore: Johns Hopkins University Press, 1994.

Stringere la pace: Teorie e pratiche della conciliazione nell'Europa moderna (secoli XV-XVIII). Ed. Paolo Broggio, Maria Pia Paoli, and Marco Cavina. Rome: Viella, 2011.

Stuard, Susan Mosher. *Gilding the Market: Luxury and Fashion in Fourteenth-Century Italy*. Philadelphia: University of Pennsylvania Press, 2006.

Sulle orme dei Bianchi dalla Liguria all'Italia centrale. Atti del convegno internazionale Assisi -Vallo di Nera -Terni -Rieti-Leonessa (18-19-20 giugno 1999). Ed. Francesco Santucci. Assisi: Accademia Properziana del Subasio, 2001.

Sznura, Franek. *L'Espansione Urbana di Firenze nel Dugento*. Florence: La Nuova Italia, 1975.

——. "Per la storia del notariato fiorentino: i più antichi elenchi superstiti dei giudici e dei notai fiorentini (anni 1291 e 1338)." In *Tra libri e carte. Studi in onore di Luciana Mosiici*. Ed. T. de Robertis and G. Savino. Florence: F. Cesati, 1998, 437–515. http://www.rm.unina.it/biblioteca/scaffale/s.htm#Franek%20Sznura, 1–41.

Tabacco, Giovanni. "Le rapport de parenté comme instrument de domination consortiale: Quelques exemples piemontais." In *Famille et parenté dans l'Occident medievale, actes du Colloque de Paris (6-8 juin 1974): organisé par l'École pratique des hautes études (VIe section) en collaboration avec le Collège de France et l' École française de Rome: communication et débats*. Ed. Georges Duby and Jacques Le Goff. Rome: l'École française de Rome, 1977, 153–58.

Tarassi, Massimo. "Buondelmonti, Ranieri, detto lo Zingaro." In DBI 15 (1972): 219–220.

Tentler, Thomas. *Sin and Confession on the Eve of the Reformation*. Princeton: Princeton University Press, 1977.

Thompson, Augustine. *Revival Preachers and Politics in Thirteenth-Century Italy: The Great Devotion of 1233*. Oxford: Clarendon Press, 1992.

——. *Cities of God: The Religion of the Italian Communes, 1125-1325*. University Park, PA: Pennsylvania State University Press, 2005.

Toch, Michael. "Schimpfwörter im Dorf des Spätmittelalters." *Mitteilungen des Instituts für Österreichische Geschichtsforschung* 101 (1993): 310–27.

Turner, Victor. *The Ritual Process: Structure and Anti-Structure*. Chicago: Aldine, 1969.

Vallerani, Massimo. "Liti private e soluzioni legali: note sul libro di Th. Kuehn e sui sistemi di composizione di conflitti nella società tardomedievale." *Quaderni Storici*, n.s. 89 (1995): 546–57.

———. "Pace e processo nel sistema giudiziario del comune di Perugia." *Quaderni Storici*, n.s. 101 (1999): 315–53.

———. "Mouvements de paix dans une commune de *Popolo*: les Flagellants à Pérouse en 1260." In *Prêcher la paix et discipliner la société: Italie, France, Angleterre (XIIIe-XVe siècles)*. Ed. Rosa Maria Dessì. Turnhout: Brepols, 2005, 313–55.

———. *Medieval Public Justice*. Trans. Sarah Rubin Blanshei. Washington, D.C.: Catholic University of America Press, 2012. Originally published as *La giustizia pubblica medievale*. Bologna: Il Mulino, 2005.

Vauchez, André. "Une campagne de pacification en Lombardie autour de 1233: L'action politique des ordres mendiants d'après la réforme des statuts communaux et les accords de paix. " In *École Française de Rome. Mélanges d'archéologie et d'histoire* 78 (1966): 503–49. Repr. *Religion et société dans l'Occident médiéval*. Turin: Bottega d'Erasmo, 1980, 71–117.

———. "La paix dans les mouvements religieux populaires (XIe-XVe siècle)." In *Pace e Guerra nel Basso Medioevo. Atti del XL Convegno storico internazionale Todi, 12–14 ottobre 2003*. Spoleto: Centro italiano di studi sull'alto medioevo, 2004, 313–33.

Vendittelli, Marco. "Malabranca, Latino." In DBI 67 (2006): 699–703.

Vengeance in the Middle Ages: Emotion, Religion and Feud. Ed. Susanna A. Throop and Paul R. Hyams. Burlington, VT: Ashgate, 2010.

Volpini, Raffaello and Antonietta Cardinale. "Giovanni Gualberto, Iconography." BS 6: 1029–32.

Waley, Daniel. "A Blood-Feud with a Happy Ending: Siena 1285–1304." In *City and Countryside in Late Medieval and Renaissance Italy: Essays Presented to Philip Jones*. Ed. Trevor Dean and Chris Wickham. London: Hambledon Press, 1990, 45–53.

Walker, Garthine. *Crime, Gender and Social Order in Early Modern England*. Cambridge: Cambridge University Press, 2003.

Warr, Cordelia. *Dressing for Heaven: Religious Clothing in Italy, 1215–1545*. Manchester: Manchester University Press, 2010.

Weber, Max. *The City*. Trans. and ed. Don Martindale and Gertrud Neuwirth. Glencoe, Ill.: Free Press, 1958 [1921].

White, Stephen D. *Feuding and Peacemaking in Eleventh-Century France*. Burlington, VT: Ashgate, 2005.

Wickham, Chris. *Community and Clientele in Twelfth-Century Tuscany: The Origins of the Rural Commune in the Plain of Lucca*. Oxford: Oxford University Press, 1998.

———. *Courts and Conflict in Twelfth-Century Tuscany*. Oxford: Oxford University Press, 2003.

———. *Sleepwalking into a New World: The Emergence of the Italian Communes in the Twelfth Century*. Princeton: Princeton University Press, 2015.

Witt, Ronald G. *The Two Latin Cultures and the Foundation of Renaissance Humanism in Medieval Italy*. Cambridge: Cambridge University Press, 2012.

Wray, Shona Kelly. "Reconciliation after Violence: Peace contracts in the *Libri Memoriali* of Fourteenth-Century Bologna." Conference paper delivered at Fordham University Conference on "Violence in the Middle Ages." 16 April 1994.

———. "Instruments of Concord: Making Peace and Settling Disputes through a Notary in the City and Contado of Late Medieval Bologna." *Journal of Social History* (Spring, 2009): 733–60.

Zanichelli, Giusi. "Pacino di Bonaguida: Un protagonista della miniatura fiorentina." *Alumina* 5.18 (2007): 24–33.

Zorzi, Andrea. *Istituzioni giudiziarie e aspetti della criminalità nella Firenze tardomedievale*. In *Ricerche storiche* 18.3 (1988).

Zorzi, Andrea. *Giustizia e società a Firenze in età comunale*. Naples: Edizioni Scientifiche Italiane, 1988.

———. "Giustizia criminale e criminalità nell'Italia del tardo Medioevo: studi e prospettive di ricerca," *Società e storia* 12 (1989): 923–65.

———. *Rassegna a base regionale delle fonti e degli studi su istituzioni giudiziarie, giustizia e criminalità nell'Italia del basso Medioevo*. *Ricerche storiche* 19–22 (1989–1992).

———. "*Ius erat in armis*. Faide e conflitti tra pratiche sociali e pratiche di governo." In *Origini dello Stato. Processi di formazione statale in Italia fra medioevo ed età moderna. Atti del convegno internazionale, Chicago, 26–29 aprile 1993*. Ed. G. Chittolini, A. Molho, and P. Schiera. Bologna: Il Mulino, 1994, 609–29.

———. "The Judicial System in Renaissance Florence." In *Crime, Society and the Law in Renaissance Italy*. Ed. Trevor Dean and K.J.P. Lowe. Cambridge: Cambridge University Press, 1994, 40–58.

———. "Conflits et pratiques infrajudiciaires dans le formations politiques italiennes du XIIe au XVe siècle." In *L'infrajudiciaire du Moyen Age à l'epoque contemporaine: Actes du Colloque de Dijon 5–6 Octobre 1995*. Dijon: Publications de l'Université de Bourgogne, 1996, 19–36.

———. "Negoziazione penale, legittimazione giuridica e poteri urbani nell'Italia comunale." In *Criminalità e giustizia in Germania e in Italia: Pratiche giudiziarie e linguaggi giuridici tra tardomedioevo ed età moderna*. Ed. M. Bellabarba, G. Schwerhoff, and A. Zorzi. Bologna: Il Mulino, 2001, 13–34.

———. "La cultura della vendetta nel conflitto politico in età comunale. In *Le storie e la memoria. In onore di Arnold Esch*. Ed. R. Delle Donne and A. Zorzi. Florence: Reti Medievali-Firenze University Press, 2002. E-book, reading 1, 135–70.

———. "Diritto e giustizia nelle città dell'Italia comunale (secoli XIII–XIV)." In *Stadt und Recht im Mittelalter/La ville et le droit au moyen âge*. Ed. Pierre Monnet and Otto Gerhard. Göttingen: Vandenhoeck & Ruprecht, 2003, 197–214.

———. "La legittimazione delle pratiche della vendetta nell'Italia comunale." In *Cultura, lenguaje y prácticas políticas en las sociedades medievales*," Ed. I. Alfonso. In *e-Spania: Revue électronique d'études hispaniques médiévales* 4 (2007) : http://e-spania.revues.org/document2043.html.

———. "Pluralismo giudiziario e documentazione: Il caso di Firenze in età comunale." In *Pratiques sociales et politiques judiciaires dans les villes de l'Occident à la fin du moyen âge*. Ed. J. Chiffoleau, C. Gauvard, and A. Zorzi. Rome: École Française de Rome, 2007, 125–87.

———. "'Fracta est civitas magna in tres partes:' Conflitto e costituzione nell'Italia comunale." *Scienza e politica: Per una storia delle dottrine politiche* 39 (2008): 61–87.

———. "I conflitti nell'Italia comunale: Riflessioni sullo stato degli studi e sulle prospettive di ricerca." In *Conflitti, paci e vendetta nell'Italia comunale*. Ed. A. Zorzi. Florence: Reti Medievali-Firenze University Press, 2009, 7–42. http://fermi.univr.it/rm/e-book/titoli/zorzi.htm.

Zupko, Ronald Edward. *Italian Weights and Measures from the Middle Ages to the Nineteenth Century*. Philadelphia: American Philosophical Society, 1981.

INDEX

Note: In order to streamline the index, I have omitted the names of both the notaries and the parties mentioned in the peace agreements. (The notary names are, however, included in the bibliography of notarial sources.)

A NOTE ON THE TYPE

THIS BOOK has been composed in Miller, a Scotch Roman typeface designed by Matthew Carter and first released by Font Bureau in 1997. It resembles Monticello, the typeface developed for The Papers of Thomas Jefferson in the 1940s by C. H. Griffith and P. J. Conkwright and reinterpreted in digital form by Carter in 2003.

Pleasant Jefferson ("P. J.") Conkwright (1905–1986) was Typographer at Princeton University Press from 1939 to 1970. He was an acclaimed book designer and AIGA Medalist.